MUIRHEAD LIBRARY OF PHILOSOPHY

An admirable statement of the aims of the Library of Philosophy was provided by the first editor, the late Professor J. H. Muirhead, in his description of the original programme printed in Erdmann's *History of Philosophy* under the date 1890. This was slightly modified in subsequent volumes to take the form of the following statement :

'The Muirhead Library of Philosophy was designed as a contribution to the History of Modern Philosophy under the heads : first of different Schools of Thought — Sensationalist, Realist, Idealist, Intuitivist ; secondly of different Subjects—Psychology, Ethics, Aesthetics, Political Philosophy, Theology. While much had been done in England in tracing the course of evolution in nature, history, economics, morals and religion, little had been done in tracing the development of thought on these subjects. Yet "the evolution of opinion is part of the whole evolution".

'By the co-operation of different writers in carrying out this plan it was hoped that a thoroughness and completeness of treatment, otherwise unattainable, might be secured. It was believed also that from writers mainly British and American fuller consideration of English Philosophy than it had hitherto received might be looked for. In the earlier series of books containing, among others, Bosanquet's *History of Aesthetics*, Pfleiderer's *Rational Theology since Kant*, Albee's *History of English Utilitarianism*, Bonar's *Philosophy and Political Economy*, Brett's *History of Psychology*, Ritchie's *Natural Rights*, these objects were to a large extent effected.

'In the meantime original work of a high order was being produced both in England and America by such writers as Bradley, Stout, Bertrand Russell, Baldwin, Urban, Montague and others, and a new interest in foreign works, German, French and Italian, which had either become classical or were attracting public attention, had developed. The scope of the Library thus became extended into something more international, and it is entering on the fifth decade of its existence in the hope that it may contribute to the mutual understanding between countries which is so pressing a need of the present time.'

The need which Professor Muirhead stressed is no less pressing today, and few will deny that philosophy has much to do with enabling us to meet it, although no one, least of all Muirhead himself, would regard that as the sole, or even the main, object of philosophy. As Professor Muirhead continues to lend the distinction of his name to the Library of Philosophy, it seemed not inappropriate to allow him to recall to us these aims in his own words. The emphasis on the history of thought seemed to me also very timely; and the number of important works promised for the Library in the near future augurs well for the continued fulfilment, in this and in other ways, of the expectations of the original editor.

H. D. LEWIS

MUIRHEAD LIBRARY OF PHILOSOPHY

General Editor: Professor H. D. Lewis
Professor of Philosophy, University College, Bangor

MORAL SENSE By James Bonar

NATURAL RIGHTS By D. G. Ritchie *3rd Edition*

NATURE, MIND AND MODERN SCIENCE By E. Harris

THE NATURE OF THOUGHT By Brand Blanshard, B.Sc., Ph.D. *2nd Impression*

PERSONALITY AND REALITY By J. E. Turner

THE PHENOMENOLOGY OF MIND By G. W. F. Hegel *Translated by Sir James Baillie Revised 2nd Edition 3rd Impression*

PHILOSOPHY AND POLITICAL ECONOMY By J. Bonar *4th Impression*

THE PLATONIC TRADITION IN ANGLO-SAXON PHILOSOPHY By Prof J. H. Muirhead

THE PRINCIPAL UPANISADS By Radhakrishnan

SOME MAIN PROBLEMS OF PHILOSOPHY By G. E. Moore

TIME AND FREE WILL By Prof Henri Bergson *Translated by F. G. Pogson 6th Impression*

THE WAYS OF KNOWING: OR, THE METHODS OF PHILOSOPHY By Prof W. P. Montague *4th Impression*

The Muirhead Library of Philosophy

EDITED BY H. D. LEWIS

THE MODERN PREDICAMENT

THE MODERN PREDICAMENT

A STUDY IN THE PHILOSOPHY OF RELIGION

Based on ~~1950-51~~
*Gifford Lectures delivered in the
University of St. Andrews*

BY

H. J. PATON

*Emeritus Professor of Moral Philosophy in
the University of Oxford
Fellow of the British Academy*

LONDON: GEORGE ALLEN & UNWIN LTD
NEW YORK: THE MACMILLAN COMPANY

1955

FIRST PU   55

PRINTED IN GREAT BRITAIN
in 11-*point Imprint type*
BY THE BLACKFRIARS PRESS LIMITED
LEICESTER AND LONDON

DEDICATED TO THE
PRINCIPAL, PROFESSORS, LECTURERS, AND
STUDENTS OF THE
UNIVERSITY OF SAINT ANDREWS

Preface

THE germ of this book first took shape as four Forwood Lectures on the philosophy of religion, which were delivered in the University of Liverpool in 1949. It developed into two series of Gifford Lectures given in the University of St. Andrews in the years 1950 and 1951. After a long process of rewriting it has reached its final form in the present work. I have to thank these two Universities for affording me an opportunity—and a stimulus—to express my views on this topic; and although I have tried to eliminate turns of phrase more suited to a lecture than to a book, I have done my best not to depart from the ideal common to both the benefactions by which I have been favoured—that of being intelligible to educated men and women who are not professional philosophers.

It is impossible for me to acknowledge adequately my indebtedness to previous writers on these subjects or to the many colleagues and pupils with whom I have had discussions; but I must thank Miss M. J. Levett, my former colleague in Glasgow, for her critical but kindly comments on my arguments and style, and also for reading the proofs. I am grateful to Professor H. D. Lewis for some valuable suggestions made at the last moment before going to press; and I must also tender my thanks to Mrs. A. Heywood, to Miss Nancy Melville, and especially to my wife, for the care and skill with which so many different versions have been typed.

In a book of this kind it may not be out of place to express also my indebtedness to my parents—to my mother for introducing me to a living religion at the most tender age possible, and to my father for introducing me, at an age only a little more advanced, to a lucid, humane, and rational theology as well. However little I may have profited, I have at least had the advantage of thinking about religious problems as soon as I was able to think at all.

H. J. PATON
Nether Pitcaithly
Bridge of Earn
July, 1954

Contents

Chapter I

PHILOSOPHY AND RELIGION

§ 1. *The task*

One function of philosophy is to think dispassionately about religion. This is the task that will be attempted here.

During the last two thousand years and more few philosophers would have questioned the propriety of such an endeavour; but this is not true of to-day. Serious objections may be raised both on behalf of philosophy and on behalf of religion, and some of these will have to be considered later. Even among people who have not reflected deeply there are many who take religion to be the illusion of a past age so that thinking about it philosophically would be a sheer waste of time. Some assume that any intelligent person must look upon religion, not merely as illusory, but as in some degree immoral. Their condemnation may arise partly because they think of a religious man as one who is indifferent to the truth, but partly also because they regard him as hide-bound and intolerant and hypocritical. If they were invited to study theology rather than to contemplate religion, their distaste would be even greater. To them all theology—even when described as 'natural' rather than as 'dogmatic'—appears as an unholy alliance in which pedantry comes to the aid of folly and thought is debased as well as emotion. This attitude is commonest among the young—I have found it most open in some of my American pupils, who are less inhibited than the English. It is not likely to be dispelled without a good deal of honest thinking.

Even those who would allow that it is possible to reflect honestly and dispassionately about this subject may distrust an enquiry which, like the present work, appears under the guise of Gifford Lectures and so is officially concerned with natural theology. This distrust was bluntly expressed by the late Professor Susan Stebbing in the preface to her book *Philosophy and the Physicists*. She remarks —quite casually—that 'Lenin and other dialectical materialists have as much an axe to grind as any Gifford Lecturer.' We must ask whether natural theology as the subject prescribed by Lord Gifford to his lecturers affords any ground for the charge most wounding to a philosopher—the charge of being prepared to tamper with the truth.

§ 2. *Natural theology*

Natural theology is sometimes supposed to be the theology that comes natural to us, and in this respect it would be like natural piety, or even natural timidity. But there is another and more technical use of the word. When we speak of natural science, we do not mean the science that comes natural to us: we mean the science of nature. So too natural theology was originally the theology of nature—the theology based, not on the book of Holy Scripture, but on the book of nature, and in particular on the evidence of God's purpose in the physical world. That is to say, it was traditionally concerned with what is known as the argument from design. From a scientific study of the order and purpose in the world human reason was supposed to pass to knowledge of the existence and attributes of a Creator who orders all things in accordance with a divine purpose; and that purpose was not uncommonly believed to be the welfare of man.

In this narrow sense natural theology—sometimes known also by the more grandiose term 'physicotheology'—was limited in scope: it tended to despise the more abstract traditional arguments for the existence of God and prided itself on close contact with the new facts revealed by science. One of its earliest exponents, Raymond de Sabunde, who published his *Theologia Naturalis* in 1438, regarded it as an infallible science which, as he said, 'anyone can acquire in a month and without labour.' In the long line of his successors, which runs from Francis Bacon to Paley, we find men influenced by the new empirical sciences and seeking to derive from them some support for religion. Because of its concern with the details of God's purpose in the world, natural theology tended to break up into a series of minor theologies, each studying the manifestations of the divine purpose in a particular field. These subordinate theologies—which are said to have been zealously cultivated by the English—were given impressive names. Thus astrotheology studied God's purpose in the stars; hydrotheology His purpose in water; ornithotheology His purpose in birds; and so on. Treatises were composed on the religious lessons to be learned from snow, thunder, insects, locusts, bees, fishes, shell-fish, and earthquakes. These edifying works are no longer read. Perhaps we may presume, even without reading them, that they contributed little of permanent value to the cause they espoused. They serve to remind us that natural theology may become highly artificial.

Fortunately there is also a broader usage in which natural theology is extended beyond the argument from design till it is identical with what is called 'rational theology' or 'philosophical theology'—that is, with a science which asks how far knowledge of God is possible for men by means of human reason unaided by revelation. Presumably it is then called 'natural' on the ground that reason is natural to man and not supernatural. Natural theology is thus opposed to a supernatural or sacred theology which rests on divine revelation and so is sometimes described as revealed theology.

In this there appears to be some risk of confusion. With all respect to theologians it may be doubted whether any theology is properly described as supernatural. Natural religion, which comes to man by his own unaided efforts, may perhaps be distinguished from supernatural religion, which comes to him by divine revelation or divine grace. But even if we accept so dubious a distinction, it is still a mistake to identify theology with religion or to transfer the attributes of one without question to the other. Theology is human reflexion about religion, and it is only too subject to human weakness, even when the religion reflected upon is said to be revealed. If there are some religious men who hold that their theology is revealed as well as their religion, they must either claim a double revelation or else deny that there is any sharp distinction between religion and theological reflexion about it.

Fewer questions will be begged if we contrast natural theology with dogmatic theology, although nowadays the word 'dogmatic' may have unhappy associations. Dogmatic theology professes to set forth the dogmas of a revealed religion; and although in so doing it proceeds rationally or reflectively, nevertheless it rests ultimately on authority or revelation. Natural theology, on the other hand, excludes, by definition, all appeals to any authority other than reason itself.

This essential prohibition means that natural theology is a branch of philosophy and cannot employ a non-philosophical method. On the other hand, it is free to adopt any method of enquiry considered appropriate to philosophy. Thus it may follow the high *a priori* line of metaphysics if this can be justified by logical argument. And equally it may start from the history of religion and the known facts of religious experience—no matter whether the religions in question profess to be natural or revealed. It may even base itself nowadays on a study of religious language. Yet it cannot itself be a kind of history or sociology or psychology or philology; for as a branch of philosophy it is not concerned with facts as such, but with their significance and value and with the principles in the light of which they are to be understood.

In all this there is no ground whatever for saying that a natural theologian—if this term may be used—must be a man with an axe to grind. But we have still to ask whether anything in the conditions laid down by Lord Gifford can justify so grievous a charge.

§ 3. *The stipulations of Lord Gifford*

It is abundantly clear, in the first place, that Lord Gifford wished natural theology to be taken in its widest, and not in its narrowest, sense. He describes the subject as 'The Knowledge of God, the Infinite, the All, the First and Only Cause, the One and the Sole Substance, the Sole Being, the Sole Reality, and the Sole Existence'. He also speaks of it as 'the greatest of all possible sciences, indeed, in one sense, the only science, that of Infinite Being'.

It may seem barely consistent with this—if one may entertain even a momentary doubt about the consistency of a benefactor— when he goes on to say, in the second place, that he wishes the subject to be treated as a strictly natural science and to be considered just as astronomy or chemistry is; for it is impossible to know the Infinite by the methods of natural science. But we may avoid the appearance of inconsistency if we suppose that the comparison with natural science is intended to hold only in one respect—namely, as he says, that the subject is to be treated 'without reference to or reliance upon any supposed special exceptional or so-called miraculous revelation'. As we have already seen, this must be so if natural theology is a branch of philosophy and is to be treated as such.

Even on this interpretation it might appear that a Gifford Lecturer is tied down to a particular view and is expected to produce a particular conclusion. Fortunately this is not so. Most philosophers to-day are unable to claim knowledge of God which would properly be described as scientific, or even as philosophical. But Lord Gifford, with admirable tolerance, allows the utmost freedom of treatment: it is permissible to argue either for or against his own views. He also goes on to specify further topics which I have so far omitted—they include 'Knowledge of the Nature and Foundations of Ethics or Morals'. What most concerns us here is the following stipulation. His lecturers may freely discuss 'all questions about man's conceptions of God or the Infinite, their origin, nature, and truth, whether he can have any such conceptions, whether God is under any or what limitations, and so on'. It is within the range of man's conceptions that I hope to say something about the nature and principles of religion, its present predicament, its grounds in experience, and its philosophical defence. This is why I prefer to describe my book as a study in the philosophy of religion rather than to claim for it the proud title of natural theology, even although I shall have to touch on many of the topics commonly considered under this head.

This preference is, I believe, typical of the present age—so far as it takes any interest in religion at all. There is something to be said for approaching these fundamental questions from the side of man, with his obscure experience, his confused conceptions, his imperfect ideals. Without claiming ability to *prove* God's existence or to *know* His nature, we may still ask ourselves what is the nature and value and justification of religion in the life of men. Is it not more becoming, and more in conformity with our limited abilities, that we should be content to consider, on the basis of experience, and particularly of religious experience, what finite man by his unaided reason may rationally *believe* and *hope*?

In thus restricting my subject I do not think I am going against the intentions of Lord Gifford or following the example of those politicians and bureaucrats who assume that any benefaction may be legitimately diverted to any purpose which in their wisdom they happen to prefer to the purpose of the original benefactor. On the contrary, I believe that I am trying to treat the subject as he would have wished it treated, had he been alive to-day. Nor do I feel that I am bound by his stipulations to grind any axe other than the axe of philosophical truth.

There are some who will maintain that this reserved attitude to natural theology is pure subjectivism, the weakness and disease of the present sick world, the mark of a failure in philosophical energy. Even so, we may perhaps plead that natural theologians require some time to adjust themselves to the ever accelerating progress of modern science, which has completely changed the background of religion; and we may doubt whether such an adjustment can be based on the philosophical concepts of pre-scientific thinkers like Aristotle and St. Thomas. In any case, if this caution, or timidity, in theological speculation is a disease, it is one which is endemic at

the present time. An account, or even a display, of its symptoms
may at least contribute to its diagnosis and so perhaps ultimately to
its cure.

§ 4. *Popularity*

A further requirement of Lord Gifford raises a problem of
greater delicacy. He wished his lectures to be 'public and popular';
and although he equates this phrase with being 'open not only to
students of the Universities, but to the whole community without
matriculation', it seems not unreasonable to surmise that he wanted
the lectures to be intelligible to the public as well as open to them.
Whether all his distinguished lecturers have succeeded in fulfilling
this stipulation it would perhaps be tactless to enquire.

The ideal of being intelligible to the public has much to recommend it. There is a danger that philosophy, especially in questions
of religion and morals, may become too technical, too inhuman, too
remote from the problems of actual life. When this happens, philosophy itself may tend to decay and wither, or at least to become a
kind of game rather than a serious occupation; and a muddled world
is left to blunder on without such modest help as philosophical
thinking can offer. It may at times be good for the philosopher
himself to come blinking out of his study and talk, like Socrates, to
his fellows in the market place or on the playing field. If he has not
wholly forgotten the language of ordinary intercourse, he may
perhaps induce some of them to consider critically the hand-to-
mouth and rule-of-thumb methods by which they usually live.
Some of our problems may be solved, or at least transformed, if only
we can look at them with detachment and intelligence.

On questions of such difficulty the ideal of popularity is far from
easy to attain, but there may be a mean between popular journalism
and a technical treatise which can be mastered only by years of
study. It is at this mean that I will try to aim, though it will be
harder to succeed when I come to the more strictly philosophical
questions in the later parts of my book. I should like to write in such
a way that any intelligent man who is willing to take a certain
amount of trouble will be able to understand what I am trying to
say, even if he has had no previous philosophical training. For this
reason I have had to omit many qualifications and reservations, and
I have discarded the customary paraphernalia of footnotes and
references which are found intimidating by so many. The result
may appear naive to the more precise among my philosophical

colleagues; but perhaps all human thinking on ultimate questions is bound to be naive. Anyhow, for the present purpose I would rather be ingenuous and intelligible than sophisticated and obscure.

Perhaps I should add that those who wish to avoid some initial difficulties may be advised to go straight on from here to the beginning of Chapter IV.

§ 5. *The starting point*

In these days there are few who would deny that we must start our enquiry from the facts of experience; but neither the word 'experience' nor the word 'fact' should be too narrowly interpreted. It is a fact of experience that bodies move; but it is also a fact of experience that men make judgements which claim to be true and may be false. It is a fact of experience that men have—or at least believe they have—an idea of perfection; and some thinkers have sought to prove from this the existence of God. Whatever we may think of such a proof, it would be arbitrary to exclude it from consideration on the *a priori* ground that no theological argument should be *a priori*.

Nevertheless, and this too perhaps will be generally conceded, the philosophy of religion must start primarily from the facts of religious experience—one might almost say from the fact of religious experience. Unfortunately the facts of religious experience are so varied as to be unmanageable. Apart from innumerable primitive religions, there are not a few highly developed religions, which may be described as great religions or world religions, and these differ profoundly among themselves. Few, if any, philosophers are likely to be familiar with them all, and we must be content to begin with a highly impressionistic view.

Our difficulties do not end there. When a scientist is studying physical bodies, he is content to look at them from the point of view of a scientist. He does not ask himself how all this business about electrons appears to a body from its own point of view: he assumes, no doubt rightly, that it has no point of view of its own. That is to say—if the spatial metaphor may be forgiven—he looks at bodies from outside: his point of view is external. As the Behaviourists have shown, it is possible to look at human activities literally from the outside: they treat human beings exactly as they treat rats and find no unbridgeable difference between the two. But if you are to understand human thinking, you must put yourself at the point of

view of the thinker and re-think his thoughts. If you are to understand art, you must put yourself at the point of view of the artist.
If you are to understand religion, you must at least try to put yourself at the point of view of the religious man, though you may
require to have a detached point of view of your own as well.

If this is true, our difficulties, already great, are enormously
increased.

Which of us can claim to have an inward experience, or a sympathetic understanding, of even the great religions of the world? If we
have been brought up on the Old Testament as well as the New—
and more and more people are coming to be brought up on neither
—we may have some slight idea of the Jewish religion, and we may
find the religion of Islam not altogether alien; but the religions of
the East are to most of us a sealed book. Even if we have taken the
trouble to study some accounts of them, this is far from enough;
for we cannot enter into the point of view of a religion unless we
know intimately the language in which it is expressed and the civilization in which it is manifested. At the most, we may be able to
recognize a religious spirit in the watchwords of a religion that is
strange to us; for example, in the great invocation of Islam 'In the
name of Allah, the Compassionate One, the Merciful'; or even in
Homer when he tells us that the beggar and the stranger come from
Zeus. We may also be conscious of a religious attitude in devotees
of a religion that is utterly remote from us, if we are fortunate enough
to be personally acquainted with them. All this is to the good, but
it does little more than reveal to us the extent of our ignorance and
the dangers of being dogmatic.

When all is said, anyone brought up in Europe or America, however indifferent or hostile he may be to Christianity, cannot but get
his main ideas about religious experience from the one religion that
is so closely interwined with Western civilisation. This means, it
may be maintained, that he is restricted to a limited point of view
from the very start: his philosophy will not merely be based on
inadequate experience, but will be influenced by bias and prejudice.
And the more we insist on the need for an understanding that is not
wholly external, the more obvious does all this become. Indeed the
starting point is more unsatisfactory than we have said, for no
thinker can have equal sympathy even with all the different forms
of Christianity. Each man must approach the topic of religion with
his own limitations—his own background, his own tradition, his
own experience, and his own peculiar temperament.

This is one reason why we must try to look at religion, not only with inner sympathy, so far as we can, but also from a detached and critical point of view. We cannot accept any one religion without further question as the norm by which all other religions are to be judged.

This can be seen easily enough if we look at religions with which we are unfamiliar. I was once told by a Hindu undergraduate that Christianity must be inferior to Hinduism because it has no sacred river. No philosopher can be content to beg such a question: he is bound to ask whether it is essential to religion, or at least to the highest form of religion, to have a sacred river. So far as he may, he must be on his guard against falling into a dogmatism based on his own tradition. In popular theological discussions it is far too common to find even professed sceptics assuming that if any one believes in God, he must be an orthodox Christian. A moment's reflexion would convince them that such a view is too narrow.

But here we begin to pass from the starting-point of a philosophy of religion to its aim or goal. Only when we are clearer about the goal can we hope to mitigate, if not to remove, the difficulties of the starting-point.

§ 6. *The goal*

In philosophy, although it is hard enough to know where you begin, it is generally even more difficult to be sure where you are trying to go. This is a problem to which different philosophers offer very different answers.

The philosophy of religion, as I see it, is concerned primarily with the norms or standards which religion must follow and by which it must be judged—with the conditions necessary for a religion to be genuine and not spurious. Some might say that it is concerned with the essence of religion. There is no harm in this if we are using popular language, but it has technical implications which few philosophers would accept to-day. Perhaps it would be best to say that the philosophy of religion is concerned with the first principles—or even simply with the principles—of religion. Strictly speaking, the word 'first' is redundant. The principles of religion state the conditions without which religion ceases to be religion and becomes something altogether different.

This usage of the word 'principle' is one of the oldest and best established in philosophy, but many modern philosophers find it obscure. It is impossible to consider here the objections to it. A simple illustration of what is meant may be found in Mr. Toulmin's book *The Philosophy of Science*. There he points out that the Recti-linear Propagation of Light is called a 'principle'—not merely a 'law'—of geometrical optics because without it there could be no such science at all. It is my belief that there are also principles of science, of art, of morals, and of religion, without which such things could not be at all, and that to formulate these principles is the first concern of philosophy.

To put forward such a claim for the philosophy of religion is no doubt bold: it sets forth an ideal which is likely to be realized very imperfectly, if at all. Yet perhaps it is not quite so bold as it may seem. It assumes that there are principles already present in ordinary religious experience, in the acts and beliefs of the ordinary religious man. These principles are not by him made explicit. They are merely taken for granted or presupposed, and yet it is by them that he determines and criticizes both his conduct and his beliefs. The business of philosophy is to disentangle and to make explicit principles which are already unreflectively adopted, and this need not be a task incapable of human achievement: it may only be to discover what is unconsciously known or acted upon by those who live a religious life.

If such principles can be formulated, what else remains to be done with them? The most obvious task is to consider whether they are consistent among themselves and consistent with the rest of our knowledge. There are also more fundamental and difficult questions concerned with their status and with the reasons why they should be accepted or rejected. Do we grasp them independently by some sort of direct intuition? Do we accept them because they are necessary if our experience, and in particular our religious experi-ence, is to be coherent with itself? Are they to be regarded as arbitrary recommendations, or decisions, about the proper use of words? Are they capable of any further justification and defence?

About these ultimate questions I propose to say little: they belong to a more general and more technical enquiry. I do try to say summarily what I think religion must be if it is to be religion at all, and I criticize what seem to me departures from its principles. But, as is perhaps inevitable at the present time, I find myself concerned most of all with the reasons put forward for accepting religious beliefs, with the difficulties of such acceptance, and with the possibility of reconciling religious belief and scientific knowledge. Perhaps the difficulties have loomed larger and larger as I proceeded, but I see little hope for religion unless these are honestly faced. On the other hand, to discuss the grounds of religious belief is also, I hope, to throw light on the nature of religious experience and on the principles of religion itself—all these problems are so closely intertwined. Even if it is a rather fitful light, I should be fully content if I could bring out some principles which would be recognized by religious men as present in their experience, or as illuminating it in any way, or perhaps as helping to distinguish the wheat from the chaff, the sense from the nonsense which is so often taken up into religious beliefs and practices. I should also like to think that I might induce some of the indifferent to consider the possibility that religion may not be all nonsense, but may contain something precious without which life may be incomplete.

Even if we take a restricted view of what can be done in a philosophical study of religion, it is clear enough that we shall be hampered by not having a wide knowledge of religions, including primitive ones. If through lack of knowledge I have been blind, or even unjust, to the religions of the East, or indeed to any religion, I can only express my regrets; but every one must do his best with such material as he has. Nevertheless the philosophical search for principles is distinct from an attempt at scientific generalization, and it does not depend on wide and exact knowledge as do the discoveries of physics or the descriptions of natural history. A man might contribute something to the philosophy of art even if his knowledge were confined to the art of Europe. It is hard to see why this should not be true also of the philosophy of religion, so perhaps we need not altogether despair. I am content to put forward what I call principles as mere hypotheses to be judged and corrected and supplemented by each man according to his own experience; but it would not show modesty in an author if he were continually reminding his readers that he is not infallible.

Needless to say, I make assumptions about philosophical method which are questioned by many; but a defence of these would be highly technical, and they will have to be judged by the way they work out. As to religion, I am making the minimum assumption that in spite of the horrors and aberrations, the cruelties and absurdities, which have accompanied it, it has at least a serious claim to be regarded as one of the great authentic human experiences, like art or morality or love. If religion were nothing but an illusion and a sham, there could be no philosophy of it. The study of it would belong to abnormal psychology.

§ 7. *Philosophy and religion*

If at least some philosophers to-day are hostile to religion, it is hardly surprising that at least some religious men should be hostile to philosophy. There is something to be said for the contention that philosophy and religion are fundamentally opposed. The spirit of philosophy is a questioning and critical spirit, while that of religion is one of simple faith. Is it possible that a philosophical investigation will tend to dry up that faith, whatever it may be, in the heart of the philosopher and in those who are unwise enough to listen to his desiccated voice? Is there perhaps a principle of indeterminacy in the philosophy of religion, as there is in physics, so that—to adapt the picturesque language of Professor Eddington—when we turn the flashlight of our observation upon it, religion, like the electron, 'will not go on doing what it was doing in the dark'. The same point was put more pharmacologically by Hobbes. 'It is with the mysteries of our religion as with wholesome pills for the sick, which, swallowed whole, have the virtue to cure, but chewed are for the most part cast up again without effect'.

Some philosophers have been deeply religious even in their thinking, yet it can hardly be denied that what may be called the psychological atmosphere of religion is very different from that of philosophy (or even of theology). Within limits it may be true that to practise one is to unfit oneself for the other—any form of specialization is bound to circumscribe a man's capacity for other ways of life. The simple believer may be well advised not to bother his head about squabbles among the doctors, which seem more likely to disturb, than to facilitate, his devotions. And the philosopher may be wise to remind himself that he is in danger of getting so absorbed in his own thinking that he begins to forget what he is thinking about.

Nevertheless philosophy is only an attempt to understand; and once the questioning spirit is awake, as it certainly is in these days, it is impossible to fall back into dogmatic slumber. Religion cannot afford to claim exemption from philosophic enquiry. If it attempts to do so on the ground of its sanctity, it can only draw upon itself the suspicion that it is afraid to face the light. If it attempts to do so on the ground of its absurdity, as in some surprising modern developments, it can only open the flood-gates of folly. If there is such a thing as sound religion—and why should we be interested in any other?—it must be tough enough to support, and even to profit by, philosophical criticism. To some men, as to Socrates, it must always seem that an unexamined life—even an unexamined religious life—is not worth living. And whatever we may lose by our first attempts at dispassionate examination, it is always possible that as we come to understand anything better, we may also come to value it more.

In any case a philosopher has no choice: he cannot always swallow his religion whole. Whatever may be the clinical results, there are times when—in spite of Hobbes—he has got to chew it.

Chapter II

THE LINGUISTIC VETO

§ 1. *The linguistic veto*

At the very outset we are faced with serious philosophical objections to our whole enterprise—almost, we might say, with a ban or veto. This ban is pronounced by thinkers who regard philosophy as primarily a study of language. Since their movement is perhaps the most original of the present century and has great influence in this country, a prohibition of this kind cannot simply be ignored. No brief discussion can do it justice, but we must try to look at it in outline and consider how far we are entitled to go on at all.

It is not easy to put the linguistic objections succinctly and yet convincingly, partly because the doctrine is always undergoing modifications—a sure sign that it is very much alive. If philosophy is concerned only with words, and we are proposing to talk about God and freedom and immortality, then naturally we must be going very far wrong. But not many thinkers would press their preference for linguistic methods quite so far as this; and there are more precise objections to the type of statements we are bound to make in a theological enquiry. These objections lead to one conclusion likely to prove fatal to any philosophy of religion. We may put it bluntly by saying that on this view the assertion 'God exists' is nonsense: strictly speaking it cannot be either true or false. Since to contradict nonsense is also nonsense, the same condemnation applies to the assertion 'God does not exist'. To the uninitiated this use of the word 'nonsense' may appear impolite; but the apparent rudeness is purely technical. We may eliminate it by writing the word with a hyphen. To say that God exists is non-sense: that is, it is to make a statement which cannot be verified by sense-perception and so must be without sense or significance.

It should not be thought that all linguistic philosophers would necessarily adopt this conclusion. Nevertheless this kind of view has played a great part in the new philosophy, and it constitutes precisely the ban or veto with which we are here concerned. The classical exposition of it is to be found in Professor Ayer's *Language*,

Truth and Logic. He would now present his doctrine less harshly than he did in his eager and enthusiastic youth—he has made a good many qualifications in his second edition. But he still believes that his point of view is substantially correct; and so do a great many other people.

§ 2. *Ordinary language*

There are two main strands in linguistic philosophy. The first uses ordinary language as a check or standard for philosophical assertions. The difference between a check and a standard is not always kept clear, but it is very important. We may agree that as a check ordinary language is salutary and yet maintain that as a standard it is impossible.

Since so much thinking, and especially philosophical thinking, is expressed in language, it is not unreasonable to suppose that the study of language will be a help to philosophy. We might become more free from provincialism in our thinking if we had a good knowledge of languages remote from our own, such as Chinese, or even if we could compare widely different types of linguistic expression. This is a topic which has lately begun to arouse interest among philologists. British philosophers, as a rule, confine themselves to standard English.

It has always been the practice of thinkers to use their own language as a means for stimulating or checking philosophical reflexion. To Socrates, for example, the process is far from unfamiliar. There can be no better way of debunking vague metaphysical statements and bringing a woolly thinker back to earth; and this kind of check has always been a favourite device of Oxford tutors. What is new about the modern movement is that it is more systematic. It owes its popularity partly to the influence of Professor G. E. Moore.

The appeal to ordinary usage is specially attractive to commonsense philosophers—to those who prefer to call a spade a spade rather than an idea in the mind of God. The language of common intercourse is practical rather than speculative. Naturally enough, it is steeped in common sense and does not trouble much about the ultimate status of the every-day things among which we live: it is content to take them at their face value. How far this makes it a safe guide for philosophers is a matter of dispute. Those who regard common-sense philosophy as superficial will not be likely to change

c

their minds merely because it comes before them in a linguistic guise.

The common-sense advocates of the linguistic method often tell us that philosophers as a class are notoriously apt to be misled by words. They sometimes seem to forget that they too are philosophers. The mere fact that a philosopher disagrees with us does not prove that he is misled by words: it is possible that he may be right. Even if he is wrong, we have *first* to show that he is wrong and *then* to show that his error arises because he is deceived by language. On the whole, philosophers are much less likely to be misled by words than are those who think less and talk more. You have only to listen, say, to an average political conversation to find this out. Yet philosophers, like other men, may at times be misled by words, and this can be shown when their arguments are based on linguistic usage. Thus it has been argued that we must have infallible knowledge because we never say that we knew something but were mistaken. This argument can be seen to be fallacious once we recognize that the word 'know', like the word 'cure', is an 'achievement verb'—to borrow a coinage from Professor Ryle. As he says, the fact that doctors cannot cure unsuccessfully does not mean that they are infallible doctors. His treatment of 'achievement verbs' is an admirable example of the philosophical advantages to be gained from the study of linguistic usage—at least when you are dealing with philosophers who base their arguments on language. Nevertheless a too exclusive concern with language may have its own pitfalls if it leads us to lose sight of what is being talked about—rather like a dog that glues its nose to the end of the walking-stick with which we are trying to point.

However valuable the study of ordinary language may be as at once a stimulus and a check, it should never be set up as a standard —as a final court of appeal—in philosophy. If we were to do this, we should show that we were blind both to the character of philosophy and to the character of language. In philosophy there can be no authorities: we are all free to think fresh thoughts for ourselves. As to language, it is a living and growing organism which is for ever being adjusted to the new thoughts men are trying to express. Every poet and every philosopher has to take liberties with language: it is impossible for either of them to write in clichés. We should be careful to avoid even the appearance of suggesting that language can be kept in a deep freeze; and it seems a pity to revive Victorian primness by telling our philosophical opponents that their language is not 'respectable'.

The study of ordinary language offers no obstacle to our present investigation: it rather provides fresh opportunities. As a result of its long history our speech is rich in expressions which originate in all sorts of past thinking: in the hands of an ingenious person it can provide support for almost any doctrine, but it can prove none. We need not trouble ourselves too much if it is used to attack religious beliefs: it could equally well be used to support them. It is shot through with philosophical and theological expressions and full of immortal longings. Even those who dislike what is sometimes called 'mind-talk'—talk which distinguishes the mind from the body—must recognize that this is much older than the English language and is found even among the most primitive peoples.

§ 3. *Ideal language*

Our real difficulties begin when we come to the second strand in linguistic philosophy. This is concerned, not with ordinary language, but with an ideal language, sometimes described as a disinfected language. It is a language that no one talks, and perhaps that no one could talk. As Mr. Bertrand Russell tells us himself, 'a logically perfect language, if it could be constructed, would not only be intolerably prolix, but, as regards its vocabulary, would be very largely private to one speaker'. Here too we can say that such a language may be salutary as a stimulus or check to philosophical reflexion; but it should not be elevated into a standard to which all philosophical assertions ought to conform.

A highly complex and continually evolving doctrine of this type cannot possibly be described in a few paragraphs, and there is a danger of giving a totally false impression of it. The precise relation between this strand and the previous one is hard to determine, but there is at least a connexion in so far as ordinary language is sometimes translated into a more ideal language: there have been, for example, elaborate discussions on the logically ideal way of saying 'Scott is the author of Waverley'. The two different methods of treating language are both commonly described as 'analysis'. It is natural enough to pass from studying ordinary language to considering how it might be improved; but perhaps it is possible to construct an ideal language entirely by itself. The construction of an ideal language is also connected with the development of modern mathematical logic, which is one of the most influential contributions to philosophy during the present century. Here again it is not easy to say precisely what the connexion is, but we may not go too far wrong if we regard the ideal language as primarily, if not exclusively, a language for mathematics and perhaps for physics.

The best introduction to this subject is probably a collection of Mr. Bertrand Russell's lectures published under the title *The Philosophy of Logical Atomism*. In this short book we can see the doctrine in process of being formed, and we are less likely to get lost in a mass of technical details which may obscure a general framework that is often now taken for granted. We can also see that the doctrine is associated in Mr. Russell's mind with the two fundamental principles of David Hume—namely, '*that all our distinct perceptions are distinct existences*, and *that the mind never perceives any real connexion among distinct existences*'. Here once more it is hard to see whether there is any closer logical link between Hume's principles and an ideal language. Whatever the connexion may be, it will not greatly recommend the ideal language to those who find themselves unable to accept Hume's philosophy.

Enough has been said to show at least that the ideal of a logically perfect language comes forward as only one part of a vast system. It cannot be discussed adequately apart from the system as a whole. Yet we may think that an ideal language will be too circumscribed for our purposes if its primary use is to talk about mathematics or even about science. We may also think that if its aim is to become a fixed or frozen language, there is a risk of its being false to the nature of language itself.

§ 4. *Analytic and synthetic propositions*

In all this we are concerned only with the ban or veto imposed by an ideal language on the kind of assertions likely to be made in a philosophy of religion. Before we can understand this, we must deal with some technical terms, especially with the difference between analytic and synthetic propositions. This distinction was first made by Immanuel Kant, and we had better begin with his account of it. A brief summary will necessarily be oversimplified.

According to Kant an *analytic* proposition is one which can be made by analysing the subject-concept (in accordance with the law of contradiction). Example: 'Bodies are extended'. The predicate 'extended' is contained in the concept of 'body'; that is, in the *concept* of the subject or—more briefly—in the subject-concept.

A *synthetic* proposition is one which cannot be made by analysing the subject-concept. Example: 'Bodies are heavy'. The predicate 'heavy' is not contained in the concept of 'body'.

It should be observed that the *subject-concept* must be sharply distinguished from the *subject* itself, which is usually a thing or class of things, and not a concept at all. Those who fail to grasp this distinction—and they are many—have only themselves to blame if they find Kant talking nonsense.

There are difficulties in speaking as if all propositions were of the subject-predicate form. This is not Kant's meaning, and hypothetical propositions, for example, can be either analytic or synthetic. If we suppose that the necessary adjustments can be made, Kant's distinction between analytic and synthetic is exhaustive. It is manifestly exhaustive so far as subject-predicate propositions are concerned.

Because in a synthetic proposition the predicate is not contained in the subject-concept, it is necessary to go beyond the subject-concept to some 'third term' if subject and predicate are to be combined or synthetized in one proposition. In most synthetic propositions, such as the example given above, Kant takes the third term to be sense-perception or sense-experience. Hence most synthetic propositions are empirical: they are verified or justified only by experience. But Kant thinks there are some synthetic propositions which are true and yet cannot be verified by experience: in other words they are *a priori*. An example would be 'All bodies change only in accordance with causal law'. This seems to be synthetic, for there is no reference to causal law in the concept of 'body' (nor even in the concept of 'changing body'). Kant thinks it the main business of philosophy to examine such *synthetic a priori propositions* and to ask whether they are possible—that is, whether they can be justified. He holds that some of them can be justified—it would be incorrect to say 'verified'—by reference, not to experience, but to what he calls 'the conditions of the possibility of experience'.

Now in all this there are difficulties into which it is impossible to enter here, and Professor Ayer—if we may go back to him as our best guide—seeks to provide more satisfactory definitions. According to him a proposition is *analytic* when its validity depends solely on the definitions of the symbols it contains. A proposition is *synthetic* when its validity is determined by the facts of experience.

It will be noted that he dislikes the word 'concept' and prefers to talk of 'symbols', but otherwise his definition of analytic propositions is at least akin to that of Kant. Synthetic propositions, how-

ever, are defined by what Kant would regard as an accident—they
are defined in such a way that they *must* be empirical. The possibility of synthetic *a priori* propositions is excluded by definition and
without argument. Indeed the possibility that any synthetic proposition could be a necessary proposition is excluded by definition;
for according to Professor Ayer empirical propositions can never be
more than probable. In the second edition he seems to recognize
that some necessary propositions at least do not look as if they were
analytic; and he meets this objection by extending his definition of
the word 'analytic' so as to cover all necessary propositions of this
type. But I may be wrong about this, and the subject is too technical
for discussion here.

What is clear is that he and Kant use the word 'synthetic', and I
think also the word 'analytic', in different senses so that even if one
says that a proposition is synthetic and the other says that it is not
synthetic, they may not be contradicting one another. Professor
Ayer's terminology may be the better of the two—most philosophers
of to-day think that it is. I am here concerned only with one limited
point. Kant's definitions admittedly require to be modified in order
to cover propositions that are not of the subject-predicate form; but
if we suppose, as I do, that this modification could be made, then
Kant's distinction between analytic and synthetic propositions is
exhaustive: all propositions must be either the one or the other even
if in some cases it may be difficult to say which. This is not necessarily true of the distinction as formulated by Professor Ayer.

§ 5. *The principle of verification*

We can now come face to face with the ban which has been
troubling us. It is to be found in what is known as 'the principle of
verification'. According to this principle *a statement is literally
meaningful if and only if it is either analytic or empirically verifiable.*
Such a requirement is, I take it, enjoined in the name of a logically
ideal language.

It should be clearly recognized that this principle has been de-
bated and discussed, interpreted and re-interpreted, by many acute
thinkers, and not least by Professor Ayer himself. To take it simply
may be to distort it. Nevertheless it is often taken very simply by
his more enthusiastic disciples and used as a kind of flail for the
smashing of philosophies they dislike. Here it can be treated only
in the most elementary way.

The principle restricts us to making only two kinds of statement: we are forbidden to make any others under pain of talking nonsense. If we make synthetic statements, they must be matter of fact sentences, like those of science and common-sense, which can be verified or falsified by ordinary sense-perception. If we make analytic statements, these will be mere tautologies which cannot be confuted by experience because they say nothing about the empirical world. Yet it is quite certain that if we talk about religion we shall want to make statements which look like neither the one nor the other. We seem to be stuck at the very beginning. All metaphysical and ethical assertions are ruled out as meaningless. We are forbidden to say that God exists or does not exist. We are even forbidden to affirm that stealing is wrong or is not wrong. In the latter case we are not stating anything but merely expressing feelings, which can have no place in philosophy; and the same will be true of any judgements of value—presumably even those which attempt to distinguish between religion and superstition.

If the prohibition merely urged us to be cautious in making statements other than those that are permitted, it would be all to the good. It is certainly the business of philosophy, not merely to make statements, but to consider what kind of statements they are and how they can be justified—although unless we first of all made philosophical statements, the second task would never arise. But all kinds of philosophical statements have to be examined on their merits and not simply condemned out of hand, as Professor Ayer would himself now agree. A blank prohibition is not tolerable. As I have already said, I see no reason to suppose that the distinction between analytic and synthetic propositions *as formulated by him* must necessarily be exhaustive.

A doubt of this kind is reinforced when we observe that in Professor Ayer's own book there are many statements which do not look as if they were either analytic or synthetic in his sense. Even the principle of verification itself is not obviously either one or the other, although it has been taken as both.

It is common nowadays to dismiss such a criticism as crude and elementary, but I have not had the good fortune to come across any short and convincing refutation. In a very clear article published in *Mind* of January, 1953, Mr. J. L. Evans seems to give the answer that the principle of verification is itself either not a statement or at least not a statement of the same logical type as the statements for which it lays down the criteria of meaningfulness. As he puts it, we do not expect a weighing machine to weigh itself. But for our purposes this is quite enough. It admits that there can be statements of a special logical type to which the prescribed criteria of meaningfulness do not apply. The admission stands even if we prefer to use some word for them other than 'statement'; and they certainly have meaning even if they are not 'meaningful' in a technical sense. If it is legitimate for any one to make statements—or pseudo-statements—of this type, then everybody must be allowed to do the same.

What is it that Professor Ayer is doing when he makes such statements? He tells us in the second edition that the principle of verification is not, as some people had imagined, an empirical generalization: he wishes it to be regarded as a definition, but *not as an arbitrary one.* He believes that his definition of the word 'meaning' is accurate when we consider the meaning of scientific hypotheses or common-sense statements, and up to a point he may well be right. But this is a rather narrow, not to say shaky, foundation for a doctrine so aggressive, and he now admits frankly that there may be other senses of the word 'meaning' and other definitions that are appropriate. This surely gives us all the freedom we need desire.

The nature of a definition raises notoriously difficult questions, which cannot be discussed here, but it almost looks, on this view, as if definitions are neither analytic nor synthetic; and this would mean that there is a gap in his classification—a gap which perhaps might even be extended. If I may describe Professor Ayer's procedure in my own language, he seems to be doing what good philosophers have always done—namely, trying to formulate principles. In his case the principles are principles of meaningful discourse: he is attempting to determine the conditions under which alone scientific discourse can be meaningful. If this is legitimate, there seems no reason why we should not be within our rights in trying to determine the principles of morality or art or religion—or, at the very least, of ethical, aesthetic, and theological discourse— even if these principles should turn out to be neither analytic nor verifiable by experience. His disjunction may even be a trifle too tidy to accommodate laws of nature or such a limited principle as the rectilinear propagation of light. We have to recognize at least that philosophical principles constitute a special type of statements, even if we think Kant's language unsatisfactory in describing them as synthetic *a priori* propositions; and on reflexion it may seem a trifle eccentric to condemn the philosophical principles of others as meaningless because they have the same characteristics (or the same absence of characteristics) as the principle in virtue of which they are condemned.

Needless to say, it would be absurd to pretend that the principles likely to be considered in a philosophy of religion will meet with the approval of Logical Positivists, if this term may be used, perhaps rather loosely, for the line of thought we have been examining. But every philosopher expects to meet with disapproval from those of a different school. All he has a right to ask is that his philosophy, so to speak, should not be strangled in its cradle.

§ 6. *Theological statements*

So far we have been defending only our freedom to formulate philosophical principles, and here we stand on ground that is tolerably firm. Theological assertions such as 'God exists' do not look like philosophical principles: they look much more like ordinary empirical statements. Yet few will maintain that the existence of God can be verified by sense-perception, and so the positivistic ban descends with devastating force. We are forbidden even to raise the question whether God exists or does not exist; for the question itself is said to be without meaning. This is a more complete rejection of religious belief than the agnostic allows himself, or even the atheist, since these admit that the existence of God may at least be reasonably questioned or denied.

Extreme as this view may seem, it is only an attempt to carry out logically the doctrine, already present in Kant, that the sense and significance of propositions must depend ultimately on some sort of reference to sense-perception. In one respect Kant goes further than Professor Ayer; for he holds that this is true of analytic propositions as well as of synthetic ones. On the other hand, Kant maintains that when we reflect on our experience of the sensible world, we are forced, not merely psychologically but logically, to entertain concepts of the world as a whole and of what may lie beyond it. For these concepts, and in particular for the concept of God, we can find no corresponding object in our sensuous experience, and so far they are admittedly without sense or significance. Nevertheless, according to Kant, we are able, and even compelled, to think of God, although we are unable to know Him; and we can understand how this thought must inevitably arise from reflexion on our experience. We can even understand how a God so conceived must be beyond our finite comprehension, and in abandoning the claim to knowledge, we can make room for faith.

We shall have plenty of opportunity to consider this type of doctrine when we come to examine arguments for the existence of God. It is manifestly not wholly out of accord with religious belief, for which, at its best, the nature and existence of God is a mystery not to be comprehended by our finite human understanding. There is no good reason why we should refuse to examine such doctrines on the ground that they cannot significantly be formulated in an ideal language constructed for a totally different purpose. Here too, as I feel sure Professor Ayer would agree, every serious argument has to be considered on its own merits. It might be possible to find an appropriate definition of 'meaning' which would allow even theological statements to become meaningful.

When the principle of verification is used to dispose of all theological statements and arguments at a single blow, this method of attack appears to many to be quite unanswerable. Yet there is a risk that a purely linguistic approach may conceal from us what we are doing and so may make an argument seem far more shattering than it really is. It is no new thing to find men who are prepared to believe only in what they can see and touch or in what can be proved by scientific method. God cannot be seen or touched, nor can His existence be demonstrated by the methods of science, as is recognized by all religious thinkers except the most naive. Hence if we choose to confine our beliefs within the limits of common-sense statements and scientific hypotheses, we can have no room for belief in God. This is so obvious that no intelligent person would question it for a moment. Yet a personal decision of this kind would not be regarded as a serious argument for refusing to examine the possibility that religious beliefs—not to mention aesthetic and moral judgements—may have grounds other than sense-perception or scientific discovery. It is not easy to see why it becomes a more serious argument simply because it appears in a linguistic dress— simply because we lay down such principles for our ideal language that in it only common-sense statements and scientific hypotheses can be meaningfully formulated. We cannot get rid of colours by excluding colour-words from our language, although we may perhaps impair our powers of vision.

It seems not unreasonable to reject the positivistic ban even on theological statements, or at least to construe it as a road-sign marked 'Slow' rather than 'Halt'. In theological assertions there is a genuine difficulty which is brought out by such a warning. Many of them look as if they were empirical statements; and yet it may be hard to see where we could find evidence for them that would be conclusive or even relevant. It may also be hard, once we have abandoned the most crudely anthropomorphic interpretation, to find in them a deeper significance which we can make intelligible to ourselves and others.

§ 7. *The linguistic method*

It would be ludicrous to deny that linguistic methods have a legitimate place in philosophical thinking: they have already added a new chapter to the history of philosophy. Even in moral philosophy, where they might seem less promising, they can be put to good use, as is shown, for example, by Mr. Hare in his book *The Language of Morals*. There is no reason why they should not also contribute to the philosophy of religion, whether by the examination of ordinary religious language or by the construction of an ideal one —so long as it is remembered that the ideal character of a language depends on what it is trying to say. They need not necessarily lead to pedestrian or sceptical conclusions, although these are generally preferred at present by most of those who favour this school of thought.

Although all this may be admitted, it does not follow that the linguistic method is the only method in philosophy or even the best one. It may escape some of the old difficulties, but it is likely to fall into new ones; and many of the old difficulties merely re-appear in a linguistic form. It may help us to avoid the illusion that we are making statements about the world when we are really making statements about language; but this is a danger against which the best philosophers have always been on their guard, even if they expressed themselves in other terms. In unskilful hands linguistic analysis may become devastatingly tedious, and each philosopher must decide for himself what is the best method for his own purposes.

If any one wishes to maintain that the linguistic method alone is legitimate, this is a further ban which must be decisively rejected.

In support of this prohibition it is sometimes maintained that science is concerned only with facts about the world while philosophy is concerned only with facts about how words and sentences are used. This is an inadequate way of distinguishing between science and philosophy. It is hard to see how 'a fact about' differs

from 'a true proposition about'; but if we are really talking about
facts, there is only one kind of fact, and linguistic facts are as much
part of the world as any others. All study of facts must be an
empirical study, but the philosophy of language is much more than
an empirical study of actual usage; and Professor Ayer himself
warns us against the danger of supposing that analytic propositions
are merely empirical statements about the way in which certain
symbols are in fact used. Even if we set aside this obvious criticism,
it is purely arbitrary to say that philosophy must be only talk about
talking. Philosophers have always exercised the right to talk about
science, art, morality, religion, and many other things besides
language, nor is there any good reason why they should abandon
this right—so long at least as they confine themselves to the search
for principles. To say that what they are doing is not philosophy is
to make a complete break with ordinary usage.

It is always unreasonable for any philosopher to tell others that
they must speak his language. This has often been done in the past,
sometimes by thinkers who imagined that the language they spoke
was ordinary English. Every language is made for a definite purpose:
it embodies various presuppositions and is adjusted to a particular
method. Once you attempt to speak the language of another you are
lost. This is not merely because you may know his language imperfectly—you may have, so to speak, only a reading, not a speaking,
knowledge and so be at a disadvantage, as you are in a foreign
tongue. The chief danger is that the language may already commit
you to the kind of propositions you wish to deny. The same sort of
trouble arises when we seek to translate the language of one philosopher into that of another. It can hardly be done without distortion;
and one impediment to our understanding of past philosophers—
I am not speaking of foreigners—is that when translated into
modern idiom, they may be made to say many things which they
would have indignantly repudiated. This is also true of discussions
between contemporaries who belong to different schools, and I only
hope I have not fallen myself into mistranslations of the linguistic
doctrine. One great difficulty about modern philosophy is that so
many different languages are used, and it is hard to get more than
a stammering acquaintance with all but a very few. But if any one
insists that you should adopt his language, he is really asking you
to follow his methods and think his thoughts. This you may be very
unwilling to do. You may prefer to have methods and thoughts of
your own.

One reason why some thinkers may prefer the linguistic method is that in talking about words they know they are at least talking about something, whereas in talking about God, they suspect they may be talking about nothing at all. This is carrying further the subjectivism from which, at least in matters of religion, so many of us suffer to-day. But religious experience is also something real. If we start from religious experience, we shall be in no worse a position than those who start from religious language. We certainly cannot begin by adopting an ideal language so designed that it is unable to say anything about God at all.

At any rate I propose to talk about religion rather than about religious language. To some readers this may possibly be a relief. Perhaps we shall be better able to talk about religious language if we have first tried to understand something of religion itself. On the other hand, we are likely to be more careful in what we say about religion, if we remember that the hounds of linguistic propriety may be hard at our heels.

§ 8. *The language of religion and theology*

Even if we decline to be bound by linguistic prohibitions, which— it is only fair to say—have been considerably watered down in recent years, this is no reason for being blind to obvious linguistic facts. Among these one of the most remarkable is the extraordinary gulf between the language of religion and that of theology. Religious men are apt to speak like poets, while theologians speak more like philosophers; and the emotional or emotive flavour of religious utterances is absent from the colder assertions of theology. According to the theologians, 'The Catholick Faith is this: That we worship one God in Trinity, and Trinity in Unity; neither confounding the Persons: nor dividing the Substance'. The religious man expresses himself more warmly and simply in such an utterance as 'O Love that wilt not let me go'.

This linguistic difference, like others, depends on the use to which language is being put. Religious speech is the expression of worship, whereas theology uses language in order to reflect, sometimes on the religious life, but more especially on the character of the God to whom worship is addressed. As reflective, theology must be dry and intellectual; and there is a danger that it will both fossilize and distort the living faith of which it professes to be the theoretical exposition. No theology can be adequate to the religious experience on which it reflects.

Although this difference is sharp, theological terms may acquire an emotional significance from their association with religion and may even become elements in religious language itself. It is possible to use a mixed language or to pass from one to the other, as in the writings of St. Paul. Traces of such a combination are still to be found in the *Meditations* of Descartes; and a writer like Martin Buber may even choose to expound his theology in the language of religion or poetry; but on the whole it is better to keep the two ways of speaking distinct.

As our present concern is with reflexion on religion, we have to use the colder language of philosophy or theology, although to religious men this may seem like offering them a stone when they ask for bread. At the best we can hope to provide only a kind of dusty blue-print and not a living picture, although there is no need to be either pedantic or inhuman. If the language of religion is to be employed at all, it will be in order to remind us of what we are talking about—not in order to exhort or edify or persuade.

Chapter III

THE THEOLOGICAL VETO

§ 1. *The theological veto*

When the Light Brigade charged at Balaclava, they found their progress impeded by the volleying and thundering of cannon both to the right and to the left. Philosophers who seek to tread the path of natural theology are in a similar plight. We have already had to meet the artillery of the Logical Positivists on the Left, but this seems almost like casual sniping when compared with the big guns of the Theological Positivists on the Right. Professor Ayer may think that natural theology is nonsense; but he is too indifferent to religion to be persistently aggressive, and if he places a ban on theological argument, he is perfectly willing to examine politely any rational arguments that may be brought forward against the ban itself. But to Karl Barth—if he may be taken as the leading representative of Theological Positivism—religion is of all-engrossing concern, and he insists that natural theology is not merely silly but positively sinful. The sin in question is intellectual pride: it may be compared to the sin of Adam in seeking, despite God's prohibition, to eat of the tree of the knowledge of good and evil. To Barth the voice of natural theology is the voice of the serpent; and what you do with a serpent is not to stare at it till it hypnotizes you, but 'to take a stick to it and kill it as soon as you see it'. Not only is the whole subject under a ban or veto, but the very ban itself is not open to rational discussion. Even the mild attempts made by Emil Brunner, his former brother-in-arms, to argue the matter out and to assign a most modest and subordinate function to natural theology are greeted with an 'Angry Preface' and a formidable 'No'.

The bitterness with which this fraternal discussion was conducted, at least on one side, is surprising at a time when all religion is under assault and the differences of sects might seem of minor importance. But family feuds are often the most fierce, and the methods of theological controversy in Germany are traditionally less restrained than in this country. It is also fair to say that the dispute arose during a political crisis, when the Nazis were threaten-

47

ing the Church with the aid of the so-called 'German Christians'. Barth seems to have believed that once natural theology, with its appeal to human reason, was countenanced by religious men, the main defence against political encroachment would be gone. Yet when all this is allowed, it must still be said that a display of anger is a poor recommendation for any form of religion.

The details of this dispute do not concern us here, but Barth is making a claim that his own orthodoxy must be exempt from all independent rational criticism: it cannot even allow natural theology to exist side-by-side with itself. This intolerant attitude does concern us as a recurrent phenomenon in religion. It is found, for example, among those Mohammedan theologians who rejected all attempts to enrich their traditional doctrine with ideas derived from Greek philosophy. Influenced by the Greek idea of justice, one school of innovators, the Mu'tazilites, dared to maintain that God was Infinite Justice, and not merely—as had hitherto been taught— Infinite Power and Infinite Love and Mercy. The orthodox banned this Hellenic novelty on the ground that since the requirements of absolute justice were expressed in terms derived from human reason, the products of human reason were being given an absolute value above the word of God. What is this but another version of Barth's veto on natural theology as setting human reason above divine revelation?

The theological veto, like the linguistic one, comes before us as part of a vast system which has undergone many changes. What is more, Barth has always taken the utmost liberties with language so that it is particularly hard not to fall into errors of mistranslation. Nevertheless, so far as I know, he has never retracted or modified his ban on natural theology—to so do would be to give up his whole position; and such a ban raises problems which it would be foolish to ignore.

§ 2. *A common scepticism*

The theological veto and the logical or linguistic veto may seem to be utterly opposed; for the first bans natural theology in the name of religion, and the second bans it in the name of science. Yet extremes often meet, and our two brands of positivist have at least a certain amount of negativism in common: they share equally in the scepticism which is characteristic of the modern world.

To Barth, as to Ayer, it is obvious that men can have no insight into religious principles and no knowledge of God either by unaided human reason or by any other human power. Both of them refuse to argue about natural theology, Ayer because such argument would be meaningless, and Barth because, besides being sinful, it would only distract attention from theology proper. According to him, real rejection of natural theology is not to be found in argument—this would merely be a fresh natural theology—but only in 'a complete lack of interest'. It may be said of both of them that they couldn't care less.

It is more surprising to find that Barth shares Ayer's scepticism about every form of rational ethics, although it is not easy to be sure that he is consistent on this subject. He appears to recognize the fact 'that our ability to distinguish between good and evil convicts us of our guilt'; and even if this ability, like all our human powers, is a gift of God, it is distinct from Christian faith. Yet if natural man can know what is good, and if what is good is commanded by God, then it would seem that he can know something, however dimly, of God's will. Such a supposition is ruled out from the start. Man is utterly corrupt in mind as well as in will; and all ethical systems are not merely impossible, but the fruit of man's fall and sin. Poor Brunner is rapped over the knuckles when he ventures to suggest that at least institutions like marriage and the State may—through the preserving grace of God—be known even to natural man as ordinances that are necessary and somehow sacred. To suggest this is condemned by Barth as 'dogmatic'—it is trying to turn the commandments of God into the commandments of men.

It looks as if man is as powerless to distinguish between good and evil as he is to distinguish between religion and superstition or between God and the devil. The plight of philosophy and of religion alike seems to be desperate indeed.

§ 3. *The rejection of reason*

In so desperate a situation it is not surprising that any one to whom religion is of supreme importance should look for some desperate remedy. He cannot be satisfied with a theological liberalism which comes to terms with scepticism by emptying religion of all that may give offence—or perhaps by substituting a philosophy of shallow optimism and vague amiability for the tragic drama of creation, sin, salvation, and judgement. He will resent the claim of science to be the sole arbiter of truth; and if he identifies human reason with scientific thinking, he will be prepared in theology to abandon reason altogether. If we suppose Barth to have undergone some such experience, we may be able to understand him better; and the experience would be all the more intense because of the political and ecclesiastical crises that prevailed in Germany between the Wars.

The remedy that Barth found was to go back to the Reformers and ultimately to the Bible. He sees the history of theology since the Reformation as a process of gradual decay—a rebellion of reason against revelation. First of all there came, in place of the old ortho-doxy, the 'rational orthodoxy' of the late seventeenth and eighteenth centuries, and this led gradually to the doctrines of the Enlighten-ment and to complete rationalism in religion. The great offence of Brunner is that after the summons to go back to the Reformers he is moving again towards a 'rational orthodoxy' which assigns some modest place to reason, and so is bound to start afresh a landslide into rationalism. Brunner does at least suppose that *after* the revela-tion has been received, all our dim thoughts about God and morality and social institutions will be illuminated and seen in their true perspective. This is a rational claim, but just because it is rational, it is rejected by Barth. If theology makes any concession to reason, it will have to retrace a course already followed and so to describe a complete circle.

In thought no circles are simply repeated, and Barth's theology, in spite of his heroic attempts to put the clock back, is different from that of the Reformers. They assumed the verbal inspiration of the Scriptures—a perfectly reasonable assumption at the time; and Calvin at least, a man as indiscriminately abused as he is little read, proceeded with complete rationality, not to say with a too relentless French logic, to develop his theology on that basis. As a result of modern criticism this foundation has been swept away. Outside the Roman Church all theologians of any standing have come to recog-nize that the Bible is not infallible, and Barth himself is too modern a man—perhaps too rational a man—not to accept the same view. Hence his theology, since it can appeal neither to human reason nor to an infallible authority, is bound to become personal and arbitrary: he may use Calvin's words, but they no longer have the same meaning. No doubt he still appeals, with supreme assurance if doubtful consistency, to the words of the Bible and the writings of the Reformers as witnesses to a divine revelation. But once the doctrine of verbal inspiration is abandoned, how can he distinguish between testimony which is worthy of trust and testimony which is not? If he does not judge by the principles of logical consistency and moral sanity and religious insight, must he not claim, and does he not in fact claim, that this distinction is revealed to him by God? If so, he seems to fall into a kind of personal dogmatism which is rare, at least in this explicit form. Yet it is further complicated by the doctrine—itself surely also a mark of modern scepticism—that revelation, although it is made by God, can never be known by man. Into this strange labyrinth of thought it is hardly possible to penetrate, and we must not forget that the doctrine has varied from time to time.

It would be out of place to consider here whether the theology of Barth is consistent with itself and with the teaching of the Bible. It is certainly full of paradoxes. Although he thinks little of history, his whole doctrine is based, not merely on the miracles and resurrection of Christ, but on the Fall of Adam considered as a historical fact; and every argument is supported by Biblical texts. Although God is hidden from mortals and the Bible is a veil which conceals rather than reveals, Barth can inform us in detail of divine events which are successive and apparently intermittent acts of God. Among these is the so-called 'act of faith', which for Him is divine and not human. This is an act of grace or revelation in which God knows man and saves him without any co-operation or acceptance or even awareness on his part; for man has no point of contact with the divine. Even the doctrine that God can be conceived, however inadequately, by means of an analogy with human relationships is swept aside. There is no resemblance between God and an earthly father. All we can believe is that God Himself has used the word 'father' to mean something that we can never know. It may be possible to descry some coherence in such paradoxes if we see them in the context of a whole system; but it is hard to believe that they do no violence to traditional Christian doctrine as well as to ordinary human reason.

In spite of all disclaimers it seems clear that in religion Barth demands a complete sacrifice of the intellect—a complete rejection of reason—except perhaps in the effort to keep theological thinking consistent with itself. This is sometimes watered down by his disciples: they suggest that he condemns only some arrogant and inappropriate ways of reasoning. If Barth were saying merely that empirical science can give no knowledge of God; or that thinking cannot prove God's existence and attributes; or that our thoughts of God cannot be adequate to the divine reality, but fall inevitably into contradictions; or that mere thinking can never be a substitute for religious experience—all such assertions would be reasonable enough, worthy of consideration, and even of acceptance, by reasonable men. At the very least they would be open to rational discussion. But Barth is saying very much more than this. What he is saying is that his theology is not open to rational discussion at all, and that if any one refuses to accept its presuppositions he is guilty of sinful pride. All man's powers are corrupted—his mind as well as his will—because of Adam's first sin. There is nothing whatever in man to which revelation can make an appeal. Still less is there anything in man which can presume to judge whether any revelation is genuine or not.

If this is not regarded as a complete rejection of reason in matters of religion, it is hard to imagine what would be. In denouncing natural theology Barth is forbidding us to apply human reason or human judgement to what he puts before us as the commands of God. We must no longer try to seek for truth: all we have to do is to render obedience.

§ 4. *The closed circle*

It is useless to argue with any one who declines all argument, but it may be worth while pointing out that Barth cannot be refuted so long as he remains within the circle of his own presuppositions.

There are times when we may be tempted to think that all philosophical arguments are ultimately circular. Thus if a philosopher holds that truth is what we know by intuition, he does so on the ground that he knows this by intuition. If another philosopher maintains that truth is what can be thought to cohere with the rest of our thinking, he does so on the ground that this can be thought to cohere with the rest of our thinking. If still another philosopher declares that truth is what works, he does so on the ground that this is what works. In all these cases we have a weighing machine which weighs itself—perhaps it would be better to say a measuring rod which measures itself: the alleged ground assumes what it is intended to prove. On the other hand, if it assumed some different ground, it would be a disproof of what it was intended to prove; and it looks as if only a circular proof could be valid. Certainly so long as a philosopher remains within his own closed circle or sticks consistently to his own assumptions, he cannot be refuted; for he can always retort that the refutation rests on suppositions which he rejects.

The same principle may apply to theological doctrines. If any one holds that the truth about God is only what is revealed by the Word of God, he may do so on the ground that this has been revealed to him by the Word of God. So long as he adheres consistently to this view his position is impregnable. Barth's position is more difficult because to him revelation is not revelation in any ordinary sense; but if we pass over this paradox, we can see why he is consistent in refusing to argue and why he is so angry with Brunner for attempting to put forward anything remotely resembling a rational defence. To argue at all is to appeal to human reason and so to abandon the whole position.

There is no doubt greater difficulty when we apply this circular method only to religious truth and not to all truth as such. The truth about God, which is known only by revelation, may be distinguished from the truth about nature (including man), which is known by our natural faculties; but it may not be easy—for example, in regard to Biblical history—to keep the two truths from clashing. Nevertheless, so long as we can maintain a complete separation and refuse to stray beyond our own magic circle, we can hope to be safe from the assaults of all the devils who seek to beguile us in the name of reason.

§ 5. *The claims of reason*

We are here concerned only with the principle involved in Barth's condemnation of natural theology—the principle, namely, that religion, which for him seems to be only his own religion, must never be exposed to independent rational thought or philosophical criticism.

This attitude is not new in the history of religion: Mr. Walzer's book, *Galen on Jews and Christians*, shows how it struck an educated Greek physician as early as the second century A.D. Yet it has not been the dominant view of Christian theology, whether Protestant or Catholic; and its extreme form is seldom found in theologians of Barth's eminence. It is utterly alien to the intellectual atmosphere of the modern world, and perhaps this is one reason why Barth goes to such extremes.

To many men to-day the only religion left—if it can be called a religion—is an absolute devotion to the truth. If they are open-minded enough to suppose that truth may be found in traditional religion, and not merely in science, they see many religions in the world and within these religions a great variety of sects. Many of

these claim to possess divine revelation, some of them to possess
the only divine revelation. Some may even declare that all other
religions are merely a form of sin. What in these circumstances is a
reasonable man to do?

It is clearly impossible for him to take one religion, even the one
in which he has been brought up, as the norm of all the rest, like
my Hindu friend with his sacred river. What can he do but ask
himself, humbly and honestly, whether an alleged revelation is
consistent with itself, consistent with the rest of knowledge, and
consistent with the ideals of morality?

In asking these questions he is making use of human reason, and
to do this, he is told, is sinful pride; for it is setting human reason
above the revealed Word of God. He not unnaturally asks 'How
can I know that this is the revealed Word of God?' The answer is
'You can never know, nor can you do anything that will help you
to know. You are completely blind and utterly corrupt. Revelation
is the work of God alone, and He reveals himself to some, and
denies himself to others, at His own good pleasure. You must
abandon your pitiful search for truth. All you have to do is to obey'.

Utterances of this type may spring from some kind of special
experience, whether prophetic or daemonic, and a reasonable man
will be willing to enquire into the nature of that experience and to
ask how it helps to justify religious belief. But this he is forbidden
to do. Yet unless he does so, he can see no way of distinguishing
between true religion and sheer superstition. A very little modesty
might suggest to the prophet that to question the truth of his
message is not the same thing as to sit in judgement upon God.
Theological arrogance can also be a form of sinful pride.

If we are to abandon all rational criticism of our prophets, the
result can only be fanaticism and chaos. We are admittedly not
entitled to assume that revealed truth must accord with our ordinary
beliefs, or even with our scientific beliefs; but we are entitled to
assume that all truth must ultimately be consistent. Above all we
must assume that revealed truth cannot be inconsistent with
morality. When we are exhorted to worship a God who is portrayed
as acting wickedly or commanding wickedness—and how often has
this been done by false prophets!—we must insist that the alleged
revelation has been inspired by some devilishness in human nature.
Without at least this negative criterion, anything whatever can be
accepted as revelation. Principles of this kind are required, not
merely in theology, but in religious experience itself.

It may be replied that we must not approach religion with our human standards of morality or set them up in judgement upon God. If this means only that religious experience may give us a new insight into moral ideals, and even into a kind of holiness which is above morality, it may well be accepted. But if it is the doctrine sometimes known as 'voluntarism', it means that murder and cruelty and treachery would have been virtues if God had so ordained. Such a conception of God, so far from being divine, is less than human. If we cannot recognize goodness even when we see it, we have no means of judging whether any command is divine or devilish. And if the divine grace bestows on us no dim idea of holiness by which we may judge the revelations presented by men or books, or even by our own hearts, then we are at the mercy of fanatics and charlatans and may find ourselves worshipping at the shrine of Satan.

To apply reason to matters of religion is only to think as reasonably as we can about all the evidence there is. It does not exclude, but rather assumes, the possibility that this evidence is to be found, not in philosophical reflexion, but in religious experience and religious judgement. It does not even deny that religious faith comes only by divine grace—*sola gratia*. To those who believe in God reason as well as faith is a divine gift which affords no ground for vanity or conceit.

§ 6. *Theological positivism*

In certain respects the Theological Positivist resembles what we may call the 'Legal Positivist'—the man who is concerned with the laws of a particular country and is indifferent or hostile to any philosophy of law. But the Legal Positivist does not ordinarily deny that there are laws in other countries than his own, nor does he attempt to make philosophical jurisprudence a crime. The theologian is less charitable than the jurist. Besides denouncing philosophical theology as a sin and sweeping aside all religions other than his own, he extends his condemnation within his own religion to other branches of the Church, and within his own branch to all who do not accept his doctrine and even to those who accept it on different grounds. All this in the name of humility!

If we may speak lightly on these serious matters, Barth is at first sight reminiscent of the Presbyterian elder who concluded his argument with a Jesuit by saying 'We must agree to differ. We are both trying to serve the same God—you in your way, and I in His'. Yet Barth will not even admit that others are trying to serve the same God in their own mistaken way. In his Gifford Lectures, which are less inhumane than his controversial writings, he has to tell us that 'the God of Mohammed is an idol like other idols'. His attitude to Emil Brunner recalls the venerable story—so venerable I almost blush to repeat it, but it is painfully apposite—of the old Scotswoman charged with believing that no one except herself and her minister could be saved. She replied 'A whiles ha'e ma doots aboot the meenister'.

It may be out of place to suggest that a sense of humour might make men less ready to claim so exclusive an insight into the divine mysteries. But we may think that it is contrary to the spirit of religion, as well as to the spirit of philosophy, to condemn as sin and idolatry even the dim gropings of men who are seeking humbly for God. Martin Buber is surely nearer to the truth when he tells us that all God's names are hallowed. Perhaps a religion may still be known by its fruits; and the greatest of these is charity.

It is difficult not to be impatient with Barth as he is impatient with others, but we must try to see some of the dangers of which, from his point of view, he has reason to be afraid.

If natural theology seeks to formulate the principles of religion, it may find these most perfectly embodied in one religion, but it will be suspicious of the claim that they are never embodied, however imperfectly, in other religions; and it certainly cannot agree from the start that only one religion is to be considered. To a prophet like Barth such open-mindedness is not a virtue but a vice —a rebellion against the true God.

If he finds danger to religion even in the starting-point, he is bound to find far more in the method, of natural theology. All philosophy is obliged to follow the argument wherever it may lead, and it may turn out to be a doubtful ally, if not an open enemy. Natural theology may be less robust in health, and less bold in temper, than it used to be: it may no longer claim to possess scientific knowledge or to demonstrate the existence of God. Yet, weak as it is, it may still be strong enough to play the cuckoo in the nest and try to oust dogmatic theology altogether. It is fear of this— a fear not unsupported by history—that arouses Barth's anger and causes him to sound the alarm.

This encroachment on the part of philosophy may not be altogether wanton. If natural theology could determine what is essential to religion, any dogmatic theology might seem to be of secondary importance so far as it is concerned with something over and above the essence. This does not mean that a natural theology could ever be a substitute for religion—no theology can be that. But it is easy to see that the risk of such an encroachment must arouse Barth's hostility and distrust.

Even if such fears are considered groundless, it is certain that natural theology will condemn in the historical religions whatever it regards as incompatible with the principles of religion as such. One great benefit of philosophical thinking is that it helps to clear away some of the rubbish with which religion tends to be cluttered up. In this undertaking it is liable to error, like all the rest of our human thinking; but it cannot abandon its office because of the danger of making mistakes. Barth may be right in suspecting that a dispassionate natural theology will reject, not only his banishment of human reason from religious beliefs, but also the extreme view of sinful, corrupt, and fallen man that goes along with it. In this respect too his attitude is fully consistent within his own circle of thought.

In the last resort it is even possible that philosophical reflexion may end in agnosticism. If Barth himself is sceptical enough to think that it must lead to this, then it is easy to see why he has to place an absolute ban on every kind of natural theology. The most extreme prohibitions are those that spring from fear.

§ 7. *The ban rejected*

Barth's extremism is doubtless the result of his zeal for religion, a zeal in every way worthy of respect. His vast system of dogmatic theology can be criticized only by experts, and even the claim that it should be immune from external criticism is unassailable within his own circle of ideas. I have made no attempt to refute his irrational ban on natural theology since this could be done only by the very reason he condemns; but I hope I have not misinterpreted it or made it seem more irrational than it is.

It is a good principle to assume that experts generally know their own business best, but it is none the less surprising to find theologians who regard philosophy with a complete lack of interest.

The dogmatic theologian cannot avoid making statements, not only about God, but about the world and man and virtue and vice. Such statements must have a philosophical character even if they claim to be made on divine authority. In Christian theology at least, if not in all theology, they are expressed in the philosophical language of the past. Can it be a matter of indifference to the theologian if contemporary philosophers declare his language to be outmoded and his doctrines to be false or even meaningless? The philosophers reach far more of the intellectual youth of the country than he does and have through them, in the long run, an immense, though not obvious, influence on public opinion. If—to take the extreme example—the philosophy of the universities insists that all talk about God is mumbo-jumbo, can the theologian afford to sit back comfortably in his professorial chair and say that this is no concern of his? He may think that theism is a poor sort of religion or no sort of religion at all; but the plain fact is that if educated men and women regard theism as false or meaningless, not many of them are likely to listen to him. To abandon reason in the modern world is to let his case go by default. To declare war upon reason is to alienate all who care for truth and to hold open the door for the impostor and the zealot.

Complete scepticism is a poor support, and a dangerous ally, for religion. The marriage between religious experience and philosophical reflexion, though subject to misunderstandings and quarrels, has been too fruitful of blessings for any wise man to approve a divorce. And every natural theologian must insist that philosophical thinking about religion, and even about God, is a necessary and desirable human activity, which may, like any other, be pursued either with pride or with humility.

Chapter IV

RELIGION

§ 1. *The conflict of opinion*

What is religion? In any philosophy of religion this is the first
question that must be asked. It is disturbing to find that there is no
commonly accepted answer. Those who have meditated on the
subject have the most varied, and indeed opposing, views.

Thus Professor Whitehead tells us that religion is 'what the individual does with his own solitariness'. To Professor Macmurray it
seems to be concerned rather with what the individual does in his
social relations: 'The field of religion', he says, 'is the whole field
of common experience organized in relation to the central fact of
personal relationship'. Matthew Arnold, we all know, defines
religion as 'morality touched with emotion'; but Hegel holds it
essential to a genuine religion that it should be revealed, and
revealed by God. Kant, again, declares religion—or at least religion
within the bounds of reason by itself—to be 'the recognition of all
our duties as divine commands'. To say this is to reject that very
mysticism which is thought by Giovanni Gentile—and by many
others—to be the essence of religion as such.

So we might go on indefinitely. For any serious view of religion
it is always possible to find another, equally serious, which seems
to be its precise opposite. It looks as if the internal conflicts for
which religion is unhappily notorious were mirrored in our dispassionate thinking about it. Nor would these surprising contradictions diminish—they would rather increase—if we turned from
neutral definitions to estimates of value. This is so obvious that it
needs no illustration.

It may be said that religion is not the only subject on which
philosophers contradict one another: such contradictions merely
bring out the amiable weakness of this eccentric class of men. But
in spite of the painful truth in this contention it remains a fact that
in the eyes of philosophers, to say nothing of ordinary men, religion
occupies a peculiarly ambiguous position. Wildly as philosophers
may differ in their theories about art or science or morals, they are,

broadly speaking agreed—no doubt with some striking exceptions—about the kind of activities characteristic of the artist, the scientist, and the good man. They would for the most part admit that Shakespeare had made some contribution to literature and Einstein to physics. Even on the more disputable topic of morals few of them would be anxious to deny that David Livingstone was a better man than Jack the Ripper. Furthermore, nearly all philosophers, perhaps all serious philosophers, would ascribe at least some value to art, to science, and to morality. It is far otherwise with religion. What some regard as religion would be condemned by others as mere superstition. There are many who regard *all* religion as superstition and hold that the only thing to do is to get rid of it. Art and science and morality may resemble religion in the devotion they receive from their followers; but religion can arouse an odium that is peculiarly its own.

§ 2. *What religion is not*

If we begin by considering religion, perhaps superficially, as something that men do, we seem to get stuck at the very outset; for there appears to be no activity which is specifically religious. The whole of human experience or human life is taken up by other activities, and there is no space left free. It may help us in our enquiry if we look for a little at what religion is not.

In the first place, religion does not seem to be a kind of thinking or knowing. It is certainly not science; it is not history; it is not philosophy; it is not even theology. From the point of view of religion I may have knowledge 'of all the mysteries and yet be nothing.

In the second place, religion is not morality, and still less is it. prudence. Perhaps morality in some ways comes closest to religion, and a religion indifferent to morals is valueless—if indeed it can be called religion, and not magic or superstition. Nevertheless religious men are usually the first to insist that religion, whatever else it is, is something more than 'mere' morality.

In the third place, religion is not emotion. If it were simply one form of emotional indulgence, it could never have played the part it has played in the history of the world. Furthermore, if we look for the highest expression of emotion, we find this in art; and the religious man will never admit that his religion is merely a form of art. In some ways art, like morality, does come close to religion, yet

—perhaps because of this—the artistic and religious attitude seem at times to be almost diametrically opposed.

Some may think that to speak in these terms is to apply a distinction now outmoded—the distinction between knowing, willing, and feeling as the three main strands of human experience. That there are dangers in this use of language, as in any other, may be admitted. It is the whole man who knows and wills and feels, and he is always doing all three: we describe him as doing one or the other according to the factor that is most prominent at any given time. But to speak in this way is not to split up man's total personality, nor does the use of abstract terms such as 'willing', or even as 'the will', commit us to some absurd doctrine of separate and independent faculties. The use of this tripartite distinction is essential if we are to understand the working of the human mind. Those who abandon the distinction usually reduce willing to the level of feeling, and by this ingenuous device they are able to assume without discussion that willing—like feeling, but unlike thinking—is totally non-rational so far as it can be said to occur at all. To take such a view for granted is to beg the most fundamental of questions and may lead to endless error and confusion. The correct analysis of the terms employed in the traditional tripartite distinction may be a troublesome business—it would demand, for example, a discussion of the difference between activities and dispositions; but, in spite of this, no other division is nearly as illuminating, not even the modern division into the unholy trinity of three rather unpleasant persons—the Ego, the super-Ego, and the Id.

This last reference suggests there may be a danger of forgetting about the primitive and the unconscious—that deep sea of which all our knowing and willing and feeling is said to be merely the surface froth. Can religion perhaps be regarded as a welling up of the primitive and unconscious? Theories of this kind are certainly put forward, though it is hard to make them precise. In this, as in other matters, we are confused by a multitude of voices. Freud condemns religion as an illusion, while Jung speaks of it as 'a source of life, meaning and beauty' and as giving 'a new splendour to the world and to mankind'. It is true that even Jung speaks of it as 'a real illusion'; but he is able to give the assurance—in the accommodating spirit of modern verbalism—that the difference between a real illusion and a healing religious experience is merely a matter of words.

If we do not trouble too much about the meaning of our terms, there is clearly some truth in the view which connects religious emotion— like other emotions and indeed like the spontaneous and creative element in aesthetic expression and even in all our thinking and acting—with the subconscious. It may be desirable to explore this connexion in detail, if such exploration is feasible—although much that has been written on this subject appears not to be very illuminating, at least to a casual reader. But in any case it would be a mistake to identify religion with the merely primitive. There is a marked distinction between primitive and developed religion, and one task of philosophy is to examine the principles on which one religion is regarded as higher or better than another.

There is one other thing that religion is not. Although it may be tempting to find the specifically religious activity in some sort of mystical experience, religion is not mysticism, unless we choose to alter the meaning of one or other of these words. In common usage the experience of the mystic is a very special form of religious awareness reserved for the gifted and favoured few; and even for them it is far from being the whole of religion. There have been many religious men who would not ordinarily be described as mystics, and it is a pity to blur the meaning of a word which marks an important difference. Even if we hold that there is an element, or at least a fore-shadowing, of mysticism in all religion, it would still be a mistake to identify the two.

§ 3. *Religion and the whole man*

It looks as if religion cannot be identified with any of the main conscious—or even unconscious—activities of the human spirit. What is there left? We may not be prepared to say that religion is just nothing or that it has to find its place among the chinks and interstices of our mundane occupations. The only alternative—and we may suspect this to be the truth—is that religion is concerned, not with some special aspect or manifestation of life, but with the whole of life or with life as a whole. For religion it is always a case of all or nothing.

Thus religion certainly claims to embrace the truth. Whatever else it gives, it offers us a view of ourselves and of the world in which we live. It is this that brings it into collision with science and philosophy. Religion may be worlds away from a creed, a dogma, a theology; but it always makes certain assumptions; and unless these assumptions can be formulated and defended theoretically, there is a danger that it may sink into a welter of vague emotion and false belief. In at least some religions we are also asked to believe in the occurrence of certain historical events. Hence religion is in a peculiar position, not because it gives rise to philosophical problems—every spiritual activity does that—but because, although it is far more than thinking, it nevertheless appears to have some kind of thinking or believing, or even knowing, as part of its very essence.

We find the same kind of interconnexion when we turn to morality, for no man is religious unless he is seeking to lead a good life. He may assent to all the articles of a creed; he may enjoy the most edifying of emotions; he may be scrupulous in the performance of ritual actions; but if he is deliberately cruel, consistently treacherous, completely selfish, and entirely unrepentant, then his religion is a sham.

Some may think that this is not true at a primitive level; but where religion is primitive, the distinction between religion and morality may not yet have emerged. On the whole, the evidence appears to suggest that this distinction does emerge very early, and it would be interesting to know whether the primitive religious man is, or is not, expected to live up to the moral standards of his community, however different these may be from our own. But, whatever the answer, we can at least say that morality is a necessary element in a developed religion. A religion which does not flower into moral goodness is apt to be an emotional indulgence, if it is not merely a convention to be followed out of inertia or prudence.

As for feeling, it is clear that religious experience is emotional, and the emotion may be of great intensity. This is borne out by the fact that it is often expressed in the language of love. If we consider religious emotion without reference to its object, it is commonly described on the humbler levels as consolation. In the mystic experience it rises to the pitch of ecstasy. Yet emotionally religion has also its darker side. The most religious man must expect at times to be deprived of consolation; and at least for some unhappy spirits the approach to religion is by way of anxiety and even despair.

The emotional side of religion has to find its expression in art, and much of the greatest art has been religious. There is beauty even in the religions which are most distrustful of beauty. Some men may refuse to adorn their temples with graven images; they may even be doubtful of so pure an art as music; but there always remains the beauty of the language in which the religion itself is expressed.

Like every other spiritual activity, including science itself, religion has developed historically out of something very primitive, and it may well have roots in the strange twilight region of the subconscious and the unconscious. The emotion of religious awe before what Otto has called the 'numinous' may be continuous with the primitive shudder at the presence of something felt to be eerie and uncanny. It is hard to see whether this is to its credit or discredit; but it may be taken as fitting into the view that religion is for the whole man and offers some satisfaction even to his unconscious needs. It would certainly be a fact of great practical importance if it could be shown, as is maintained by Jung, that religion with its creeds and dogmas, its ritual and symbols, is able to offer healing for the neuroses which spring from the depths of the unconscious mind.

All this raises questions about the relation of soul and body; for emotions, and primitive emotions in particular, are bound up with the bodily structure we have inherited from our ancestors. Every religion has its ritual—the bodily expression of an inward attitude and at the same time the means of its evocation; and it has been said that for primitive man religion is a thing which has to be, not thought out, but danced out. Here too it seems to be concerned with the whole man, and so with the body as the instrument or partner of the soul.

Thus it looks as if religious men were somehow seeking to become whole, or healthy, and this is borne out by the use of the word 'holy', which is perhaps the key-word in religious language. Religion appears to aim at a whole in which our intellectual ideals, our moral aspirations, our emotional needs, and even our sense of beauty, may all alike find their satisfaction. If this is so, religion cannot be a matter of negligible interest, and we may reasonably demand of it that it should be sound or sane.

§ 4. *Man and the whole*

There are many reasons why the account so far given is bound to seem inadequate and incomplete. Religion may possibly aim at some sort of integrated personality—if this modern jargon may be forgiven—but surely a man can be an integrated personality without being religious, and he can also be religious without being an integrated personality.

It certainly seems as if a man might be a whole man, and might lead a balanced intellectual, moral, and emotional life, without being in any way religious. Perhaps some may think that religion is more likely to upset such a balance than to create it. Yet from the religious point of view it would have to be said, not only that without religion a balance of this kind is precarious, but that the wholeness or harmony of a non-religious life is imperfect. There would still be something lacking; and the reason why we have failed to see this, the reason why our analysis has gone astray, is that we have been regarding the religious life merely as the activity of isolated and finite individuals. If the finite individual is to become whole, he cannot do so either by himself or even in his relation to other finite beings: he must somehow in some sense become at one with *the* Whole—the ultimate whole beyond which there is nothing else. Such seems to be the minimum claim of developed religion. And perhaps we should add that—at least in the West—the Whole is taken to be no mere object of our contemplation, but something like a subject in its own right. To express this in the language of Martin Buber—there is always in religion some relation of self to the Other, to what is sometimes spoken of as 'the Absolute Thou.'

Our account was not merely theoretically inadequate: it was also morally misleading, being altogether too self-centred and egoistic. Every ideal can be degraded by man in practice, and it is only too true that for many men religion becomes one form of selfishness, a prudent effort to avoid eternal punishment or at best a vivid concern with personal salvation. All this is as false to religion as it is to morality. What the religious man seeks is not primarily to receive favours or consolations or even to win salvation for himself—the very word 'salvation' at least lends itself to misunderstanding. Religion does not exist in the isolated individual soul, but in man's relation to something that is other and greater than himself.

If reflexion on religious experience leads men to talk about the Whole which is also the Other, this suggests a close connexion between religion and metaphysics. Metaphysics too, as the supposed science of ultimate reality, is concerned with the Whole, and it employs very similar language—even to the extent of using initial capital letters. This practice is often derided to-day, and it would be out of place in philosophy if its only aim were to be awe-inspiring. Yet it may serve to indicate that we are concerned, not with limited wholes (of which the number is infinite), but with the one ultimate whole of which all limited wholes are only parts. Hence 'the Whole' becomes almost akin to a proper name—the

E

name of something that is individual—and so is written with a
capital. Since no finite individual can be the Whole, the Whole is
also known as 'the Other', and this expression too is treated as akin
to a proper name.

It must not be thought that relationship to the Other is confined
to religion.

Even in thinking there is always a relation to the Other—a relation, not only to other selves with whom we share our thoughts and
to a world not made by us which we seek to know, but ultimately to
a whole system of reality, of which other selves and the world as we
know it are only parts. In knowing bits of reality we seek to know
them together in their relation to one another and so as parts of a
wider whole—ultimately as parts of the one all-comprehensive
whole. Such knowledge is the ideal, conscious or unconscious, of
all our thinking, even although it is beyond our intellectual grasp.

But perhaps it is in action that we are most aware of our relation
to the Other. In all action there is a relation to other selves who
co-operate with or resist our will and to a world of things which is
at once an instrument and an obstacle; but when we rise to the
level of morality, we find, not only that we are seeking to realize a
systematic whole of human co-operation, but that this ideal cannot
be attained without something like the co-operation of the whole
universe of which we form a part. It is this that brings morality so
close to religion.

With art the case is rather different, for every work of art appears
almost to be a little universe in itself.

So far the Other has been spoken of as if it were something out
there for us to know, to work with or against, and so on. But many
men, and these by no means necessarily religious, have at times a
feeling that in their thinking and acting, especially when these are
at their best, it is not they who are thinking and acting, but something other that is thinking and acting through them; and the artist
may have a similar experience. It may almost seem as if what I call
our activity is given to us from without and so far is passive—even
although we have at least to hold it together in time if it is to be *our*
experience. Some may connect this experience with the unconscious,
or even with some sort of collective unconsciousness, but it is
specially prominent in religion. Whatever importance we attach, or
refuse to attach, to feelings of this kind, they at least suggest the
possibility that the Other may not merely be the object of our
thought or the aid to our strivings, but may be active in us and so

perhaps not wholly other than ourselves. If this were so, the Other would be, not merely the Whole on which we depend, but also the Whole of which we are somehow a part.

Talk of this kind is highly abstract and even metaphysical, but it is one of the ways in which philosophers try to formulate the Idea of God.

§ 5. *The Idea of God*

As hitherto described, the character of the Other has been left extremely vague—too vague to satisfy the religious consciousness, yet not vague enough to be free from contradictions. It is hard to see how the Other can also be the Whole, yet this is how it appears to be experienced, or at least felt, by religious men. To them God is certainly the Other, but He is also conceived as somehow 'all in all'.

Views of this kind are apt to arouse the ire of analytic thinkers who regard clarity as the supreme intellectual virtue. They forbid us to talk about the Whole, and are naturally pleased to find that when we ignore their prohibition, we begin to talk nonsense—not merely by making assertions which cannot be verified, but by using concepts which are mutually contradictory.

No easy answer can be given to this criticism. Nevertheless our concern with limited parts of the world inevitably raises questions as to the Whole, unless we deliberately restrain our thoughts by an arbitrary act of will. We may, reasonably enough, regard these questions as unanswerable and so may prefer not to attempt an answer; but we go too far if we ignore their existence or elevate our personal preferences into categorical prohibitions. It may be possible for us at least to understand how these questions must arise, and even to understand how we must fall into contradictions when we seek to apply to the Whole, by some kind of analogy, words whose ordinary use is to describe only the parts. But in any case our present task is to make clear what seem to be the claims of the religious consciousness. There is no attempt here to justify these claims.

The question whether the religious man feels a relation to something which is the Whole or the Other, or is somehow both, is akin to the theological question of God's immanence or transcendence. Some doctrines of Buddhism, if an Irishism may be used, make God so immanent that He ceases to be God, and we may become doubtful whether we have here one form of religion or merely a special way of morality. It is also possible to consider God as so transcendent that He becomes inconceivable and consequently indistinguishable from nothing. If we are to believe in God at all, we must think of Him as immanent in the self and in the world at least to the extent of being conceivable, however imperfectly, by man; and we must also think of Him as transcendent in the sense of not being wholly conceivable by finite beings.

Of greater interest to the religious man is the question whether God is to be conceived as personal or impersonal.

Mr. Aldous Huxley tells us that mystics who go far enough in recollection and meditation always end 'by losing their intuitions of a personal God and having direct experience of an ultimate reality that is impersonal'. This conclusion appears to have his moral approval since he also informs us that 'whenever God is thought of, in Aristotle's phrase, as the commander-in-chief rather than as the order of the army . . . persecution always tends to arise'. Such generalizations seem too sweeping; but the fact has to be faced that there are religions—especially in the East—which are content with a God (if this term may be applied) who is characterized only by metaphysical attributes, such as first cause or ultimate reality, and not at all by attributes derived from human personality, such as wisdom and goodness. In the Western world God is more commonly conceived, not merely as ultimate reality, but also as a subject of thought and action and as in this respect akin to a human person. This is what is meant by speaking of Him as 'the Absolute Thou'. Those who use this language conceive of God as somehow personal or more than personal and of man's relation to Him as somehow akin to a possible relation between men. Here is the great cleavage within religion itself, and many of those who take the Western view would regard any other as more of a philosophy than a religion. Even so, it has to be recognized that to speak of God in terms of personality is at the best to make use of a human analogy, which must be inadequate to the divine nature. It is possible that these sharp theological distinctions are the product of reflexion rather than of religious experience itself, but I propose to use in the main our Western terminology, which has at least the advantage of being familiar. Its difficulties will no doubt force themselves upon us later.

In spite of all these uncertainties it may perhaps be as well to say boldly that for the religious consciousness God must be and must be perfect.

To say that God must be is to say that the religious consciousness is not satisfied by the mere conception of an ideal. Religious men will not be content with an imaginary God any more than business men will be content with imaginary dollars. If the view is accepted that religious experience is not self-centred, but is, as it were, focussed upon the Other, then it is not enough for it to have what has been called an imaginary focus—a *focus imaginarius*. If a religious man is convinced by his critics that he is worshipping an ideal which is not also real, he will seem to himself to be descending from religion to morality.

The statement that from the religious point of view God must be perfect is almost equally obvious. It is true that in primitive religions the gods may be merely objects of fear and gratitude and so may be regarded as little more than beings who certainly possess power and may possibly exercise benevolence. But as religion develops, the divine nature is less crudely conceived. Even in the narrowly self-centred view with which we began it was assumed that religion must be able to satisfy our intellectual ideals, our moral aspirations, our emotional needs, and our sense of beauty. If so, God must be characterized in the light of such satisfaction; and we find this confirmed in the language which speaks of Him as the all-wise and all-knowing, the all-powerful and all-loving, the all-glorious, and the all-holy. Once we pass to the more genuinely religious view which is not self-centred, it seems evident that only a God so conceived can be an object of worship.

It may be thought that the concept of perfection is altogether vague and incapable of supporting analysis. This may be so, but we have to remember that analysis is not the dominant interest of religion. I have here interpreted perfection in the traditional language of Western religions, but the statement that God must be perfect need not be incompatible with a considerable variety of beliefs. It might be accepted by a man who used the word 'perfection' in a purely metaphysical sense for the self-sufficient or the complete. It might even be accepted by a man who regarded perfection as a state bordering upon nothingness. We may think this a queer idea of perfection, but it is not more queer than the idea that blessedness is a complete absence of feeling.

§ 6. *Worship*

If the word 'God' may be used for the Other who appears to the religious consciousness to be somehow also the Whole, to be utterly remote and yet revealed in all creation, to be personal or more than personal, but above all to be and to be perfect, is it possible to describe further the relation between the religious man and his God?

Here again we have to start from religious experience, an experience in which feeling is a prominent factor. The emotional side of religion runs the whole gamut from despair to ecstasy, but on the humbler levels it may be most fittingly described as consolation. It could also be described as peace—an inner peace even in the midst of strife—but these words make religious experience seem too self-contained unless it is added that the peace and consolation in question seem to be given and received: they are not acquired by our own efforts. In order to make it clear that religious experience seems to be more than a state of the individual, it may be said— with Schleiermacher—that the predominant religious feeling is one of dependence. Whatever he may have meant by this, I take it to be an immediate feeling of dependence on the Other—not a self-contained feeling of helplessness from which we make a dubious inference to something else as its cause. Otto prefers to speak of a 'creature-feeling'; but this—apart from its revolting character as a word—again suggests an intellectual theory of the relation between the creature and the creator, although what he has in mind is something very different. Perhaps the feeling in question could be described better as a feeling of trust or even of self-surrender.

The religious feeling of dependence may be one of *utter* dependence, involving awe as well as trust; but we should surely hesitate to connect it too closely with fear and horror and shuddering. However strong such feelings may be in primitive religion, and even in the initial, or sometimes the recurrent, experiences of the sadder saints, they seem most appropriately directed to the uncanny which is still undifferentiated and may be devilish rather than divine.

If the religious feeling of dependence is taken to be one of awe as well as of trust, the religious attitude may be described most simply as worship.

So far it is the *feeling* of dependence that has been emphasized; but if religion is for the whole man, there must also be both an intellectual recognition of this dependence and a voluntary acceptance of it as a basis for action.

Of these two the voluntary attitude is the easier to characterize. It may be described as one of service or, better, of dedication. The religious man seeks to put his whole life at the service of God and in doing God's will to serve others. His aim is not his own personal spiritual progress but the coming of the Kingdom of God; and all the duties incumbent upon him in that enterprise he sees as divine commands.

The factor of intellectual recognition is much harder to describe, for it is here that religion passes insensibly into theology, and so the subtle begins to prevail over the simple. The religious man recognizes that he can do nothing of himself and that everything comes to him by divine grace. This is the ground of his humility and gratitude; but it must also be remembered that only in divine service does he feel himself to be free. Furthermore, in recognizing his own dependence he recognizes also the dependence of all creation. In particular, he conceives goodness as effective in the world only through God's will; and this conception may be described as at least one aspect, the intellectual aspect, of what men call 'faith'. There is implicit in it a theory of God's nature and of His relation both to the world and to human beings. Yet the theory is taken for granted rather than explicitly conceived: it is felt, so to speak, as an awareness of reality rather than as the acceptance of propositions. If we wish to avoid the emphasis on theory which is too often associated with the word 'faith', we may prefer to go back to a word already used in connexion with the feeling of dependence—the word 'trust'. The religious man trusts in God that in spite of appearances He will do all things well and will not allow any effort towards goodness to be made in vain. It is this that gives the saint an assurance of strength and peace.

§ 7. *What religion is*

Religion is for simple people, and so must itself be simple. A theory which ignores this simplicity must be mistaken. Perhaps it may be hoped that we have not gone too far wrong if we have described religion as worship, dedication, and trust; for all of these are possible even for the simplest of men.

It may be tempting to connect worship with feeling, dedication with willing, and trust, as I have described it, with thinking or belief; but these connexions were only provisional devices for trying to find what we sought. Religious experience is always an experience of the whole man as a whole in his relation to the Other or the Whole. Like everybody else, the religious man will at different times be specially concerned with acting or thinking or feeling. Indeed this must be so if, ideally at least, his whole life is religious through and through; but he is not more religious in virtue of the

predominance of one factor rather than another. The religious life
is not lived in compartments. Alike in worship, in dedication, and in
trust the whole man is feeling and willing and even in some ways
thinking or knowing, if we use these words in their most general
sense; and his whole life—not merely different phases of it—is trust
and dedication and worship. Each of these is inseparable from the
other two, and indeed they are not three things, but only one. This
one thing which is the essence of the religious life may be described
most simply and appropriately by the single word 'love', provided
love is understood as worship and dedication and trust—not as
sickly sentiment without intellectual content or practical results.
And, like all love, it may seem to come as a favour or a gift—not by
our own efforts, but by divine grace.

   To say this is merely to formulate what all religious men are
supposed to know. I began by speaking about religion as concerned
with the wholeness of the individual in his relation to the Whole or
the Other. These cold and vague phrases might be filled up in
various ways, even in negative ways that regard the wholeness of
the individual as something to be found only through absorption in
the Whole, and so through self-annihilation. I have filled up these
phrases positively in accordance with our Western tradition. On
this view what the religious man seeks is that grace may be given to
him to lead, in co-operation with his fellows, a life of worship and
dedication and trust, not for the sake of his own wholeness, but as
his contribution to an all-comprehensive whole beyond himself, or
even as a manifestation of his love for God and God's love for him.
This may remain a true description even if he is the victim—the
happy or pathetic victim—of an illusion. In spite of widespread and
growing indifference to religion, I am inclined to think that at least
it is the description of a human aspiration and a human need.

Chapter V

RELIGIOUS ABERRATION

§ 1. *Aberrations and obsessions*

Religion would have aroused less hostility if it had displayed only the characteristics so far ascribed to it. What has been depicted is an ideal towards which religious men aspire, an ideal which may be realized in some of them to a greater or less extent. But, as Aristotle remarked of morality, there are many ways of going wrong, and only one way of going right. Whatever may be thought about the second part of the statement, it is impossible to doubt the truth of the first. The ways of going wrong in religion may be called mistakes or aberrations: to speak of them as errors would be to make them too intellectual. It is now our ungracious task to review some of these possible aberrations. If they can be seen as deviations from the ideal, this may help to make the ideal itself more intelligible. It may also show how some of the hostility to religion springs from its aberrations rather than from religion itself.

If the religious life is a balanced one in which different factors—intellectual, moral, emotional, and even primitive—have their part to play, each of these factors by going wrong may warp the religion in which it plays a part; but an attempt to trace all these possible deviations would be concerned with the sum total of human folly. The enquiry may be narrowed by supposing that perhaps the most serious deviations from the ideal may occur when one of these factors is over-stressed at the expense, or even to the exclusion, of others. This may be used as a clue for the discovery of religious aberrations, which, it need hardly be said, vary greatly in degree. In extreme cases they may be called religious obsessions; for in some ways they resemble fixed ideas which disturb the harmony, and destroy the completeness, of the religious life.

There are thus four possible aberrations to begin with, each having its own distorted vision of God: (1) the obsession with the primitive, (2) the obsession with emotion, (3) the obsession with thinking, (4) the obsession with morality. Unfortunately there may be many more.

§ 2. *The obsession with the primitive*

A genuinely primitive religion is not the perversion of something higher, but the first clumsy effort of the human spirit to rise above the level of the brute. As such it has a claim to sympathy and understanding; and it may at times show a simple insight which the modern townsman, with his artificial environment and his sophisticated thinking, may have almost entirely lost. The religion of primitive peoples has to be judged in relation to their own society and environment, not in relation to ours. When it is so judged, much that to us seems arbitrary or meaningless, or even revolting, may become intelligible. Nevertheless complacent talk about the noble savage is less justified to-day than in the time of Rousseau, for we can speak with fuller knowledge. When we consider the ignorance and superstition, the cruelty and bloodshed, and above all the dread and horror, which make up so much of primitive religion, we cannot lightly indulge in the language of unmixed eulogy.

The aberration which concerns us here is a falling back to the primitive from a higher level. In religion, as has been already suggested, there may be some satisfaction of unconscious needs, especially in the ritual which is the bodily expression of an inward attitude and is also the means of its evocation. There is a return to the primitive wherever ritual is practised as having value in itself apart from any inward attitude. If ritual is employed as a direct means for winning divine favour or—still worse—as a method of manipulating the divine will, religion is degenerating into a form of magic. This may be seen in far Tibet in the use of the prayer-wheel —a mechanical device for economizing spiritual energy. It may be seen nearer home wherever religious ceremonies are performed with no thought behind them or only the thought of personal advantage. There are countless examples, and they are the mark of a dead or dying religion. In all ages reformers have had to insist that religious ceremonial is of no value in itself and that the only way to please God is by justice and mercy and humility.

There is a wilder side to all this. As we are constantly reminded to-day, there are dark forces in our mental underworld, and the modern tendency to worship these would be comic if it were not so tragic. The two great primitive drives are pugnacity and sex. Some men seem inclined, as it were, to take out their religion in fighting and others in sexual indulgence—the latter leading at times to a morbid fear of sex which may itself also be something primitive at

a further remove. Among the religions marked by a primitive wildness the best known is the religion of Dionysus, in which the ecstasy
seems often to have been independent of wine—although on this
point different authorities take curiously different views. In some
kinds of modern revivalism, both in this country and more especially
in America, there are other forms of religious excitement which
appear to be in no need of alcoholic stimulus. Primitiveness may be
manifested, not only in a dying religion, but in one that is struggling
to be reborn.

Some reversions to the primitive are little more than a homesick-
ness for the mire. On a slightly higher level there may be an eruption
of the primitive in the glorification of fighting and in the worship of
the will to power; but this may be merely a substitute for religion
rather than a religion itself. A more genuinely religious perversion
is the obsession with fear and trembling, anxiety and despair, which
is for ever recurring and has found literary expression in the works
of Kierkegaard and his disciples. Whatever value such literature
may have as a corrective of complacency, and however deserving of
pity may be the painful experiences at its root, this obsession is not
merely primitive, but neurotic—a mark of disease and not of health.
It resembles that terrible obsession with demons and devils which,
in an even cruder way, tormented the lives of so many mediaeval
saints.

§ 3. *The obsession with emotion*

The obsession with religious emotion is sometimes indistinguishable from obsession with the primitive, but it requires to be looked
at for its own sake. Every human activity tends to be accompanied
by some sort of feeling which, as it were, takes its colour from the
activity and is closely connected with our judgements of value. To
this rule religion is no exception: it is always emotional, and sometimes strongly emotional. Nevertheless religious feeling should be
regarded as no more than an accompaniment, however precious, of
the religious life. Those who make it their primary aim are likely to
lose interest in the religious life itself and so to lose or to distort the
emotion that accompanies it.

There is a special danger of this when religious emotions fail to
issue in action. Religion then becomes a form of selfishness or self-
absorption; and like selfishness in general it leads only to a sterile
narcissism and an emptying of the individual's life. When divorced
from action, emotion has to find its outlet in vague day-dreaming,

in a world of phantasy out of relation to the real world. In any case religious emotion, like every other, is by its nature transient. This is recognized by writers like Thomas à Kempis, who insists— possibly too much—that the religious man must set himself to endure toil and hardship, and not to enjoy supernatural delights.

Sometimes the obsession with emotion takes the form of a sickly sentimentality, which is glorified too often by the sacred name of 'love'. The love we are bidden to show to our neighbours, and even to our enemies, is interpreted, not as genuine consideration and active kindness, but as an emotional fervour which would be excessive if directed towards our nearest and dearest and is impossible as a permanent state of mind. Insistence on this so-called love can lead only to a natural and very proper revolt. A sane religious view may enable a man to think more warmly and kindly of his neighbours and to regard every individual soul as having—at least potentially— an absolute worth in the sight of God. But this is worlds away from directing towards others a spurious emotion and subjecting them to a treatment repugnant alike to common sense and self-respect. The family of those known to the Americans as 'sob-sisters' are a menace to religion as to any healthy form of moral and practical life.

The same principles must hold even of the emotional side of mysticism. From the accounts given of it, the mystic ecstasy seems to be something which seizes upon the individual, not something to be sought and cultivated, although the way for it may be prepared by leading a specially exacting moral and contemplative life. Even mystic emotion is not to be divorced from the other factors in religion. 'It sufficeth for me', says one of the English mystics, 'to live in truth principally, and not in feeling'. And St. Teresa herself, speaking of the genuine union 'which consists in making our will one with the will of God', says 'This is the union which I desire and should like to see in you all: I do not covet for you those delectable kinds of absorption which it is possible to experience and which are given the name of union'. There may well be emotional aberrations connected with the mystic experience; but if there are, few of us are likely to suffer from them.

There is no need to speak too harshly of the obsession with emotion, and it should be added that in some people concern with religion is mainly aesthetic: it has little bearing on action and less on truth. Such an attitude may be unsatisfying to those whose religion is more whole-hearted; but it may have its own value and may flower into works of art, even in a sceptic like Dante Gabriel

Rossetti. It is an error to draw too hard and fast a line in these matters, and there may be all sorts of shades between an experience which is mainly aesthetic and one which is decisively religious.

§ 4. *The obsession with thinking*

Another religious aberration may be described, perhaps rather misleadingly, as an obsession with thinking, or at least with the theoretical element in religion. There can hardly be too much thinking in religion, except in the sense that it is possible to substitute theory for the religious life, to become a critic rather than a practitioner. This is not very common except among philosophers (professional or amateur) and possibly theologians. What I have in mind is a fixed or closed thinking which may cease to be thinking altogether—the kind which works out, or takes over, an elaborate theology and claims that every clause must be adopted as an article of faith. Here an exaggerated importance is assigned to the acceptance of theoretical propositions, and there arises an intellectual intolerance which is not only fatal to thinking but dangerous to religion itself.

Intolerance of a kind is a danger to all religions, but intellectual or doctrinal intolerance seems a special temptation to followers of the Christian faith. The traditional method of asserting that a brother theologian has fallen into error is to call down a curse upon him—'*anathema sit*'; and this practice has its roots even in St. Paul. It sometimes looks to the pessimist as if the subtlety of the Greeks and the zealotry of the Jews and the legalism of the Romans had all combined for the purpose of destroying the religious spirit. On the creed which goes by the name of Athanasius it may be permissible to quote the good English common-sense of Richard Rolle, a mystic of the fourteenth century. 'This psalm', he says charmingly, 'tells us much of the Trinity, but it is not necessary for every man here to know it, since a man may be saved if he believes in God and hopes that God will teach him afterwards what is necessary . . . . But God forbid that men believe that every man must believe expressly every word that is said here, for few or none are in that state, either Greeks or Latins'. If this gentler spirit had prevailed, we should have avoided, not merely the bloodshed and persecution which have stained the annals of Christendom, but also the embittered controversies between sects, and the agonizing spiritual conflicts within the souls of individual men, which have turned religion into a kind of nightmare. Modern criticism has done a great service in helping to diminish the force of such intellectual obsessions, but there is always a danger of their recurrence.

It would be foolish to depreciate the value of thinking on religious questions. Apart from cool reflexion religion may become vague and sentimental and even extravagant. But such theological thinking must be free and spontaneous and, above all, modest—claiming at the most to offer us the best light available at the time and willing to modify itself with further insight. In some ways religions are like rose-bushes: they cannot flourish unless from time to time the dead wood is cut away.

There is always a temptation for the theologian to believe that he alone is right. He sees so clearly what he does see, and he can be so blind to what others see. It is as possible for the innovator to be intolerant as it is for the traditionalist. The traditionalist may even claim to be the more modest of the two inasmuch as he has behind him the wisdom of the ages; but the corporate intolerance of the priest may be more deadly than the personal intolerance of the prophet. All I maintain here is that the theologian, however much he may cling to his own views, ought never to claim that their acceptance is the condition of salvation. Still less ought he to impose his views by force. To do this is to be guilty of what I have called obsession with the theoretical element in religion.

§ 5. *The obsession with morality*

It is equally possible to be obsessed with the moral element in religion. This is a mistake in practice as well as in theory, and is consequently commoner, since most men are but little concerned with theory. In some ways it may be a more dangerous mistake; for experience suggests that religious life may flourish side-by-side with an exaggerated emphasis on theories, and even on monstrous theories, whereas an absorption in what is sometimes called 'cold' morality may mean the emptying, or possibly the death, of religion itself.

It may seem absurd—and indeed it is absurd—to suggest that the religious man can be too moral: we might as well say that a circle can be too round. But there is a parallel here to what was said about thinking. Morality may become a substitute for religion; but, broadly speaking, the danger to religion comes, not from a living and warm morality, but from a cold morality that is fixed or closed.

This might be better described as a kind of legalism or pharisaism, an unintelligent and even fanatical adherence to a code of rules from which the spirit of morality has departed.

This kind of mistake (along with others) is to be found in the harsher forms of Puritanism, but Puritanism is not confined to a particular movement in sixteenth or seventeenth century England: it is a tendency manifested in all ages, and in nearly all religions—not to say in movements which need not be religious at all. What is more, even some of its harsher forms may be an exaggeration of something good; for a measure of austerity towards oneself, and possibly—though with more circumspection—towards others, may be a healthy element both in morality and in religion. Even moral rules are not entirely otiose, and it is foolish to imagine that a total lack of discipline is likely to make for the well-being either of the individual or of the race.

A cold morality may have two main forms. The first takes moral ideals seriously, but shows to the sinner a harshness which sometimes springs from an uneasy feeling that his temptation is particularly attractive to ourselves. The second is shallow and displays a complacent satisfaction with mere convention: it worships at the shrine of the great god Respectability and so is different from Puritanism, which can be too wild to be respectable. Respectability is not altogether to be despised: it may be an appropriate butt in an age of decorum, but in a period of coarseness and violence it may even become precious. Yet in the eyes of the religious man it trifles with the great issues of good and evil. Here we have a too common form of religious decay, and also of moral decay, although it is less harmful than an abandonment to magic and superstition.

Where morality is living and creative, the position is different. Here all persons are already regarded as possessing, at least potentially, an absolute value, and men seek to establish a society whose members will act freely on the principle that every one should be treated in this spirit. Such a morality may come very close to religion, and the distinction between those who accept or reject this principle is more fundamental than the distinction between those who accept or reject religion. The religious man may find this morality incomplete, but he will be short-sighted if he fails to see in it an attitude akin to his own. A living morality without religion is better than a religion without morality; nor should it be difficult to understand how good men have felt obliged, or even eager, to be content with it, and have feared to clutter it up with beliefs for which they can find no intellectual justification. Such men follow good as they see it and are willing to leave the ultimate issue to whatever forces may control the world. But it may be hard to maintain this attitude unless they can at least hope that these forces may be somehow on the side of goodness; and to have that hope, however faintly, is already to have something of the religious spirit.

§ 6. *The spirit of intolerance*

The aberrations so far considered arise because one element in religious experience is exaggerated at the expense of the whole. Curiously enough, there is another and very grave aberration which springs from an obsession with the wholeness of religion. A whole-hearted religion may become a totalitarian religion—so closely do defects, like a kind of shadow, follow on the heels of even our best qualities.

Here again it would be absurd to suggest that a man can be too whole-hearted in religion. His religion claims the whole of him, his emotions, his art, his thinking, and the entire practical conduct of his life. It claims, moreover, to be valid for all men and even to reveal the will and purpose of God. Concern with all this may produce an inner tenseness and rigidity, which is fatal, not merely to humour and practical sense, but to that relaxation without which no great thing can be achieved. It is fatal also to the spirit of tolerance in dealing with others. Religion to its devotees seems at times to spread so slowly, and to meet with such blind and sinful opposition, that young men in a hurry, and middle-aged men who have lost the high hopes of youth, and old men whose time is short are all alike prepared to impose their beliefs and practices on others by every means in their power. The greatest danger of religion, because of its very whole-heartedness, is intolerance. Think as I think, feel as I feel, do as I do, worship as I worship, or else it will be my sacred duty (and perhaps my secret pleasure) to destroy the miscreants who so impiously rebel against the righteous demands of my God—and of myself as his chosen and dedicated instrument. In face of the savagery which has been the darkest shadow of religion—and not least of religions of love—it is not surprising that men have felt with passion, and still feel with passion, that this truly devilish thing must be swept away.

If intolerance were a monopoly of religion, it would be hard not to agree with them. Unfortunately we have seen in our day, and are

still seeing, that the fires of persecution may flare up whenever men
are whole-hearted in any cause, even the most irreligious. It is
impossible to get rid of intolerance and cruelty by abolishing
religion, for these things have their roots in the lowest depths of
human nature. But the bullying saints ought continually to remind
themselves that a persecuting religion is the worst form of
blasphemy.

§ 7. *Wildness and rigidity*

If intolerance is not peculiar to religion, but is rather, as it were,
the shadow cast by zeal and whole-heartedness in any human
endeavour, it may be asked whether other religious aberrations may
not spring from the common defects of human nature, although
they take their special colouring from the setting in which they arise.

In all human achievement—if so bold a simplification may be
permitted—there is a tension or equilibrium between spontaneity
and discipline. Where this tension or equilibrium is destroyed, so
that spontaneity becomes undisciplined or discipline unspontaneous,
there is inevitably failure and aberration. Spiritual activity must be
free, but it must also be controlled; and as freedom may degenerate
into anarchy, so control may degenerate into rigidity. All the aberrations in religion may be understood as a failure to maintain the
proper balance of two opposing tendencies. In the obsession with
the primitive and the obsession with emotion, and indeed in all the
wildness and enthusiasm of religion, men seem to abandon control
in favour of an unregulated and disordered spontaneity. A similar
abandonment may be suspected in those who seek to substitute
what they call 'guidance' for moral judgement and common sense.
The danger of rigidity has already been seen in the obsession with
thinking and the obsession with morality; but it may also be found
in the obsession with the primitive so far as this is manifested in a
mechanical use of ritual. It may even be present in the sentimentality which substitutes spurious for genuine emotion—as in those
who adopt a fixed religious smile. But the different strands of aberration are so closely intertwined that it may also be possible to combine a kind of wildness with a kind of rigidity. Intolerance, for
example, may be wild and rigid at the same time.

Whatever be the truth in these complicated matters, the history
of religion offers us the spectacle of a continuous oscillation between
reform and decay. In periods of reform religion may be a revolutionary force and may suffer from wildness and extravagance. But

F

these reforming movements are apt quickly to lose their impetus, and men fall back into a kind of spiritual fossilization in which the letter triumphs over the spirit. Religion becomes a matter of habit and external observance with little breath of life. When this is so, external observances, naturally enough, will cease to inspire, and even those professionally concerned with religion may lead a worldly, if not a sensual, life under the cloak of their official position. Although there may be no complete collapse, there may be a tendency to substitute some other interest for religion—at best an interest in morality, but sometimes an interest in the welfare and power of the institution in which religion finds its outer embodiment.

It would be fair to add that between the movement of reform, which may be living without necessarily being wild, and the period of decay, which may never be complete, there may be a time of balance when religion is at its best. There are, so to speak, relatively level stretches of religious history as well as ascents, which may be quick, and descents, which may be gradual. There are also minor ups and downs in the religious life both of individuals and of communities. But at present our concern is with religious aberrations, and a picture of these in isolation is bound to be over-simple.

§ 8. *The deviation into politics*

On the whole, wildness is a lesser danger to religion than rigidity; for wildness, although it may be most offensive, tends to work itself out in a short time, and it is at least a sign of life, while rigidity is a mark of mechanism and even of death. The victory of mechanism over life is most conspicuous where an ecclesiastical institution becomes more important than the religion it was intended to serve. This might be described as the obsession with politics.

The fundamental aberration here is not the attitude of religious men or institutions to secular politics. This raises complicated questions, and too often the fixed conservatism so often found in religion itself has resulted in an equally fixed antagonism to necessary political change. But the main problem is one rather of ecclesiastical politics—the politics inseparable from the religious institution known in the West as a Church.

A Church is indeed more than a religious institution. The Idea of the Church—for ultimately there can be only one—as a community of all the faithful in heaven and earth is in itself one of the great religious ideals. But the Church on earth can hardly exist except as organized in some sort of institution or institutions; and through this ecclesiastical or political organization it spreads out, as it were, visibly in space and time. Without such an external organization no Church can either expand or endure. This is obvious where religion is bound up with a priesthood claiming authority from a long line of predecessors. But it is true also in a religion, like that of Islam, whose ministers make no claim to priestly powers. There must always be some sort of organized religious institution, and for the present purpose any such institution may be described as a kind of Church.

Every human institution may fail to adjust itself to changing circumstances and growing knowledge, and so may become stiff and mechanical. To this rule Churches, even if they claim to be also superhuman, form no exception. Indeed they are peculiarly liable to become victims of that blind conservatism which is one of the most common religious aberrations: like a naval convoy they tend to move at the pace of the slowest ship. This may spring from the sheer difficulties of government—difficulties so often ignored by the doctrinaire. Partly, however, it may arise from preoccupation with the mechanism of an institution at the expense of the religion whose instrument it is supposed to be. The mechanism may become ossified and petrified, and in the end it may become a positive impediment to religion. At the worst it may become primarily a political organization seeking to glorify its own agents and increase its own power.

This deviation into politics is not so much a religious aberration as a tendency to replace religion by something else. It is nevertheless a weakness to which religion is exposed so far as it is embodied in institutions, and this form of aberration is one main reason for the distrust and hatred with which religion is so often regarded. Some religious men have wished to abolish ecclesiastical institutions altogether. In so doing they have failed to take into account the necessities of human nature, but there are times when it is hard not to feel sympathy with their ideal.

§ 9. *Hypocrisy*

Besides the aberration into politics there are others made possible by religion even if they do not belong to religion itself. Religion constitutes a kind of magnet which, by its mere existence, attracts unbalanced emotions and unbalanced personalities. Even more than philosophy, it has an irresistible fascination for cranks, and the enthusiasm of the unbalanced leads sometimes to religious mania. For such abnormal phenomena religion itself cannot be held responsible; but there is a way of leading the religious life which, while not abnormal, is slightly morbid and perhaps a trifle self-conscious and even affected. This may be called religiosity; and, naturally enough, it is a source of prejudice against religion. It may shade gradually into sanctimoniousness and ultimately into hypocrisy.

The most serious of the vices made possible by religion, and to a lesser degree by morality, is hypocrisy. It is usually based on self-interest rather than on a lack of mental balance, and consequently is to be distinguished from religiosity. But at times it may be pursued almost as an art for art's sake. It may become for some people a kind of dramatic exercise in which they begin by deceiving others and end by deceiving themselves.

Hypocrisy is essentially parasitic: it can flourish only where there is a genuine regard for virtue. Hence decay in religious belief brings with it the compensation of a corresponding decline in religious hypocrisy. The present age is on the whole not a hypocritical one, and the most blatant hypocrisy is to be found among totalitarian politicians rather than in religion. Yet it is hard to deny that a successful religious institution may give scope, if not for hypocrisy, at least for failure in the finer points of intellectual honesty.

§ 10. *The significance of aberration*

Such are some of the main mistakes or aberrations connected with religion. I have described them as if the religious life were more or less self-contained; but all of them, so far as they belong to religion itself, are reflected in the character ascribed to God by the worshipper. In them God may be regarded as a being who can be manipulated by magic rites or pleased by fulsome adulation, as a stickler for intellectual subtleties or moral rules, and even as a tyrant and a tormentor. This is why they have to be regarded, let it be said in all charity, as forms of idolatry; and this is why I described a persecuting religion as the worst form of blasphemy.

There may be other aberrations arising from the fact that the religious life is not self-contained but is centred in God—the aberrations of other-worldliness and contempt for all human excellence. But these may be regarded by some as not aberrations at all, and their character will have to be examined later. They belong to what is known as the way of negation, which demands consideration by itself. And anyhow we seem already to have aberrations enough.

When we contemplate this distressing catalogue, we may feel drawn to the mediaeval belief that religious men are specially exposed to the assaults of the devil. We may even feel inclined to draw the conclusion that religion is just one big aberration from which we should seek to free ourselves as quickly as possible.

Those who hold the latter view would maintain that our first account of religion as an ideal was merely a fancy picture which must give way before reality, and that even the darker side has been all too lightly sketched. The ignorance and superstition, cruelty and bloodshed, dread and horror, which I have ascribed to primitive religions, they would attach, with some show of plausibility, to religion as such. They would remind us that the inflexibility in thinking, and the legalism in morality, by which religion has placed obstacles in the way of progress, have often led to a fierce and frightened condemnation of human thought, human virtue, and human beauty. On this view religion should be classified, not with science and morality and art, but rather with an institution such as war—something closely intertwined with human nature, perhaps inevitable in desperate situations and at certain levels of culture, capable at times of indirectly furthering progress and even of furnishing the occasion for displays of human excellence, but in the last resort, in spite of the glamour with which it has been surrounded, a curse from which we must hope that men will some day be entirely freed.

It is important to grasp this view if the present predicament of religion is to be understood. Religion must seem to be a menace unless we are allowed to attach to it that saving grace of sweet reasonableness which Barth and others so ardently condemn. The manifold aberrations of religion, more than anything else, bring out the need for intelligent human criticism—except to those who prefer the authority of an infallible Church. Yet all these aberrations are at least not incompatible with the view that religion may be aiming at a wholeness which is more than a merely personal equilibrium. We could not recognize or describe aberrations unless we were conscious, however dimly, of some sort of norm from which they are a departure; and it is this norm that I have attempted to adumbrate, whether the attempt has been successful or not. Even if we take a low view of human nature, it is difficult, though perhaps not impossible, to believe that religion attracts men only because of its aberrations, and not in spite of them. It is not as if religion made its appeal only to the vulgar and insensitive: in all ages there have been among its devotees some of the best and ablest men who have ever lived. Aristotle was right in asserting that wherever there is a standard, there are countless ways of departing from it; but these departures are not to be blamed on the standard itself. The very richness of religion may multiply its possible aberrations, and the corruption of the best may be the worst; but this is no reason why we should reject the best.

This problem—except in so far as religion may seem to be in conflict with known truth—is not to be settled by philosophical argument: it is rather one for personal decision in the light of our experience and our knowledge of the world. All that philosophical discussion can do is to clear the issues and get rid of confusions. The one thing quite certain is that the general answer to these questions will determine, for good or ill, the whole character of our civilization. To dismiss them as of no importance is the greatest aberration of all.

Chapter VI

THE WAY OF NEGATION

§ 1. *The way of negation*

A strange and striking characteristic of religion, and certainly one which makes it distasteful to the average sensual man, is a tendency to what may be described as negation. We are so often bidden to suppress human desires, to reject human pleasures, to renounce the world and all its ways. This tendency can be pushed to extremes, and we find religions hostile, not merely to sensuous pleasures and worldly ambitions, but even to human wisdom and human virtue, not to mention human beauty.

It may seem artificial to use a logical word like 'negation' to describe this type of religious attitude. Why not speak more simply of self-denial or self-renunciation? The answer is that these words are still too narrow. Those who follow the negative way—the *via negationis*—to the end are not content merely with renouncing, or even annihilating, the self. In the extreme case they regard all human life as an illusion and deny reality alike to the world and to God.

The most extreme negation is to be found in the religions of the East. In these there are also more moderate views, but the general direction is clear enough. Lao Tzu, for example, speaks thus: 'The five colours blind the human eye; the five notes (of music) deafen the human ear; the five tastes spoil the human mouth; racing and hunting madden the human mind; the highly-prized treasures degrade human conduct'. This might perhaps be taken as a moderate view showing hostility only to worldly pleasures. But others go so far as to tell us that the highest truth is 'absolute emptiness' and that we should seek to attain the goal of 'absolute vacuity'. Wisdom and bliss are to be found in 'the state without a specific reality'. Here the way of negation is not a way to anything positive: it is pursued for its own sake and it ends in nothing.

The goal of religion always corresponds with a view of God, and it has been said that all the major religions of the East affirm what in the West would be regarded as atheism. Such a pronouncement is too

sweeping; it is manifestly in need of explanation and expansion;
but there can be no doubt that Buddhism, at least in some of its
forms, may not unreasonably be described as atheistic.

In Christianity and the religions of the West negation is seldom
carried to such lengths, but the same tendencies can be observed
there also. How often have men been told that they must mortify,
not only sensuous desires (however innocent) and worldly ambitions
(however moderate), but even the most harmless of personal affections! This is a commonplace of much devotional, and especially
monastic, writing. According to St. John of the Cross this deadness
to the world is 'the dark night' of the senses which the soul must
enter in its journey to God; but there is a second and still deeper
darkness to be faced—a darkness not of the sensuous, but of the
spiritual or rational, part of the soul. Understanding, memory, and
will must all alike be emptied or darkened; and in this second
darkness the rational part of the soul is deprived of the light of
reason or 'to speak more clearly' is blinded. We are even told that
solid and perfect spirituality consists 'in the annihilation of all
sweetness in God, in aridity, distaste, and trial, which is the true
spiritual cross'. The soul is compared to a window which must be
free of stains and mist, wholly pure and clean, if the light of God is
to shine through it. It looks as if the way of salvation were the way
of complete blankness.

This extreme language is at times watered down, perhaps not
quite consistently, to mean little more than the utter abandonment
of self-love for the love of God. Nor should it be forgotten that for
St. John of the Cross this way of darkness is not an end, but only a
means to perfect union. Nevertheless the unregenerate may have
more sympathy with the good feminine sense of St. Teresa when
she says 'It would be a bad business for us if we could not seek God
until we were dead to the world'.

There is also a way of negation which consists in aiming, not at a
blank zero, but at what may be described as a minus quantity. The
mortification of all desire and the rejection of all pleasure may
become the pursuit of pain, the glorification of suffering. This is a
yet darker aspect of religion from which Christianity has not been
free. As a form of masochism it is primarily a problem for abnormal
psychology; yet at its best it has been ennobled by a wish, however
misguided, to share in the sufferings of Christ. St. John of the Cross,
who is himself not immune from these tendencies, does at least
recognize their danger. Where men kill themselves with penances,

and weaken themselves with fasts, by performing more than their frailty can bear, this, he tells us, may be 'no more than the penance of beasts, to which they are attracted, exactly like beasts, by the desire and pleasure which they find therein'. He considers this to be a form of 'spiritual gluttony' and his remedy for it is obedience to a spiritual superior—a cure which to some of us may seem almost as dangerous as the disease.

§ 2. *Self-love and negation*

The negative way in religion is often connected with metaphysical views about reality, but perhaps it can best be approached from the side of action. Let us begin by considering enlightened self-love. This is below the level both of morality and of religion; and since we are all moved by self-love, even if it may not always be enlightened, any negation present in it may perhaps be easier to understand.

When we follow enlightened self-love in our actions, what we pursue is our own good. Our own good may be described as happiness—our own happiness. Many thinkers have regarded happiness as an excess of pleasant over painful feeling distributed over a whole life. This attaches too much importance to pleasant feeling, which is only one object of desire among many others; and happiness is better described as the maximum satisfaction of desire distributed over a whole life. It may also be described as the maximum harmonization of our ends; for the objects of our desire are ends, and these may clash with one another. To seek such a goal is reasonable for a being who, although affected by momentary impulses and desires, is not directly determined by them like an animal, but has the power of looking beyond them to the satisfaction of other desires in the future.

A life of enlightened self-love should not be regarded as a purely selfish life which shows no consideration for others. The ordinary man has desires for human society; he wants to co-operate with his fellows in work and play; he likes to give affection as well as to receive it; and he can be interested in the future happiness of those he loves even if he will not be alive to share it. He may also become aware quite early in life that if he shows consideration for others, they are more likely to show consideration for him. We need not describe him as selfish: he may be intelligent enough to see that systematic selfishness is likely to impoverish his own life. But he is

self-centred: if he seeks the happiness of others, his main reason for
doing so is that in this way he is likely in the long run to get what he
wants, whether for itself (where his desires are generous) or as a
means to something else. He has no use for a standard which may be
independent of his desire for his own happiness.

To lead this kind of life successfully requires intelligence and a
firm will and some mastery over appetite. A man of this type may
believe that he will be happiest if at times he removes the check
upon impulse, for there must be spontaneity as well as control; but
he will repress inclinations likely to interfere with his happiness in
the long run. The life of enlightened self-love demands some sort
of discipline.

It is obvious that one and the same principle of self-love may be
applied very differently according to our different circumstances,
our different temperaments, our different views of the world. In
seeking our own happiness our motto, if we are by nature adventu-
rous, may be 'Live dangerously'; if we are timid, it may be 'Safety
first'.

In this second motto we begin to find what we are looking for—
the way of negation on the level of self-love. Negation is in a sense
present in the discipline or repression of refractory impulses, but
there it is only a means—even the man who lives dangerously may
have to repress his fears; and it has been said that if you want to live
dangerously, you should do so as carefully as possible. But if we are
timid—if we find the world a vale of tears in which pain prevails
over pleasure and frustration over achievement—we may seek our
happiness in moderating all our desires. If we can't have what we
like, we may try to like what we have. We are still seeking the maximum satisfaction possible, but negation, so to speak, has begun to
affect our goal.

This moderate negation is an ever-recurrent attitude, and it finds
its classical expression in the philosophy of Epicurus. It is most
prominent, not in ages of expansion and achievement, but in periods
of frustration and decay. Naturally enough, it does not appeal to the
young and the hopeful: it is the philosophy of middle age. There is
a well-beaten track which begins with sensuality and passes through
disgust to a rather smug detachment. The pilgrims who tread this
road we have always with us, even though they may be unconscious
that it has ever been trodden before.

The extreme limit of this negative attitude is utter pessimism
both about ourselves and about our world. Desire leads only to

pain, effort only to frustration, thought only to a heightened awareness of the horrors of life. The one thing that a wise man can do is
to abandon thinking, to cease from willing, to get rid of desire. We
have nothing to hope for but death and annihilation and the end of
trouble. This is the everlasting NO. The negative goal of self-love
is a dreamless sleep.

§ 3. *Morality and negation*

Enlightened self-love has often been mistaken for morality, but
there is a sense in which the life of self-love and the moral life are
fundamentally opposed. A good man is one who takes the moral law
as his *supreme* principle of life to which all other principles, including
that of self-love, must be subordinated: he seeks his own happiness
only so far as this may be compatible with obedience to the moral
law. The man who makes self-love his *supreme* principle obeys the
moral law only so far as this may be consistent with his own happiness. He may be a respectable citizen or an average sensual man or
an out-and-out villain, but he has no part or share in morality. What
morality seeks is not *my* happiness or *my* advantage or *my* good, but
the good; and *the* good is not determined by what *I* happen to want
or even by the maximum possible satisfaction of *my* desires.
Morality differs from self-love in not being self-centred.

It must not be thought that this is already the way of negation in
morality—that it is hostile to desire as such and condemns, not only
pleasure, but even happiness. It does say that a man is not morally
good in virtue of being good at furthering his own interests, and that
a good man may find it his duty to give up his happiness and even
his life for the sake of some higher good; but surely we all know this
already. It says too that a good man may have to repress and discipline his desires, as must happen even on the level of self-love. But
it does *not* mean that it can never be right for a man to seek his own
pleasure or pursue his own happiness. Still less does it mean that
morality consists in finding out what you want to do and then doing
the opposite. On the contrary, a man has every right to pursue his
own happiness so long as he does not transgress the moral law.
Indeed it may be one of his duties to do so inasmuch as gloom is apt
to be a source of bad temper in himself and distress in others.

The way of negation in morals is found when the discipline or
repression of desires is practised, not as a necessary means, but as
an end in itself. The moral law is then supposed to forbid all

pleasure and all pursuit of happiness. This view, like that of Epicureanism, may arise when we live in an age of frustration and are pessimistic about our world or disgusted with its pleasures. Indeed it is not always clear whether it is a moral principle or merely one of self-love. We find it in the Stoic ideal of 'apathy', which is not an ideal of indolence, but of complete freedom from pleasure, desire, anxiety, and fear. This is not an ignoble doctrine, but it is a mistaken one. A good man's actions admittedly must not be determined by his desires; but this does not imply that he should have no desires or even that he should never satisfy them.

Complete freedom from desire can be found only in death, and the logical conclusion of this negative morality in its extremest form would be suicide. The Stoics were willing to go through this 'open door' in order to preserve virtue when life was too beset with obstacles, but they did not glorify suicide for its own sake. To do so would be to abandon the moral struggle altogether in favour of non-existence. This is a counsel of despair, and it seems to bring us back again to the negative goal, not of morality, but of self-love.

§ 4. *Self-love and religion*

Self-love is ubiquitous and seeks to insinuate itself even into Paradise. Its crudest form in religion is found when men serve God in the hope that he will bless them with earthly goods, with food and raiment, flocks and herds, sons and daughters. But its essential character is not altered when they are willing to endure hardships in order to enjoy the blessedness of Heaven or to escape the pangs of Hell. A long-term prudence is still distinct from morality, and when it passes for religion, it may even become nauseating.

In religion, as elsewhere, self-love need not be so crude. It may take subtle forms and mingle itself with higher motives so that good men are often confused both in what they practise and in what they preach. For John Bunyan as for St. Bernard fear of the wrath to come was at least the first motive which induced men to turn their backs upon the world and give themselves up to a religious life. Even in the search for personal salvation self-love may be more prominent than the love of God, and the language commonly used is too often ambiguous.

To be free from these ambiguities, alike in theory and in practice, is as important as it is unfortunately rare. To attain such freedom is no easy task, but what interests us here is something simpler. We are concerned with the negative way in religion, and it should be manifest that restraint of desires and renunciation of the world so far as these proceed, whether intelligently or stupidly, from self-love are without religious, as well as without moral, value.

The same judgement must hold if self-love is the dominant motive in seeking a blessedness which is even more negative than the way to it. In such terms we may perhaps describe, at least in some cases, the salvation or emancipation that is to be found in Nirvana. When Sariputta had asserted that Nirvana is blessedness, he was asked 'How can there be blessedness since here is no feeling?' His answer was 'It is in this that it is blessedness, that here is no feeling'. This ideal may correspond to a longing for unbroken rest after toil and disillusionment and despair; but so far as it is sought merely from such a longing, it too is without religious value.

It may be thought that a desire of this type cannot spring from self-love since it is a desire for something that comes very near annihilation of the self. This objection seems to be merely verbal. When we despair of the world and seek to be free from its pain, our search may be not only self-centred, but even selfish. A policy of escapism is no less self-centred because it proceeds to the uttermost extreme.

§ 5. *The negative way in religion*

Only when some of these ambiguities have been dispelled is it possible to consider the negative way in religion. So far as this way is religious, it can have nothing to do with self-love. We have seen that morality cannot be self-centred. Still less can religion be self-centred, unless it is to fall below the level of morality. The essential thing about religion is that it should be, not self-centred, but God-centred. When we ask what is the place of negation in religion, we must assume that the religious life is centred in God.

If we make this assumption, the life of self-love and the religious life are fundamentally opposed to one another. The man who leads the life of self-love has as his *supreme* principle 'My will be done'. The religious man has as his *supreme* principle 'Not my will, but Thy will be done'. This emphasis on will, it should be noted, is found even in the Christian mystics who lay most stress on con-templation. In the last chapter St. Teresa was quoted on this point, and here is another quotation from St. John of the Cross. Speaking of the supernatural union of likeness that springs from love, he says that 'it comes to pass when the two wills—namely, that of the soul and that of God—are conformed together in one, and there is naught in the one that is repugnant to the other'.

It is clear enough that the religious man must be ready to give up his pleasure, his happiness, his personal affections, even his life, if this should be in accordance with God's will; and it is foolish to imagine that such readiness would be possible without some discipline of his desires. Everything said by the ascetics under this head is so far fully justified: it accords with what we know even of morality. But the same mistake found in regard to morality may also be found here. It is a fallacy to suppose that this doctrine tells us what God's will is. We have no right to argue from it that God wills every religious man to be miserable in this life. Still less have we any right to argue that the best way to discipline desires is to root them out.

The way of negation in religion, as in morals, is to be found when the discipline or repression of desires is practised, not as a necessary means, but as an end in itself. But in this matter there are all sorts of degrees, and we may suspect that discipline, even when professedly it is only a means, can be so disproportionate that it becomes something very like an end. There is much more to this question than elementary confusions of thought, and we have to respect the experience of religious men, especially in regard to rules of discipline which may be repugnant to our natural inclinations. But when they tell us on authority that such and such is the will of God, we can only say that we must have some light to distinguish the priests of Jehovah from those of Baal, the ministers of God from the envoys of Satan. When they condescend to argue with us, as the wisest among them do, we must take their arguments seriously; and if these are confused, we must point this out. We must also hold that anyone who tells us that God wills men to do what is wrong is clearly mistaken. Thus, for example, when St. John of the Cross tells us that all the affections which the soul has for creatures are pure darkness in the eyes of God, and backs this up by the argument that 'he that loves a creature becomes as low as that creature, and, in some ways, lower', we may not find this very convincing—not even when he adds that as light is incompatible with darkness, so the love of creatures is incompatible with the love of God. Similarly the love of beauty incurs his condemnation because when compared with the beauty of God the beauty of creatures is the height of deformity. This is the way of negation, and it is easy to see how he comes to his conclusion that the only method by which the soul can prepare itself for union with God is to strip itself of everything. It would be truer to say that we should love all creatures because they are creatures of God, and that he who loves God must love his neighbour. We may charitably suppose that he has confused two quite different propositions—the proposition that the love of creatures should be wholly subordinated to the love of God, and the proposition that the love of creatures is excluded by the love of God. St. John seems to waver between the two without observing how different they are.

So far as the problem of spiritual discipline is concerned only with means, it is an empirical one; but with all respect for the experience of those who have given themselves entirely to the religious life, we may doubt whether the total repression of sense and desire, not to speak of thinking and willing, is most likely to lead to spiritual progress. When we have exorcised one devil, we may only get seven more devils in its place. This is the great danger of the way of negation even when an exaggerated discipline is said to be adopted only as a means. It is a still greater danger if we suppose it to be God's will that our will should be broken rather than transformed.

In the extreme case the annihilation, or at least the complete emptying, of the will is made the goal of religion. This is especially associated with some Eastern religions, although it must be remembered that even the most extreme views may, whether consciously or through mere confusion, admit positive elements on the way to blank negation.

The way of complete negation, so far as it springs from a pessimistic longing to escape from a world of sin and trouble, can hardly be considered as other than a special manifestation of self-love. Is it possible for life with a purely negative goal to be God-centred rather than self-centred and so to be one form of religious life?

The ideal aimed at in a religious life is always mirrored in a corresponding conception of God or—if you prefer to put it the other way about—the conception of God is mirrored in a corresponding religious ideal. When a writer like St. John of the Cross empties the religious life of all personal affections, he so far empties also the conception of God. With him this emptying may be only a means; but where emptiness is the recognized end of the religious life, there has to be a corresponding emptiness in the conception of God. This is presumably one reason why Buddhism, at least in some of its forms, has to be atheistic.

When the goal of religion is emptiness, and God—or at least the supreme reality—is also emptiness, can we say that the religious life is God-centred? Clearly in a sense we can, for it is centred in emptiness and emptiness is God—the only God there is. It would be harsh to define religion in such terms as to exclude this way of life, especially if we find in it many characteristics which we unhesitatingly regard as religious. Apart from questions of verbal usage, it is dangerous to pass judgement on these matters without a much fuller knowledge than most of us possess; but at least some points seem to be fairly clear.

The positive and negative ways may coincide over a great part of their course if there must be in every form of religion the self-control and self-denial which are also an essential factor in moral goodness. Both ways may be exposed to the aberration of making self-discipline and even self-mortification something very like an end in itself. Yet the ultimate goals are manifestly incompatible. I have taken the ideal of religion to be perfect and harmonious and active life in union with a perfect, harmonious, and active whole. To those who follow the negative way this ideal, together with any belief in the grace of God, is based on illusion—on a false and anthropomorphic vision of reality. If we accept the Western ideal, the negative way cannot but be regarded as a failure in insight or in faith, a distrust of life and of reality, and so in itself, and not merely in its accidents, a religious aberration, however disinterested and worthy of respect. We may even find in it a self-contradiction so far as a love of emptiness must be an emptying of love. But we have also to remember that what is conceived as negative may be felt as positive, and that the way of negation may be one way of conceiving a mystery that is beyond human understanding.

§ 6. *Must willing be self-centred?*

It is possible to argue that all willing must be self-centred, and that consequently what has been said here about morality and religion is nonsense. If this is true, we cannot cease to be self-centred without ceasing to be, and the only way to escape self-centredness is to end the life, not merely of the body, but of the soul.

The argument may be supposed to run like this. Even if I could say that I took the moral law as the supreme principle of my actions, seeking to obey its positive injunctions and to refrain from everything which it does not at least permit, it would still be I who willed my actions. Hence my goal must still be self-realization, and the realization of my will must still give me personal satisfaction. In the long run we do only what we happen to want; and morality and religion alike must be as self-centred as any other human choice.

This view contains a number of assertions which must be dealt with very summarily.

First of all, we have a statement of the tautology 'I will what I will'. This no one would be anxious to deny. We cannot infer from it anything about the character of my will. In particular, we cannot infer that my will must be self-centred, unless by saying that it is self-centred we mean merely to repeat the tautology that it wills what it wills.

Secondly, we are asked to infer that if I succeed in doing what I will, this will give me personal satisfaction. No doubt it will, and this satisfaction may be present even when I am miserable because I have had to thwart desires and sacrifice happiness. But if the inference is that in acting morally I act only in order to secure a feeling of personal satisfaction, this is not even plausible. I cannot obtain the feeling of *moral* satisfaction unless I act for the sake of doing what is right. As to the term 'self-realization', it is so ambiguous that it is better avoided. In the present context to talk of self-realization is either to repeat the tautology 'I will what I will', or else it is to make a fallacious inference from the tautology.

The real sting of the argument lies in the assertion that I do only what I happen to want. This merely sweeps aside dogmatically the distinctions we have made. Broadly speaking, men act either on impulse or for the sake of their interests or for the sake of the moral law. Only the first of these is properly described as doing what we *happen* to want—into both the others there enters a factor of reasoned judgement. Anyone who infers that because I will what I will, therefore my actions must be determined by impulse, falls into a patent fallacy. And what he says has no bearing on the difference between self-love and morality.

There are many who dislike talk about the moral law, especially when no attempt is made to define it, and we shall have to return to this question later. At present it is necessary to stick to the level of common sense. On this level we must assume that men sometimes know, or at least reasonably believe, that some things are right for them to do and others wrong; and, furthermore, that 'what is right' does not mean 'to my advantage' any more than 'what is wrong' means 'to my disadvantage'. This is the basis of the distinction

G

between self-love and obedience to the moral law, between a self-centred life which seeks my own advantage and a moral life which seeks to follow a standard independent of my own advantage. If there are any who deny the distinction, there is no more to be said—except that they are not entitled to infer that I always seek my own advantage from the mere tautology that I always will what I will.

Hence there seems to be nothing in the objection that all willing must be self-centred, and I mention it only because it so often takes in the simple-minded. I would add that what a good man seeks is that the moral law should be realized, and only incidentally that it should be realized through him. He is specially concerned with goodness in his own life only because this is the only life *he* can make good; for a good life is one that must be freely willed by the person who lives it.

All this can be applied to religion. What the religious man seeks is that God's will should be done, and only incidentally that it should be done through him. He welcomes consolation as a gift of God's grace, but he does not seek to do God's will for the sake of consolation. And the tautologous assertion that he wills what he wills has no bearing on the truth or the falsity of these statements.

§ 7. *Nihilism*

The way of negation can be understood most easily as an ideal of action; but corresponding to ideals of action there are always theories, or at least assumptions, about the nature of the world and—in the case of religion—about the nature of God. Even if theory springs out of practice, it may also react upon practice. Thus where emphasis is laid on God's transcendence, it may seem natural to regard the world as worthless or evil; and the task of religion is to turn from the world and seek satisfaction in God alone. If God is taken to be immanent in the world, the duty of the religious man may be to live in the world and play his humble part in a divine enterprise. Here we can find the difference between world-denying and world-accepting religions. A world-rejecting religion is apt to regard all earthly desires as obstacles to the religious life and so to be rooted out. A world-accepting religion, on the other hand, assumes that the satisfaction of natural desires may find its place in a disciplined religious life. The first way—the negative way—may become harsh and intolerant, while the second may end in the abandonment of religion altogether.

The philosophical theories of immanence and transcendence are too complicated to be dealt with shortly, and it may be doubted whether if we accept one, we must reject the other. Indeed those who venture into theological speculation may find themselves impelled to accept views which, if they were concerned with finite objects, would be self-contradictory. But to the modern man of the West the way of negation in religion seems so strange that it may be illuminating to sketch briefly one metaphysical theory of the universe which is its ground or background. I am indebted here to a remarkable essay published by Professor Northrop of Yale University in a volume entitled *Philosophy — East and West*. As it would take too long to explain his elaborate terminology, I must try to put the main point in simpler language of my own. I may be unable to make it intelligible to those not already versed in Greek philosophy—or perhaps even to those who are; but it came to me as a flash of light, and those who fail to grasp my exposition may be referred to Professor Northrop himself.

This theory may be called 'nihilism', and it can be summed up paradoxically by saying that what is is what is not.

We start with the assumption that only what is immediately apprehended is real. Since only what is sensed can be immediately apprehended, only what is sensed can be real. What we sense are the objects of our five senses (such as colours and sounds) and the objects of introspection (such as images and feelings). Objects of this kind we may call 'sensed objects', and they alone are real.

All we can see is colour, and all we can hear is sound. But we have objects of another kind as well. This colour that I see I take to be the colour of a chair or a table, the colour of a body. A very little reflexion will show us that a body is not immediately apprehended: it is not a sensed object, but rather a 'postulated' object—an object postulated to account for what we see. The material bodies of our common-sense beliefs and the mysterious electrons of the scientist are all alike postulated objects. So too are the triangles of the mathematician and the space of the physicist, and also the universals (or Forms) of Plato and Aristotle. Similarly, mind is a postulated object, and so is God. None of these objects can be immediately apprehended or directly sensed. We get at them by some kind of thinking even if this must start from what we sense.

For the believer in nihilism all postulated objects are unreal— presumably in the sense that they are merely fictions or creations of our own minds: nowadays we might call them 'logical constructions'. Although it is expressed in different language, this view is very like the modern positivistic doctrine known as 'phenomenalism', to which we shall have to return later.

For the present purpose we may ignore postulated objects. We come to the distinctive doctrine of nihilism if we turn back to the sensed objects themselves.

I have said that all we can see is colour and all we can hear is sound. But this should not be taken to mean, as it is by David Hume and some of his modern followers, that colours and sounds are distinct existences—that they are, so to speak, atomic objects isolated from one another. On the contrary, what we apprehend immediately by sight is a continuous field which is white here and blue there and shades off into something without any colour at all—on the periphery of our vision we are all colour-blind. In more technical language the object of sight is a *differentiated continuum*; and the same is true of all the objects we sense, whether by our five senses or by means of introspection.

Now within the differentiated continuum of sense we can attend, and we usually do attend, to the differentiations—that is, to the different colours and sounds and so on. But we can also relax attention and ignore the differentiations. What we then sense—it is still supposed to be a matter of sense only—is an *undifferentiated continuum*. We are perhaps at times aware of something rather like this as we sink gradually into sleep.

Colours and sounds and all other differentiations of our sensuous continuum are transitory and evanescent, as was pointed out long ago by Plato. From this it is concluded—as he also concluded, though it is rather a big jump—that the differentiations are unreal or illusory. The only thing that is real is the *undifferentiated* continuum, a blank uncharacterized reality which is barely to be distinguished from nothing.

We can follow the same line of thought about the objects of introspection. The feelings and images we introspect are also mere transitory differentiations of a continuum and so are unreal. What is real in the self is only the undifferentiated continuum, and—since there can be no differences between undifferentiated continua—this is identical with the undifferentiated continuum apprehended by our five senses. The self and the world are the same undifferentiated continuous reality. In the technical language of the East the Ātman and the Brahman are identical.

We can now see where we stand—it can be put most simply in

the language of Plato. The sole reality is not to be found, as he imagined, in the determinate, intelligible, and timeless universals—such as Goodness itself, Beauty itself, and so on—to which he gave the name of 'Forms' or 'Ideas': it is to be found in what he called 'matter' or 'the indeterminate' or 'not-being'. This is why the doctrine of nihilism can be summed up by saying that what is is what is not. The novel feature of this Eastern nihilism is that we are supposed to apprehend this not-being *immediately* by means of *sense*: we do not merely conceive it theoretically as the ideal limit of a process in which all differentiations are gradually thought away. The doctrine is indeed supported by many subtle forms of negative dialectic, but it is ultimately based on direct sensuous intuition.

The ascetic discipline known as 'the Yoga' is one way of attaining this intuition, in which the self is completely merged and lost in the ultimate reality which is nothing—or perhaps just not nothing. Another way—I quote Professor Northrop—is 'the practice of the early Indian sages of sitting on their haunches in the heart of an Indian forest, so overwhelmed with the diversity and complexity of its tropical foliage that the mind loses all capacity to distinguish differentiations and is left to contemplate the unfathomable and ineffable intensity and the inexpressible immediacy of indeterminate experience itself'.

This doctrine is beautifully consistent with the way of utter negation in religion, with pessimism about the whole temporal world of illusion, and with denial of a personal God and personal immortality. It also raises questions about what really happens to those who follow St. John of the Cross by emptying themselves alike of sense and desire and memory and understanding and will. We may find it hard to see why the dreamless sleep which is the sole reality should ever have been disturbed by our painful human dreams, or why we cannot escape from these dreams by death instead of by the difficult ways of self-denial and contemplation and dialectic. Professor Northrop himself thinks that in comparison with those who follow this negative way Westerners have tended to become emotionally and spiritually starved—a surprising judgement unless it is confined to the weakness of modern industrial civilization, aggravated perhaps in America where so many men have been cut off from their ancient roots. As a view of the world this nihilism is at least less terrible than a doctrine which reserves eternal bliss for the chosen few and eternal torment for the vast mass of mankind. It would be impertinent to dispose of it in a few words either as a

system of thought or as a way of life. Here at least, with its many
varieties and elaborations, we have one of the great philosophies—
a far more thorough-going positivism (or negativism) than any
known to us in the West. It is, I believe, right in maintaining that
purely immediate apprehension—if such a thing were possible—
would give us an object barely distinguishable from nothing. But
this might be a reason for basing ethics and theology on something
other than purely immediate apprehension.

Chapter VII

INTELLECTUAL IMPEDIMENTS

§ 1. *Different types of impediment*

There are many impediments to religion. Among these human wickedness—or human sinfulness, if we use the language of theology—is the most formidable, but it is by no means the only one; and under this head we ought not to include the sin of thinking about religion, as is sometimes done by those who are guilty of the sin of thinking too little. Another obstacle is to be found in the aberrations of religion itself and in the unworthiness of its professed followers. These impediments are patent enough from the religious point of view. We must now take a more detached standpoint and consider some of the alleged incompatibilities between religious belief and the rest of our knowledge. This ungrateful task may be described as a study of the *intellectual* impediments to religion. The views with which we have to deal are commonplace among thinkers, and are dimly apprehended even by the unthinking masses, so that it would be foolish, and indeed wrong, to pass them over in silence or to pretend that they are not serious.

§ 2. *Religion and science*

Intellectual impediments to religion are made possible by the intellectual element in religion itself. Every religion, and certainly every developed religion, offers us a doctrine of man, a doctrine of history, a doctrine of the universe, and a doctrine of God. The exact status of such doctrines may be difficult to determine, and obsession with theory may be one of the major religious aberrations. Nevertheless religion cannot get on without some sort of doctrine, even if this be reduced to the barest minimum.

Doctrine necessarily claims to be true, and this means that it enters into competition with other doctrines also claiming to be true. We may hold that one doctrine is true from one point of view and another from another; but ultimately there can be only one truth, or one comprehensive system of truths, in which divergent points of view are reconciled. We may not be able to effect this reconciliation, but to abandon the belief that such a reconciliation is possible is to abandon reason altogether and to have no defence against lunacy.

What are the doctrines with which religion, so far as it is doctrinal, may, and does, come into conflict? They can all be summed up in one word—science. But this bald statement is in need of some further elucidation.

In the first place, science has to be interpreted widely. It includes, not only the natural sciences, but also the mental and social sciences, such as psychology and anthropology. It covers also the modern methods of historical and literary criticism. The development of all these disciplines in the last four hundred years has brought religion face to face with a situation very different from any that existed before.

In the second place, it may be objected that there is no such thing as science—there are only sciences in the plural—and that all this talk about a conflict between religion and science is too vague to be profitable.

In such an objection there is some truth, and we ought always to be chary of those who are in the habit of telling us that Science (with a capital S) teaches us this or that and admits of no further argument. Assertions of this kind often spring, not directly from science, but from semi-popular philosophy, and some of the impediments to religion may fall under this description. Nevertheless we are blind if we fail to see that in method, in outlook, and in what can be described as atmosphere, science—all science—may be opposed to religion. Even if scientific knowledge is ultimately compatible with religion, it does not appear to be so at first sight; and indeed it seems to contradict a great deal formerly considered by theologians to be necessary for a saving faith. Furthermore, whatever may be true as regards logical compatibility, there is at least a psychological opposition between the scientific and the religious attitude. The gradual spread of the scientific outlook—and we are all affected by it even if the scientists say we are not nearly as much affected as we ought to be—has tended, not so much to refute religious belief, but rather to make it fade and wither. To quote Professor Price: 'it has led to that inner emptiness and lack of faith . . . which is our fundamental and, as it seems, incurable disease'.

It may be replied that all this is very much out of date—a mere survival of Victorian rationalism long ago abandoned. Those who comfort themselves thus are, I am afraid, deceived. It is true that science to-day—apart from the followers of Karl Marx, who was more of a prophet than a scientist—is not so cocksure as it once was about the finality of its teaching and is more prepared for revolutionary discoveries. It is also true that the note of hostility to religion is often, though by no means always, less strident than it was in the past. All this is to the good, but the main reason for the lesser stridency is that the modern rationalist no longer considers himself to be battling for victory: he supposes that the victory is already won. The greater amiability of present-day discussions is no doubt a straw that can help to show which way the wind is blowing; but those who clutch at that straw may only give the impression that they are drowning men.

§ 3. *Religion and physics*

The tide of science which threatens to submerge religion began to flow when Copernicus discovered that the earth was not the centre of the physical universe, but only one of the planets revolving round the sun. This tidal movement became more perceptible when Galileo confirmed his discovery and began to develop the modern methods of observation and measurement which have led to such astonishing triumphs. As if aware of the impending danger, the Church reacted violently, and condemned these doctrines as incompatible with Holy Scripture. Yet in spite of its utmost endeavours the tide has flowed relentlessly for more than four hundred years. Its rise has continuously accelerated and is certain—unless there is a world catastrophe—to accelerate more and more. During the whole of this period—if we may change the metaphor—religion has been fighting a rearguard action, abandoning one position after another till it is uncertain how much is left.

Why is it that the amazing achievements of modern physics and astronomy have seemed so inimical to religion? It is not merely that they overthrow primitive Biblical speculations about the physical universe—although, when a book has been regarded as divinely inspired throughout, to contradict the least part of it may seem to destroy the authority of the whole. Nor is it merely that man is seen as the creature of a day, clinging precariously to a whirling planet in a solar system which is itself utterly insignificant amid the vast reaches of interstellar space and astronomical time. These and many other considerations all play their part; but perhaps the main im-

pediments to religion arise from two things—from the character of
scientific method and from the conception of the world as governed
throughout by unvarying law.

On scientific method little need here be said, although psychologically it may be the strongest influence of all. A scientific training
makes it difficult or impossible to accept statements on authority,
to be satisfied with second- or third-hand evidence, to believe in
marvels which cannot be experimentally repeated, or to adopt
theories which cannot be verified by empirical observation. There
may be exceptions to this rule; for some scientists seem to lose their
critical power once they stray beyond the narrow limits of their own
subject. But there can be no doubt that in this respect the influence
of science is both powerful and pervasive, and that it is unfavourable
to much that passes for religion. How far that influence may in its
turn lead to error or extravagance it is not here necessary to enquire.
For our present purpose it is enough to recognize that the whole
attitude, not merely of scientists, but of thoughtful men brought up
in a scientific age, towards all the problems of life, whether secular
or sacred, has been affected to an extent which it is almost impossible
to exaggerate. Here may be found perhaps the greatest impediment
to the unquestioning acceptance of any simple and traditional
religious faith.

It is more difficult to gauge the effects which follow from conceiving the physical universe as subject to laws which admit of no
exceptions. As late as the eighteenth century many thinkers regarded
the discovery of physical laws as a revelation of the divine plan by
which the universe is governed ; and the very simplicity and comprehensiveness of the plan was taken to be a proof of divine benevolence and wisdom. Yet at least as early as Descartes it was already
realized that physical laws were independent of, if not opposed to,
the idea of purpose in the universe. It is this second interpretation
which has prevailed. When Laplace, speaking of the existence of
God, said 'I have no need of that hypothesis', he meant that the
conception of God's activity or purpose played no part in his
formulation of scientific law, as it had done in the work of other
thinkers, including the great Isaac Newton himself. In that specific
sense the dictum of Laplace is the universal assumption of science
to-day.

If modern physics is unfavourable to belief in a divine purpose
or plan, it is still more unfavourable to belief in miracles. So far as
these are considered to be breaches of physical laws, they cannot be

accepted without rejecting the most fundamental presuppositions of science. Hence it is not surprising that they have become some- what of an embarrassment to religion. At one time they were invoked to guarantee the truth of revelation. Now, if they are defended at all, it is revelation that is invoked to guarantee the truth of miracles, and their occurrence is explained as the manifestation of some higher law.

So far as physics is incompatible with miracles and has no use for a divine purpose in the universe, it is hard to see how we can retain the idea of providence in general and of special providences in particular. But this is not the worst. The character of scientific law appears to require a universal determinism which applies to the movements of human bodies as much as to the movement of the smallest electron or the remotest star. This cuts at the roots of all morality and so of religion as well.

There are some who seek to escape from this gloomy situation by reminding us that the old-fashioned mechanical views of physics are now abandoned. The concepts of mechanical cause and effect have been given up, and in place of causal laws we are left only with statistical averages. Physics itself even recognizes a principle of indeterminacy and so leaves at least a chink for human freedom. Hence perhaps the future before religion is not quite so black as it has been painted.

Without any wish to be dogmatic on these difficult subjects we must still ask ourselves whether those who find comfort in such considerations may not also be clutching at straws. To abandon the old-fashioned view of causation is by no means to give up the universality of law: all it amounts to is that the laws have a different character. The microscopic space left open by the principle of indeterminacy is far too small for the exercise of human freedom— if indeed we can conceive human freedom at all as manifested only in the apparent chinks and interstices of the physical universe. The late Professor Susan Stebbing was right when she said 'It cannot be maintained that all that is required for human freedom is some amount of uncertainty in the domain of microphysics'. And if we wish to argue that the new physics is less unfavourable to religion than the old, we must take into our reckoning what is called the second law of thermodynamics, according to which the universe is steadily running down. It is hard to see how this can offer any ground either for moral optimism or for religious faith.

The general effect of the modern scientific outlook is summed up in the eloquent, and by now familiar, words of Mr. Bertrand Russell. 'That man is the product of causes which had no prevision of the end they were achieving; that his origin, his growth, his hopes and fears, his loves and beliefs, are but the outcome of accidental collocations of atoms; that no fire, no heroism, no intensity of thought and feeling, can preserve an individual life beyond the grave; that all the labours of the ages, all the inspiration, all the noon-day brightness of human genius, are destined to extinction in the vast death of the solar system, and that the whole temple of man's achievement must inevitably be buried beneath the débris of a universe in ruins—all these things, if not quite beyond dispute, are yet so nearly certain, that no philosophy which rejects them can hope to stand. Only within the scaffolding of these truths, only on the firm foundations of unyielding despair, can the soul's habitation henceforth be safely built'.

If Mr. Russell's views be regarded as suspect, let us listen to the less eloquent, but hardly less despairing, words of a deeply religious thinker—Dr. Albert Schweizer. 'My solution of the problem', he says, 'is that we must make up our minds to renounce completely the optimistic-ethical interpretation of the world. If we take the world as it is, it is impossible to attribute to it a meaning in which the aims and objects of mankind and of individual men have a meaning also.'

§ 4. *Religion and biology*

If the first great wave that threatened to engulf religion came from physics, the second came from biology. The Darwinian theory of evolution overthrew the belief that each species was the object of a special creation and possessed a fixed and unchanging character. This served to upset the authority alike of Aristotle and of the book of Genesis. But still worse than this, the process of evolution appeared to be mechanical rather than purposive, blind rather than intelligent, and so to render nugatory the argument from design, which was commonly regarded as the most cogent proof for the existence of God. Furthermore, from a human point of view evolution in its working seemed wasteful and even cruel, and the main qualities making for survival appeared to be lust and violence and deceit. It gave less than no support to belief in the wisdom and benevolence of the Creator or to the view that the end of creation was the furtherance of virtue. But perhaps the greatest shock of all came from the discovery that man, far from having been specially

created in the image of God, was himself the product of this unintelligent process of evolution and must look back to a long line of
ape-like ancestors. Nowadays we take all this calmly in our stride,
partly perhaps through lack of imagination. We may even feel in a
curious way that it unites us more intimately with the world of
nature of which we form a part. But it should not cause us surprise
if to our Victorian grandfathers it seemed that

'The pillar'd firmament is rott'nness,
And earths base built on stubble.'

In comparison with this the other shocks from biology may seem
unimportant, but we have to remember that the effect of scientific
discoveries is cumulative. Of these further shocks we need mention
only one.

It has always been recognized that the soul is in some ways
dependent on the body; and we all know from ordinary experience
how a minor indisposition, or even fatigue, may dull our mind and
blunt our emotions and weaken our will. But the development of
physiology began to show in ever minuter detail how close is the
connexion between mind and body, and how utterly we depend on
the structure of our brain and nervous system. The very existence
of the soul began to be questioned. Why should we postulate a soul
instead of recognizing that mental functions are completely dependent on bodily functions? Above all, why should we suppose,
against all the empirical evidence, that the soul could exist as a
separate entity after the death of the body? The belief in immortality, one of the strongholds of religion, or at least of many
religions, was being steadily undermined. Conclusions based on
these detailed discoveries were supported further by the general
theory of evolution, which abolished the sharp separation of man
from the other animals, as also by the general theory that physical
laws govern the movements of all bodies, not excluding the organic
bodies of plants and animals and men. Some philosophers and
scientists hold it out as a possibility, and indeed as an ideal, that the
laws of biology, and even of psychology, may one day be reduced
to laws of physics.

One general result emerges from all this. Man displays his intelligence in discovering laws of nature and then awakes, perhaps with
horror, to the fact that these laws apply to himself: for science he
is only one object among many others and has to be understood in
the same way as the rest. Thus man is finally entangled in the
meshes of the net that he himself has woven; and when we say this,

we must add that it is true, not merely of his body, but of his soul. Science is, as it were, a machine constructed by man in order to master the universe; but the machine has turned against its maker and seeks to master him as well.

§ 5. *Religion and psychology*

The third great wave threatening religion comes from psychology, which is, at least etymologically, the science of the soul. This is a more recent wave; and as we disappear gasping under its onrush, we are hardly yet in a position to study its shape. Indeed its shape is perhaps not yet definitely formed. Its exponents at times contradict one another with a freedom ordinarily reserved for philosophers; and some of them indulge in a boldness of speculation from which a respectable philosopher would shrink. We are offered a choice between different schools of thought.

Thus there is a Behaviouristic school, which, as a further expansion of physiology, makes still more formidable the impediments already considered. The Behaviourists ignore in practice, if they do not also deny in theory, the mental phenomena formerly considered open to introspection—our thoughts, our emotions, our volitions, and so on: they are content to study only the bodily behaviour of human and other animals, and so to blur still further the dividing line between man and the brutes. A very different method is adopted by the schools of psycho-analysis which originate from Freud, both by those which seek to carry further the work of the master and by those which attempt to modify and improve it. All of them start from an examination of human consciousness, especially of human dreams; and they claim on this basis to bring under scientific investigation the vast and obscure domain of the unconscious, whose existence had been merely suspected and whose character had not been seriously explored. According to them the human mind is like an iceberg, by far the greater part of which is under water and not amenable to direct observation. By means of inference they attempt to describe in detail these murky nether regions; and they have been able, as it were, to draw up from the ocean's depths many strange, and on the whole unpleasing, objects for our contemplation and instruction.

The schools which consider human consciousness to be worthy of scientific attention take up different attitudes to religion. As we have seen, they may regard it as a harmful illusion or as a healing and even 'real' illusion, whatever that may be. But, broadly speaking, even at the best they offer cold comfort to religion, and the attitude of Freud himself is conspicuously hostile. Besides, they exhibit the general tendency to assume determinism in mental processes; they encourage the view that reason has little or no part to play in human behaviour; and even if they regard mind as a possible object of study, it is for them only one object among others and requires no special principles for its understanding. All psychology is an example of what I meant when I said that the soul is entangled in the meshes of the scientific net which man has devised for the better understanding of the physical world. And many psychologists believe that religious experience can be explained—or explained away—in accordance with the ordinary laws that have been found to account for other mental phenomena.

This third wave is perhaps logically less intimidating to religion than the other two, if only because psychology is not yet fully developed as a science. Psycho-analysis has called attention to mental phenomena hitherto neglected; it has thrown light on dark places; and it has done mental healing a service for which the world must be grateful. Whatever be its defects, it has opened up the way for fresh advances, but has it already advanced so far that even its fundamental concepts are firmly established? Sometimes it may seem not to have got much beyond a stage like that in chemistry when the phenomena of combustion were explained by postulating a hypothetical substance, now forgotten, which was known as 'phlogiston'; or at least—if this is too depreciatory—not beyond the comparatively recent stage in physics when 'ether' had to be postulated as an elastic substance permeating all space and forming a medium through which rays of light were propagated. It may be heretical to say so, but it seems to me rather improbable that our old friends, the Ego, the Super-Ego, and the Id, will occupy permanent niches in the scientific pantheon.

Nevertheless, even if this third wave may not yet be so very imposing logically, psychologically—partly perhaps by its very vagueness—it is to-day almost the most formidable of the three, at least as far as popular or semi-popular thinking is concerned. In spite of attempts to make use of it in the interests of religion, it produces an emotional and intellectual background so different from that of religious tradition that the combination of the two becomes very difficult. What is sometimes said of philosophies is even more true of religious beliefs—they are usually not refuted, but merely abandoned. When the spiritual climate has altered, they may simply fade away; and we seem to be witnessing something rather like this at the present crisis of our civilization.

§ 6. *Religion and history*

There are other human sciences besides psychology, and their influence has also tended to be psychologically, if not logically, unfavourable to religion. Anthropology, for example, tends on the whole to blur sharp distinctions between the primitive and the developed, and among heathen superstitions it finds parallels even for the most sacred mysteries of the higher religions. It suggests that religion is a survival of something primitive in the experience of the race, just as psychology suggests it is a survival of something primitive in the experience of the child. Even economics takes a hand in the unholy assault. The classical economists may have been tempted at times to suppose that the 'economic man' was, not a mere useful abstraction, but the only kind of man there is; and this tendency has been hardened into a dogma by the Marxists. They tell us that our bourgeois religion, like our bourgeois morality, is only an ideology—that is, an illusory 'rationalization' of purely economic factors—and one of the main impediments to human progress. All these human sciences, among which sociology also may be included, have the common characteristic of treating man as one object among other objects: they tend to explain his thoughts, his actions, and his emotions as the effect of forces outside himself— forces whose influence can be determined, and even controlled, in accordance with ascertainable scientific laws.

Here then we have a whole series of little wavelets, not perhaps very impressive in isolation and colliding at times with one another, yet all driving inexorably in the same general direction. But belonging to the same series there is one special wave so menacing that we may be inclined to call it the fourth great wave—the wave of historical method and historical criticism.

The modern development of the historical method is particularly menacing to Christianity, since of all the great religions Christianity has laid most stress on history—the history of the Jews, the history of the Founder, and the history of the Church. Modern criticism has undermined first the authority of the Old Testament and then the authority of the New in such a way that the traditional belief in an infallible Book, written down by God's penmen at His dictation, can no longer be accepted by any intelligent man of independent judgement who has given serious consideration to the subject. We have instead a most fallible human record compiled by mortal men, who, even if they were gifted with a special religious insight, were unacquainted with the canons of historical evidence and unfamiliar with the ideals of historical accuracy. Christian thinkers have made great and creditable efforts to adjust themselves to this new situation —the other world-religions are probably not even yet fully awake to their danger. The methods of modern scholarship may be able to sort out what is reasonably certain from what is at least doubtful as well as from what is in all probability fictitious. On these points there are, and are bound to be, differences among scholars, and it is only experts who can profitably form an opinion. Hence it is always possible, and it may often be justifiable, to dismiss the arguments of laymen in these subjects as ignorant or exaggerated. Nevertheless the plain man used to be faced with a plain situation which he could understand. He was told that every historical statement in the Bible, or at least in the New Testament, was true. He has now to be told that while the religious teaching in the Bible retains its unique value, some of its historical statements are true, while some are untrue, and others have been traditionally misunderstood. Even if he is sensible enough not to hold that if anything goes, the whole thing goes, he yet feels that he does not know where he stands, and that he is ill-equipped to come to a decision in matters about which the doctors differ. This is a new impediment to the simplicity of religious faith.

To the thoughtful man all this opens up questions which are philosophical rather than historical. He has been told, in traditional language, that religious faith is necessary for salvation, and the question he asks himself is this. Granted that religious faith is very much more than an intellectual belief in historical facts, can a belief in historical facts be necessary for salvation, and so for religious faith, when only the most expert scholarship is competent to decide whether these alleged facts are historical or not? If he answers in the negative, if indeed he comes to the conclusion that no belief in historical facts and no skill in historical scholarship can be necessary for what he calls salvation, his view of what is essential to religion has undergone a revolution, and he has entered a new path, not knowing where it may lead.

§ 7. *Religion and philosophy*

I have not mentioned philosophy as one of the waves with which religion has to struggle. Philosophers do not speak with one voice, and the best of them are more anxious that men should think for themselves than that they should accept any doctrine dogmatically. But if we may speak of general trends, the movement of philosophy in this country has been, on the whole, away from religion. The Oxford Idealism which prevailed at the end of the Victorian age did at least have religious sympathies. The Realism which tended to replace it later, if it was not always sympathetic, was seldom other than neutral. The more modern school of Logical Positivism, which owes its rise to the great influence of Mr. Bertrand Russell, is often openly hostile or indifferent. We have moved far from the days when philosophy was the handmaid of theology. Like other hand-maids at the present time, she now considers herself to be not only as good as her mistress but—if the colloquialism may be pardoned— a damn' sight better; and if she were inclined to enter again into domestic service, it would be as the handmaid, not of theology, but of science.

So far as Logical Positivism places a linguistic ban on theology and even on ethics, it has already been examined briefly in Chapter II; but it would be a mistake to regard the doctrine that all statements about God are nonsense as the central feature of the modern linguistic movement as a whole. There is already a marked tendency to get beyond the earlier dogmatism, and even to display an interest in religion as well as in other problems more akin to those which have occupied philosophy in the past. As originally expounded Logical Positivism sweeps so much away into one comprehensive rubbish heap that it is difficult not to feel there must be something wrong with it; but its boundaries are becoming so blurred that it is almost time the name was dropped. All I wish to point out here is that a modern philosophy which had—and may still have—a very great following, especially among the younger intellectuals, is, perhaps I should not say hostile, but politely con-temptuous, towards everything in the nature of religious belief. In this respect, as in others, it would seem to be a faithful mirror of an attitude widely prevalent at the present time.

§ 8. *The predicament of religion*

I have no wish to pretend that the contentions I have put forward are conclusive or that they are all equally sound. Like Logical Positivism itself, they sweep so much away along with religion that we may begin to doubt their validity. What I have stated is the case which is widely accepted and has got to be answered. Nevertheless it is folly not to see that the case is very strong and that, although in certain respects it may be specially menacing to Christianity, it is a threat, not to a particular religion, but to all religion as such.

There are doubtless many other reasons, some of them less creditable, for the growing indifference to religion; but reasons of the type I have described are worthy of special consideration since they spring, not from human wickedness and folly, but from the highest achievements of human thought. They affect, not only the intellectuals, but also, through them, the immense mass of men who take their opinions at second and third and fourth hand. The whole spiritual atmosphere is altered, and even the ordinary religious man speaks to-day in a different tone about special providences and the hope of immortality, if he speaks of them at all.

In such circumstances it is unconvincing to tell us that the conflict of religion and science is now happily out-moded, that so and so has put forward new theories about scientific methodology and somebody else has confirmed some statement in the Biblical record from a newly-discovered papyrus or from some archaeological remains. This is mere tinkering with the subject; and we should not be surprised if those who have been brought up in the new atmosphere and have little or no experience of religion are apt to dismiss the easy optimism of some religious teachers as springing from blindness or ignorance, if not from hypocrisy. Nor can it be denied that they sometimes have ample excuse. The situation to be faced is one unknown to St. Paul and St. Augustine, to Aquinas and Duns Scotus, to Luther and Calvin; and it can be met, if it is to be met at all, only by a new effort of thinking at least as great as any of theirs. So long as this is lacking, the modern world is bound to suffer from a divided mind and from a conflict between the heart and the head. If religion has to satisfy the whole man, its demand is that the men who follow it must be whole-minded as well as whole-hearted. The very wholeness at which religion aims is impossible unless the spiritual disease caused by the fatal rift between science and religion can receive its own specific intellectual cure.

Chapter VIII

RESPONSES

§ 1. *Responses*

We have examined, if only in outline, the challenge offered by modern science to every form of religious belief. Our next task must be to consider, though once again only in the barest outline, some of the possible responses to this challenge.

An examination of such responses should not be confused with an attempt to answer the formidable case which has been presented. A satisfying answer, if it can be provided even for our own day and generation, will require a rare combination of philosophical and religious genius, and it certainly could not be given in one lecture, or even in a whole series of lectures. I have chosen the word 'responses' deliberately, for this covers both a mere reaction and an adequate answer as well as the whole range stretching from the one to the other.

The various responses to be examined need by no means be exclusive of one another: they may be combined in many different ways. Even considered by themselves each of them may take a great variety of forms.

The purely negative response I propose to pass over. Many honest thinkers abandon religion altogether and seek compensation in the pursuit of scientific knowledge, which alone can give some mastery over nature; and also in the practice and enjoyment of art, which can afford some of the emotional satisfaction formerly obtained from religious worship. If there is any truth in the account I have given of religion, this would involve a loss of spiritual health or wholeness. And if the negative response means also that we must reject human freedom and deny objective standards in morality, it is not one to be lightly approved.

§ 2. *The way of the two compartments*

One way of dealing with an obstacle or impediment is to pretend that it does not exist. This may avoid embarrassment, but it does

116

not make for progress. In its extremer forms it might be described
as the way of the ostrich, but this common aspersion on ostriches is
said to be unwarranted. Perhaps we had better describe it as the way
of the two compartments. We may keep one compartment of life for
religion and another for science, and we may be careful to arrange
that there should be no communicating door between.

This way is sometimes followed even by those who are undis-
turbed by intellectual difficulties. The late Sir Henry Jones used to
tell a story about an old lady distinguished for her piety. She
happened to meet one day a traveller who told her he had just
returned from Jerusalem, and this took her completely aback.
'Young man', she said, 'do you mean to tell me that there really is
such a place?' For her the world of religion, however precious, was
a dream world which had no disturbing contact with reality. A more
sceptical example of this attitude is that of the little girl who said,
'Of course I know Santa Claus isn't real, but I don't want anybody
to tell me so'.

Especially in moments of crisis or despair, men may continue to
use the familiar language of devotion when it no longer represents
their intellectual beliefs; but I am thinking rather of those who are
unable to reconcile their religion with the rest of their knowledge
and yet cling to both in the belief that both are good. They may be
justified in doing so if they feel that these matters are too difficult
for them and that they lack the intellectual equipment necessary to
effect a reconciliation. In this there are many different grades, and
even men who have abandoned most of their religion intellectually
may be able at times to recapture their old feeling, and renew their
former attitude, without troubling themselves too much about
logical consistency. This latter experience finds its classical expression in the now hackneyed lines of Robert Browning which begin

'Just when we are safest, there's a sunset touch,
A fancy from a flower-bell, some one's death,
A chorus-ending from Euripides, — . . .'

Bishop Blougram's attitude was complicated with self-interest and
so with hypocrisy, but in itself the experience is not hypocritical: it
is only the mirror of a divided mind.

The policy of the two compartments may offer some sort of
temporary practical solution, but if exalted into a theory it merely
re-states a problem which it has not solved. However comforting,
and even necessary, it may be to the individual, it belongs to a
religion which has a past rather than a future.

§ 3. *The way of archaism*

Another way of dealing with an obstacle is to re-trace one's steps. We may meet the crisis of religion and science by going backwards into the past. This might be called the policy of putting back the clock; but perhaps we had better borrow a term from Dean Inge and call it the way of archaism.

The way of archaism is not uncongenial to religion: it fits in with the conservatism of so much religious thought and practice. Priests, as Dr. Inge reminds us, continued to use stone knives long after iron had been discovered. The extreme of archaism is a reversion to the primitive, like the Nazi effort to revive the ritual of the ancient Germans. But its commonest form is the appeal to tradition, and ultimately the appeal to authority—an appeal characteristic of most, if not all, religions at certain stages of their development. We find this in Fundamentalism and in the attempts of Barth and his followers to get back to the Reformers and ultimately to the primitive Church. It is perhaps most conspicuous to-day in converts to Roman Catholicism.

The Roman Church does not fall into Barth's error of condemning natural theology and repudiating reason. On the contrary, it declares authoritatively that the natural light of reason can give us knowledge of God by means of philosophical argument and can establish the fact of divine revelation by historical proofs, notably by the record of miracles and prophecies. Yet when this result is achieved, the believer is commanded to accept without question, not only an inerrant Bible, but also a vast unwritten tradition, on the authority of an infallible Church. This is not an entirely closed circle to those who believe it can be approached, if not entered, by means of rational thought; but once within the circle there is no further scope for independent thinking. The doctrine of the divinity of Christ and that of the Immaculate Conception—and even the recent pronouncement that the Blessed Virgin Mary was taken up bodily into Heaven before death—have to be accepted with equal piety and veneration solely on the ground that they are vouched for by an infallible authority. There is no room left for argument except in order to support conclusions already assumed to be true.

The flight into the past, whatever form it may take, may be one way of not facing the impediments of the present, one way of carrying out the policy of the two compartments: we transport ourselves in imagination to a period when our present difficulties had not yet arisen. The dream world to which we retire for safety gains a certain measure of reality because something like it is supposed to have existed once; it has the charm of things that are old; it gives room for play to the aesthetic imagination; by shutting out the present it embodies the wholeness for which modern men seem to seek in vain; by offering a block belief or monolithic doctrine which has to be swallowed whole on authority it can free men from the painful responsibility of thinking and enable them to concentrate on the religious life; it can also remove from them the burden of difficult personal decisions; and in all these ways it can afford consolation to troubled, and even to sceptical, spirits, especially to those who find themselves unable to cope with the complexities, and perhaps the flatness, of the actual world.

Needless to say, it is only natural to cling to a past tradition and to derive inspiration from it—the most revolutionary movements make use, even if unconsciously, of what has gone before. Nevertheless we keep a tradition alive, not by accepting and repeating and elaborating what previous thinkers have thought, but by meeting our own problems in the same spirit as they met theirs. Religious thinkers in the past made assumptions which cannot reasonably be made to-day, and it is this which sets the modern problem. Mere archaism, intellectually considered, is an evasion of the problem. If it hardens into an abandonment of independent thought and an unquestioning submission to ecclesiastical authority, it is likely in the end to be as fatal to religious, as it is to intellectual, life.

§ 4. *The way of absurdity*

It is possible in religious matters, not merely to abandon thinking, but to spurn and deride it, to welcome paradox and to glorify inconsistency. This may be called the way of absurdity. It is another way, and a mad way, of pretending that obstacles do not exist. Once we take this path, we are free to do exactly as we like—to accept any religion or no religion as the whim seizes us.

Those who adopt this attitude surrender themselves frankly to unreason. Here is a terrible quotation from Martin Luther. 'All the articles of our Christian belief are, when considered rationally, just as impossible, and mendacious and preposterous. Faith, however, is completely abreast of the situation. It grips reason by the throat, and strangles the beast'. On this Karl Barth makes the cryptic comment 'He who can hear this, let him hear it; for it is the beginning and end of history'. It sounds more like the end of human sanity.

This rejection of reason finds its most elaborate modern expression in the voluminous writings of Kierkegaard, and his popularity to-day is a sign of the dangerous pass to which we have come—a mark of desperation and despair. He wrote, it is true, before the Darwinian theory and before the development of Biblical criticism; and he shows no interest in science or in the bearing of science on religion. The rationalism threatening religion he found principally —and perhaps not without justification—in the philosophy of Hegel and his followers. But what is most interesting in him, and also most modern, is that he denies any objective basis for religion: there must be a leap of faith into paradox and absurdity. His motto is '*Credo quia absurdum*', and he carries it to the utmost length. Thus he exalts 'the knights of the faith' above the moral law; he believes in a 'teleological suspension' of ethics; and he becomes almost maudlin in his admiration for Abraham's willingness to offer up his son Isaac as a human sacrifice. This is expounded in the book called *Fear and Trembling*; and what makes it nauseating as a professedly religious work is that, as he himself has said, it is a 'mystification' which reproduces his own life. In other words, it is an account of his unhappy love affair with Regina Olsen, an account in which his own deplorable behaviour is supposed to be similar to that of Abraham. We may pity his unhappy and diseased temperament, but neurosis is a poor qualification for setting up as a religious guide. We should be particularly on our guard when the guide makes no pretence at objective thinking, which stands or falls by the argument independently of the personality of the thinker, but rests his case on the inwardness of his own personal experience. If ever a person was self-centred it was Kierkegaard: he hardly ever thinks of anyone but himself. Self-centredness is the very antithesis of religion; and if the paradox of faith is—as he says—a willingness 'to do the terrible and to do it for its own sake' (as well as for God's sake), then the less of this kind of faith we have the better.

It is not with the aid of such a leader that religion can be defended. Kierkegaard's thought may perhaps be winnowed into something of value for the philosophy of religion, since even his morbid vanity does not always overpower his natural shrewdness; and Gabriel Marcel has developed some of his ideas in a saner way. It is reasonable enough to recognize the limits of human knowledge and to

insist that in the religious life there must be a decision or commitment which is not the result of discursive reasoning. But once we
enter on the path of absurdity with a whole heart, there is no limit
to the nonsense that may be talked. Fortunately or unfortunately,
religion has no monopoly in absurdity, and it cannot be recommended on the ground that 'humanly speaking, the knight of the
faith is mad'.

§ 5. *The way of the kernel and the husk*

If religion is to retain its sanity, it has to adjust itself to the new
knowledge. One way in which men begin this adjustment is by
attempting to separate the core of religion from its accretions of
myth and dogma and legalism, and indeed from all the aberrations
of which we have already spoken. This may be called the way of the
kernel and the husk. It means the giving up of something, even of
much, that was precious to our fathers; but perhaps obstacles can be
most easily surmounted by those who are content to travel light.

This way is often pursued within religion altogether apart from
intellectual difficulties. In all ages and in all religions the greatest
teachers have recalled men to simplicity, to the spirit as opposed to
the letter. When this happens there is a great liberation of religious
energy—a feeling of escape from the trivial to the serious, and from
slavery to freedom. These movements within religion have often a
moral, rather than an intellectual, inspiration, and so are positive as
well as negative.

The modern movement towards simplicity in religion is partly
moral, for much that used to be accepted without question is morally
revolting to the men of to-day. But we are here concerned primarily
with the theoretical difficulty of reconciling religious belief and
scientific knowledge. This intellectual approach, though it may be
pursued in a religious spirit and may indeed be more truly religious
than a lazy acquiescence in traditional doctrines, is not in itself a
source of religious inspiration. Its task is rather to cut away dead
wood and so to secure space for the new shoots that may sprout in
due course. But the cutting away may seem at first to be sheer loss.

The way of modernism, as this intellectual movement may be
called, is directly opposed to the way of archaism, whose followers
regard it with horror. They sometimes assert that a minimal theology must result in a minimal religion, but it is not obvious why
this should be so. The teaching of Jesus in the synoptic gospels

might be said to contain a minimum of theology, but a maximum of religion; and there are at least some men, perhaps even many, who, like the Quakers, find religion most compelling when it is reduced to its simplest terms—the love of God and of our neighbour. Modernism, even if at times it may seem to lack positive inspiration, is at least an attempt to meet, and not to evade, the intellectual difficulties of to-day. So far as it is a theology, it only constructs— like any other theology—a framework within which the religious spirit may manifest itself. So far as it is a religion, it too may have its saints.

On one point we should be under no illusion. Although it may get rid of some difficulties, modernism by itself is no answer to the scientific challenge since this affects the most essential of religious beliefs—belief in God and in objective standards of morality. Hence the unhappy modernist is assailed on two sides. He is charged with being half-hearted both in faith and in thought, with satisfying neither the religious nor the scientific spirit. He may be said to make the worst of both worlds. All this goes to show that from an intellectual point of view modernism is incomplete without a philo- sophy of religion. Even the central core of religion can no longer be accepted as a matter of general agreement.

In spite of what has been said about the attraction of a simple religion it may be urged that besides doctrine and an effort to lead the good life in the service of God and man, there is need of a symbolism, a myth, a ritual. These may be necessary to satisfy the primitive side of our nature, to kindle our imagination, to move our hearts. Yet they must develop gradually, and they are most effective when hallowed by tradition. Is there not a danger that modernism may leave only the thin ghost of a religion which will quickly lose its influence among ordinary men?

§ 6. *The way of allegory*

There is admittedly a danger that a religion which is, so to speak, disembodied may be too rarefied for ordinary men: it may become more like a philosophy, and this is not an adequate substitute. Ulti- mately the religious spirit must be left to evolve its own symbolism and ritual, but where it is not strong enough to do so, men have always tried to meet this situation by what may be called the way of allegory: they have interpreted what traditionally seemed to be plain statements of fact as myths or parables which reveal a higher truth.

Those who adopt this course are commonly attacked, or even despised, both by the upholders of orthodoxy and by those who wish to sweep all religion away. They are spurned as half-hearted and dishonest triflers by men who, for quite different reasons, unite in insisting that religious statements must be taken with absolute literalness. Thus from the religious point of view Theodore of Mopsuestia assailed Origen long ago for teaching that Adam was not Adam and paradise was not paradise and the snake was not a snake. Yet the allegorical method is far from being uncongenial to religion: it is practised at all levels from the simple use of parable to the most elaborate methods of exegesis—witness, for example, the traditional interpretations of the Song of Solomon; and it becomes extravagant only in the stage of decline, as when the old Greek religion was near the point of death. There are few who would support Theodore against Origen to-day, and even Karl Barth once declared that 'it did not matter whether the serpent spoke, but what he said'.

The way of allegory was employed by Immanuel Kant, perhaps more for the benefit of his pupils than of himself. He believed that the historical element in religion served only 'to illustrate and not to demonstrate' the rational truths of religion and morality: its value lay in the fact that it could be interpreted as revealing these higher truths. This is certainly a fundamental departure from the traditional beliefs of Christianity, and his attempt to preserve Christian doctrine in an altered form was as unwelcome to an orthodox thinker like the Prussian archbishop Borowski as it was to a 'convinced heathen' like Goethe. It is harsh and unjustifiable to condemn as dishonest those who seek in this way to maintain continuity with the religion of their fathers or to recover the purity of a faith which they think has been corrupted; but there must be a limit to the possibility of preserving an ancient symbolism or ritual or doctrine while reading into it a different meaning. This is a transitional method, and there may come a time when it can no longer be followed with an undivided mind and heart. In the words of the Moslem philosopher Al Ghazali, 'Whenever a man knows that the glass of his traditional faith is broken, that is a breaking that cannot be mended, and a separating that cannot be united by any sewing or putting together, except it be melted in the fire and given another new form'. Nevertheless until breaking-point is reached, there may be effective continuity in a faith which finds very different intellectual interpretations at different stages of its development.

§ 7. *The way of religious experience*

It may be thought that the account so far given of responses to the modern challenge is altogether too intellectual. Must not the only satisfactory response be based on the fact of religious, and perhaps of mystical, experience? Only if we fall back on experience can the scientist be met on his own ground.

The position unfortunately is not quite so simple as that.

Naturally enough, the religious man must respond by continuing to live the religious life. He may also reasonably claim that only those who attempt humbly to do so are likely to be granted the vision of God. Furthermore, religious experience is actually felt, not only as a contact with ultimate reality, but as a communion, or even union, with God, a communion which is not mere knowledge, but is also love. Perhaps it may even be felt, not as one-sided, but as mutual love. This is a tremendous, and indeed a staggering, claim; yet without something of this character religion—so far as it is more than morality—is reduced, at the worst to an emotional indulgence, and at the best to a form of art, perhaps to a form of art which, after the fashion of Coué, directly influences conduct by means of the imagination. The religious man may feel that his experience is its own guarantee, and that for him it is impossible to doubt the reality that is experienced. This may be sufficient for him in practice; but unless he is prepared to think further, he has not escaped from the way of the two compartments and is still in need of intellectual defence against criticism, especially if his experience is to be used for the persuasion of others.

There is a further point. Religious experience may be in fact the main reason why men continue to believe in God, but it may be doubted whether they have always recognized this. In the past such experience developed against a hard background of theological doctrine and took much of its colour from this background. Even a mystic like St. Teresa would, I think, have been surprised to be told that the ground of faith was religious or mystical experience. She always displayed a proper respect for learned men—perhaps not without a tinge of irony—and was ready to withdraw at the behest of the Church anything that she had said. The divine favours specially granted to a few chosen spirits she would have regarded as a strong confirmation, rather than as the very foundation, of religious belief.

Even from a religious point of view we must ask how far religious experience claims to be knowledge of God. It is a ground for faith; but faith is not knowledge, and the religious consciousness itself seems to shrink from any claim to know God as He is. Nor is the position altered if we appeal to the mystics. It would be unreasonable to doubt that some favoured men and women have experienced in a kind of trance or ecstasy what they feel with absolute assurance to be union with God. On this evidence some are prepared to say with Mr. Aldous Huxley that in these experiences 'the God who is both immanent and transcendent, personal and more than personal, may reveal Himself . . . in his fullness'. This is too hurried, even if we set aside a possibility suggested by our account of the negative way—the possibility that the mystic union may be a sinking back into that undifferentiated continuum which is supposed by some Eastern philosophies to be the ultimate reality. The mystics themselves are full of warnings that any claim to knowledge of God is subject to the severest limitations. Let me quote again from St. John of the Cross. 'One of the greatest favours bestowed on the soul transiently in this life is to enable it to see so distinctly and to feel so profoundly that it cannot comprehend God at all. These souls are herein somewhat like the saints in heaven, where they who know Him most perfectly perceive most clearly that He is infinitely incomprehensible; for those who have the less clear vision do not perceive so clearly as do those others how greatly He transcends their vision'.

Religious and mystical experiences must be of the utmost importance for any philosophy of religion. Yet it is abundantly clear that they are in need of philosophical interpretation and defence if they are to satisfy the mind as well as the heart.

§ 8. *The way of psychical research*

If our intellectual difficulties arise mainly from empirical science, it may be thought that we must seek the main, if not the sole, defence of religion from empirical science itself—namely, from that branch of it known as psychical research. Here surely we shall be able to meet the natural scientist on his own ground.

This view has been advocated by thinkers so eminently worthy of respect that it cannot be passed over even if we feel, as I do, some qualms about it—possibly as the result of what Professor Broad calls 'unconscious resistance'. It is held, for example, by Professor Price, and he has rather ambiguous support from Professor Broad, whose sympathy with religion is less conspicuous.

The subject of psychical research suffers from its relation to spiritualism and to what is known as 'the occult'—that hideous breeding-ground of credulity and fraud—but we should not allow this to prejudice us against it. Having studied the evidence, Professor Price considers that telepathy and clairvoyance have been scientifically established. In telepathy—I quote his words—'one mind exercises a direct influence upon another mind, without any known physical intermediary'; and in clairvoyance 'a mind has a veridical "impression" of an object or event (often a distant one) without making use of physical sense-organs'. From this he proceeds to argue that in these occurrences 'the brain apparently plays no part', and consequently that psychical research 'has already in principle demolished the materialistic theory of human personality'. Needless to say, he does not propose to base religion on such experiences, but he considers that these discoveries go some way towards making tenable a belief in personal immortality and so in divine justice. These two beliefs he regards as essential to religion.

We may have the utmost sympathy with this attitude, and yet doubt whether the evidence will bear the weight of all his conclusions. As these psychical events have happened, so far as we know, only to living beings possessed of a brain, it is hard to see why they should be any more independent of the brain than is, for example, the solution of a mathematical or philosophical problem. The evidence seems only to suggest possibilities which scientists may be too ready to exclude. Every encouragement should be given to further enquiry; and if our research produces genuinely scientific results, we are entitled to make use of these results as a corroboration for philosophical theories of the relation between mind and matter. So far we may agree with Professor Price. But the religious man must hesitate to let his case stand or fall by reference to facts which are admittedly not open to all observers and which may be susceptible of different theoretical explanations. Unless religion can maintain itself even on the supposition that there is complete correlation between mental and cerebral processes, it is putting itself at the mercy of further scientific discoveries.

In recent years psychical research has increased its scientific respectability by moving into the laboratory and taking the name of 'para-psychology'. In his book, *The Reach of the Mind*, Professor Rhine expounds, with rather less subtlety, a doctrine not unlike that of Professor Price; and he supports it with a careful account of the experimental evidence for extra-sensory perception (ESP) and psycho-kinesis (PK). He experiments mainly with dice or cards, and he claims to have demonstrated, not only that some individuals can foretell the fall of dice more often than the theory of mathematical chances would warrant, but also—more surprisingly—that they can, by willing, influence the fall of dice to an extent that is mathematically significant in the same sense. All this is extremely interesting, and, as he himself recognizes, it opens up the possibility that telepathy, as tested in the laboratory, may be reduced to precognition of the record that has subsequently to be written down by the sender of the telepathic message. What concerns us is his view that here at last we get experimental proof that man is something more than a merely physical being. I should have thought that every scientific experiment, and indeed that every act of thinking, was already a proof that man was more than a physical being. The failure to consider this possibility illustrates the modern tendency so to concentrate on the observed experiment that the mental activity of the experimenter is entirely overlooked.

We ought not to make light of these recent attempts to support religion by the aid of scientific experiment, but it is necessary to get them into perspective. Professor Broad tells us that psychical research offers the religious man the *only* possible gift-horse in the field of the sciences; but he adds the warning that it may turn out to be a Trojan horse. In spite of the ambiguous character of the animal he would, he says, hesitate, if he were a religious man, to look it quite so superciliously in the mouth as the leaders of religion habitually do. Superciliousness is certainly unbecoming to leaders of religion; but the mouth of a possibly Trojan horse should be scanned with the most anxious care—especially if we are invited to put our shirt on it.

Professor Broad's warning should be taken seriously. We cannot let our philosophy, and still less our religion, turn on empirical evidence which is dubious in character and limited in scope. Such evidence can be too easily upset or at least re-interpreted. We may look to it for corroboration, but we cannot make it the foundation of a philosophical or theological system without the risk that at any moment the whole structure may topple about our ears.

§ 9. *The need for philosophy*

Religion, as I think Professor Price would agree, must stand or fall by the authenticity of religious experience; but if, like a crab, it is to grow a hard shell adequate at least for a time, it must look to a philosophy which is broadly based and is ready to take into account all the evidence there is.

This appears to be the main conclusion which emerges from the survey of the various possible responses. It will be unwelcome to those who deny to philosophy the right, or even the power, to deal with ultimate questions; but most of those who take this view are not concerned with religion, and the few who are so concerned must be left to find their own way out of the present difficulties. Our conclusion is not incompatible with most of the responses that have been considered—not even with the way of the two compartments, unless this is adopted as a permanent principle and not merely as a temporary device. There is only one response to which it is diametrically opposed. Between the way of philosophy, or of sanity, and the bad, mad way I have called the way of absurdity there can only be war to the knife.

Chapter IX

THE WAY OF EXPERIENCE

§ 1. *Religious experience*

Thinkers who maintain that religious experience is a sufficient warrant for theological beliefs are under a plain obligation to describe this experience and to explain why it should be regarded as a guarantee of its own validity. The same demand may also be made of those who prefer to speak of revelation rather than of religious experience; for a revelation, if it is to be something more than the words written down in a book, must become—or at least must have been—a revelation to individuals in a personal experience. Unless such experience can be described, the plain man does not even know what to look for, and he is given no help to recognize a revelation or to understand why he should trust it.

Perhaps we should not expect this demand for a description to be adequately met—religious men, like artists, may be more interested in having experiences than in describing them; but even the most modest expectations are too often disappointed. Many of those who lay the greatest stress on religious experience seem unable or unwilling to tell us anything about what that experience is. They speak freely enough of the content of revelation, but far too little about the way in which that content is revealed. Yet once they abandon the view that a revelation is literally dictated by God, the need becomes urgent. It is not enough to say, with St. John of the Cross, that 'God without the sound of words . . . teaches the soul—and the soul knows not how—in a most secret and hidden way'. From Barth— to take one striking example—it is hard to find out anything more than that the Bible becomes the Word of God when it overpowers or masters us (the German word is '*bemächtigt*'). We ought to be told more than this.

It is sometimes said that such a request is unreasonable—that if we could explain what divine revelation is, what we explained would be precisely *not* divine revelation. 'We may not pretend', says one writer, 'to usurp the office of the Holy Spirit'. But this is a complete misunderstanding. Nobody expects that a description of aesthetic experience will itself be a work of art or that a description of religious experience will itself be a divine revelation. But we should like at the very least to be told something about the emotions which accompany religious experience, and about the way in which they differ from emotions of a more ordinary kind. Without some light on these and kindred matters we cannot hope to see why religious experience should be exalted above other emotional experiences and regarded as an apprehension of divine reality.

§ 2. 'The Idea of the Holy'

The theologian who seems to have grasped most clearly the nature of what is required is Rudolf Otto in his book 'Das Heilige'; and he has been fortunate enough to find in Professor Harvey a competent and sympathetic translator, who has given us an English version under the title 'The Idea of the Holy'. This work combines wide learning with psychological insight: it is rich in delicate distinctions which are too often overlooked. It can be commended also as a study of religious language; for we may attain greater subtlety and precision in linguistic usage if we are trying to find words for things rather than things for words, although the two processes must go on side by side. As an account of the origin, development, and nature of religious experience it is in a class by itself, and we must try to see what we can learn from it.

At the very outset it should be emphasized that if we approach this topic as philosophers, we may get it a little out of focus. A philosopher is concerned with description and analysis, not for its own sake, but as a basis for the claim that religious experience is the apprehension of a transcendent reality. This is the claim which has to be critically assessed, and it is one on which Otto himself is insistent; but he may be better as a psychologist than as a philosopher, and the merits of his description will remain even if the theories based on it fail to carry conviction.

There is a further point which must be kept in mind if we are to grasp, let alone criticize, the doctrines set forth in this remarkable book. Wide as is its range, it lays special stress on one aspect of religion—the non-rational aspect. Otto recognizes clearly enough that there are both rational and non-rational elements in religion, and that these, in his own metaphor, constitute its warp and woof. He is concerned with both these elements and with their interaction or interpenetration; but he pays more attention to the non-rational element because he believes it has been too much neglected in the past. Unless we make allowance for this, we may think his view very one-sided.

§ 3. *The rational and the non-rational*

The rational is commonly identified with thinking and the non-rational with feeling, but Otto extends this distinction to cover the *objects* of thought and feeling. To him an object is rational if it can be thought or conceived clearly; it is non-rational if it can merely be felt but not conceived. Thus the rational element in religion is what can be conceived. God, for example, may be conceived as Spirit, Reason, Good Will, Supreme Power, and it is the very mark of a religion's high rank that it should have no lack of *conceptions* about God. Without these religion would be mere feeling, not belief, and it would be indifferent to morality. Yet we might entertain theological concepts without being at all religious. In religious experience there must be something more; and Otto claims that our rational concepts have to be predicated of a non-rational or supra-rational Subject which eludes conceptual understanding, and yet must somehow be apprehended in a different way. This different way is the way of 'a unique original feeling-response' which is non-rational or non-conceptual. It is present at all levels of religion and constitutes its 'real innermost core'.

In all this there are serious initial difficulties.

In the first place, no concept can be adequate to its object: the most insignificant mongrel has more to it than we can think in our concept of 'dogness' or 'dogginess'. And it is impossible to suppose that even the rational attributes of God, such as omniscience, can be adequately grasped by any concept of ours.

In the second place, it is hard to see how Otto can talk about religious feelings and their object without making use of concepts, or at least of conceptual words. No doubt these concepts will not be definable like the concept of a triangle; and the words, if they indicate a feeling, will mean nothing to any one who has not experienced that feeling. But, after all, the same might be said about the word 'red'. Otto himself attempts to avoid this difficulty by describing as 'ideograms' the words which refer to specifically religious emotion. Curiously enough, the word 'ideogram' is normally used for a letter or mark that indicates, not a sound, but an idea or concept, as in the writing of the Chinese. Otto uses it for an ostensive sign or mark or token which points directly to some experienced feeling.

Even if there may be some confusion in all this, there is at least a real difference between thinking and emotion; and it will be a great service if our attention can be drawn to a distinctive religious feeling.

To religious feeling Otto applies the adjective 'numinous', derived from the Latin word '*numen*'. He maintains—and this is his central doctrine—that non-rational numinous feeling is an essential element in religious experience and is part of its compelling power. By calling it 'numinous' he wishes to insist that it is not dependent on theoretical or moral concepts, but is something original and even primitive. The crux of his doctrine lies in the claim that by numinous feeling it is possible to apprehend both the existence and the value of a corresponding numinous object.

§ 4. *Mysterium tremendum*

If the argument is to be followed, we must do our best to describe this numinous experience in a summary fashion; but a bare outline may be misleading, and will certainly be jejune, where so much depends on distinguishing the finer shades of feeling by means of words which are emotionally precise. What is still more serious, we shall have to refer to ordinary natural emotions which are merely analogous to numinous emotions differing, not in degree, but in kind; and the words we use must be taken, not as conceptual, but as mere 'ideograms' for emotional 'moments' that are unique. The numinous cannot be conceived, or at the most it can be conceived only negatively—that is, we may be able to conceive what it is not; but what is conceived negatively may be *felt* as in the highest degree positive—as, for example, when St. Paul says: 'Eye hath not seen, nor ear heard, neither have entered into the heart of man, the things which God hath prepared for them that love him'.

To those who have never experienced any religious emotion it will be as if we were trying to explain colours to a blind man on the analogy of sounds.

The numinous object—that is, the object of numinous feeling— is said to be *mysterium tremendum*. The phrase is perhaps better left untranslated, since to express it in our own language is to conceptualize it and make it less of a mere ideogram. Perhaps the Latin words indicate the numinous by their sound better than by any idea they may convey, and those who do not know Latin will be here in at least as a good position as those who do. The religious man is in the presence of a mystery which arouses dread and stupefaction and fascination rather than conceptual thought.

Let us begin by considering the adjective '*tremendum*'.

The first aspect of the object thus indicated is its 'awefulness': the object arouses an awe or dread akin to natural fear. This is found in a perverted form in our dread of ghosts, in shudders and creepings of the flesh before the eerie, the uncanny, and the weird. In the cruder manifestations of religion it is a daemonic dread, like the horror of Pan. In the higher religions it becomes genuine awe, a feeling of personal nothingness before the awe-inspiring object directly experienced. To this object we ascribe something analogous to wrath—the Wrath of God, the mysterious *ira deorum*, which likewise has a different character at different levels of religious experience. In it there is an element which may be indicated by the phrase 'absolute unapproachability'.

In the *tremendum* there is a second aspect which may be called 'majesty'—or again 'power' and 'might'. It is especially before this majesty that we are conscious of being 'dust and ashes'—conscious of the annihilation of the self before the 'transcendent' or 'overpowering', which is the sole and entire reality.

There is in the *tremendum* yet a third aspect, which may be called the 'urgency' or 'energy' of the numinous object. This is said to be most perceptible in the Wrath of God and to be present at all stages from the daemonic level up to the encounter with the 'living' God. It 'clothes itself in symbolical expressions—vitality, passion, emotional temper, will, force, movement, excitement, activity, impetus'. Even the love of God may be felt as a consuming fire.

These three aspects of the *tremendum*—its 'awefulness', its 'majesty', its 'urgency'—seem to be closely connected. If we turn to the noun '*mysterium*', we find further—and more sharply distinguishable—elements in the numinous feeling and the numinous object. The *mysterium* may be called the '*mysterium stupendum*': it is a mystery which arouses stupor and amazement as distinct from dread—an astonishment which strikes us dumb. In its everyday sense a mystery is merely a secret which baffles us, something alien, uncomprehended, unexplained; but in its religious sense it is the 'wholly other', which is entirely beyond the familiar, the usual, the intelligible. Here we have the non-rational, the non-intelligible—something beyond nature and beyond the universe, or even, in Plato's phrase, beyond being, something 'whose kind and character are incommensurable with our own, and before which we therefore recoil in a wonder that strikes us chill and numb'.

There is one last factor in our feeling for the *mysterium*—perhaps the most important factor of all. The numinous object does not fill us merely with dread and amazement: it also attracts and charms and entrances, and indeed fascinates. This fascination Otto connects with the transport and fervour, the ravishment and intoxication, the exaltation and ecstasy, of the Dionysiac element in religion. But he finds it also in the solemnity and calm of public prayer and private devotion, in the peace of God which passes understanding. This factor we might expect to be associated, not so much with the worship of Dionysus as with that of Apollo—unless this God is reserved for the rational element in religion; and the rational concepts of love, mercy, peace, and comfort, which are said to be parallel to this numinous fascination, seem to be connected more with religious calm than with religious transports. Yet it may be that Otto is right in not making too sharp a separation between ecstasy and tranquillity; and both of these may be covered when men speak in decisively religious terms of the bliss and beatitude of the worshipper and the divine grace of the object of worship.

If the numinous object were merely dreadful, religion would be concerned only with expiation and propitiation. Because this object is felt also as fascinating, there can be religions of salvation in which there is a self-surrender to the *numen*, in which God may be loved for His own sake—not merely for the material or spiritual benefits He can bestow. Here also parallels are to be found at the lowest levels of religion—in the half-magical, half-devotional attempts to identify the self with the *numen* or to be united with it in ecstasy. Where possession of and by the *numen* becomes an end in itself, there we have at least the beginnings of religious life.

Such in bald outline is Otto's analysis of religious experience, or rather of its non-rational elements considered in relative abstraction. He may seem at times to lay too much stress on fear and wrath and even, like A. E. Taylor, on feelings of pollution. In the last case especially we have to ask ourselves whether such feelings are a mark of spiritual profundity or a symptom of mental disease. Some men will always prefer to worship at the shrine of Apollo rather than of Dionysus, and will find true religion in the writer of St. John's Gospel, in St. Francis and St. Teresa, rather than in the more daemonic saints. They will lay greater stress, as I have done, on such feelings as 'gratitude, trust, love, reliance, humble submission, and dedication'. But Otto may well be right in claiming that these are far from covering the whole range of religious life; and he is fully aware that primitive emotions have to be transmuted or transformed at the higher levels if they are not to be a source of religious aberration. The balance as well as the richness of his thinking can be grasped only by those who are willing to read the book itself.

§ 5. *The faculty of divination*

We may agree with Otto that religious feeling is unique in the sense that, as he says, it is distinct from 'pleasure or joy or aesthetic rapture or moral exaltation'. We may also grant that some men have a special aptitude or susceptibility for religious feeling, just as others have for music or poetry or mathematics. But it is a very big jump from this to postulate, as he does, a special religious faculty, termed appropriately enough 'the faculty of divination', which, although originating in feeling, is aware both of a transcendent reality and of its objective value, and is even able to grasp and appraise itself.

This special faculty of divination is supposed to be present in all men, though in very different degrees, and to be at work throughout the development of religion: it is not to be superseded or absorbed by philosophical thinking or moral action. Although manifested at first, so far as it is cognitive, in mere inklings or surmises, and associated with the primitive experience of shudders and creeping flesh, it propels us towards an ideal, but non-rational, good known only to religion. This shows, according to Otto, that 'above and beyond our rational being lies hidden the ultimate and highest part of our nature'. The mystics call it the deep places of the soul, the *fundus animae*. It is a predisposition which may be called 'pure reason' in the profoundest sense—an odd nomenclature for a faculty expressly non-rational; and it has to be 'distinguished both from the pure theoretical and the pure practical reason of Kant, as something yet higher and deeper than they'.

To use words like 'faculty' may be misleading if we suppose that a faculty is an agency or cause by which phenomena can be explained. We in no way explain how opium can put us to sleep by saying that it has a soporific faculty. The danger of being misled is increased when we speak of a faculty as 'propelling' us or as 'being hidden in the depths of the soul'. But we must try to understand Otto's language and not merely to find fault with it.

If we use the word 'do' in its widest sense, men, according to Otto, are able to do something in a greater or less degree—namely, to feel emotion that is specifically religious. To say that they have a faculty of divination is to say this over again. What Otto wishes to add is that this faculty—or this emotion—gives rise to 'an *a priori* category' by which it is possible to know God.

Nothing could be more shocking to a modern ear, which is trained to connect the phrase '*a priori*' only with analytic or tautologous propositions. In the face of such an obstacle it is difficult to make Otto's meaning clear.

The *a priori* may be equated with what is *not* derived from given sense-impressions (although it may be manifested on the occasion of sense-impressions): it is a product of spontaneous mental activity. The most obvious example is the concept of 'ground and consequent'. We have this concept only because we think: to think is to distinguish between ground and consequent. This distinction could never be derived from sense-impressions, even if thinking could not take place without sense-impressions. Thus the concept of ground and consequent is an *a priori* concept—one produced by our own activity in thinking.

Otto extends this usage very far—perhaps altogether too far. Feelings are commonly classed with sense-impressions even although they may be roused by association. Otto, however, wishes to regard the religious feeling-response and its development as *a priori* inasmuch as it is a spontaneous activity which depends for its character on an original predisposition of the soul.

We need not quarrel with the word 'predisposition', which may be given a perfectly good sense; but one difficulty about all this is that the usage of the term '*a priori*' becomes so wide that there would hardly remain any mental phenomenon which was not *a priori*.

Clearly all emotion would become *a priori*: we could not, for example, experience sexual emotion unless we were, so to speak, made that way. Seeing a colour would become *a priori* so far as it depended on a predisposition or power to see. Instinct itself might be described as the *a priori* of animals.

Even if we are not dismayed by this prospect, we have to ask what it is that the faculty of divination is supposed to do.

The whole of Otto's book is his answer, but we may try to sum up the doctrine in his own words. The religious predisposition becomes a 'religious drive or impulsion' (*Triebe*). 'In undirected, groping emotion, in seeking and shaping representations, in continually striving onwards to the generation of Ideas, this impulsion endeavours to become clear about itself, and it does become clear about itself by laying bare that obscure *a priori* foundation of Ideas out of which it itself sprang'.

The trouble about this statement (in which I diverge a little from Professor Harvey's translation) is that the faculty of divination seems to do too much. It is not merely that Otto wants it to be cognitive as well as emotional: he also wants it to be self-conscious and self-critical. There may be a sense in which religious consciousness claims to be all this; but when it comes to laying bare its own *a priori* foundations, it is hard to deny that it is becoming very rational indeed.

There is, however, one fundamental difficulty which overshadows all the rest. If the faculty of divination by its own spontaneous activity 'shapes' representations and 'generates' Ideas *a priori*, how can it possibly grasp reality, let alone a transcendent reality, by means of such apparently subjective representations and Ideas? Otto seems unaware of this difficulty although it is the fundamental question raised by that very philosophy of Kant which he is attempting to develop further.

§ 6. *Otto and Kant*

It would require at least a chapter by itself to deal with the relations between Otto and Kant. Even so, the result would be intelligible only to those who had a fair grasp of Kant's philosophy. Here I can only touch on some of the technical terms borrowed by Otto from his master. Readers who shrink from technicalities had better pass on hurriedly to § 7.

Kant holds that the mind in thinking uses *a priori* concepts like 'ground and consequent', and can make these concepts clear to itself by subsequent reflexion.

Among *a priori* concepts he recognizes what he calls 'Ideas of Reason'—Ideas with a capital I. These are concepts of the absolute or unconditioned, and they spring from the drive in our thinking towards completeness or totality. We can, if we like, include among them Ideas of absolute reality, absolute power, and so on. As we can never experience anything absolute or unconditioned, Ideas by definition can have *no* objects in experience.

There are other *a priori* concepts called 'categories of the understanding'. These are concepts of what *every* object must be if it is to be an object of experience in time and space. Kant holds, for example, that the states or qualities of every object must be subject to causal law and so have to be thought under the category of 'cause and effect'. He holds also that a category can be applied *only* to the spatial and temporal objects of experience, so that for him no category can be predicated of God.

Otto lumps together Ideas and categories—he uses the words interchangeably—and assumes (by twisting the meaning of both) that the category or Idea of 'the holy' can give us knowledge of an object which transcends ordinary experience altogether.

There is in Kant a more complicated doctrine which I can only state summarily. According to this doctrine the category of cause and effect—like all other categories—is complex and contains two distinguishable elements.

First of all, there is in it the *a priori* concept of 'ground and conse-quent', to which we have already referred. Whatever be the view of modern physics, we commonly regard a cause as a *ground* (or condi-tion) of an effect which is its *consequent* (or is conditioned by it).

Secondly, there is a temporal element which may be called 'regular succession'. Whenever a cause occurs, its effect must follow in time. Without regular succession in time we could never think of one event or state as the ground or cause of another. Regular succession is described by Kant as the 'schema' of the category.

Thus the category of cause and effect is a complex category made up of (1) the *a priori* concept (sometimes described as the *pure* category) of ground and consequent, and (2) the schema of regular succession. A cause is a ground which regularly precedes its effect (or consequent) in time.

The essential characteristic of a schema is that it is nearer to sense perception and so enables us to *apply* the category to a real object of experience. Thus the schema is the *non-rational* element in the category. For reasons into which we need not enter Kant connects it with imagination—with the construction of complex images—rather than with thinking.

All of this terminology is taken over bodily by Otto. For him the complex category of 'the holy' is also made up of rational and non-rational elements. The non-rational element has already been con-sidered—it is the numinous, the *mysterium tremendum*. The rational element we have still to examine; but it may be observed at once that, with a strange perversity, Otto reverses the meaning of the terms he has borrowed. The pure rational concepts belonging to the category of the holy are described as the schemata of the non-rational instead of *vice versa*. Furthermore, as these rational concepts, although called 'categories', are really Ideas and so by definition can have no objects in experience, they are of all things the least suited for the function of schemata—namely, the function of enabling us to apply an *a priori* concept to an object. Otto no doubt talks as he does because he wishes to regard the non-rational element in religion as somehow 'higher'—in an unspecified sense—than the rational. But Kant must have shuddered in his grave.

§ 7. *The numinous and the holy*

Otto's account of the category—or Idea—of the holy must be stated in his own terms, however unsatisfactory these may be.

On his view the 'holy' means more than the numinous in general, more even than the numinous at its highest. We understand by it 'the numinous completely permeated and saturated with elements signifying rationality, purpose, personality, morality'. To neglect the numinous is to impoverish religion and to turn the Church into a school of ethics and theology. To neglect the rational and above all the ethical, is equally fatal: it is the source of fanaticism and other religious aberrations. Where then are we to discover the rational schemata, so-called, which must 'permeate and saturate' the numinous if we are to have a sound religion? The details are very briefly as follows.

According to Otto, the *tremendum*—the 'aweful' or dreadful aspect of the *numen*—finds its schemata in our rational concepts of justice and morality: it then becomes what he calls the holy 'Wrath of God', which may seem to some to loom too large in his theology. The *fascinating* aspect of the *numen* finds its schemata in the concepts of goodness, mercy, and love; and thereby it becomes what is known as 'the grace of God'. The *mysterium* itself, the fundamental character of mystery, has its schema in 'the *absoluteness* of all rational attributes applied to the deity'.

All of this is not only ingenious, but admirable, as a contribution to the psychology of religion—so much so that it seems a shame merely to expose its bare bones as I have had to do here. Otto is surely right in finding a close connexion between feelings of the numinous and the 'rational' attributes of *absolute* justice, *absolute* goodness, and so on. He is mainly concerned with moral attributes;

but what he says applies also to any attributes taken to be absolute or unconditioned, such as absolute power or knowledge. Concepts of the absolute are Ideas of reason and so are always beyond our powers of understanding: indeed—though Otto denies this—they may themselves be the source of numinous feeling. Hence even if they are not to be identified with the mysterious, they are well suited to be—in Otto's sense—the 'schemata' of the mysterious, 'which lies altogether outside what can be thought and is alike in form, quality, and essence, the utterly and "wholly other".' We shall be in a better position to understand this when we come to consider the traditional arguments for the existence of God.

At present, however, we are concerned with Otto's attempts to uphold the validity of religious experience. At times he speaks as if no intellectual justification of religious 'intuition' is possible; but he also wishes to show that it is at least not unreasonable to believe in a transcendent reality which is the object revealed to numinous feeling; and his account of the special faculty of divination and of its relation to human reason is partly directed towards this end. Hence the first question before us is this—Does he rest belief in God's existence on reason or on divination?

It seems pretty clear that he bases religious belief, at least primarily, on divination and not on reason. If so, he ought to reverse his terminology—that is, to make numinous feeling the schema of rational Ideas instead of *vice versa*—and say something like this. In the obscure yearning and feeling and groping which is called 'divination' we have from the beginning some inkling of the *mysterium* which lies behind the world of sense, although at first we misunderstand or misconceive it. Only in the Ideas of unconditioned reality and absolute goodness can we find concepts whereby we can conceive, however inadequately, the object of our yearning and groping. By themselves these concepts are purely rational and not religious; but if we combine them, as we must, with the numinous, considered as a non-rational schema, we get the complex concept— the specifically religious category or Idea—of the holy, under which alone can be conceived the object of worship and adoration so far as it can be conceived at all. Even this complex concept is totally inadequate to the divine reality which is directly felt as a *mysterium tremendum* beyond all comprehension. The non-rational element of feeling remains essential to religion; but it has become purified into a feeling, not of the merely dreadful or fascinating or daemonic, but of the august and holy; and through this purified feeling or direct awareness our empty Ideas of reason can find their object in a living and holy God.

For Kant such a doctrine would be mere mysticism or *Schwärmerei*; but it is the most plausible adaptation of his philosophy to the needs of the religious consciousness as described by Otto. We must try to consider it on its merits.

§ 8. *The appraisal of religious value*

It must be obvious even from the few quotations already given that Otto's language, however suited to the description of religious emotion, is logically too imprecise and metaphorical for the purpose of philosophy. To clarify it may be to distort it. Yet it seems clear enough that what he calls numinous feeling is assumed to be cognitive as well as emotional, and that it has two functions, which for him are not distinguished: (1) the appraisal of religious value and (2) the apprehension of God's existence. The first of these functions is plausibly connected with feeling, although the feeling must be 'permeated and saturated' with something more than feeling.

If we speak of God, after Otto's fashion, as the *object* of numinous feeling, our language is not altogether happy; for God must be much more than an object. But in this terminology it is reasonable to say that numinous feeling is an appraisal both of the object and of the subject. The religious man *feels* at once God's holiness and his own unworthiness. Otto's description of this can hardly be bettered.

It is also reasonable enough to say that numinous feeling appraises itself—that is to say, as it becomes more refined, it may reject what once it accepted. The analogy for this is the feeling of the artist. We know from experience that the aesthetic feelings both of the creative artist and of the lover of art may become more sensitive and more discriminating in a life given up to the pursuit of beauty. A similar development may be found in those who lead the religious life.

On the other hand, it would be a mistake to suppose that the reflexions of the artist or the religious man on his experience are merely a matter of feeling. When these reflexions become philosophical and begin to lay bare 'the obscure *a priori* foundation' of art or religion, they have moved out of the realm of feeling altogether.

There remains a further question. How can religious feelings claim to be objective—that is, to be valid for others as well as for the individual? Here again we may find some guidance from the analogy of the artist. Whatever philosophers may say, no artist or aesthetic critic can accept the view that the judgements of the Philistine who prefers pushpin to poetry are as worthy of attention as his own. In spite of philosophical difficulties—and they are many—we may, at least provisionally, allow to the religious man a like independence and assurance, and also a like fallibility, in his judgements of religious value. The crucial question for philosophy is the claim that by numinous feeling he is able to apprehend the existence of God.

§ 9. *The apprehension of God's existence*

So far as divination is a feeling, or a source of feelings, we have to face the difficulty that no mere emotion can by itself give us knowledge of the existence of God. The difficulty is only increased and not diminished, if divination is supposed to produce *a priori* Ideas from the deep places of the soul. How can Ideas so produced have any contact with external reality, let alone with a transcendent reality which is 'wholly other'?

The analogy of the artist fails us here. What he produces is an imaginary world, and an imaginary God cannot satisfy the religious man.

Otto's answer to our question is so cloudy that it is impossible to give any clear summary; but some of his obscure and conflicting statements may be quoted.

First of all, he assures us that numinous feeling is a *feeling of reality*. 'This "feeling of reality", the feeling of a "numinous" *object* objectively given, must be posited as a primary immediate datum of consciousness'. Yet on the crude level it is attached to 'objects, occurrences, and entities falling within the work-a-day world of primitive experience'. The beliefs and feelings involved in the numinous experience, he further tells us, 'are themselves not perceptions at all, but peculiar *interpretations* and *evaluations*, at first of *perceptual data*, and then—at a higher level—of *posited objects* and entities, which themselves no longer belong to the perceptual world, but are *thought of* as supplementing and transcending it' (the italics are mine). The inconsistencies here are too glaring.

The word 'posited' can cover a multitude of philosophical sins; but we should like to know whether 'positing' is the work of feeling or of thought or of both together. This we are never told, but the main view appears to be that the religious man not only *believes* in a reality beyond the senses, but also '*experiences*' it: he not only has Ideas of the holy, but may become 'consciously aware of it as an operative reality intervening actively in the phenomenal world'. Otto is prepared to speak of 'the experience of God' and of 'the actual discovery of and encounter with very deity'.

One of the queer things in his doctrine is that he seems to identify *belief* with inner revelation (or general revelation) and *experience* with outer revelation (or special revelation). Apparently we find mere *belief* when 'the holy and sacred reality is attested by the inward voice of conscience and the religious consciousness, the "still, small voice" of the Spirit in the heart, by feeling, presentiment, and longing'. Religious *experience*, as opposed to belief, is found when the holy and sacred reality is 'directly encountered in particular occurrences and events, self-revealed in persons and displayed in actions'.

We should naturally have expected experience to be concerned with inner feeling and belief with outer events, especially as the German word for 'to experience' is '*erleben*', which indicates a minimum of thought. An outer revelation is not a revelation to us at all until it becomes an inner revelation; and it might seem as if history could give us only second-hand belief in what to the writers themselves was an inner experience. But in spite of Otto's curious reversal of terms he does recognize, unlike Barth, that we could not discover the divine in history unless we already possessed, at least potentially, 'an inward standard that defies expression', namely, the *a priori* category of the holy. And indeed he identifies the faculty of divination with the inner witness of the Holy Spirit—'*testimonium Spiritus Sancti internum*'.

The word 'history' is probably the clue to Otto's strange choice of language. For him the main outward revelation of God is to be found, not in the experience of nature which meant so much to a poet like Wordsworth, but in the Old and New Testaments, particularly in the prophets and 'in one in whom is found the Spirit in all its plenitude'. 'Such a one is more than Prophet. He is the Son'.

There is another strain of thought which is borrowed from Schleiermacher with at least a qualified approval. When confronted 'with the vast, living totality and reality of things as it is in nature and history', a religious mind may grasp in intuitions, as it were, 'a sheer overplus' in addition to empirical reality. The import of these intuitions is 'the glimpse of an Eternal, in and beyond the temporal and penetrating it'. They are *surmises* or *inklings*, and must

certainly be called 'cognitions'; yet they are not products of reflexion, but 'the intuitive outcome of feeling'. Whatever we may think
of these details, it is a fact that numinous feeling may be 'occasioned'
by an effort to comprehend reality as a whole.

All this may have value as a description of the ways in which
numinous feeling can be aroused in men; but it does not help us to
understand why numinous feeling should be regarded as giving
knowledge of the eternal. What theory there is appears to be self-
contradictory; for although the holy reality is said to be 'directly
encountered', the events in which it is encountered are described as
'signs'—signs which on the cruder levels are not signs 'in the true
sense'. It is not easy to see how a 'direct encounter' can take place
by means of signs, or how awareness by means of signs can be
properly described as a feeling. No attempt is made to explain how
we can pass from the sign to the reality of the thing signified; and
it is hard to believe that this could be done without the aid of
concepts.

The philosophical problem is not solved by elevating feeling into
a special faculty of divination capable of producing its own *a priori*
category. Even in the philosophy of art nothing is gained by postulating a special faculty of aesthetic feeling. But the problem of
religion is entirely different; for religion claims, not merely to assess
or produce spiritual values, but to afford knowledge of ultimate
reality—even if it be a knowledge that comes by faith—in a way that
art as such never professes to do. For this purpose a faculty of
religious feeling is altogether inadequate. And although Otto, very
properly, seeks to supplement this faculty with rational Ideas, he
does not pretend that these Ideas enable us to grasp the existence
of that 'supra-rational' subject of which they are said to be
'predicated'.

§ 10. *Religion and philosophy*

It would be a mistake to end on a note of mere negation. On the
strength of Otto's analysis the religious man may say to himself
something like this. 'I have enjoyed experiences which seem to me
to be experiences of a divine presence. These experiences, which
may occur in many ways, I find to be authentic and compelling, and
they are shared by many others besides myself. Hence I am willing
to trust them, to cultivate them, and above all to act on them. I
cannot analyse or justify them further, but I believe that in them

God reveals Himself; that He is no mere product of my imagination; and that I must conceive Him under such concepts as the absolutely powerful and the absolutely good. I am aware that these concepts are obscure and that no concepts of mine can be adequate to His nature, but only a God whom I think by means of these concepts can be the object of my worship; and I know from experience that only if I live by these beliefs can my whole life have meaning and my whole soul find peace'.

Such an attitude may be enough for religion, but it is not enough for philosophy. What Otto has done is rather to supply material for philosophical reflexion. He is right in warning philosophers and theologians that religion is by no means to be reduced to the acceptance of theoretical propositions or to the living of a moral life. He is right also in emphasizing the element of mystery; for in a world without mystery there could be no religion. Yet the mystery of the world may be more obvious to our advanced thought than to our primitive instincts; and indeed there can be no mystery except to a being who thinks as well as feels. Otto has done a great service in attempting to describe the development and purification of religious emotion, although this development cannot possibly work itself out, as he sometimes suggests, 'purely in the sphere of the non-rational'. The main result emerging from his discussion is rather that the various strands of the religious life are inseparably intertwined, and that if we wish to do justice to religious belief, we must not rest it merely on feeling, but must look more closely at the theoretical arguments for God's existence and also at the convictions bound up with moral action. If religion is of the whole man, it cannot be understood without taking into account his experience as a whole.

K

Chapter X

THE MYSTIC WAY

§ 1. *The claims of mysticism*

Direct awareness of God, and even consciousness of union with Him, is the special claim of mysticism. There are many to-day who, whether or not they follow one of the historic religions, look to the testimony of the mystics as the best assurance and ground of religious faith. To others of a more rationalistic type of mind the mystic experience is one source of the emotionalism and mystification by which religion is bedevilled.

The mystic union appears to be an outcome or development of ordinary religious experience, and it is not confined to one special form of religion. Although it is coloured, as might be expected, by the theological beliefs of the individual mystic, there is a widely accepted claim that it takes similar forms, and passes through similar stages, in votaries of very different religions. It is this which is said to give it special importance, particularly in the eyes of those who seek for a common element in religion as such. Whether it be regarded as the highest attainment of the religious spirit or as a mere aberration, there can be no doubt as to its reality and its compelling power. Although it is reserved for men and women with special susceptibilities, and although these may have to prepare themselves for it by certain ways of life—whether by prayer or asceticism or moral action or thought or communion with nature—the experience itself seizes upon the mystic: it is not anything which he can do or acquire or control by his own volition.

The difficulty of discussing this way of religious life is that we have to deal with something wholly outside the experience of most of us. Hence we can have no hope of confirming it for ourselves, or even of understanding it when it is described. The mystics are apt to say that it is ineffable, although they are themselves not always noticeably silent. We have to take it on trust, but we may find grounds for doing so in the character and intelligence of those who have had such experiences and are prepared to speak of them by way of analogies and images. Because these experiences cannot be tested by others, there is opened up a wide field of opportunity both for charlatans and for the mentally diseased. But this fact, though it may present difficulties and disturb confidence, is no reason for denying either the reality of the experience or its importance for the understanding of religion.

Even from an external point of view the subject can be treated adequately, if at all, only by those who have made a prolonged study of the relevant literature. In the absence of expert knowledge the best course, especially for a brief discussion, is to follow a reliable guide, checking him so far as one can by other authorities and by one's own reading of the mystics themselves. The guide I have chosen for this purpose is Father Poulain, a clear-headed, good-hearted, simple-minded Jesuit, who has written a widely read treatise called '*Des grâces d'oraison*': it is translated into English under the title '*The Graces of Interior Prayer*'. His treatment of the subject is dry, scholastic, and matter of fact; and this is all to the good in dealing with a topic which lends itself to cloudiness and emotion. The combination of literalness and logic may give us confidence that we are getting at least the external facts, which are all we can hope to understand.

In so vast an enquiry it may be a positive advantage that he is concerned almost exclusively with Catholic mystics. He is specially interested in St. Teresa, whose charming, but at times inconsequential, writings he reduces to a system. An authority whom he follows almost as closely is St. John of the Cross, a more philosophic writer than St. Teresa, although one not so conspicuous for natural healthiness of mind. But Father Poulain casts his net very wide, and he gives us an anthology of Catholic mystical writings arranged under appropriate headings, as well as his own conscientious analyses and precise definitions. If at times his credulity induces him to offer us a certain amount of dross along with the pure gold, even this may serve to remind us of the need for caution.

It is not my ambition to explain within the limits of an hour what mysticism is, although Father Poulain assures us that this can be done. As in the case of religious experiences generally, the topic is here being approached from a special point of view—from a desire to find, if we can, some indications of the way in which the mystic experience claims to give men knowledge of God. This epistemological interest is not that of Father Poulain, who treats the subject, not as a philosopher, but as a director of souls. This in no way diminishes the value of his evidence, for we are trying to find out

what the experience claims to be in itself. I will follow him at first
without criticism.

§ 2. *Ordinary prayer*

If we are to get any conception of the mystic union, we must
contrast it with ordinary religious experience. Ordinary prayer, we
are told, has four stages or degrees of progress: (1) vocal prayer;
(2) meditation or discursive prayer; (3) affective prayer; and (4) the
prayer of simple regard or of simplicity. The first two stages are in
no need of explanation. The last two—and especially the last—are
more difficult, and more relevant to our present enquiry.

Affective prayer differs from the prayer of meditation in two ways.
In the first place, the thinking involved becomes simpler: it contains
less reasoning and more intuition, and it tends to be dominated,
though not exclusively, by one main idea. In the second place,
emotions, and also practical resolutions, begin to play a larger part.

This double process, as it is carried further, passes into the
prayer of simple regard, the prayer of simplicity. Here intuition in
great measure replaces reasoning, while the emotions and resolutions show little variety and are expressed in few words. There is a
thought or sentiment which 'returns incessantly and easily (although
with little or no development) amongst many other thoughts,
whether useful or no'. The persistent recurrence of one idea and the
vivid impression it produces constitute, when prolonged, the
prayer of simplicity. Broadly speaking, this is a 'prayer of loving
attention to God', not one of meditation upon God. Although other
subjects are not excluded, they are of secondary importance.

In all this there is a gradual transition, a gradual simplification,
and a gradual diminution of reasoning: but we are still in the realm
of ordinary prayer, which can be cultivated by human efforts
although not without divine grace. The prayer of simplicity may
even pass gradually—perhaps by way of what St. John of the Cross
calls 'the first dark night of the soul'—into the prayer of quiet,
which is the lowest stage of the mystic experience. Nevertheless the
two prayers are not to be confused, for the prayer of quiet is different, not merely in intensity, but in kind. At all levels of ordinary
prayer—and here Poulain seems to differ fundamentally from Otto
—we have only abstract knowledge of God, a thought of His
presence and a feeling of love towards Him. The mystic experience
is always more than this and is reserved for the very few.

§ 3. *The mystic way*

In the mystic experience or the mystic union there are also four stages or degrees: (1) incomplete union, or the prayer of quiet; (2) full union or semi-ecstatic union; (3) ecstatic union or ecstasy; (4) transforming union or the spiritual marriage. The first three grades have a certain unity or continuity: they differ primarily in strength or intensity so that the first may be compared to a spark, the second to a flame, the third to a conflagration. The transforming union or spiritual marriage, on the other hand, completes the three previous grades, not by strengthening them, but by modifying them. It must be put in a class by itself.

The first three grades, in spite of their continuity, differ in more than strength or intensity. At each stage a new fact emerges, and by means of this the different grades can be distinguished.

In the prayer of quiet the soul is still subject to the distractions of imagination. In the semi-ecstatic union the soul suffers from no distractions, but it is still in possession of the bodily senses and able to control bodily movements. In ecstasy the communications of the senses are entirely, or almost entirely, interrupted, and voluntary movements are impossible. The mind is in a state of trance.

So far we have only a negative description of the different grades. We must try to be more positive.

The first and essential characteristic which distinguishes the mystic union from all ordinary prayer is this. The mystic does not merely think of God's presence with love: he feels or experiences union with God and has what is called 'an experimental, intellectual knowledge' of His presence. Such knowledge or feeling is said to be produced by God's own action, not by anything that men can do. In the prayer of quiet this knowledge may be obscure, but it increases in distinctness as the union becomes of a higher order. Although from its description the prayer of quiet may seem very like the ordinary prayer of simplicity, the difference in actual experience is said to be unmistakable, and the prayer of quiet is at first received by beginners with surprise and even with distrust.

The phrase 'experimental, intellectual knowledge' is not familiar to us in English. I take it to mean knowledge derived from sensation (not from reasoning), but from sensation that is spiritual and entirely distinct from bodily sensation. This special spiritual sensation is the second essential characteristic of the mystic union, and it bears a resemblance to Otto's faculty of divination. By it the mystic is

said to know a present object as existing and as operating in order
to make itself known.

Spiritual sensation, we are told, in spite of its uniqueness, shows
certain analogies with the bodily sensations through which we become aware of material objects. Curiously enough, although there is
a spiritual sight without images and a spiritual hearing without
words, these are not the senses of which the mystics most commonly
speak. As regards sight in particular, we cannot say, save in
exceptional cases, that God is 'seen' in states inferior to ecstasy.
The spiritual senses to which the mystics usually refer are those of
taste, smell, and—above all—touch. At all stages of the mystic union
the presence of God is felt as of something within, something which
penetrates the soul. The sensation is one of absorption, fusion,
immersion, and to this Father Poulain gives the name 'interior
touch'.

This may seem surprising and over-literal, even although it
means only 'that everything happens *as if* there were touch'. It is,
I suppose, a way of saying that God is felt almost as we feel the
presence of our own bodies—a view confirmed even by ordinary
religious experience and expressed in Tennyson's line: 'Closer is
He than breathing, and nearer than hands or feet'. In a sceptical
and scientific age, on the other hand, it may raise difficult psychological questions, especially when, as so often, it is elaborated in the
language of love; but into these questions I do not propose to enter.
I must also pass over the subsidiary characteristics ascribed to the
mystic union. Most of these reinforce the doctrine that the mystic
state is one which we do not control and do not fully comprehend.
Perhaps the most extraordinary characteristic is the presence, at all
stages—although in varying degree—of what is called technically
the 'ligature' of the faculties. This is some sort of impediment to the
voluntary production of interior acts—even such acts as the repetition of a customary prayer. In ecstasy it amounts to complete
suspension of the faculties.

§ 4. *Ecstasy and the spiritual marriage*

Alienation of the sensuous faculties—an incapacity to see, hear,
feel, or move—is the external and corporeal characteristic of
ecstasy. A positive and internal characteristic is a very intense
attention to some religious subject. We are here concerned with this
only so far as it professes to give knowledge of God.

Ecstasy may occur gently and gradually. When it is sudden and violent, it is called 'rapture'; and it is at the stage of rapture that we get, not a mere feeling that God is in us and we in Him, but an intellectual vision of Him—that is, a vision which excludes images.

This vision is said to be sometimes a vision of the Blessed Trinity; and Father Poulain is of opinion that even without the Church's teaching we should come to know, by way of experience, how many Persons there are in God, and how they proceed One from the Other. Other writers have held that the vision is generally of an impersonal God, even in the case of Christian mystics. We can say at least—with the agreement of Father Poulain—that St. John of the Cross, unlike St. Teresa, describes the vision even of the spiritual marriage as the contemplation of the divine attributes, not as the contemplation of the Trinity.

Although at the level of rapture the mystic has an intellectual vision, not merely a spiritual touch or feeling, of God, the vision is still experimental—that is, it does not depend on reasoning or inference. Furthermore, it is never without a certain obscurity. It is as if we were blinded partly by the divine light and partly by some of the attributes that are manifested. Certain attributes, such as beauty, justice, mercy, and intelligence, can be reflected in creatures, and we are able to receive their radiance. But there are also incommunicable attributes which can be possessed by no creature—such as infinity, eternity, creative power, universal knowledge. These, though they are manifested in the vision, are to us incomprehensible, and they produce the terrifying obscurity known as 'the great darkness'. This great darkness is sometimes pierced by the blaze of a rapid flash of light which is readily interpreted as the light of glory, because it seems to show God as He is. But Father Poulain shares the opinion of the majority of theologians that even the mystic vision is not a sight of God as He is in Himself. It consequently differs in kind from the beatific vision, which is reserved for the saints in Heaven.

Less need be said about the transforming union or spiritual marriage. There seems to be some doubt whether this highest form of union introduces a claim to any different kind of knowledge. The intellectual vision of God is said to become permanent, though it may vary in clearness. There is, however, also a 'transformation' of the higher faculties such that the mystic is conscious of divine co-operation in their use. 'God is no longer merely the *object* of the supernatural operations of the mind and will, as in the preceding degrees.' He shows Himself as being 'the joint cause of these operations'. Our own acts appear to us as in a way divine.

Another remarkable characteristic of this transforming union is not only that it is almost permanent, but that it persists even amid ordinary occupations and yet does not interfere with them. The spiritual marriage appears to be a time of peace after storm. It contains fewer ecstasies, but its inner calm is unbroken by the trials and tribulations inseparable from human life. Much of the language used of it by St. Teresa herself reads rather like the language of ordinary religious experience—except that this experience seems to have become more stable and more secure. So far as I can judge, the view that there is a mystical transformation of the higher faculties comes mainly from St. John of the Cross; but something like it may be found in St. Paul, when he says, for example, 'I am crucified with Christ: nevertheless I live; yet not I, but Christ liveth in me . . .' This claim has been echoed, not always with sufficient qualification, by many religious men.

§ 5. *The element of suffering*

There could be no greater mistake than to suppose that the mystic way is merely a path of consolations and spiritual delights. It is, on the contrary, full of trials, and the intensity of spiritual delight is accompanied by a similar intensity of spiritual pain.

I will not attempt to follow Father Poulain in his long chapter on the trials that beset the contemplative life. He enters into almost too many details, some of which are not wholly convincing, as, for example, his circumstantial account of the way in which many saints have been mercilessly beaten or bitten by devils. There is, however, conclusive evidence that mystics have often to suffer long periods of aridity—that is, of desolation in prayer—during which they experience tedium and even disgust. If some of this arises from a mistaken attempt to wind human nature too high, a recurrent aridity may none the less be inescapable in the religious life and even in ordinary intellectual life as such. What is more important is that ecstasy itself may be followed, and even accompanied, by spiritual pain. As we have already learned from Otto, the vision of God's holiness and our own unworthiness may produce a feeling of dread and even horror; but there appears to be in, or after, the experience of ecstasy an element of suffering which is not to be so rationally

explained. This suffering may be made light of, or even welcomed, in relation to the experience as a whole. In itself it may be extreme.

§ 6. *The element of negation*

Although pain is opposed to pleasure it is at least more than a mere negation. What are we to make of the negative element in the mystic's experience?

It may have been observed that progress in ordinary prayer was already described as a process of simplification—a process of becoming dominated by one idea so that variety in thought and even in emotion was gradually diminished. This process is continued further in the mystic union. At first there may still be distractions and a considerable measure of self-control. With further advance the distractions disappear, and finally in ecstasy or rapture the senses cease to function and voluntary movement becomes impossible. Is this further process of simplification an emptying of the mind, or is it one of greater concentration and clearer awareness? Is it knowledge of a reality unknown in ordinary experience?

This is the crucial question, and we may be tempted to think—especially when we remember the negative way as practised and explained by Eastern mystics—that the end of the progress is an apprehension of nothing, or of an undifferentiated continuum which is barely distinguishable from nothing. Some of the language used even by Christian mystics lends support to this supposition. Insistence on the complete emptying of the mind if God is to make His presence known seems to be carried further into nihilism. Thus we are told by Meister Eckhart that 'all creatures are one pure nothing'. We are even told by Scotus Erigena that 'God in virtue of his excellence is not inappropriately spoken of as nothing'.

There could be no other end to a process that was solely one of emptying. But there is still the possibility that what has to be thought by means of negations is felt as something positive. The use of negative language may be necessary to describe indirectly attributes which cannot fall within ordinary experience. This view is held both by Otto and by Poulain, although the latter, unlike the former, refuses to extend it to the practice of what he calls 'certain Hindu Buddhists': he considers their ecstasies to be counterfeit and asserts that they are 'immersed in the great All, that is to say in the great nothing'.

Without personal experience it is hard to see how one could decide these questions between rival mysticisms; but we may incline to think that the more charitable view which recognizes common elements in the different varieties is also likely to be the more correct. The one thing which appears certain is that in the most intense mystic experience there is no conscious reasoning or inference. This need not mean that there is no element of judgement or of what Father Poulain calls 'understanding'. We may take it to be at least the orthodox theory of Catholic mysticism that even in ecstasy the understanding is enlarged as well as overwhelmed.

§ 7. *The difficulties of criticism*

It may seem a mere impertinence if we pass from an external and summary description of the mystic union to the question of its validity. Only those who have had the experience are entitled to judge, and they will need no help from a detached philosophy. For them the experience itself is the guarantee of truth, and their conviction of its validity is absolute.

On this point the evidence is conclusive, but philosophical criticism is required, not in order to strengthen the conviction of the mystic—this would indeed be an impertinence—but in order to assess the claim that mystical experience is to be accepted as a ground for religious belief by those who have had no such experience themselves.

Even in this more modest endeavour it must be recognized that we are moving in the dark, and it is only right to display caution as well as humility. The account I have chosen to follow makes an absolute separation between ordinary religious experience and the experience of the mystics, and it postulates a special religious faculty which is wholly denied to others. If this were entirely true, the evidence of the mystics would be so unintelligible to us as to be useless. We must be able to suppose that at least the beginnings of what the mystic enjoys in its fulness are present dimly and gropingly in the experience of his less favoured brethren. We must also be able to suppose that his special awareness has some relation to ordinary cognition and is not dependent on a new faculty or a sixth sense. We must even be able to suppose that if God reveals himself to mystics in a special way, there must at least be analogous ways in which He reveals Himself, even if more obscurely, to others. These suppositions may be mistaken; but if they are, I do not see how the topic can profitably be discussed at all.

To many at the present time discussion will in any case seem unprofitable and even childish: the topic on their view should be reserved for abnormal psychology. Such a contention is encouraged by talk of special faculties and also by the fringes and accompaniments of mystical experience, some of which are accepted all too readily by such a writer as Father Poulain in spite of his honesty and natural common sense. We must agree that the subject is a proper one for investigation by psychology, although it would be more polite—and perhaps more scientific—not to specify the character of its particular branch before the investigations are completed. But if religion is partly concerned with questions of value, we need not accept without criticism everything that we may be told by psychologists, just as we need not accept it as an enlightening account of art when we are informed, on dubious evidence, that some supreme artists were certifiable. If we are allowed to judge by our native intelligence, many of the great mystics seem to have been conspicuously sane.

Besides the special difficulties inevitable in attempting to criticize the claims of the mystics—and indeed of any religious man—to possess assured knowledge of God, there are also more general difficulties which have to be met whenever the validity of knowledge, even of mundane knowledge, becomes subject to question.

Consider, for example, our supposed knowledge of physical bodies. This must be based on what is given to sense; but it may be hard to say what is given to sense, if by 'given' we mean 'given without any mental activity on our part'. Even if this difficulty be ignored, how can we pass from the given to something that is not given? Are bodies posited entities or postulated entities or inferred entities? Are they entities at all or mere 'logical constructions'? Similar questions may be raised about the atoms and electrons of the scientists. Philosophers differ widely in their answers.

Again, how can we know that we have minds and that other people have minds like our own? It used to be supposed that we know our own states of mind by introspection, but this possibility is sometimes denied to us to-day. Even if such introspection be admitted, how can we pass from given states of mind to knowledge of the mind which 'has' them? Some philosophers maintain that we have no minds to know. But even supposing we do know our own minds, how do we get from this to the minds of other people? Are we to believe that from certain sights and sounds and feelings we first of all infer that there are bodies, then that some of these bodies

are alive, and, finally, by an analogy with our own bodies, that some of these living bodies are connected with, or animated by, minds like our own? This seems an elaborate inferential process to take place before a child can recognize his mother as a person like himself.

No doubt we should distinguish between the *process* by which we come to a belief and the *grounds* on which the belief is to be justified; but so far as our belief in the existence of other persons is concerned, it is not easy to find an entirely convincing account of either. All these commonplace difficulties will reappear if we try to think about the mystic's knowledge of God as if it were analogous to our knowledge of other human beings; and incomparably greater difficulties will arise from the fact that God is not to be conceived as a finite person and cannot be known or encountered as if He were.

§ 8. *The question of validity*

If we ask how far religious faith is to be supported by what is known of mystic experience, the answer will depend on what we believe the character of that experience to be. On this point it may be possible to make some tentative suggestions if the analogy with our knowledge of other persons is borne in mind.

First of all, it should not be supposed that the claim to have experimental knowledge of God rests on an inference from an effect to its cause. There is no such causal inference in our awareness of other people, or even in our awareness of physical objects. Hence it is not too difficult to accept the claim that the mystic's awareness of God is direct and is not the result of reasoning.

This admission should not lead us to the opposite extreme. There is no ground for supposing that mystical experience—unless possibly in some forms of 'nihilism'—can be one of pure feeling unadulterated by thought. This experience, like any other, takes some of its form and content from previous experience and previous thinking, as is obvious from the evidence of the mystics themselves. How could unmixed feeling seem, even on subsequent reflexion, to know God as infinite and eternal and omniscient, or again as just and merciful?

The thought present in mystical experience is admittedly not inference, but some mystics claim also that it is not 'discursive'— that is to say, it does not use abstract concepts in order to run over a number of instances or to pass consciously from one member of a class to another.

This claim also is not difficult to accept. Even on the humblest
level of thought we can solve an anagram by running through the
possible permutations and combinations, but sometimes, perhaps
immediately or after a night's sleep, the answer, as it were, leaps
into our mind. Similar sudden insights may be given to poets and
even to philosophers—perhaps all poems begin in this way, and it
has been suggested that philosophies are often the working out of
some simple original intuition, which may from time to time be
renewed. Whatever conceptual elements may be present, the
mystical experience as a whole is presumably more like feeling or
aesthetic creation than like discursive thinking, and it is only natural
that it has to be expressed in something more like poetry than like
philosophy. Some mystics may find their way to the vision by means
of dialectic; but even for them it is the vision, not the dialectic, that
is fundamental.

Perhaps we should not go too far wrong if we said that in the
mystic union *judgement* must be present, as it is in aesthetic appreciation, or in recognizing a footstep, or even in an approach shot at
golf; but the word 'judgement' should not be taken to mean the
conscious application of abstract concepts to a given reality, and still
less the utterance in words of a theoretical proposition. What is
meant is something different from this, something with which we
are all familiar, although we have no accepted name for it. A failure
to take this factor into account leads men to speak as if sensation—
whether spiritual or non-spiritual—could by itself be knowledge of
the existence of an object. But we have no sensation of existence,
and knowledge of existence requires more than mere sensation. This
'something more' has to be described as a thought, a concept, a
judgement, though it is neither a discursive thought nor an abstract
concept nor an explicit judgement—or at least it is none of these
until it has been made clear by reflexion. We may, if we like, call it
a 'positing', but this only explains the obscure by the more obscure.
The mere fact that we find it so hard to describe this commonplace
factor in our ordinary experience of finite objects may help us to
understand the difficulty of the mystics in describing their experience of an object which to them is infinite.

Strictly speaking, there can be no experience of an infinite object,
and the judgement present in the mystic vision must be strained
beyond the limits of our finite powers. Hence it is not surprising
that the mystics feel themselves to be in the presence of a mystery
before which thoughts and words alike are poverty-stricken and

unavailing. We may hope to get more light on this when we come to consider the intellectual element in religious experience. Here it is enough if we can see—so far as we can see at all—that the conceptual factor in the mystic union, as in ordinary religious experience, is not accidental, but necessary: it is not merely read into it by commentators or by the mystic writers themselves. This is very obvious in the poetic vision with which this chapter ends. Even if—as might be suggested—Father Poulain is reading the theology of his Church into the mystic vision, and even if St. Teresa is obviously anxious to do the same, this does not do away with the need for judgement both in the experience itself and in the descriptions of it. On the other hand, it would be a gross error to suppose that the mystics are merely dressing up an accepted theology in poetical language. It is their personal experience which makes them speak as they do. They have a marked tendency to leave the theological rails altogether and so to get into trouble with their ecclesiastical superiors. Even the good Father himself seems not to have been free from difficulties of this kind.

An attempt to isolate the cognitive element must distort the whole picture, but in spite of this we have to ask how far it is reasonable for those who have no inside knowledge to rely on the reports of mystic experience as a ground for religious belief.

So far as the mystic vision is granted only to those in a state of partial or complete trance, this is likely nowadays to inspire doubt rather than confidence. Yet this objection is not in itself conclusive; for something not wholly unlike a trance may be required for the highest achievements in art and literature—perhaps even in science. All creative work seems to depend on the unconscious, and it demands an intensity of concentration that excludes attention to ordinary perceptions. But whatever defence may be made, it must be admitted that an abnormal condition of body is no guarantee of spiritual insight into a transcendent reality. Similarly, if the so-called 'ligature' of the sensuous faculties is made the basis for a claim that God, as it were, seizes upon the soul, this too must be received by a workaday philosopher with caution if not with distrust.

Some thinkers may be inclined to sweep aside the whole of mystic experience as a kind of self-hypnotism or even as a mental aberration; but such a conclusion would be reckless unless it were supported by a vast body of unbiased psychological evidence. It would be equally reckless to accept without question the claims of Mr. Aldous Huxley, who speaks as if it must be manifest to any impartial thinker that in the mystic way God is revealed 'in His fullness'. There is no reason why we should have to choose between unquestioning acceptance and utter rejection. It is hard to resist the conclusion that a dispassionate decision must ultimately turn, not on the mode of reception, but on the positive content of the mystic vision as conveyed to us, however dimly, by analogies and images. This must be judged—if it can be judged at all—only by its continuity with ordinary religious experience, and perhaps also with aesthetic experience and even with philosophical reflexions and moral aspirations.

On this basis it is not unreasonable to maintain that mystics may grasp vividly in a sudden flash of insight what is laboriously sought and dimly seen by lesser mortals. Hence their writings may be of the utmost value to a philosopher in his attempts to understand the nature of religious experience. Nevertheless if these writings are to be used as evidence, it would be a mistake to regard them as exempt from philosophical criticism or to suppose that there was no need for a much wider enquiry. Although mystics may claim with complete sincerity and absolute assurance that they have experimental knowledge of God's presence and nature and even of His actions, this cannot be interpreted as if it were on all fours with our knowledge and understanding of a human friend. If these claims are taken in a literal and matter of fact way, which the mystics would be the first to reject, there is a danger of falling back to a very primitive level of theology.

From the religious point of view men may have their faith strengthened if they find in the mystics reports of a supreme experience which is at least remotely analogous to their own and may even seem to be, as it were, its crown and goal. But they too cannot base their beliefs simply on the evidence of experts, as most of us have to do in physics; for religious belief is nothing apart from personal experience and personal conviction. Hence the meaning of the mystic vision even for them depends on the light which it throws on their own faith.

I have chosen to examine a cloistered mysticism because it is the best documented. It is confined to those who, besides accepting a traditional theology, have given themselves up to devotion and in a lesser degree to good works. It is indifferent to argument; and it is far from being inspired by any contact with nature or with natural beauty, which it tends to regard as a snare. So far as it can be said to look outward at all, it looks only to God. If it stood alone, it would have a weaker title to our consideration, but there are other ways of mysticism—including the practice of dialectic and of communion with nature—as well as the way of prayer. All these different ways are often said to lead by similar stages to the same vision and so to establish a very special claim on human credence.

Although there are striking resemblances in the works of very different kinds of mystic, this sweeping statement should be received with some reserve. Father Poulain would himself repudiate it. We may perhaps suspect that he makes the stages in the mystic way a little tidier than they really are; and I should like to see further evidence that different ways have the same stages—this obviously cannot be true of dialectic—and still more that they lead to the same vision of reality, no matter how different may be the background of life and thought in which mystical experiences have their origin. But this caveat may be taken as an expression of ignorance: I have no wish to deny that there is at least a strong *prima facie* case which demands further investigation.

§ 9. *The voice of poetry*

Mysticism, like religion, finds its natural expression, not in prose, but in poetry. My prosaic account, and perhaps even the language of my learned guide, may seem external, pedantic, niggling, and possibly repugnant. If we wish to look at a living mysticism, not at one carefully docketed in the cabinets of a museum, we may turn to the writings of Emily Brontë. She is a nature-mystic and a lover of liberty. Her inspiration comes from the Yorkshire moors,

   'Where the grey flocks in ferny glens are feeding;
   Where the wild wind blows on the mountain-side'.

Yet the lines of her experience are strangely close to the pattern drawn from the study of the cloister. I quote from three poems and add no comments; but after the fashion of my Jesuit friend I will arrange the passages under appropriate headings, without, I hope, doing too much violence to their original context. Every word in them deserves the closest scrutiny.

   The experience :
   But, first, a hush of peace—a soundless calm descends,
   The struggle of distress, and fierce impatience ends;
   Mute music soothes my breast—unuttered harmony,
   That I could never dream, till Earth was lost to me.

Then dawns the Invisible: the Unseen its truth reveals;
My outward sense is gone, my inward essence feels:
Its wings are almost free—its home, its harbour found,
Measuring the gulf, it stoops—and dares the final bound.

The suffering :
Oh! dreadful is the check—intense the agony—
When the ear begins to hear, and the eye begins to see;
When the pulse begins to throb, the brain to think again;
The soul to feel the flesh, and the flesh to feel the chain.

Yet I would lose no sting, would wish no torture less;
The more the anguish racks, the earlier it will bless;
And robed in fires of Hell, or bright with Heavenly shine,
If it but herald death, the vision is divine.

The vision :
O God within my breast,
Almighty ever-present Deity!
Life, that in me has rest,
As I, undying Life, have power in Thee.

With wide-embracing love
Thy Spirit animates eternal years,
Pervades and broods above,
Changes, sustains, dissolves, creates, and rears.

Though earth and moon were gone,
And suns and universes ceased to be,
And Thou wert left alone,
Every existence would exist in Thee.

There is no room for Death,
Nor atom that his might could render void:
Thou—THOU art Being and Breath,
And what THOU art may never be destroyed.

The response :
Strange Power! I trust thy might; trust thou my constancy.

L

Chapter XI

I AND THOU

§ 1. *Experience and encounter*

When we try to think about religion, there is a risk that we may ask the wrong questions and use the wrong language. Hitherto we have been enquiring into the nature of religious and mystical experience considered as a ground for belief in God. It is hard to see how this language can be avoided, but it may fail to bring out the difference between religious experience and our ordinary experience of bodies and minds.

Ordinary experience may be supposed—in spite of many philosophical difficulties—to pass from given sensations to belief in the existence of finite objects. Hence religious experience may be supposed—by analogy—to pass from some special sensation, or special feeling, to belief in the existence of God. It may even be supposed to do so by means of some special faculty—a faculty of 'divination'. But an appeal to special sensations or feelings or faculties, though it may direct attention to some psychological truth, is bound to be unsatisfactory as an attempt at philosophical explanation. As to the passage, if there is one, from religious feeling to religious belief, we have so far found only the vaguest statements, mainly from Otto, about 'positing' or about passing 'from the sign to the thing signified'.

There is a still more serious difficulty. Ordinary experience is experience of finite objects in space and time—objects that are subject to the laws of nature. God is not a finite object in space and time, nor is He subject to nature's laws. Hence it may be misleading to speak of Him as an object of experience. The relation of a religious man to God may not be one of subject to object but of subject to subject. It is possible that God is not 'experienced' but rather 'met' or 'encountered'? Does religious faith differ from ordinary belief, not in being directed to a special object, but in requiring a wholly different point of view?

Here perhaps we may look for help to Martin Buber, who offers an answer to these difficult questions in his book *'Ich and Du'*: it is translated into English under the title '*I and Thou*'. He expresses himself in an unfamiliar idiom—in the language of a Jewish prophet turned philosopher. This may discourage some would-be readers: at times it makes him obscure, and on a first acquaintance it may be difficult to see what he is talking about. Nevertheless, like some of the best poetry, his book is crammed with thought, and this gradually becomes clearer with repeated study. I may have failed to master it, especially in its most crucial part; but I will try to put what I take to be his central doctrine in a more sombre prose, which I hope may be at least partially intelligible.

For the benefit of English readers I will follow Mr. R. G. Smith's translation pretty closely, although in his difficult task he does not always use the words I should have chosen myself.

§ 2. *I-Thou* and *I-It*

In accordance with modern fashion Martin Buber approaches his problem from the side of language.

Language, he tells us, develops out of primary words. These are not isolated words but combined words; and they do not signify things but intimate what he calls relations. Of these primary words there are only two: (1) the combined word *I-Thou*; and (2) the combined word *I-It*. Each of these expresses one aspect of man's two-fold attitude to the world, and in accordance with this two-fold attitude the world is a two-fold world to him. Although both these words are said to be primary, it is clear that on this view the word *I-Thou* comes before the word *I-It*. There is no *I* taken by itself, and the *I* of the primary word *I-Thou* is said to be a different *I* from that of the primary word *I-It*.

We may try to put this less linguistically.

The fundamental relation in our life is a relation of subject to subject, of person to person, of the child to his mother. Out of the first obscure consciousness of this relation there gradually emerges the distinction between *I* and *Thou*. It would be a mistake to call this the distinction between self and not-self. I become conscious of myself as against you—almost (though this is not Buber's language) as a differentiation within one total personality. I do not first discover myself, and then make a precarious inference to your existence. You and I were there all the time, and only gradually am I able, so to speak, to sort myself out. Only after I have sorted myself out from you, can I become aware of a world of things, which are not *Yous*—not persons, but just *Its*. Only then can I use the primary word *I-It*; but the *I* that uses this word is merely cognitive, a subject in relation to an object. This is the reason for saying that the *I* is a different *I*; and also for saying that the word *I-It* can never be spoken with one's whole being. Only the word *I-Thou* can be so spoken.

The word *I-It* belongs to the language of common experience, the language of science. The word *I-Thou* belongs to the language of what Buber calls 'relation' or 'standing in relation'. As the word 'relation' is ambiguous—there is after all a relation between subject and object—perhaps I may be allowed to speak of 'living relation' when I mean the relation of *I* and *Thou*. This is not a merely cognitive relation, but a relation of life, a relation of living subjects to one another.

All this is elaborated with great ingenuity by Buber both as regards the primitive savage and as regards the child.

§ 3. *The world of living relation*

We get into greater difficulties when we begin to explore the world of living relation, which is said to arise in three different spheres—in our life with nature, our life with men, and our life with intelligible forms.

First, our life with nature. In this the living relation is said to cling to the threshold of speech, and even to sway in gloom, beneath the level of speech.

Here we might expect to find the attitude of the nature-mystic, which is closely connected with the beauty of landscape, and especially of hills. Buber himself seems to be mainly interested in living creatures—although he refers in one place to a fragment of mica and in another to a streak of sun on a maple twig. One of his examples is a tree when we cease to classify it and measure it and generalize about it and even—curiously enough—to look on it as a picture. This recalls the neurotic vision of the tree in Jean-Paul Sartre's novel '*La Nausée*', but Buber's becoming bound up in living relation with the tree seems to be sane. A more remarkable example is that of living relation with a cat—an example which, however serious, is in danger of sounding merely funny in English. If I understand aright, the usual glance of a cat expresses anxiety, the tension of a creature 'between the realms of vegetable security and spiritual venture'. The account continues as follows:

'Sometimes I look into a cat's eyes. The domesticated animal has
not as it were received from us (as we sometimes imagine) the gift
of the truly "speaking" glance, but only—at the price of its primitive disinterestedness—the capacity to turn its glance to us prodigi-
ous beings. But with this capacity there enters the glance, in its
dawn and continuing in its rising, a quality of amazement and of
inquiry that is wholly lacking in the original glance with all its
anxiety.'

We need not follow the professor in his attempts to translate the
cat's amazed enquiries into human speech—perhaps these go better
into German—but we may note that he has no experience of a
consciousness in the tree similar to our own.

As to our life with man, it is here that our living relation takes
on the form of speech. We can give and accept the *Thou*. The relation seems to be best described as a relation of love, but love is
something more than an emotion. Love is the responsibility of an *I*
for a *Thou*.

Our life with intelligible forms is the life of the creative artist. A
man is faced by a form which claims to be made through him into a
work of art. Here the living relation is without speech, but begets it.
We feel we are addressed and we answer. Our answer, I presume,
need not be in words: it may be in the colours of the painter or the
notes of the musician. By speech in this wide sense the intelligible
form is embodied in the work of art.

We might imagine that the thinker stood in a similar living relation with the thoughts he embodies in speech, and even that the
intelligible forms might cover the Platonic Ideas. This does not
appear to be the case: Martin Buber is no Platonist. He refuses
recourse to 'a world of ideas and values'; he appears to regard
general thoughts as belonging only to the world of *I-It*; and,
departing from his customary charity, he even asserts that the man
who addresses Ideas with an abstraction or a password, as if it were
their name, is pitiable.

The difficulty in his account of these spheres of living relation is
that he wants this relation to be mutual or reciprocal so as to prepare
the way for the relation to the eternal *Thou*. Thus he has to speak,
not only of 'man's loving speech', but also of 'form's silent asking'
and of 'the mute proclamation of the creature'. We may be tempted
to regard the last two as metaphorical or merely fanciful, but they
should not be dismissed without due consideration.

More important is the account of the way in which the *Thou* is envisaged by the *I*. I do not experience the *Thou* as one object among many: I encounter or meet him as a whole, not split up into qualities and not bounded by others. I do not meet him at some particular time or place. He has no neighbours but fills the heavens. This does not mean that nothing exists except himself. But all else lives in *his* light. In this sense he is boundless or exclusive. He lives in a spaceless and timeless present.

All this becomes more intelligible when we contrast it with the world of *I-It*. It is, we are told, 'the exalted melancholy of our fate, that every *Thou* in our world must become an *It*'. A work of art, a creature, my fellow man, and even my self—all of these can be looked at as one object among other objects, one thing among other things, occupying a particular position in space and time, capable of being measured and analysed, and subject to causal laws. This on the side of thought is the world of science, the ordered and detached world which is reliable and has density and duration, the world of common objects. On the side of action it is the world we use, not the world we encounter or meet or love. And the *I* belonging to this world of *I-It* has shrunk from substance and fulness to a functional point, to a mere subject which experiences and uses—to something, it would seem, rather like Kant's transcendental unity of apperception.

Every *Thou*, after the meeting or encounter, *must* become an *It*. Every *It* *may* enter again into living relation and become a *Thou*. It is not possible to live in the bare present of the *I-Thou*, but it is possible to live in the bare past of the *I-It*. To those who live habitually in the solid, reliable world of experience and use, 'the moments of the *Thou* appear as strange lyric and dramatic episodes, seductive and magical, but tearing us away to dangerous extremes, loosening the well-tried context, leaving more questions than satisfaction behind them, shattering security—in short, uncanny moments we can well dispense with'. 'Without *It* man cannot live. But he who lives with *It* alone, is not a man.'

§ 4. *Some difficulties*

So summary an account of Buber's starting point must fail to do him justice. The luxuriance of his language may seem repellent when fragments of it are torn from the consistent fabric of a philosophical prose-poem. Nevertheless he describes well the attitude and world which are expressed in the *I-It* language of the scientist and the economic man. There appears to be no place for religion, no place even for morality or for freedom, in the world as seen from this point of view.

He is surely right in saying that there is another attitude and another language—that the world can be looked at from another point of view. But has he described, or even hinted at, one consistent attitude? Is the language of the *I-Thou* one coherent language?

Even in our life with men this language seems to suggest at times the high moments of intense love; at other times the morally good life in which men treat each other as ends in themselves; at other times ordinary co-operation in work and play when our fellows are our collaborators and not our tools. It may sometimes apparently even cover the language of philosophical and scientific dialogue; for Socrates too is said to speak the language of *I-Thou*. But in all this there is response—although even love may be unrequited. When we pass to our life with creatures and with 'intelligible forms', our difficulties increase. We may feel a certain partnership and friendship with our dog—perhaps even with our cat—and for many of us at times inanimate nature may seem to speak with a living voice. There may be in all this some kinship with aesthetic experience, and a work of art, both in being created and in being enjoyed, may fill our universe. Perhaps in love and loyal co-operation and art we are in contact with the concrete and the real—not with abstractions like universals and laws and measurements and physical objects. Martin Buber is certainly not just indulging in emotional nonsense, and a life restricted to a scientific view of the world—still more one confined to profit-making and power-seeking—would be impoverished. But it is not clear that what is opposed to such a life falls under one head or is expressed in one language or meets with a like response.

I have also difficulties about the *I* which is the subject of the *I-It* language, and has to be distinguished from the *Me* which is expressed by the *It*. The latter may be an object among other objects, subject to causal law and bound by fate. But may not the former be free and—if I may fall into my mentor's style—go forth even in thinking to meet its destiny?

§ 5. *The absolute relation*

We have at best discovered only a possible line, or lines, for further reflexion, but even with this insufficient preparation we must try to go forward. The way is beset by difficulties. Buber's thought is too compact to be crammed into a smaller space. The style becomes more lyrical, and perhaps it ought not to be turned into prose. I may be asking the wrong questions and trying to translate the language of *I-Thou* into the language of *I-It*; or, what is worse, I may be mixing up the two languages. I shall have to use a good many of Buber's phrases, which may go ill with my own, and those who seek further light must turn to the original.

The world of *It* is set in the context of space and time. The world of *Thou* is not set in the context of either of these. Its context is in the 'Centre', where the extended lines of living relation meet—in the eternal *Thou*. Every particular *Thou* is a glimpse through to the eternal *Thou*. Particular limited living relations may be completed only in a relation to God which may be called pure, absolute, and unconditioned.

We must first try to understand this relation, so far as we can.

Every *Thou*, it will be remembered, was said to be boundless— that is, not bounded by others—and every living relation was said to be exclusive. The last word is perhaps misleading; for it means, not that nothing else exists except the *Thou*, but that all else lives, and is seen, in his light. This exclusiveness might therefore just as well be described as inclusiveness. Hence it is not surprising to be told that in the relation with God unconditioned exclusiveness and unconditioned inclusiveness are one; for everything lives, and is seen to live, in the light of the eternal *Thou*. Here we find a living relation that gathers up and includes all others.

Particular *Thous* were also said to be in a timeless present. Yet these timeless presents are of brief duration, and every *Thou* must fall back into the world of *It*—must enter the chrysalis state of the *It* in order to take wings anew. If I may revert to the encounter with the cat, this living relation was only momentary: 'morning and evening flowed pitilessly mingled together, the bright *Thou* appeared and was gone'. By its own nature the eternal *Thou* is eternally *Thou*. It is only *our* nature that compels us to withdraw it into the world and the talk of *It*.

Correlative with the boundless and eternal *Thou* is the united *I*— the whole man in a living relation with the all-embracing God. At times Buber seems to speak as if man has to become one *before* he can go out to encounter God. I take him to mean that the concentration and exaltation found in art or in human intercourse may be a condition of this encounter, a stage from which we may go forward or back, but that complete wholeness is to be found in the encounter itself. The way to God is not by mortification of the desires or withdrawal from the world. 'Men do not find God if they stay in the world. They do not find him if they leave the world. He who goes out with his whole being to meet his *Thou* and carries to it all being that is in the world, finds Him who cannot be sought'. Furthermore the encounter is an encounter and not a merging or a soliloquy. Those who regard the ecstatic union of the mystics as a fusion or absorption concentrate on the living relation and forget the *I* and *Thou* without which there would be no relation at all. Those who bid us take refuge in the One thinking Essence, in the Pure Subject, who say to us 'This is the real, the Self, and Thou art the Self', are compelled to make the world and God mere functions of the soul and so to destroy the possibility of living relation altogether.

It would take too long to explain how by virtue of this pure living relation there exists the unbroken world of *Thou*, how the isolated moments of living relation are bound up in a life of world solidarity, how there arises a 'community' through the common quality of living relation with the Centre. Still more difficult is the connexion between the world of *Thou* and the world of *It*, and the way in which they are necessary to one another: there is only one world which is two-fold because of man's two-fold attitude to it. We must note, however, that man's thirst for continuity is unsatisfied by the life-rhythm of pure relation: he longs for extension in time and in space. Because of the first longing God becomes an object of faith or belief; because of the second He becomes the object of a cult or Church. In this way God is manifested in history, and there is said to be a new 'form' of God in the world, form being apparently a mixture of *Thou* and *It*.

§ 6. *The way to the encounter*

More important for our purposes is the way to the encounter. As we have already learned, God is not to be inferred—the encounter is immediate and direct. Our life with nature, our life with men, and our life with 'intelligible forms' are three gateways leading into the presence of the Word, but it is our life with men which is the main portal. 'The relation with man is the real comparison for the relation with God ; in it true address receives true response; except that in God's response everything, the universe, is made manifest as language.'

This is perhaps the clearest statement that we can get from Buber as to the nature of God's response. From the religious point of view it may be wrong to ask for further analysis of this response, and still more wrong to ask with what justification it is to be called the response of God—we may be committing ourselves to the inappropriate language of *I-It*; but to this point we shall return.

According to Buber we know our own way to the encounter, but not God's way: our concern is with our own will, not with God's grace. 'The *Thou* confronts me. But I step into direct relation with it. Hence the relation means being chosen and choosing, suffering and action in one.' On the one hand I know that I am given over for disposal; on the other that it depends on myself. This seeming contradiction or antinomy, like many others in the religious life, is overcome, not in thinking, but in living.

There is said to be no such thing as seeking God, for there is nothing in which He could not be found. Before the encounter there is nothing to do but wait. We are even told—this is surprising —that there are no precepts of action or meditation which a man can follow in order to prepare himself. As we have already seen, it is useless to withdraw from the world or retire into the depths of the self. There is indeed a process of 'reversal', but this seems to be the same as 'stepping into direct relation'—it is 'recognition of the Centre and the act of turning again to it'. Reversal seems to follow, at least sometimes, from the despair which is the result of exclusive absorption with the world of *It*—with theoretical knowledge and the use of men only as means. It is a change of movement and not merely of goal. Broadly speaking, we do not get beyond the view that the encounter with the eternal *Thou* is a development of encounters with particular *Thous*. 'If only we love the real world . . . really in its horror, if only we venture to surround it with the arms of our spirit, our hands will meet hands that grip them.'

§ 7. *The mark of revelation*

Is there any way in which we can check or test the reality of the encounter? So far as an answer is given to this question, it is to be found in what is said about revelation.

The essential mark of revelation is that 'a man does not pass, from the moment of the supreme meeting, the same being as he entered into it'. Something has *happened* to him; something has been *given* to him; and this something appears to supply him with new strength.

'We receive what we did not hitherto have, and receive it in such a way that we know it has been given to us.'

Is it possible to specify more precisely what it is that is given and received?

What man receives is not a specific content, but a Presence, a Presence as power. This Presence and power include three things, which can be considered separately, although they are undivided.

First of all, there is said to be 'the whole fulness of real mutual action'. This looks like another expression for the encounter itself, but we get the new assertion that it does not lighten man's life—it makes it heavier, but heavy with meaning.

Secondly, there is 'the inexpressible confirmation of meaning'. The word 'meaning' is notoriously treacherous, and we should have liked a fuller exposition at this stage; yet there is sense in saying that we may find life meaningful or meaningless. This is the sense intended by Buber when he tells us that meaning is assured and that the question of the meaning of life is no longer there. The meaning of life is not something to be exhibited or defined, to be formulated or pictured—not something to be explained, but something to be done. If I may put this in my own prosaic language, the religious man, by means of the encounter, has the assurance that his own life, and indeed all life, is not something isolated and ineffectual, but is part of one great enterprise and is to be understood—and lived— as such a part. To say that an action has meaning as part of a wider teleological whole is perfectly good sense; and it is surely something like this which men find in religion and sadly miss without it.

The third point is that this meaning is not that of another life or another world, but of this life and this world. We are told also that this meaning 'can be proved true by each man only in the singleness of his being and the singleness of his life'. But this 'proving true' is not a matter of knowledge, and the riddle of life remains unsolved. If I understand aright, the 'proving true' is to be found in action and not in thought. The religious man does not understand the universe as a complete teleological whole, for that no man can do; but in living his life as part of such a whole he finds in himself a wholeness and peace, a strength and insight and assurance, which confirm and justify his choice.

§ 8. *The God of reflexion*

Even from this short account it will be obvious that the doctrine of *I and Thou* is open to criticism from many sides. Yet it contains at least two principles without which religion can hardly hope to stand at the present stage of civilization.

The first principle is that religion and science are not two rival theories professing to explain the world in different ways. If they were, there is no doubt that one would have to be abandoned, and we cannot abandon science. But it is possible that they may represent two different points of view from which the world may be regarded, or—perhaps this is a better way of putting it—two different attitudes which may be taken to the world and in virtue of which the world itself may appear two-fold to us. I do not clearly see how Buber himself works this view out in detail, and it is dangerously near to invoking the doctrine of double truth, which was formerly put forward in defence of science, and is now put forward in defence of religion; but it is a view which merits further investigation.

The second principle is the one I have propounded from the first —that religion is for the whole man. Religion cannot be based on a special faculty, an extra sense, a unique feeling, even if these are uneasily attached to rational concepts. Buber makes a real advance by insisting that religion must be an attitude of the whole man, an attitude necessarily accompanied both by feeling and by thought, and one which can be tested and confirmed in actual living. But here too we may ask ourselves whether he has done justice to the element of thought and its relation to our ordinary thinking.

It is stupid to blame a man for not writing a different book from the one he has written or for not answering questions he has not chosen to ask. Buber's book, as I have said, is crammed with thinking, as only a poem can be, although its bony structure may be veiled in metaphors. But we have got too little light on the validity of religious experience—if such language may still be used in spite of its misleading associations. This is a theoretical question, and perhaps one which on his view we ought not to ask.

Why is it considered wrong to raise questions of this kind? The answer is that we are proposing to reflect about God, and to reflect about God is to turn Him into an *It-God* who is no longer a *Thou* and so is not God at all. God can be spoken to, but not spoken about. Reflexion makes God into an object—and this is just what God cannot be. If instead of allowing God's gift to work itself out, we reflect about the Giver, we shall merely miss both. 'Meeting with God does not come to man in order that he may concern himself with God, but in order that he may confirm that there is meaning in the world.'

Such a view, although it offers an attractive picture of a genuine and undogmatic religion, seems to rule out all theology, including natural theology, from the start. And certainly much theology treats God like other objects, or even as one among other objects, as also does much popular preaching with its reckless claims to familiarity with God's purposes and God's plans for this or that. To Buber such thinking is concerned with God's way to us, and this is wholly beyond our ken: it is enough if we can say something of our way to Him.

To some this will mean that Buber is affected by the modern disease of subjectivity. Yet even these should take warning that much thinking about God is an attempt to bring Him under human categories which may be necessary for us but are wholly inadequate to Him. This has always been known to wise men, even if at times they have forgotten it.

On the other hand, if we dismiss reflexion too lightly, we may fall into a welter of emotions, a spate of attitudes, a mist of incoherence. After all, what is Buber doing himself? His own book is more than a poem and more than a prayer. He is not merely using one language: he is also talking about two languages and their relation to one another. He is not merely addressing God, but reflecting on the way to Him; and it is impossible to think about the way without also thinking about that to which it is the way. As a warning against idle speculation his doctrine is wholly sound; but at least we have to reflect further on the intellectual and moral elements in religious life and on the limits of our finite understanding. With such a proposal Buber himself would, I think, have no quarrel.

Chapter XII

THE ARGUMENT FROM PERFECTION

§ 1. *Religious thinking*

If religious life is bound up with belief in God's existence and attributes, it must contain an element of thinking. Religious men may reasonably claim that their thinking is neither inferential nor discursive—that it is more like intuition or feeling than like reasoning; and they may be right in asserting that if it is explicitly formulated as a philosophical argument, it is likely to be emptied or distorted. We are now, it is to be hoped, in a better position to appreciate these real difficulties and dangers; but the conceiving or thinking or judging that must be present—under whatever name— in man's living relation to God, is manifestly in need of closer study.

There are many ways in which this almost unmanageable task might be attempted, but a brief discussion may perhaps be made a little easier if we consider some of the traditional arguments for the existence of God.

It may be thought that to do this is to abandon the basis of religious experience and to take refuge in the arid region of scholastic discussions as remote from ordinary thinking as they are alien to modern philosophical taste. Such an objection cannot be accepted without further enquiry. The traditional proofs may be unconvincing as abstract arguments and may be inadequate to the intellectual factor in religious experience, but they have grown out of such experience: they are ways in which men of great acuteness have attempted to justify or defend their religious beliefs, and it is in relation to religious experience that they should be examined.

We must proceed at first along a well-beaten track—it has been trodden by many pilgrims before us and may be called the Hill of Difficulty. The arguments in question have been elaborated with the utmost subtlety and complexity, perhaps in order to meet the objections of critics. The subtle and the complex must here be passed over if there is to be any hope of making natural theology intelligible to those who are not professional philosophers. There may even be advantages in this avoidance of the subtle; for although an invalid argument may be made valid by further premises, the very complexity of an argument may conceal its fallacies. To simplify these proofs, so far as one can, may mean a failure to do them justice; but at least it may open up a possible line of enquiry, and any errors can be checked and corrected by more elaborate expositions, of which there is no lack.

§ 2. *Arguments for the existence of God*

The theoretical arguments traditionally supposed to prove the existence of God may be grouped under three main heads.

First of all, we may argue—according to some philosophers— from certain thoughts or *conceptions* of our own; for example, we may argue that a perfect being must exist since existence is contained in the very concept of a perfect being. Secondly, we may argue from our *general experience* of the world; for example, we may maintain that since anything in the world must have a cause, there must therefore exist a first cause, to which we give the name of 'God'. Thirdly, we may argue from *particular experiences* of special features in the world; we may hold, for example, that the organs of living creatures are so marvellously adapted for purposes of life that they must be the product of a supremely intelligent designer or creator.

Put thus nakedly, these possible lines of argument must seem unconvincing, however much they may have carried conviction to men in the past—or at least may have reinforced convictions already held on other grounds. In actual thinking they are not so sharply distinguished from one another as the classification might suggest. Rather they run into one another and may afford each other mutual support or corroboration. On the other hand, so far as they provide separate links in a chain of argument, the whole chain will have the strength only of its weakest link. Nor can it be denied that they rest on assumptions which are not readily made to-day.

Even at first sight it may seem that all these types of purely intellectual argument have a common defect: they seek to pass from non-religious premises to a religious conclusion. Admittedly, even from the religious point of view, they are concerned with intellectual abstractions; but we must be careful not to take the word 'religious' too narrowly. It seems to be a conviction of religious consciousness itself that God is revealed (or reveals Himself) in two ways—firstly, in the world that He has made, and, secondly, in the heart of the worshipper. We have been concerned with the second way, the way of the heart, in attempting to examine the numinous feeling and the mystic union and the living relation to the Absolute Thou. So far as we are now to be concerned with God's revelation in the world, we are bound to start from our ordinary experience of that world. And so far as we are to be concerned with the way of the head, we are bound to consider even the most abstract thinking about God. We are not entitled to set all this aside at the outset on the ground that it can in no sense be a factor in religious experience and so cannot lead to a religious, or even to a theological, conclusion.

There is one further general point. It is impossible to establish the existence of anything without some conception of its character. Hence the alleged proofs of God's existence must be in some way concerned also with His nature and attributes.

§ 3. *The ontological argument*

This double concern is obvious in the argument from the concept of a perfect being to His existence: it is an inference from God's nature to His reality.

This argument, which was formulated first by Anselm and elaborated by such thinkers as Descartes, Leibniz, and Hegel, is commonly known as the ontological proof. It has many variations but may be put most simply as follows.

God is by definition a perfect being and indeed—if we may speak of degrees in perfection—a supremely perfect being. But it is self-contradictory to regard a supremely perfect being as non-existent; for to lack existence must be an imperfection. Hence a perfect being must exist, and so God must exist. This conclusion is said to be as certain as the mathematical theorem that a triangle must have the sum of its interior angles equal to two right angles.

Such an argument may be in need of further premises: perhaps we ought to show that a perfect being can be conceived without contradiction and also that there can only be one perfect being. Into these complexities it is not necessary to enter. The crux of the argument is the contention that we are entitled, and indeed obliged, to pass from the thought or notion of God's perfection to knowledge of His existence—to knowledge that He must necessarily exist.

There is something very peculiar about this attempt at a proof. Arguments to the existence of anything usually start from knowledge that something exists and go on to maintain that if this exists, something else must exist—if there is smoke, there must be fire. Such arguments are based on experience, if we take experience to be sensuous experience of something existent in time and space. All theoretical proofs of the existence of God except the ontological one start from experience of an existent world and argue to the existence of its first cause or its creator. The ontological argument is unique in not being based on experience of an existent world. It is not based on any experience of any existent at all—not even on what men sometimes claim to be religious experience of an existent God. It is based on the bare concept of perfection—on pure thinking unsullied by thought or feeling. It professes to pass from the pure thought of perfection to knowledge of God's existence, or to enjoy such knowledge by means of this pure thought alone.

From the religious point of view the concept of perfection, in spite of its vagueness, is the most satisfactory basis on which to rest any attempt at an ontological proof: the religious man can worship only a God who is and is perfect. But the concept from which the argument starts can be expressed in other words. Anselm, for example, took the concept of God to be the concept of that than which nothing greater can be conceived. Others have taken it to be the concept of the most real being, the supreme being, the being of beings, and so on. These concepts have the advantage of appearing less anthropomorphic, and they are metaphysically preferable to the concept of perfection, except when its human associations have been removed. But unless they cover the notion of perfection, they will not, from the religious point of view, offer a satisfactory basis for any proof of the existence of God. From a logical point of view they may lead only to the empty tautology that whatever is most real must be most real.

In whatever form the argument is stated it will be instinctively rejected by common sense. Some may see in it a pitiable exhibition of human weakness. How is it possible that men of outstanding intellectual ability should have been taken in by so manifest a sophism? We can never be entitled to infer from the mere thought of an object that the object itself must exist. No purely verbal definition can give us knowledge of reality.

The attitude of common sense in this matter seems to be fundamentally sound. Nevertheless it is a mistake to suppose that we can take an argument apart from its context and dismiss it summarily without regard to the whole philosophical system of which it forms a part. This particular argument merits a little more consideration

M

because of the importance attached to it by thinkers whose eminence in other fields is beyond dispute.

§ 4. *The philosophical background*

For Anselm the ontological argument had a background of Platonism imperfectly understood. In such a context the argument becomes more plausible. Common sense ascribes existence and being, at least primarily, to the world we perceive—to the ordinary world of stars and planets, rivers and mountains, tables and chairs, plants, animals, and human beings. Whatever else may exist or be, these things exist and are. But Plato did not agree with common sense. In his language the ordinary world is in a state of flux and cannot be said to be but only to become: it tumbles about between being and not-being. Things can be said to be only if they are eternally what they are and so are outside the flux of time. Such things he found in numbers and mathematical figures, but above all in what we call universals and he called Forms or Ideas—for example, in beauty itself, goodness itself, and so on. Though beautiful things come into being and pass away, beauty itself neither comes into being nor passes away, but remains eternally what it is. Only of the Forms (and such other things as may be grasped by thought and not by sense) can it be truly asserted that they are.

Thus it can be said that for Plato the objects of thought, not the objects of perception, are real; but by this he did not mean that they existed merely as objects of thought. On the contrary, they are for him eternal or timeless realities in their own right, whether we think about them or not. No doubt we come to know beauty itself (or beauty in itself) by a process of thinking stimulated by the sight of beautiful and perishable objects in the changing world; but even this process is to be described, at least mythologically, as the 'recollection' of a reality known in some former life.

Such a doctrine about our knowledge of universals cannot legitimately be extended without further argument to our knowledge of individual souls and of God, even although the intellectual element in the soul is said to be akin to the Forms; but at least the claim to know such Forms in virtue of this kinship helps to make knowledge of ultimate reality by means of pure thinking less suspect and eases the obvious difficulty of the ontological argument.

The philosophy of Plato with its claim to know by pure intelligence an eternal world more real than our perceptible world of

change will always have a special attraction for religious men; and
no one who has not been at one time a Platonist can know fully what
it is to enjoy philosophy. But perhaps we must now say that Plato
exaggerated the importance of universals as some modern philosophers exaggerate the importance of words. Men who make a
philosophical discovery generally make too much of it.

In view of the Platonic doctrine it may be suggested that the
ontological proof is misdescribed when regarded as an inference
from our thinking, or even from our concepts, to the independent
reality which is thought or conceived. What we conceive, it may be
said, is a real essence, a timeless and independent universal; and the
inference to existence—if it is an inference—is based on this real
essence, and not on our thinking and conceiving.

Few philosophers would now hold that by pure thinking we are
able to know real essences; and many would maintain that such a
doctrine is unintelligible. But even if we set aside these grave
objections, it is still hard to see how we can infer from a real essence
to the existence of an individual who partakes of this real essence or
in whom the essence is embodied. From our knowledge of beauty
itself (if we have such knowledge) we cannot infer that beautiful
things must exist. The argument must turn on the special character
of the essence in question: it must be an essence such that only one
individual can be its embodiment; and the individual must be such
that it embodies only the essence and nothing more. In short, the
ordinary distinctions of individual and universal—or of matter and
form—must be overcome. In accordance with such a view God has
been described as pure form, and the distinction between His
essence and His existence has been denied. We are told, for
example, that it is a mistake to say 'God is good'. If we speak
strictly, we must say 'God is goodness'.

All this raises questions as to the sense in which God is said to
exist. The doctrine does not mean that God exists as a universal
exists, or even as a real essence exists. It means that He exists both
as an individual and as a universal; and we have here a real essence
which is supposed to determine one individual, and only one individual, through and through. This may seem merely to repeat the
ontological argument in different language. But, in any case, if
God's essence and His existence are indistinguishable, there can be
no inference from one to the other. The ontological argument has
become an assertion, intelligible, if at all, in the light of a whole
philosophy.

A similar development may be found in philosophies of a very different kind. An idealist, for example, may reject the common-sense distinction between our thinking and what we think, and may tell us that to be real is to be thought—no doubt in some rather special sense of the word 'thought'. As is sometimes said—not without risk of ambiguity—'The real is the rational, and the rational is the real'. In such a setting the ontological argument may again find its place, although it will no longer be a simple inference, but rather the assertion of a principle which is worked out in a whole philosophy and must stand or fall with that philosophy as a whole. Doctrines of this type are found in Hegel and his followers, and the philosophy of Hegel is not to be disposed of in a couple of paragraphs. It is enough to say that it makes claims to a knowledge of ultimate reality which are not easy to accept.

Even if we are willing to adopt such theories, it is hard to see how the ontological argument can be valid for us unless we can have knowledge of God's perfection, and indeed of His essence, as He is in Himself. So bold an assumption is not to be lightly made. Philosophers and saints alike may be shocked at Hegel's claim for his own logic, when he says that 'The content of logic is the representation of God as He is in His eternal essence and before the creation of nature and any mortal mind'. If St. Thomas rejected the ontological argument on the ground that no human being can know God as He is in His eternal essence, perhaps he is to be congratulated on his modesty and good sense.

§ 5. *The concept of perfection*

So far nothing has been said about the origin of our concept of perfection. How do we arrive at it? Is it merely a concept that we happen to have?

The simplest view would be that we derive it from our acquaintance with degrees of excellence. We find, particularly in human beings, a gradation from the less powerful to the more powerful, the less wise to the more wise, the less good to the more good. We suppose this gradation to be completed ideally in a being that is most powerful, most wise, most good—or even all-powerful, all-wise, all-good. We conceive certain human qualities as raised, so to speak, to a higher power—indeed to the highest possible power—and we apply them by analogy to God. Thus we speak of God as possessing absolute might, absolute wisdom, absolute goodness, and it is such characteristics that are conceived in our concept of perfection. If we believe in degrees of reality, we may also suppose the divine perfection to cover the possession of supreme or absolute reality. This is the basic supposition of the present argument.

Some thinkers would hold that by this means we get no clear concept at all—we use the word 'perfection', but we have no corresponding concept. Even if we have such a concept, it must be inadequate to God's nature since it is derived mainly from human qualities known to us. In any case we have now adulterated the ontological argument with elements drawn from experience— precisely what we are claiming to avoid.

It may be replied to this that so far from our concept of perfection being drawn from experience, it is, on the contrary, pre-supposed by experience—if the word 'experience' may be used to cover awareness of degrees of excellence. We can say that one man is more wise or more good than another only because we already possess the notion of absolute wisdom and absolute goodness—even if this notion is first evoked by experience of lesser degrees of wisdom and goodness. How could we know that anything is imperfect unless we already had some notion of perfection?

This kind of argument is unfashionable at the present time. It does not follow that it is invalid. But even if we accept it, there is at least a risk that we are still contaminating the unsullied purity of the ontological argument. There is a danger that we may now be arguing, not first from knowledge that the imperfect exists to our concept of perfection and then from our concept of perfection to the existence of the perfect, but directly from the existence of the imperfect to the existence of the perfect. This is quite a different kind of argument: it is no longer an ontological argument from pure thought to existence. The direct argument from existent imperfections to an existent perfection, as we shall see later, comes much more naturally to ordinary men than the ontological argument; and it is probably true that unless the argument from existent imperfections had already been used (and perhaps found incomplete), the ontological argument would never have been invented. But this does not justify us in confusing two arguments that are fundamentally different.

In Kant's *Critique of Pure Reason* we can find a much more elaborate account of the concept of the most real being (*ens realissimum*) as the basis of the ontological proof. He arrives at it by considering such abstract logical questions as the synthesis of all possible predicates and the relation of negation to affirmation. Such complexities lie outside our present scope. We must try to look at the ontological argument free from all possible accretions; and in order to do this most effectively it is safer for the present to regard the concept of perfection as like the high priest Melchizedek—without father, without mother, and without descent.

§ 6. *Existence*

Let us turn to the 'being' or existence' we are supposed to infer legitimately from our concept of perfection.

There is much ambiguity in the word 'exists' and still more in the word 'is'. We say readily enough that the conspiracy existed only in his imagination or even that centaurs existed only in Greek mythology. This usage is frowned on by sticklers for precision, but at least we can be sure that such imaginary existence is the last thing the supporters of the ontological argument wish to ascribe to God. Similarly we might perhaps say that some things exist as objects of thought—for example, propositions or even mathematical triangles. Some philosophers would prefer to say that these 'subsist' rather than 'exist', while others would repudiate such language altogether. But here again the ontological argument manifestly does not seek to prove that God exists or subsists as an object of thought. On the contrary, it seeks to pass from the premise that God exists as an object of thought (an object thought under the concept of perfection) to the conclusion that He must exist in Himself, independently of all our thinking. It is precisely this transition that is so difficult to follow.

We do not help ourselves very much when we say that if anything exists in any strict sense, it exists in itself independently of our thinking and imagining; for we are only using the word 'exists' over again. Perhaps it is impossible to say more than that existence is existence, and that if we do not know what existence is, then nobody can tell us. But in the case of finite things, like tables and chairs, we can indicate the conditions under which we are prepared to say that they exist. It is not enough to say that we must be able to see or touch them; for in certain pathological states (perhaps even when artificially induced) men are credibly said to see, and even to touch, things that do not exist at all. Material objects exist only if they are open to public inspection and have a determinate position in public time and space. This means that they must be subject to causal laws—or at least to laws accepted by physics and in some degree by common sense. If we believe that such things as electrons exist, we do so on the ground that although they cannot be observed themselves, they are connected by physical laws with objects open to public inspection. It is more difficult to speak of finite minds even in this over-simplified way, because they appear to have a determinate position in time but not in space—except in the sense that they are connected somehow with a body which is in space. But these refinements we can here neglect.

When we say that God exists, we do not mean to assert that He occupies a determinate position in public time and space or that He is subject to physical laws. The conditions under which we assert His existence are not the conditions under which we assert the existence of material objects or even of finite minds. Hence if we choose to define existence by reference to the conditions under which finite objects are said to exist, we cannot say that God exists. The word 'exists' like any other word can be applied to God only by analogy with our ordinary usage. We have to think away the conditions under which the word is applied to finite beings; and this is why it is hard to be certain what we are thinking when we say that God exists.

There are some who infer from such considerations that it is meaningless to speak of God's existence. But there are others who infer that the concept of God's existence is supremely intelligible because it can be grasped by pure thought without any reference to the conditions under which we have sensuous experience of finite objects. These are the two extremes, and the second of them is the one which finds expression in the ontological argument.

It is wise not to be too dogmatic on either side. If a thinker proposes to apply the word 'exists' only to finite things in time and space, then—for him—a statement that something exists outside time and space is by definition meaningless. He has made it impossible for himself to say significantly that God exists; he has perhaps closed his own mind to problems hitherto considered important; but he has not even contradicted, much less disproved, the theological assertion that God exists; for no reputable theologian would affirm that God exists as a finite object in space and time. On the other hand, he has challenged the theologian to explain what can be meant by the existence of an infinite being, not in time and not in space.

The theologian, in his turn, can afford even less to be dogmatic;

for he has to admit that he ascribes existence to God only by analogy. The thought that something not finite may exist, though not in space and time, may be a necessary thought (if we allow our thinking to stray beyond the problems soluble by science); but it is purely negative and tells us nothing about the positive character of such a possible existence. To find any positive character the theologian may have recourse, perhaps he must have recourse, to a consideration of the existence of finite minds; and he may say that to exist is to be active in thinking and willing. But here again he has to ascribe such activities, and consequently such existence, to God only by analogy. Furthermore, if to be temporal is to be finite, he has to say that God's thinking and willing is not in time, and to face the objection that in that case we cannot understand it as thinking and willing at all.

The theologian has to admit that he sees God in a mirror—in a riddle. He is even forced into paradoxes. For him God is everywhere, and yet nowhere. If the expression may be used, God is everywhen, and yet nowhen. God must be conceived as thinking, but not as we think; as willing, but not as we will; as existing, but not as we exist. It may be possible to show that these paradoxes necessarily arise from the limitations of our own finite thinking; but to say we know that God must exist because we understand so clearly the nature of His existence is to arrogate to ourselves an insight wholly beyond our finite human powers.

§ 7. *The inference from perfection to existence*

With these considerations in mind we can now try to look at the ontological argument as a bare logical inference which professes to be valid in itself.

Unless perfection, when ascribed to God, were understood in a very special sense, the inference to God's existence would not even be plausible. We do not argue that a perfect man must exist, because if he did not exist, he would not be perfect. Such an argument would be received only with derision. But parallels of this kind always arouse the ire of those who champion the ontological argument. They tell us—not always too politely—we must be stupid not to see that the argument holds for one special concept and for that only. This, however, is precisely what they are being asked to prove. Those who seek to refute the argument by the use of such workaday parallels hold it to be a characteristic of concepts *as such* that we cannot pass from them to the reality of what is conceived; and they deny flatly that any concept can be so special as to justify an exception to this rule. All you can do with any concept by a purely logical operation is to analyse it and so to make clearer what you are already thinking. You cannot argue from a concept to an existent object. You can only argue from one existent object to another.

If we take an ordinary empirical concept, like the concept of elephant, we should never dream of saying that we could prove the existence of elephants merely by analysing the concept. In order to show that elephants exist we must, as it were, go beyond our concept and appeal to observation or experience. In technical language 'Elephants exist' is a synthetic, and not an analytic, proposition.

From a logical point of view the proposition 'A perfect being exists' is on exactly the same footing. If we could go beyond our concept of perfect being and appeal to experience of God—whether by means of a unique feeling or a special sense or a faculty of divination—we might say that we had shown the existence of a perfect being adequate to our concept. The extreme difficulty of any such claim we have already seen; for no feeling, however unique, and no sense, however special, can by itself be experience of a perfect being. But this difficulty need not trouble us here. The whole point of the ontological argument is that no such experience is necessary: we can show that God exists merely by analysing the concept of a perfect being.

This is surely a quite incredible claim. Even if we admit that the concept of a perfect being includes within itself, not only the concept of absolute goodness, absolute wisdom, and so on, but also the concept of absolute reality, we have still to get somehow from the concept of absolute reality to absolute reality itself. If these are different, how can we make the transition? If they are identical, how can there be a transition at all? Are we perhaps combining two contradictory views and supposing ourselves to pass from one to the other on the hidden assumption that there is no difference between them?

It is no use telling us in this connexion that all our concepts must refer to reality and that we are making a false separation between conception and reality. If our concepts can refer to reality, the separation has already been made. And although all our thinking may in some sense refer to reality, this is the reason why our judgements can be false as well as true. Our concept of chimaera refers in some way to reality; for it is the concept of an animal with a lion's head, a goat's body, and a serpent's tail. But, in spite of this, when we judge that chimaeras exist, our judgement is false. Similarly we all, let us hope, have some experience of wisdom, of goodness, and even of existence; but if it be granted that these can be conceived as absolute and as all combined in the concept of a perfect being, it does not follow that we make a true judgement when we say 'A perfect being must exist'.

It would be sheer sophistry to tell us that even if we can infer the existent only from the existent, we can nevertheless infer the existent from a concept since a concept is itself an existent. This is a mere abuse of language; for concepts do not exist in the same sense as things. If the statement that concepts exist is taken to mean that a particular thought occurs at a particular time, we are no farther on. The ontological argument is based on what I am thinking, not on the fact that I am having a particular thought now.

§ 8. *Existence is not a quality*

It will be replied, with some acerbity, that the concept of perfect being is still being treated as if it were an ordinary concept: it is a very special concept with the special property of guaranteeing the existence of its object. To say this, however, is only to repeat once more what we are asking to be proved and not merely asserted. And even those who use this language assimilate the concept of a perfect being to ordinary concepts in certain respects. Some of them tell us we can know that a perfect being must exist as certainly as we can know that a triangle, defined as a three-sided figure, must have its three interior angles equal to two right angles.

Here I must confess that I am in the unhappy position of not even being able to infer from a mere analysis of the *concept* of a three-sided figure that a three-sided figure must have three angles. In order to see this I have first of all to consider how a three-sided figure can be constructed either on paper or in imagination; but this disability may be due to a lack of acquaintance with the higher mathematics. I am, however, able to infer from analysis of the concept of a three-sided figure that a three-sided figure must have three sides; and I am willing to suppose that all mathematical thinking can be reduced to similar analytic operations.

What are we to make of this parallel between mathematical thinking and the ontological argument? It appears to imply that existence is an extra quality which is thought in the concept of perfect being

along with other qualities like absolute wisdom and absolute power
—just as three-angledness is an extra quality which is thought in the
concept of a three-sided figure. But it is sheer error to regard existence as one quality among others. Existence is not a quality at all.
A thing with all its qualities either exists or it does not. It receives
no additional quality by existing. The dodo as an animal species is
unfortunately now extinct; but the concept of dodo, even if it could
be a concept of all the qualities in the dodo, is precisely the same
concept whether the dodo exists or not.

The objection to the ontological argument may also be put in
linguistic terms. If we decide to say that a being is perfect only when
we are able to say that it exists, we are entitled to say that a perfect
being must exist. But this alleged necessity is a logical necessity
based on the use of language, and it should not be mistaken for an
insight into the real necessity of things. If, in spite of protests, I may
again resort to ordinary concepts, we might also decide to say that a
thing is an elephant only if it exists; and after all how could it be an
elephant unless it did exist? But if we inferred from this that an
elephant must exist, meaning anything more than that we should
refuse to call anything an elephant unless it did exist, we should
merely be deceiving ourselves. The existence of a thing does not
depend on the usage of a word.

Such a linguistic interpretation would—with complete consistency—be repudiated by those who claim to know real essences and
their interconnexions by means of pure thinking. Even if we are
unable to agree with them, we may find at least plausible the
doctrine that human beings can 'see' a necessary connexion between
being good and being intelligent, or even between being supremely
good and being supremely intelligent—a necessary connexion based
on something more ultimate than an arbitrary use of words. But
when we are told that they can also 'see' a necessary connexion
between being perfect and actually existing, the position is far
otherwise. The relation between perfection and real existence cannot be assimilated, except by the grossest confusion, to a relation
between interconnected qualities.

If this contention is sound, it is fatal to any ontological proof of
God's existence; and, in spite of a recent attempt to prove otherwise,
it is equally fatal to any ontological disproof of God's existence. If
the ontological argument is ever to become valid by being incor-
porated into the structure of some philosophical system, it will have
to suffer a sea-change in the process. Yet the fallacy, even in its

simplest form, is not so easy to detect that we need despise men who accepted the argument in circumstances very different from our own; and not many of us would be able to say where the argument had gone wrong if we were meeting it for the first time.

§ 9. *Theoretical argument and religious conviction*

It may seem that a great deal of energy and time has been spent on arriving at a purely negative conclusion, which most of us could reach by inspection—namely, that the ontological argument is not valid. But we may also have gained something more positive— perhaps a slightly better understanding of some of the concepts men have used in trying to think about God. At least we may have seen that concepts applicable to finite beings cannot be used literally in thinking about God, but only by some sort of analogy. This may warn us against accepting a too crude theology, which inevitably leads to an equally crude rejection of theology.

We embarked on this enquiry, not for its own sake, but in the hope of getting some light on the intellectual factor in religious experience. Perhaps we have not been too successful even here. The plain religious man, and even the saint, may make little use of the concepts we have considered in abstraction, but they do make some use of them. Furthermore, it is true to say that what is nowadays— sometimes rather confusedly—called an 'attitude' presumes a certain character in its object, even when there is little or no attempt to set forth this character in conceptual terms. The religious attitude is an attitude of worship, and we may say that it presumes an object of worship which is and is perfect. We may even perhaps say that it presumes an object of worship which not only exists but exists necessarily and unconditionally—which has no source or ground in anything other than itself.

Some of us may think it would be better for religion if men worshipped perfection without what has been called its 'fallacious existential trimmings'; but this fails to satisfy a religious need which has its roots very deep in human nature. Men can worship only a God who is. Perhaps those who elaborated the ontological argument were working out unconsciously, on a high level of abstraction, some more obscure, and perhaps more fundamental, process of thought and feeling deeply involved in religious experience. This does not make the argument valid and may even be taken to throw doubt on the deeper process which it is alleged to express. We may be told that the ontological argument is a fallacious rationalization of an irrational process which is equally fallacious—a mere projection of our own desires, a kind of wishful thinking now made only too clear.

Whatever we may think of this, it seems that pure thinking, detached from experience and from life, is unable to give us knowledge of God's existence—or of His non-existence. In this respect it resembles pure feeling detached from thought. But pure feeling permeated by thought may be at least a source of personal religious conviction, even if this fails to pass the test of philosophy. If religious experience is of the whole man, it is unlikely to fit neatly into our tidy pigeon-holes; and in it feeling and thought appear so to interpenetrate that to some minds the very thought of a perfect or most real being whose existence springs from, or is identical with, his essence may be a source of numinous feeling and so of religious conviction. Perhaps after all we have learned something of the intellectual factor in religious experience. Even although the ontological argument is the one that comes least naturally to us, it does seem to express in its own arid intellectual way a demand of religious consciousness itself.

Chapter XIII

THE ARGUMENT FROM IMPERFECTION

§ 1. *The cosmological argument*

If we are unable to derive knowledge of God's existence from the bare concept of perfection, we may perhaps hope to infer His existence from our experience of the world. But here we must distinguish between *particular* experiences and *general* experience (or experience as such). The ordinary religious man, so far as he argues at all, would probably argue to God's existence from particular experiences of what he takes to be manifestations of a divine purpose—from the beauty of the hills, from the marvellous construction of living things, and so on. But it is possible to argue from some characteristics of *all* objects of experience—from a categorial characteristic, as it may be called. Thus it may be held that all objects of experience must have a cause, and therefore there must be a first or uncaused cause, to which we give the name of 'God'.

Even if, as is often done, we begin with one particular existent thing—for example, myself—and maintain that since this must have a cause, there must be a first cause, we are not arguing from any *special* characteristic distinguishing this object of experience from others: we are arguing from a universal or categorial characteristic—the characteristic of being caused—which it shares with all other finite objects of experience; and we start from this particular object only because we know that it exists.

All arguments of this type are varieties of what is called the 'cosmological' proof: they seek to make an inference from some categorial characteristic of an experienced object or objects to the universe or cosmos as a whole, and so to the God who is its cause or ground. Because they appeal to experience, they can begin with something known to exist and thus escape the paradoxes of the ontological argument. Yet they appeal—and this is the essential point—not to a rich and full and diversified experience, but to its bare bones. The inference, so to speak, is not from the living body of experience, but only from its skeleton. Hence the cosmological argument is arid, and it may be asked whether it is worth while trying to make these dry bones live.

If the ontological proof is described as the argument from perfection, the cosmological proof may be described by contrast as the argument from imperfection. In it we have no need to struggle from a mere concept to existence; for if we begin with the imperfect, we have only too much assurance that it exists. But the imperfect must here be taken to be the incomplete, the finite, the contingent. The imperfect or contingent is what it is only because of some cause or ground beyond itself; and all objects of experience are in this sense imperfect. A perfect being, on the other hand, is supposed to be its own ground or cause; and this is why men have thought they could argue from the concept or essence of a perfect being to its existence without having recourse to anything beyond the concept itself.

The cosmological proof, as an argument from imperfection, must also be contrasted with the argument from design. The argument from design too rests on experience, but on a more rich and diversified experience—on experience of perfections in the world. An inference may be made, for example, from the perfection of living creatures to the perfection of their designer or creator. Such an inference rests on a particular experience of some objects in the world, not on a general experience of finite objects as such; and the perfection from which it argues is a special kind of perfection—the perfect adaptation of organs to what is supposed to be their purpose.

If the cosmological argument holds at all, it must hold for any world in which objects are the effect of causes other than themselves. Hence it would be valid even if the only world we experienced were Hell—provided we were able to trace a relation of cause and effect between one torment and the next. As we should hardly be justified in conceiving as God a first cause whose sole known product was an Inferno, it seems that the cosmological argument, even if it can prove the existence of something, cannot prove without the aid of further premises that this 'something' is God. The difficulty is thus, so to speak, the reverse of that found in the ontological argument ; for this, even if it may have a more adequate conception of God, is unable to prove the existence of anything.

In order to remedy the fatal defects of these two arguments when taken separately it is not surprising that men should run them both together—or confuse one with the other. Such a procedure should be subjected to the closest scrutiny. We are not very likely to get one valid argument by combining two that are in themselves invalid; and if we are serious in our attempts to support religious beliefs by a theoretical proof, we must be very sure that the proof is not fallacious.

§ 2. *The five ways of St. Thomas*

If the cosmological argument, in its many forms, were solely of historical interest, we might pass it by in respectful silence. At present it finds little support or even consideration outside the followers of neo-scholasticism, but we cannot say that it is everywhere abandoned. The Roman Catholic Church is heavily committed to the teaching of St. Thomas Aquinas by the encyclical *Aeterni Patris* of Pope Leo XIII in 1879, not to mention others of more recent date. Furthermore, although modern man may not find this type of argument convincing, at least it does not strike him as merely artificial—which the ontological argument most certainly does. Even the relatively unthinking may find themselves asking questions about the origin of the world and of themselves. If the present distaste for metaphysics and for religion itself were to give way to some other fashion, the old questions, and even the old answers, might arise from their graves and show signs of renewed life. To the sophisticated they may appear moribund, even if they are not wholly dead; but at least they are not unnatural, and we are not entitled to assume that they can throw no light whatever on the intellectual factor in religious experience.

The classical exposition of the cosmological argument may be found in the *Summa Theologica* of St. Thomas—in the famous 'five ways' of proving the existence of God.

As we are here concerned only with forms of the cosmological argument, two of these 'ways' may be ignored; for one is an argument from design, and another an argument from the inferior value of finite things—from their imperfection in a narrower sense than the one I have used. Even if we chose to regard the second as a special form of the cosmological argument, we should be unlikely to find it more convincing than the others.

We have therefore only three ways of argument to consider. The first is from the fact of motion to the existence of a first or unmoved mover. The second is from finite things as effects to the existence of a first or uncaused cause. The third is from finite things as contingent beings to the existence of a non-contingent or necessary being. And, according to St. Thomas, whether we speak of a first mover, a first cause, or a necessary being, this is what all men speak of as God.

It is obvious that the first argument is only a particular application of the second, which in its turn is only a particular application of the third. As the first argument is thus the least abstract, a brief summary of it may serve as the most concrete illustration of the general line of thought.

According to St. Thomas, whatever is in motion must be put in motion by something else; and if that something else is in motion, it too must be put in motion by something else. But this regress, he tells us, cannot go on to infinity because then there would be no first mover, and therefore no other mover—that is, there would be no movement at all. Consequently there must be a first mover put in motion by no other; 'and this everyone understands to be God'.

We need not examine this argument in detail. The proof is based, not merely on the metaphysics of Aristotle, but on his physics; and the not inconsiderable advance of physics since his time makes it necessary, at the very least, to readjust the whole argument. The more general proofs may not be affected to the same extent, but all the 'five ways' can be understood properly only by reference to an Aristotelian background (such as the doctrine of the four types of cause). With great honesty and acuteness St. Thomas used the best knowledge available at his time to support and expand doctrines which he believed were already firmly established by revelation. But there is no blinking the fact that much of what he took for granted would be questioned, or denied outright, by most philosophers and scientists of the present day.

§ 3. *The conditioned*

We must try to look at the cosmological argument in a general way without troubling too much about its varied historical forms.

The argument starts by assuming that we know something to exist. This 'something' is not uncommonly taken to be myself, partly because accomplished doubters have found it harder to doubt their own existence than that of other things, and partly perhaps because we have a personal interest in our own existence. But we can begin just as well with any object of experience if we are certain that it is not a mere product of our imagination. We are trying to get down to some hard fact with no nonsense about it.

N

Whatever we may choose as our starting point, we are not concerned with its special characteristics. What interests us is merely that its existence depends on something else. This we express variously by saying that it is finite or limited or incomplete or imperfect. We can put this point more technically by saying that it is *contingent*. The whole argument is sometimes described as the argument from the contingency of the world or—more briefly—as the argument from contingency.

The word 'contingent' has many different meanings, which it is impossible to pursue here. We may say that a thing is contingent if it might have been otherwise. My existence is said to be contingent if I might not have existed. But this is not enough for the cosmological argument. In it we assume that anything contingent is dependent on something else. It would not be what it is but for something else; and indeed it must be what it is because of something else.

This is puzzling. The contingent is *opposed* to the necessary—opposed to what is taken to be necessary in itself or to what could not conceivably have been otherwise. Yet the contingent is also said *to be* necessary—necessary, not in itself, but subject to some condition or cause other than itself. The contingent is thus the *relatively* necessary: it is opposed to the non-contingent or *absolutely* necessary.

Perhaps we are making too heavy weather of all this. For the purposes of the argument—it may be thought—I have only to assume that I should not be what I am, and indeed that I should not be at all, but for some cause other than myself. And the same would apply to any object of experience.

The relation of effect to cause is certainly the simplest case to keep in mind when we try to follow the cosmological argument. But the argument itself is aiming, as we shall see, at something more general, something harder to put in ordinary words. It takes the cause to be the *condition* or *ground* of the effect and not merely to be something that invariably precedes the effect in time. What it is concerned with is the general relation of the condition to what it conditions; and it takes the relation between cause and effect to be only one case of this more general relation (which may be called the relation between the condition and the conditioned or even between ground and consequent). We speak of cause and effect only when the cause precedes the effect in time. But there are other cases where the condition does not precede in time what is conditioned by it.

For example, if we think that space is the condition of motion, we do not mean by this that space must first exist by itself and that motion comes into existence later as its effect.

Thus, speaking generally, *the contingent is what depends on a condition other than itself ;* hence it may be described also as the conditioned (as opposed to the unconditioned or the absolutely necessary). But we should not assume that its condition must necessarily be its cause or must precede it in time. The reason for insisting on these complications will be seen later.

It must be said at once that to many modern philosophers all this is a complete muddle. They do not regard causes as the condition of their effects ; and they consider it sheer confusion to speak of one real object as the condition of another. Like David Hume, they are unable to perceive any 'real connexion among distinct existences'. For them the whole assumption confuses purely logical relations with real ones.

This is a formidable objection. It is hard to deny that supporters of the cosmological argument fell into confusions of this type; and it is certain that they did not adequately consider the difficulties. We may not be prepared to accept the objection as it stands, and we may believe that the philosophy of these critics is itself inadequate and unsatisfactory, but we cannot afford to dismiss as unimportant the questions which they raise.

It would, however, take us far beyond our present scope even to touch on the fringe of these problems. All that need be said here is this. The cosmological argument rests on the common-sense assumption that things which exist do so under a condition—for example, they exist only if they have been caused to exist by something else. If this assumption is mistaken, the argument fails.

§ 4. *The unconditioned*

If we can conceive a contingent being, it requires no supreme effort of metaphysical genius to conceive a non-contingent being— a necessary or unconditioned being. At the very least we are all able to prefix the word 'non' to the word 'contingent', and to equate the combined word 'non-contingent' with the word 'necessary'. But why should anybody want to do this? We may perhaps be able to understand why, if we go back to the more concrete relation of effect to cause.

We find that something exists, but we think it might not have existed, and we wish to understand *why* it exists. It exists, we may be told, because it has been caused to exist by something else. But this 'something else' too might equally not have existed, and so in its turn must have been caused to exist by another 'something else'. We seem to have embarked on an infinite regress; and if this is so, we shall never find any cause that is not just as contingent as the thing with which we began. Hence we get no satisfactory answer to our original question, and we remain as dissatisfied as we were at the beginning, seeking an explanation, but finding none. We are tempted to say that if the world is to be intelligible, we must in time come to a first cause which has no further cause, one which is not contingent but absolutely necessary—which does not need to be explained by anything else, but is, so to speak, its own explanation and the explanation of everything else.

But there is more to the argument than this. Let us suppose that the regress is infinite—that we could go back and back from one contingent cause to another for ever and ever. Even so, if some contingent being exists, then all its preceding causes must have existed; for otherwise it would not be at all. We are therefore logically obliged to conceive the sum total (or totality) of its causes. What is more, we are obliged to conceive that totality as itself existent—in the sense that all its members must have existed. But this totality of causes, if it is a totality (whether infinite or not), can by definition have no further cause. Considered as a totality it must therefore itself either contain or be an uncaused existent. If so, it must itself either contain or be a non-contingent or unconditioned or necessary being. In short, if something exists, a necessary being exists.

This may help to explain why men come to use the concept of a non-contingent or unconditioned or necessary being, and why they feel entitled to say that a necessary being must exist. If we allow further that the totality of conditions for any contingent existent must be the universe or cosmos, we begin to understand why this is called the cosmological proof. What we have not yet been able to understand is why it should be regarded as a proof of the existence of God. To see this we must take another step.

§ 5. *Time and the unconditioned*

We seem to be faced with two alternatives, to each of which there are serious objections.

On the first alternative we suppose that we could in time come to a first cause, and that this first cause would be the first member of the whole series of causes. If this is so, the first cause—or at least its causal action—must be an event in time, and this at once gets us into difficulties.

Every time seems to be conditioned by a previous time—can we seriously think of a time which had no preceding time, of a present without a past? Is there any sense in asking ourselves 'At what time did time begin'? And since time can be known only by the events in it, can we seriously believe that there could be any event without a previous event? The sole reason why we entered on our argument was the supposition that every event must have a preceding cause. Why should we abandon that supposition now—unless we do so merely because we are getting tired? And if we are prepared to do so now, why should we not regard every event as a first cause and a necessary being in itself? Why should we ever have started out on this weary pilgrimage? It seems that if there can be a first cause or a necessary being, this must be something that cannot exist in a part of time at all—it must exist outside time altogether, and so can never be an object of experience.

But perhaps it might exist throughout the whole of time: we might be able to regard the whole infinite series of causes itself, if not as a first cause, at least as an uncaused or unconditioned or necessary being. This is our second alternative, but it seems no less unsatisfactory.

St. Thomas, it will be remembered, says roundly that the regress of causes cannot go on to infinity; but he might not have been so sure of this if he had not already learned from revelation that the world had a beginning in time. We may hesitate to say *a priori* either that the world must, or again must not, have a beginning in time—still more to say that time itself must, or again must not, have a beginning. But even if we allow that the totality of causes is infinite; even if we allow that as a totality it can have no farther cause; it still seems absurd to say that a totality of causes each of which is admittedly contingent must itself be unconditionally necessary. If we do say so, can we attach any positive meaning to our statement?

We can get no light on this question from experience, for we experience nothing but contingent events. If the totality of contingent events could be an object of experience, it too would be a contingent event like any other. Hence on this second alternative also it seems that we must look beyond experience, beyond events in time and even beyond the totality of events in time, if we are to find any being which can plausibly be described as non-contingent and as necessary in itself. We must also look beyond events in space, although space has been neglected for the sake of brevity.

Considerations of this kind have led men to believe that if the world is to be intelligible, there must be a non-contingent and necessary being which is not itself in space and time, but which is the first cause of all contingent beings in space and time. Since the word 'cause' has always a reference to time—the cause precedes the effect—it is here applied by analogy to what is timeless, to the ultimate *condition* or *ground* of all conditioned beings. This ultimate condition, we are told, must itself be unconditioned and so must be a necessary being. It is this necessary being to which we give the name of 'God'. If anything exists, He must exist. The whole spatio-temporal cosmos is itself contingent: it has its ground in a God who exists necessarily and is neither spatial nor temporal.

When we say that God is a necessary being, we do not mean merely that we must necessarily assume Him to exist if the universe is to be intelligible. God is not necessary merely as the postulated cause of some effect, nor could He conceivably be necessary as the effect of some cause. What we mean is that God is necessary, not relatively to something else, but absolutely and in Himself. If the universe is contingent—and this is the whole point of the argument —it must have an uncaused cause, an unconditioned condition, an ungrounded ground; and only a being necessary in Himself can be such a cause or condition or ground.

§ 6. *Necessary being*

In the cosmological argument we begin with a contingent thing known to exist and we progress by means of three steps—or perhaps we should say jumps. First we jump to its condition in time and space. Then we jump to the totality of its conditions in time and space. And finally we jump right outside time and space to an unconditioned condition, which we describe as a necessary being. These jumps become progressively more difficult—or at least they become more and more repugnant to many modern philosophers. But even if we can dispose of all objections, where have we finally landed? We made each jump because we felt our footing to be precarious. Have we found firm ground at last?

Our conclusion appears to be curiously negative. We are told indeed that God exists and is the cause or condition or ground of the universe. All these terms admittedly can apply to God only by analogy; but when we ask for further light on their meaning as applied to God, we seem to be answered by pure negations. God does not exist in time and space; and He has no cause, no condition, no ground, other than Himself. Even when we are told that He is a necessary being, we are not using the word 'necessary' in the sense in which it is applied to contingent beings. As applied to God it does not mean 'necessary subject to a condition': it means 'necessary subject to no condition'. When we drop the condition which is ordinarily supposed to make necessity intelligible, do we get an absolute necessity which can be regarded as supremely intelligible? Or are we merely playing with words?

So far the concept of God as an absolutely necessary being is entirely vague and indeterminate. Something is supposed in some sense to exist, but we are told nothing more about it except what it is not. If we are to mean anything definite, we must make the negative concept of a non-contingent or necessary being into a positive one. How is this to be done?

The first step is to say that a necessary being is its own ground, its own condition, its own cause. This statement is itself sufficiently bold, and we may wonder in what sense, and with what justification, these words are now being used. If we ask what all this means, we are invited to take yet a further step. A necessary being is one whose non-existence is inconceivable—that is, it is one whose essence is the ground of its existence.

These words have a familiar ring. We have been edged back gradually to the old ontological argument, which we are now asked to take for granted. The non-existence of a being can be inconceivable only if we possess a concept which guarantees the existence of its object—the concept of an essence which is also a ground of existence.

Unless we can show that we possess such a concept—whether it be the concept of a perfect being, a supreme being, or a most real being—the whole cosmological argument must fail to prove the existence of an absolutely necessary being in any positive sense. If our previous discussion was sound, there is no concept which can guarantee the existence of its object. And if we could prove by analysis of any concept that its object must necessarily exist, there would be no need to bolster up our proof by an appeal to the dubious inferences and indeterminate concepts and mainly negative conclusion of the cosmological argument.

If this is true, it is hardly necessary to remind ourselves that even if the cosmological argument were valid, it would not be a proof of the existence of God. Since it would hold for any universe, however diabolical, in which there were contingent beings, the most it could prove without further premises would be that a being existed with the divine attribute of self-sufficiency. Even the ontological proof would not be a proof of the existence of God unless the concept of perfection were a concept of more than self-sufficiency—or unless it could be shown that it is impossible for the devil to be self-sufficient.

To sum up—the cosmological argument cannot prove the existence of God without the aid of the ontological argument, and this may be the underlying reason why the ontological argument had to be invented. If the ontological argument is valid, the cosmological argument is superfluous. If the ontological argument is invalid, the cosmological argument must be invalid too. The religious man has to walk by faith and not by sight; and in view of the difficulty of this discussion he may be tempted to thank God that it has pleased Him not to save His people by means of dialectic.

§ 7. *Metaphysics*

Metaphysical arguments, as was pointed out earlier, may look very different within the context of a whole philosophy; but if those we have considered are fair samples, it is hard to resist the conclusion—at least the provisional conclusion—that the existence of God cannot be demonstrated by pure metaphysics. Quite certainly it cannot be demonstrated by any kind of scientific proof; and if we have made up our minds to listen only to scientific proofs, there is no more to be said.

How is it that supremely able men have entertained such difficult concepts and indulged in such abstruse arguments, asking themselves unanswerable questions about the physical universe as a whole, and about what may lie beyond it? Some modern philosophers appear to hold that these problems spring from elementary confusions about words, but this view is perhaps a trifle ingenuous. Others regard interest in these questions as pathological. The nature of the disease in question is seldom diagnosed in any detail, but we are sometimes offered a system of philosophical therapeutics which professes itself able to effect a cure.

There are critics inconsiderate enough to throw doubt on the scientific character of the therapeutics; but there is a prior question to be raised. Is an interest in such ultimate matters properly diagnosed as a form of mental disease, or at least of mental disability?

It is certainly not unnatural or artificial to ask questions of the kind described; but if these questions cannot be answered, it may seem plausible to condemn them as diseased. It is not unnatural, but it may be diseased, when men with weak heads on a precipitous path keep thinking about the dangers of a fall or are unable to avert their eyes from the fatal depths below. They may be well advised to keep their eyes on the immediate situation, and their minds on the next step. On the precipitous path of life perhaps some men will fare better if they do the same. Even from a religious point of view Cardinal Newman could say

'I do not ask to see
The distant scene—one step enough for me'.

But perhaps he would not have felt this to be a religious attitude, had he not been aware of the encircling gloom as well as of the kindly light. If a philosophical therapeutics has been devised to circumscribe the view of those who are afraid to face the distant scene, we may wish it every success. Yet it may be unhealthy to induce an artificial myopia, as it is unhealthy to ignore or forget hidden feelings of fear or guilt. The best way to deal with hidden troubles is to bring them into the open; and in intellectual matters the fatal error is to deceive ourselves, whether by pretending we have solved a problem when we have not, or by pretending that there is no problem to solve.

All these questions, and the concepts—or 'Ideas'—they employ, spring inevitably from the drive in our own thinking towards wholeness or completeness. This movement in thinking is supremely healthy: without it thinking would stop altogether instead of going on, as it does, from cause to cause, from narrower to wider generalizations, from isolated observations to systematic theories. This process is precisely what men have regarded as the function of reason, without, if I may say so, imagining that reason was a mysterious entity exercising some sort of pressure—or prod—on what we think or do. We are only carrying on the same function if we ask ourselves whether the process itself could be completed, and what kind of knowledge we should have if it were. It is true we fall into error or illusion if we suppose that by such reflexions we can acquire scientific knowledge of ultimate reality; but the cure for this can only be a deeper understanding of what it is that we are doing.

It may be a positive gain to grasp the limits of scientific reasoning, and indeed of all human reasoning. If we try to work out the logical implications of our scientific thinking and to apply our fundamental concepts, not to a part of reality, but to the whole, we are bound to fall into contradictions and paradoxes—to meet difficulties we are unable to surmount and questions we are incompetent to answer. In particular we are bound to ask whether the world as it is known, or even as it could be known, to science is intelligible, and whether we are entitled to entertain, however obscurely, the concept of a 'something' beyond time and space, or at least of a blank—perhaps even of a vaguely God-shaped blank—outside the bounds of our ordinary experience. It is not too hard to see how concepts of the kind we have examined must arise from the very nature of human thinking, and how they have to be used in thinking about God, if we think about Him at all. It is not even too hard to see how they must be mainly negative, and how they must be inadequate to anything that could be regarded as an ultimate reality.

There are many to-day who regard such thinking with repugnance, and they are justified in saying that the manipulation of such concepts—though it has certainly a logical grammar of its own—can become pretentious, dogmatic, and even silly. They have every right to concern themselves with more mundane affairs; but if they say there can be no other world than this, they go too far and become dogmatic in their turn: we are not entitled to say *a priori* that the boundaries of science must be the boundaries of reality.

Metaphysical arguments, however invalid as proofs, at least bring us face to face with a question—a question we seem unable to answer with a plain 'Yes' or 'No'. They force us to consider unverifiable possibilities which seem at least to be conceivable, and yet in another way to be inconceivable by us. Even the word 'possibility' is itself ambiguous. We require no metaphysical arguments to assure us that God is not possible, if by saying that something is 'possible' we mean that it could be experienced as a finite object in time and space; for to describe God as possible in this sense would be self-contradictory. Yet the thought of a being who is not temporal, not spatial, and not contingent—and even of one who is the ground of his own reality—is at least logically possible in the sense of not being self-contradictory. That men have actually entertained this concept is indubitable; and perhaps they are obliged to entertain it unless they stop their thinking at some arbitrary point. They are unable to prove that an object exists—still less that it must exist —in correspondence with their concept; and the best of them are acutely conscious that if it does exist, no concept of theirs can be adequate to its reality. Their dry conceptual thoughts take on the colour of what may be called rather an inkling or a surmise—perhaps even of a personal conviction and a basis for action. If this should happen, they can reasonably claim that their belief is at least as immune from scientific refutation as it is incapable of scientific proof.

§ 8. *Metaphysics and religion*

This kind of thinking may seem thin and dry and dusty to a religious man who is no philosopher: it is utterly remote from his warm convictions, his holy peace, his ecstasy and despair. Yet here too the philosopher may be working out, on a high level of abstraction, a kind of thinking actually present in religious experience itself. If his thinking is mainly negative, we should not forget that what is thought as negative may be felt as positive. Even as negative, these thoughts serve at least to bring out the ultimate mystery of the universe without which religion is impossible.

Religious experience is intimately bound up with a feeling of dependence. The religious man does not speak of the finite and the contingent, but he feels himself to be weak and helpless; and as he contemplates the forces which master him, and the endless chain of causes which have made him what he is, he is acutely conscious of his own insignificance. Yet he may also be uplifted as he realizes that in spite of his insignificance he is able to contemplate these forces and in a way to rise above them. In so doing does not he too cherish, however obscurely, the thought or feeling of a supreme reality which is above and beyond this endless chain of meaningless causes and effects, a reality without beginning or end and without cause or ground other than itself? Indeed is it not at least partly by this thought or feeling that he finds himself brought, as it were, into the presence of a *mysterium tremendum*, at once utterly near and utterly remote, at once fascinating and fearful by its very incomprehensibility, and yet the whole in which alone his imperfect life could find its meaning and completion?

At least to some philosophers even this kind of metaphysical thinking, with all its dryness and abstraction, seems to come very near to religious experience—perhaps almost against their will. No

one has done more than Immanuel Kant to discredit the traditional
proofs as a source of knowledge, and no one has been more hostile
to the view that feeling can give us insight into the ultimate nature
of reality. Yet, although he is not commonly regarded as an emotional
writer, he is moved to speak of unconditioned necessity as 'the very
abyss of human reason'. 'We cannot', he goes on, 'ward off the
thought, nor yet can we endure it, that a being, conceived as the
highest of all possible beings, should, as it were, say to itself "I am
from eternity to eternity; beyond me is nothing save that which
exists solely by my will; but whence am I?" Here everything gives
way beneath our feet.'

All of this may be subject to different interpretations. We may
discredit such metaphysical thinking as a mere rationalization of an
obscure experience made up mainly of desires and emotions, conscious or unconscious; and we may discredit the experience because
of weaknesses in the metaphysical thinking to which it gives rise.
No other conclusion is possible if we have made up our minds to be
content with scientific thinking and to admit nothing more. We may
even say that all this argumentation is only a device for enabling us
to believe anything we please. On the other hand, we may think that
such an attitude is itself dogmatic and arbitrary—the product of an
irrational determination to close one's mind to possibilities suggested
by experience and even by thinking itself. From a purely intellectual
point of view the obvious solution is to suspend judgement; but
there may be other points of view as well.

Even from a theoretical point of view our examination of the
thinking in religious experience is manifestly incomplete. The traditional arguments are supposed to be valid for any one who thinks
about any kind of universe, or at least about any kind of ordered
universe in which there are finite beings. Religion, as we know it,
arises in our own particular and variegated universe, and it is this
curious world of ours that now falls to be considered if we are to
round off our sketch of the intellectual element in religious faith.

Chapter XIV

THE WORLD AND ITS DESIGN

§ 1. *The common world*

The world is a large subject. It is coupled with the flesh and the devil as a source of temptation. Here it has to be considered as the vast stage on which men and women are said to be only players. There is a sense in which every human being—perhaps even every conscious animal—lives in a world of his own. But our concern at present is with what we take to be the common world—the world in which we all live together, the world of common sense.

The common world is also the world of science, which may be regarded as a kind of glorified or systematized common sense. In these days we all take it for granted that the world is described most accurately by scientists, and many of their ideas have seeped through into our ordinary thinking. Popular science bulks so large in the modern outlook that our present topic might be described as the world of science, or the world of the scientist, considered from the limited point of view of common sense. But we have also a special purpose in mind: we are trying to see what bearing this common world of ours has on religious belief. Does it give any support to the argument from design—perhaps the most widely accepted of all the arguments on which men have based their belief in the existence of God?

So large a subject can be treated only summarily at the best, but there is a special difficulty at the present time. Science is advancing with such ever-increasing rapidity that the layman is left breathless if he tries to trail along behind. What he says about it, if not sheer platitude, is likely to be antiquated and even absurd. I will endeavour to avoid absurdity, so far as I can, and will use circumstantial detail only in order to bring the obvious home to the imagination. If I borrow some of the details from Mr. Fred Hoyle's book on *The Nature of the Universe*, it is because he is so good at making his theories vivid. Even if the details are mistaken, this will not affect my argument.

Since I first drafted this chapter, it has been suggested that Mr.

Hoyle's figures should be doubled; and there has also been discovered by means of radar the presence of who knows how many new stars invisible to any telescope; but even if the figures given here had to be multiplied by a million million, the effect on the mind of the ordinary layman would not be noticeably different.

§ 2. *The great and small*

Perhaps the first thing that strikes us about the world is its sheer size. Distances are so great that the astronomical figures in which they are expressed leave us numbed.

The diameter of our earth is some 8,000 miles, and those of us who have travelled as much as 1,000 miles can form some dim picture of its extent. We may perhaps grasp vaguely something of what is meant when we are told that the sun is 90,000,000 miles away; but even then we have scarcely begun our celestial explorations. If we are not to be overwhelmed with meaningless agglomerations of cyphers, we have to measure distances by the time light takes to travel over them. Light moves at the modest speed of 186,000 miles a *second*, and it takes about eight minutes for a ray of the sun's light to reach the earth. Hence we may say that the sun is eight *light minutes* distant from us; but with our modern telescopes we can see, or at least photograph, stars which are 1,000,000,000 *light years* away. Within this observed range there are some 100,000,000 galaxies, each one containing anything from 100,000,000 to 10,000,000,000 stars comparable with our sun. Theoretically, we could observe galaxies which are 2,000,000,000 *light years* away. Beyond the theoretical limit of possible observation—though this statement must be taken as controversial—there may be constellation upon constellation, and galaxy upon galaxy, continuing indefinitely for ever.

Why is it that these further systems could never be observed, no matter how much we improved our instruments? According to Mr. Hoyle, it is because these galaxies are moving away from us faster than light. This he expresses—for reasons hard for the layman to understand—by saying that while these bodies are not themselves expanding, the space between us and them is stretching with a speed greater than that of light. If so, the light they radiate can never reach us even in an infinite period of time.

Time, like space, appears to go on and on and on for ever. Our own galaxy is said to have come into existence some 5,000,000,000

years ago; and even our earth is believed to have had a life of something like 3,000,000,000 years. The history of man himself may have
to be 'measured, not in centuries, but in tens and perhaps in hundreds of thousands of years'. In such a context the individual human
span is utterly dwarfed; and even the most stable institutions like
the Roman Empire or the Christian Church or human civilization
itself seem to be momentary bubbles on the vast ocean of physical
events.

If we turn to consider what is contained within so small an object
as a drop of water, we soon come again to measurements by which
the imagination is overwhelmed. There are said to be millions upon
millions of molecules in a drop of water, but even a molecule is a
relatively large object to modern physics. Each molecule of water
contains two atoms of hydrogen to one of oxygen. If we confine
ourselves to the hydrogen, an atom of hydrogen has under normal
conditions a diameter of about a hundred-millionth of a centimetre.
Even so, this atom, although it is the simplest of all atoms, is itself
a kind of solar system containing a central nucleus and a revolving
electron. The whole atom is supposed—if this view is not already
out of date—to be a hundred thousand times as large as the electron;
and the electron is said to go round its tiny orbit about 7,000,000,000
times in a millionth of a second.

Some writers have taken comfort in the thought that if man is
insignificant when compared with the vastness of the universe, he
is himself vast in comparison with the electrons of which his body is
composed. To many of us the second statement is no less disturbing
than the first.

§ 3. *Energy*

In contemplating the universe we are confounded, not merely by
the vastness of its extent and duration, the smallness of its constitu-
ents, and the speed of its motions, but also by its energy or power.
Here too we have our own tiny human standards of measurement,
which come within the scope of our senses and imagination—the
effort necessary to lift a weight, to propel a motor-car, to fire a gun,
or to explode a shell. In these days we have had to face fearfully the
explosive power of an atomic bomb and to recognize that new and
better bombs are on the way. But the explosion even of a hydrogen
bomb is as nothing compared with the explosions which take place
in nature—for example, in the stars known as supernovae. When

such a star explodes, the effect is equivalent to the explosion of a million million million million hydrogen bombs all going off at the same time. Most of the material is blown out into space as a cloud of incandescent gas, which moves at the speed of several million miles an hour and radiates as much light as all the 10,000,000,000 stars in our galaxy put together.

According to Mr. Hoyle, such a supernova was a companion star to our sun. When it exploded, the bulk of its matter moved off into space, and the few remnants left within the gravitational influence of the sun formed a rotating circular disk out of which the earth and other planets were condensed. Our quiet earth was born in the extremity of violence.

There are some who hold that not only our planetary system, nor even our own particular galaxy, but the whole of our known universe started life a finite time ago in a single explosion. On this theory the universe is steadily running down, and all life on this planet will ultimately perish of cold. Mr. Hoyle takes a different view. He holds that the universe is formed by what he calls a process of condensation; and that as galaxy after galaxy moves beyond the range of the theoretically observable universe, this universe, so far from emptying, will still contain as many galaxies as before by the continuous creation of new galaxies to take their place. That is to say, the new galaxies will be condensed out of a background material which is continually appearing from nowhere, is not made out of anything, and in that sense is literally a new creation. But this, even when supported by his belief that there is life on many planets belonging to many suns in all these many galaxies, affords no ground for human optimism. The vast forces of the universe will go grinding on, and all life will ultimately perish in the solar system, not because the sun will become too cold, but because it will become too hot—so hot that the very oceans on the earth will boil. The sun itself will expand in this grilling process till it swallows, first Mercury, then Venus, and finally the earth.

§ 4. *Law*

Whether these illustrations are accurate or not, the continuance of human life depends on a precarious balance of forces wholly beyond our control, and the power and vastness of the universe are such as to confound the imagination of man. Yet the fact remains that man, in spite of his insignificant size and weak vision and feeble power, has been able to form such theories, to make such measurements, and to check and correct them by the observation of phenomena within the range of his senses. He is able to do this, provided he has the necessary intelligence and training, only on one supposition—the supposition that the same laws hold throughout the universe. The third outstanding characteristic of our world, and the one which is the condition of our knowing the others, is what is variously described as the uniformity of nature or the reign of law.

These phrases conceal many ambiguities, against which we must be on our guard. We must not let ourselves suppose that the word 'reign' implies a ruler or the word 'law' a lawgiver. The very notion of law is subject to modification, and we are now forbidden to speak of causal laws or of those laws of interaction between physical bodies which were good enough for our grandfathers. We are no longer allowed even to speak of things or bodies, but only of events. Perhaps we might express the universal prevalence of law by saying that events are similar in different parts of space or of space-time, or even—with Mr. Hoyle—that one bit of infinite space will behave in the same way as any other bit. Yet in this too there are obvious ambiguities. Even if the same laws prevail throughout the universe, their manifestations may be amazingly different. The prevalence of law and order does not mean blank identity everywhere, and still less does it mean an unbroken peace. The explosion of a supernova is as much an instance of law as the gentle falling of a drop of rain.

However difficult it may be to define our terms, science proceeds on the assumption that it is possible to discover laws in nature. The scientist is not content with elementary generalizations: he seeks to bring ever wider ranges of phenomena under ever more general laws and to formulate these laws mathematically—as when Newton brought the fall of an apple and the motion of the moon under the one law of gravitation. Similarly, Faraday gave a formula to cover the phenomena of electricity and magnetism, and then Clark Maxwell provided a higher formula, which covers, not only electromagnetic waves, but light as well. Einstein in his latest work has attempted, whether successfully or not, to formulate a law covering not only the phenomena of electro-magnetism but also those of gravitation. In the last few years—I quote Professor Bronowski—men have discovered that 'gravitation does not get everywhere instantly, but travels in waves like electro-magnetic waves, and at the same speed, which is the speed of light'. It seems only yesterday that I put a question on the speed of gravitation to the two Haldanes,

o

father and son, and was told with a kindly smile that in science such a question could not properly be asked.

These brief allusions may serve to illustrate, not merely the rapidity of scientific advance, but the law-abiding character—if such a phrase can be used—of the universe, a character at once assumed and confirmed in every scientific success. If we did not assume this, we could know nothing about the universe at all.

§ 5. *Nature and law*

It is in relation to this world of unimaginable vastness, energy, and law, that we have to examine the argument from design—the teleological proof, as it sometimes is called. On the basis of the design supposed to be found in nature men have inferred that the world must have a maker or creator, and that this creator must be, not only most powerful, but also most wise and most good in His choice of means and ends.

This theological inference undoubtedly mirrors a process of thought and feeling present in religious experience itself. The religious man finds God, or feels God, to be revealed in nature, perhaps without arguing at all; and he is ready to consider the argument from design with great respect. But it must be said at once that the modern scientific attitude is—to put it mildly—most unpropitious to any argument of this kind. Even to discuss the question will be taken by many as a sign that one is, not merely tenderminded, but soft-headed. The theologian here is trespassing into the domain of science itself, and he should not be surprised if he is treated as a marauder.

The argument from design, it must be remembered, did not arise originally in the scientific world that has here been so summarily described. Nothing could be more primitive than the tendency to look for a mind or spirit behind all the happenings in nature. It may seem that the teleological proof of God's existence, even if more sophisticated and refined, is a survival of primitive animism and must now be jettisoned as useless lumber. Some modern thinkers would even regard statements about the mind of man himself as a similar survival and would be happy to get rid of the concept of mind altogether. It is inevitable that they should have no use for any reflexions on the mind of God.

Even if we are not prepared to accept so drastic a repudiation of all past thinking, it must be admitted that the physical universe, as

we know it to-day, offers no cheerful prospect for theological arguments based on teleology. Suppose we grant that all this vastness and
energy has an intelligent being as its maker and ruler, the means
seem utterly disproportionate to the end (or *telos*) if this is taken—
in accordance with tradition—to be the happiness or the salvation
of man. The Infinite, no doubt, is not to be judged by our straitened
ideas of economy; but if we are looking for an argument to God's
wisdom, and not merely to His power, we can hardly pretend to
find it in all this reckless prodigality. The argument from design
must rest primarily on the prevalence of law and order throughout
the universe.

Why should men argue from the laws of nature to the presence of
design and so to the existence of a wise creator? The laws of nature
are descriptive—not prescriptive like the laws of men; and it is
sometimes suggested that the argument is based on confusing two
different senses of the word 'law'. This explanation—so far as I
know—is not supported by empirical evidence: Greek philosophy
already distinguishes very sharply between law (as convention or
prescription) and nature. What seems more likely is that men failed
to distinguish between mechanical and teleological laws: even to this
day the word 'mechanism' suggests a machine intelligently constructed in accordance with a design or purpose. It is not unnatural
to suppose that the alternative to design or purpose or intelligence
would be pure chance and so chaos. The argument is not scientific,
but neither is it verbal: it rests on the analogy either of human
action or of the machines made and controlled by men. As philosophers, if not as scientists, we are at least entitled to ask what are
the implications of there being laws of nature.

A subtler form of the same argument is based on the suppositions
of science itself. The scientist assumes, not only that there are
mutually consistent laws of nature, but that these can be brought
under higher or more general laws. This assumption was originally
made with the minimum of evidence—it bears some resemblance to
a religious faith. It has been confirmed amazingly by success, but it
still remains an assumption, and indeed an assumption without
which there could be no science at all. Does the scientist himself
suppose, even if unconsciously, that the universe is adapted to our
human intelligence? Or at least can we say, more modestly, that it
looks *as if* the universe were so designed as to be intelligible to
scientific thinking?

This has the merit of talking about a particular design, and not merely of design in general. It is certainly most surprising that the universe seems in the mind of man to be coming, as it were, to consciousness of itself; and some of us may still feel—to use no stronger word—that this could not have happened by accident. But from the scientific point of view all this is utterly naive, and we are getting hold of everything the wrong way round. What we ought to say is that the human mind is adapted to understand the universe—not *vice versa*; and even this is so only because the minds (or the bodies) which failed to understand were eliminated by a process of natural selection. The unintelligent were unable to survive. This contention diminishes, if it does not wholly remove, the mystery of what has happened; but it concerns the nature of man rather than the nature of the world.

Apart from more fundamental difficulties, an argument to the wisdom and goodness of God cannot rest merely on the prevalence of law, or even on the prevalence of discoverable laws: it must depend on the character of the laws that in fact prevail.

§ 6. *Nature and design*

It is in the laws governing the life of organisms that men have seemed to themselves to discover the most convincing evidence of intelligent design in nature.

This has the initial disadvantage that these laws—the laws of biology—apply only to the tiniest fraction of the whole universe, even if we suppose life to exist on other planets than our own. If we can find evidence of design in living organisms, we still have to connect that limited design with the design of the universe as a whole, and it is obvious that this will be far from easy. The subject is too vast for summary treatment, but a few elementary considerations may be put forward on the level of common sense.

Words like 'design', 'plan', and 'purpose' are taken from our descriptions of human action and are applied by analogy to organic life and ultimately to the universe as a whole.

Even as regards human action these words are not free from ambiguity. They may suggest something thought out consciously beforehand, like the blue-print made by an architect before he begins to construct a house. But we all know that as a rule action is not in the least like that. If we sometimes think first and act afterwards, we at least as often act first and think afterwards. Nevertheless if an action is to be regarded as our action, we must at the time be conscious of what we are doing or are trying to do: we must will our action as an action of a certain kind. We call such an action 'purposive' without committing ourselves to the view that it was all thought out beforehand. We also call any observed action of others 'purposive' when it looks *as if* it had a design or plan and *as if* there were an attempt to adjust means to an end. In using this language we do not commit ourselves to a belief that the design or plan or purpose was thought out beforehand, but we do suppose that other men, like ourselves, are aware of what they are trying to do. Apart from this supposition we should not regard their actions as human actions, but as mere animal behaviour.

When we extend the use of a word like 'purpose' to cover the functioning of an animal organism, we drop the idea of *conscious* purpose altogether. If we are simple enough to say that the purpose of the stomach is to digest, we do not mean that the stomach is conscious of what it is trying to do—much less that it has thought out beforehand a purpose or design or plan of digestion. Nor do we mean that God has made the stomach to fulfil a purpose in accordance with His wise design: this would be at most an inference from the facts we are trying ingenuously to describe. We all recognize, even the simplest among us, that we are here using the word 'purpose' only by a kind of analogy with conscious human purpose. We are supposing that the stomach has a function, the function of digestion, and that this function is to be understood only within the total activity of the whole organism. The stomach looks *as if* it had a design or plan, *as if* it were aiming at a purpose, *as if* there were an attempt to adjust means to an end; and beyond this we do not intend to go.

The word 'function', or even the word 'purpose', is not just a comfortable word like 'Mesopotamia'. It really is hard for the lay-man to see how a science like medicine can distinguish between health and disease without some reference to the functions or pur-poses of the bodily organs. It would never occur to him that the stomach was not subject to mechanical law; but he does suppose that in the structure and functioning of such a bodily organ there is something which cannot be explained by mechanical law alone, as the motion of a cricket ball can be explained by the motion of its parts. Even when he is told that the functioning of organs can be explained by a combination of mechanical laws and natural selection —by the fact that animals with organs which fail to function are simply killed off—he does not readily believe this. He still tends to think there must be something more—something which makes the organ develop as a whole in a body which develops as a whole and is not a mere aggregate of parts.

We can understand the impatience of the scientist when he is told that this 'something more' must be the will of God or even a principle of life. These are not scientific hypotheses at all: they cannot be tested by any experiment; and it would be the death of science if we were content to explain why anything is what it is by saying that it was made so by the good pleasure of God. We make a real advance if we can say that some special gene has the function of making the whole develop as a whole, the organism develop as an organism. Yet even here, so long as we use words like 'function', 'whole', and 'organism', we are using biological rather than physical terms—unless these terms have also to be introduced into physics.

A vast amount of nonsense has been talked on this subject, and I have no ambition to add to its bulk; but some things seem to be fairly clear. The scientist—very rightly—claims to push the mechanical explanation of life as far as it will go. He also repudiates the use of words like 'purpose' and 'design' because of the very crude meanings sometimes given to them. What is not so clear is whether he repudiates the distinctions intended by those who used these words with greater subtlety or merely claims that he can state these distinctions with more precision.

Some philosophers hope that we shall be able ultimately to reduce the laws of biology to those of physics; but it is doubtful if this is a scientific belief or even a scientific assumption—it is sometimes derided by biologists, although their language is not always free from ambiguity. A most distinguished biologist, having impatiently denied that biology had any use for purpose, was heard a few moments later speaking blandly about the purpose of the eye. When the discrepancy was pointed out to him, he was merely puzzled; and it was hard not to believe that he was using the word 'purpose' in different senses in the two different contexts.

Modern biologists still use freely expressions like 'organization' and 'self-regulating systems'. So long as they do so, without also using them with the same meaning in physics, we are perhaps entitled to say that they still assume living organisms to have a distinctive character—the character that was meant, however obscurely, by those who formerly spoke of 'purpose' and 'design'. But the new terms do not commit us, as the old terms were sometimes wrongly supposed to do, to a mind which has purposes and executes designs.

No doubt it is still open to us to argue that organisms or self-regulating systems could not exist without a divine maker. We can still claim that there is something very remarkable about the growth and reproduction of living things and about the mutual dependence of their parts. But we are unlikely to maintain that there is a special divine intervention in each case. The argument must be rather that a universe which contains such perfections must be the work of a divine agent; and what we now know about the imperfections of living organisms makes the argument more difficult.

§ 7. *Nature and beauty*

Men have also found evidence of design in the fact of natural beauty—in our aesthetic experience of the world. Apart from the theoretical consideration of magnitude and energy and order and life the direct aesthetic contemplation of nature—for example, of 'this brave overhanging firmament, this majestical roof fretted with golden fire'—is in itself an experience akin to worship. In it nature looks like art: nature looks *as if* it were designed for human delectation and wonder, and this experience of nature may be felt as communion with something familiar and friendly and comforting and even holy. From this direct awareness of natural beauty philosophers may pass to the thought that nature is adjusted or adapted to the aesthetic needs of the human mind or, in religious language, that it is a revelation of divine beauty—that the Heavens declare the glory of God.

Such a thought, although it may draw out the implications of a direct experience, is worlds away from a scientific theory. From the point of view of science, if this terminology is permitted at all, it is the mind which is adapted to nature. Aesthetic sensibility does not, like scientific intelligence, have an obvious survival value, unless possibly as bound up with sexual attraction; but the intensity of aesthetic delight may be regarded as a mere outgrowth or accident, like that intensity of physical pain which seems to have no direct utility in the process of evolution.

§ 8. *The argument from design*

In the argument from design—or the physicotheological argument, as it is sometimes more grandiloquently called—we seem first of all to derive the concept of purposiveness from our acquaintance with human action and to apply this concept by analogy to the living organisms observed on the surface of our planet. We then, by an immense leap, extend it to cover the whole of the vast universe, perhaps on the ground that this also is governed by law, although by law of a different kind; and we may feel this extension to be confirmed by our experience of the beauty in nature. Finally we argue that purposive activity in beings without intelligence must be directed by an intelligence outside and beyond themselves; and so we pass, because of the magnitude and power and order and beauty of the world, to the existence of an all-powerful and all-wise intelligence, to which we give the name of 'God'.

Let us look summarily at this argument in a spirit of complete intellectual detachment.

It is obvious that an argument based throughout on analogies is unscientific. If we say that the universe as revealed to us by science must have an omnipotent and all-wise creator, or that God must be a mathematician, we pass to a totally different point of view where we can no longer devise mathematical formulae and test them by empirical observation. You may feel, and I may feel, that a world like this necessarily has a creator, or at least probably has a creator, or—to put it in the most modest way—possibly has a creator; but in such statements words like 'necessarily', 'probably', and 'possibly' have no longer their ordinary scientific meaning. It is difficult enough to say what we mean by these words even in their ordinary sense; but, to confine ourselves to the word 'probably', there is in it at least a reference either to the mathematical calculation of chances or to observed repetitions or to both. In what we are now saying there is neither. Our statement seems to be based on some obscure feeling in ourselves. We feel that so amazing a world cannot just have happened to exist for ever and ever, and cannot have come into existence by pure chance. Hence we seek to find its explanation in something outside itself.

Even so, our own analogies suggest that the world may have an architect or builder (if not many architects or builders) rather than a creator—that it may be made out of pre-existent materials rather than created out of nothing. But here we must remember that the different strands of argument for the existence of God are all interwoven: there is a danger that we may be picking out the individual threads and then declaring the fabric to be shoddy. If we suppose that every ordered universe must have as its ground a non-temporal, non-spatial, unconditioned, and self-sufficient being, we are bound to suppose this of our own ordered world. On such a supposition we are already beyond the analogy of a human architect and are at least closer to the concept of a creator. What the argument from design has to show is only that this creator must be wise and benevolent; and this it has to do from the study of our own particular world. The burden of proof is then lighter, though it would still be hard to infer absolute wisdom or absolute benevolence. On the other hand, if the argument from design depends on the validity of the cosmo-logical and ontological proofs—if perhaps its limitations led to their invention—then it must stand or fall as they stand or fall; and we have not been able to show that they can stand.

If we set aside this supreme difficulty, and are willing to assume the existence of a creator, can we discern in the universe we have described a divine plan or purpose such as warrants an inference to His supreme wisdom and benevolence?

From the vastness, energy, and order of the world we can perhaps infer that its creator must be of immense power and intelligence. Yet even if we suppose that we are entitled to judge the universe by our human standards of what is best, it seems impossible to claim that we are able to grasp intellectually the aim and purpose of all this vastness and energy and order or to assess the excellence alike of its means and of its end. Few of us are ready to assert with St. Thomas that bodies act 'always, or nearly always, in the same way, so as to obtain the best result'. It is significant that even he has to add the honest, but disquieting, qualification 'nearly always'—so remini-scent of the captain of the Pinafore; but the whole phrase seems meaningless unless we are able to specify the end. We have seen no sign, apart from the bare fact of our own existence and our capacity for scientific discovery and aesthetic appreciation, that the whole creation is directed to the attainment of values we can appreciate or understand. Still less is there any indication that the purpose of the universe is the welfare of living organisms or the perfection of the human race.

Even within the limited range of animal life we have to face the fact of pain: some animals, for example, have to die slowly as over-grown horns or tusks press gradually into their brains. The horrors of nature are as real as its delights, and even if pain is overbalanced by pleasure, this can be of little comfort to a creature dying in agony. We have here events not to be understood by human standards of kindness; and few of us will think the problem made any easier by the explanation, sometimes put forward even to-day by men of intelligence, that the pain of animals has been inflicted by God as a consequence of Adam's disobedience. An easy rational solution of problems like these is as unsatisfactory from a religious, as it certainly is from a scientific, point of view. If we are to be intellectually honest, we must frankly admit that we can detect no purpose or meaning in the vast distances and wild eruptions of the universe —and certainly no purpose centred on the welfare of man. Even in our own little world as judged by our own human standards, while there is much to call forth our admiration, there is also much that is wholly at variance with ideas of human kindness.

The argument from design has in the past made claims to be closely based on science, but science can have no direct part in discovering God. Science is concerned with facts and laws, not with purposes and values. It can find relations between different parts of the universe, but it ceases to be science if it tries to find relations between the universe and God—perhaps even if it begins to speak about the universe as a whole. If philosophy seeks to follow closely in the steps of science, it must impose upon itself the same limitations. If it refuses to be bound by such a self-denying ordinance, if it endeavours to think out the implications of what I have called the drive in our own thinking towards wholeness or completeness, what can it offer us? Certainly not a scientific proof or demonstration of God's existence or God's goodness, but at the most a mystery, a paradox, a question, a surmise, and perhaps a hope.

§ 9. *Religious experience*

It is hard to know what to make of all this from the point of view of religion. Men cannot worship size or duration or energy or even law. Yet contemplation of these things, and still more contemplation of the marvels of life and the beauty of nature, arouse emotions and attitudes which are not merely akin to those of religion but are elements in religious experience itself. Here too the dry argumentation of the traditional philosopher seems to express, however inadequately, something of the intellectual factor in religious life.

Before the vastness and energy of the universe man cannot but feel his own insignificance and helplessness. Even his shudders at its violence and seeming remorselessness are not unlike those attributed by Otto to consciousness of the daemonic. However insignificant and baffled he may feel himself to be, these very feelings spring from his own ability to grasp the laws of nature, and so to measure the immeasurable, to weigh the stars in a balance. The spectacle of universal law is itself awe-inspiring, but the power of being able to grasp such law carries with it a kind of exaltation. Thus man is uplifted as well as cast down; and as he strains to envisage the whole universe of which he is dimly conscious, a whole beyond his powers of imagination and even of thought, he experiences an emotion which is at least akin to reverence. Little wonder if he feels himself to be in the presence of a mystery, perhaps in the presence of a mind infinitely greater and other than his own.

By some thinkers such an attitude is considered worthy of rebuke. Professor Susan Stebbing, for example, reprimanded Jeans and Eddington, not merely—perhaps with justice—for the confusion of their thought, but also for the impropriety of their emotions or of the emotions they tried to convey to others. As she pointed out, the imaginative contemplation of the universe revealed to astronomers is to be distinguished from direct awareness of the beauty of the night. Both of these experiences may arouse something like religious emotion—they may even reinforce one another; but for some reason she commended the second as much as she condemned the first. Like a just, but kindly, schoolmistress, she combined her reprimand of Jeans and Eddington with a little pat on the back to Kant because —according to her—his well-known awe before the starry heavens was a simple aesthetic experience which could be enjoyed by any ignorant shepherd. Seldom can magisterial commendation have been less deserved. Had she taken the trouble even to glance at the context, she would have seen at once how wrong she was. What moved Kant was not merely what he calls 'the noblest spectacle presented to the eyes of man', but rather its connexion with the endless magnitude of worlds upon worlds and galaxies upon galaxies and with the boundless times of their periodic motions, their beginning and their duration. Failure to appreciate such emotions may spring, not from clarity of thought, but from lack of imagination, or at least from an unwillingness to exercise it. It is easy enough for some of us to close our minds, but this practice should not be elevated into a philosophic virtue.

We have to recognize a similar distinction—and this is particularly true in our contemplation of living things—between our direct enjoyment of the beauty in nature and our quasi-aesthetic admiration for the adjustment of part to part and of the whole to its environment. Besides our aesthetic pleasure in the shape and colour and flight of a swallow we may also have, as it were, a technical admiration for the perfect efficiency of its wing-structure—an admiration comparable to the reverence which a good engineer has for his engines. These emotional experiences in combination (as is well brought out by Kipling in *M'Andrew's Hymn*) lead very naturally and easily to an attitude of worship, especially when they are connected with the mystery of the world as a whole and with a feeling of thankfulness that these wonders should be given to us without any effort of our own.

But what of the darker side of human experience—of the pain and suffering and waste and cruelty and savagery of animal life? Does the religious man shut his eyes to all of this and seek in religion for a way of escape?

Plain and honest men cannot but have a proper feeling of repugnance when a theologian or philosopher ignores the horrors of the world—still more when he tries to have it both ways and tells us that the good in the world is a proof of God's goodness, while the evil shows that we cannot expect to understand the mystery of the divine will. It would be more reasonable to say that the religious man seems to himself to see some things as a manifestation of divine goodness and hopes one day to have a similar vision even of the things that baffle him now. It is hard to speak of this problem without smugness and self-deception, but even this simple, and perhaps ingenuous, rational solution does not adequately describe religious experience. The religious man, even apart from his darker thoughts of sin, is genuinely troubled by the evil in the world, and this trouble seems almost to be a part of his religious faith. Religious faith is not to be identified with a shallow optimism: it seems to contain in itself an element more akin to tragedy. The suggestion may be a foolish one, but it almost seems as if the bafflement inevitably experienced in the effort to understand the size and power and order of the world were as inevitably experienced in the effort to appreciate its goodness—and as if this very bafflement were an essential factor in religious experience itself.

Religious experience, made up as it is of thought and emotion, is certainly a source of religious conviction. Some may compare it in its own sphere with the practical assumption of the scientist that the universe is governed throughout by discoverable law. They may even claim it to be a kind of divination of the nature and existence of God. To the scientific mind this so-called divination is at best an assumption which can in no way be confirmed; the thoughts into which it is articulated are manifestly fallacious; and the emotions are merely so many psychological events to be scientifically explained. The religious and scientific points of view are fundamentally opposed. There seems no hope of a reconciliation unless from a philosophy which is at least not unwilling to consider what can be said or believed about the universe as a whole and about the different points of view from which it can be contemplated.

Chapter XV

THE APPEAL TO HISTORY

§ 1. *The appeal to history*

If the traditional arguments for the existence of God are found to be inconclusive, this does not mean that philosophers have no further questions to ask about religion: their task may be only beginning. But some religious men may be inclined to abandon all hope of philosophical help. They may think that philosophers are looking in the wrong places when they try to discover in abstract speculation or in biological science a basis, or at least a support, for religious faith. Religion, it may be said, has its roots, not in philosophy or science, but in history. Unaided reason may be unable to find in physical nature, or even in the general history of mankind, a plan or pattern of divine action analogous to the plan or pattern of a rational human enterprise. Nevertheless in the history of one human and yet perfect life there may be revealed, though not to unaided reason, the divine plan for creation and the very nature of God Himself. There may be, as it were, an empirical knowledge of God which, like other empirical knowledge, is independent of philosophy and must be accepted as a basis for philosophical thinking. It would seem to be a grave omission, not to say a dereliction of duty, if nothing whatever were said about the philosophical problems raised by so remarkable a claim.

The appeal to history is specially Christian, but it is also to be found in other religions. Even Buddhism, for example, is sometimes said to make a similar appeal. Although it is, so to speak, officially atheistic, yet in its popular form it may treat the Buddha as a Saviour-God: it then becomes a religion of salvation through faith in a personal Saviour, a faith which rests on the historic vow of the Buddha not to enter into bliss until he had brought light to his fellows. Apart from other parallels the examples of Christianity and Buddhism are more than enough to compel discussion of the relation between religion and history. In natural theology such a discussion must be intellectually detached and must be concerned with a general problem. Yet even in considering the general prob-

lem those who inherit the traditions of Christendom cannot but
have in mind the Christian doctrine. It is better that this should be
made explicit, although the intricate questions of dogmatic theology
lie beyond the scope of a merely natural theologian, even if he were
qualified to deal with them.

From the side of human needs it is not difficult to see the attraction of an appeal to history, and especially to the history of a single
human life. To ordinary men, and even to philosophers in their
more human moments, the God of philosophy may appear remote,
impersonal, and vague: elaborate argumentation about the ultimate
concepts and timeless truths of a philosophical theology are unlikely
to move the heart. What man seems to want is a personal Saviour.
His instinct is to worship what has been called, not too happily, 'the
concrete God' or, in more religious language, 'the living God'—a
God who meets human weakness and human love with an unfailing
response. Such a God can be portrayed only in a myth or story, not
in a metaphysical treatise; and if He is to be known as real—such is
the common belief—the story has to be a history and the myth a fact.

A distaste for abstractions and a quest for concrete reality is not
unknown even among philosophers. Modern existentialists, especially the Christian ones, would claim to be moved by such considerations; but so too would empiricists and even, in their very different
way, the followers of Hegel. It might almost be said that every
philosopher, no matter how abstruse, would assert emphatically
that he is trying to get near to concrete reality or even to common
sense. But it is Hegel and his followers who have in fact laid most
stress on history and have been conspicuous in treating historical
events as the temporal embodiments of eternal principles. If their
doctrines fail to satisfy the needs of the religious man, this may be
because he suspects that in this philosophy the events may be
swamped by the principles and time be swallowed by eternity.

History itself can be exposed to no such danger, and it seems
more likely than any philosophy to give us knowledge of concrete
individual reality. It combines the vividness of art with something
like the precision of science; and its concern is not so much with
general laws as with actual individuals. So far as it ventures, unlike
science, to pass judgements of value, it may give life and body to the
abstractions of the philosopher and so bring them within the range
of common understanding. Some history is too scientific to allow
itself this indulgence, and there may be reasons for its austerity; yet
a history of art, for example, would not obviously be improved if it

ited itself from all aesthetic standards. History has even been
garded as the completion of philosophy; and philosophical speculation may be thought profitable only so far as it becomes also
historical insight.

If any such view can be justified, it is not unreasonable that
religious men should expect the historian rather than the philosopher to be the defender of their faith. History has some of the
wholeness and comprehensiveness claimed for religion; for it too is
concerned with the whole of human life. And if God is to be conceived by the help of an analogy with human ideals, the history of
a perfect man might afford a unique manifestation or revelation of
God such as would be most appropriate to our limited human
understanding. An ideal man who was also real might, so to speak,
be a mediator between man and God.

On the other hand, it would be an error to identify historical
knowledge with religious faith or even to suppose that history could
supply a proof of the goodness of God or the divinity of Christ.
History is concerned only with the finite; it can work only with
human categories; and its explanations must be psychological rather
than theological. This may be expressed in Barth's aphorism 'Who-
so says history, says non-revelation'. If history is to be the source of
a religious faith, it must, we are often told, be illuminated by 'the
inward witness of the Holy Spirit'—*testimonium Spiritus Sancti
internum*. Its message is sometimes said to be accessible only to those
who already believe.

Hence appeals to history cannot enable men either to dispense
with religious experience or to disregard philosophical questions
about its validity. When considered as a source of revelation history
can be only one strand, even if an essential one, in the web of faith.

For natural theology the fundamental question is this—What
must be the character of a history which may reasonably be regarded
as a vehicle of divine revelation?

It may be suggested that the history must, in the first place, be
true: otherwise we might as well be content with a parable or a
myth. In the second place, since it cannot depict an eternal and
infinite reality, it must portray a finite, but ideal, character—the
character of a man whose perfection can be recognized, and whose
life and teaching can arouse admiration and love and even awe. In
the third place, the history must be susceptible of a theological
interpretation: it is, for example, not enough for Christian theology
that the ideal man portrayed should be used as an analogy in our

human thinking about God—he has to be regarded as the Son of God or even as God Himself.

There are thus three questions to be raised about what may be called a religious history: (1) a question of fact; (2) a question of evaluation; and (3) a question of theological interpretation. These questions, although they would be appropriate in considering any history that formed the basis of a religion, have a direct bearing on the doctrines of Christianity.

§ 2. *The question of fact*

The history traditionally accepted as the basis of Christian doctrine extends far beyond the human life of Jesus of Nazareth. It includes within itself the story of the Jews and lays special stress on their prophecies of the coming Messiah. It covers also the story of the Church on earth, which has followed Jesus as its Master and Lord. Beyond these stories it looks back to the Creation and the Fall of Man, and forward to the Last Judgement. It appears as a great drama played, as it were, in Heaven as well as on earth—a complete history of mankind in which the centre is Jesus Christ, who is both Man and God. That part of it which concerns the Church after the death of the first disciples has no authoritative record and is interpreted differently by Protestants and Roman Catholics; but for both alike (apart from minor differences about the Apocrypha) the remainder is contained in one sacred book—in the Bible which is also the word of God; and the whole Biblical story from beginning to end has been taken to be a true chronicle of historical facts.

This traditional belief is stated with admirable clarity in the Encyclical *Providentissimus Deus* promulgated by Pope Leo XIII as recently as 1893. 'All the books which in their integrity the Church receives as sacred and canonical, with their parts, were written by the dictation of the Holy Spirit, and therefore exclude all possible error'. Among the possible errors excluded we must presumably reckon errors of fact as well as of doctrine. This inerrancy was equally accepted by the Reformers, although they appealed to the authority of the Holy Spirit rather than to that of the Church. They maintained further that natural reason, if not competent to prove that the Scriptures are the infallible word of God, is at least able to establish their credibility against the criticism of unbelievers.

We need not enquire too closely into what is meant by the 'dictation' of the Holy Spirit: at one time it seems to have been

P

taken literally. What is important for our purposes is this. During the last hundred years and more there has gradually taken place, outside the Church of Rome, a radical revolution in theological thinking about the Bible. Apart from a few Fundamentalists, who make up in zeal what they lack in scholarship, theologians are no longer able to accept what used to be the common belief of Christendom. The accounts of the Creation and the Fall, whatever their religious significance, are recognized to be myth and not history. Much in the history of the Jews is seen to be legend; and all of it is exposed to errors found in the early history of other nations. Even the prophecies are no longer interpreted in the literal way that is accepted as obvious by New Testament writers as well as by later theologians.

Questions of fact—and it is only with these that we are at present concerned—have to be determined in a critical age by competent scholars on the basis of empirical evidence: they cannot be decided by appealing to a revelation which is taken to be exempt from criticism. This is the clear principle which has to be accepted by religious men to-day if their faith is not to be regarded as superstition. Here again the Church of Rome forms a notable exception. So far from questioning the historical inerrancy of the Scriptures it claims a similar inerrancy for its own traditions; and it has recently promulgated as a dogma to be accepted by all Christians the statement that the body of the Blessed Virgin Mary was taken up into Heaven before death. Unless this factual assertion can be established by dispassionate examination of historical evidence—and it is not easy to believe that it can—it must presumably be guaranteed by revelation. It would be hard to find a more direct clash of principles between theology and science—if under the head of science we may include historical criticism.

It may be objected that if we have already accepted, on whatever grounds, the other elements in a revelation—in particular its evaluative judgements and theological interpretations—we may be entitled to believe in historical facts other than those which could be established by a dispassionate historian. Such a contention is not without difficulties, especially if evaluation and interpretation have in turn to be based on the historical facts; but it is not unreasonable to claim that a historical revelation has to be judged as a whole. On the other hand, if the great religious drama of God and man has been declared for centuries to be historical fact from beginning to end, and if we have now to admit that some of it is myth and some of it is legend, we are faced with a new situation and a new need for criticism. It becomes all-important to discover how much is factually true, and this is a work for scholars rather than for saints. The old assurance has been lost, and it is impossible to decide *a priori* where the line may have to be drawn between historical fact and religious myth.

§ 3. *The historical Jesus*

Even if many of the ancient props have given way, it is still possible that the central narrative—the life of Jesus of Nazareth—might stand fast as history. Yet here too the eroding activity of Biblical critics has been long at work, and it appears to be now undermining—I again except the Church of Rome—the very citadels of positive and orthodox theology.

It is impossible to outline this critical movement in a few words. A brief and yet comprehensive account of its modern developments, and one which—if I may say so—manifests a rare combination of the critical and the religious spirit, is to be found in Professor D. M. Baillie's book *God was in Christ*. Here there is no room to do more than mention the most recent school of Form Criticism—or *Formgeschichte*—as it is called, whose leaders in Germany are Professor Rudolf Bultmann and Professor Martin Dibelius. Its exponents study the Gospels historically—I quote Professor Baillie—'by distinguishing the various "forms", the various types of anecdote, parable, apophthegm, wonder-story, homiletic reminiscence, that were used in the preaching of the early Church about Jesus and grew into the Gospel tradition'. This inevitably suggests that it may be impossible to get behind the primitive Christian '*Kerygma*' (or message) to the historical Jesus. The issue is controversial, but if the present situation is to be understood, it is necessary to note the kind of conclusion reached by some of the most eminent Biblical critics, whether they belong to this school or not. In order to avoid misrepresentation I quote their actual words, though even these may be misleading when considered apart from their context.

Professor Bultmann tells us that 'we can know almost nothing concerning the life and personality of Jesus'. 'It seems then', says Professor R. H. Lightfoot, 'that the form of the earthly no less than of the heavenly Christ is for the most part hidden from us'. 'To practise Christology', writes Professor Tillich, 'does not mean to turn backwards to an unknown historical past or to exert oneself about the applicability of questionable mythical categories to an unknown historical personality'.

These are not the utterances of professed sceptics, but of outstanding theologians in Germany, England, and America. Even if we turn to those who have a reputation for the most rigid orthodoxy, the story is not very different. Thus Emil Brunner can say: 'Faith presupposes, as a matter of course, *a priori*, that the Jesus of history is not the same as the Christ of faith'. And Karl Barth himself can make the astonishing statement: 'Jesus Christ, in fact, is also the Rabbi of Nazareth, historically so difficult to get information about, and when it is obtained, one who is apt to impress us as a little commonplace alongside more than one other founder of a religion and even alongside many later representatives of His own religion'.

It would be wholly unfair to take these isolated declarations as expressing adequately the beliefs of their authors; but we may perhaps descry in them a common appeal from the historical Jesus —'the Christ who died at Jerusalem', to quote the words of James Nayler, the Quaker preacher—to the Christ who lives and reigns. The truth or error of their historical views can be judged only by those who have given their lives to Biblical scholarship—some weighty criticisms are supplied by Dr. Baillie himself. Yet—from the point of view of natural theology—it seems hard to resist the conclusion that, in an age of questioning, religion cannot be established or defended, as is sometimes thought, by a simple appeal to known historical facts.

A further difficulty has been brought into prominence by Professor Bultmann in an essay on *The New Testament and Mythology*. This is published in a volume entitled '*Kerygma und Mythos*', which contains also criticisms from other theologians: the title of the English translation is '*Kerygma and Myth*'. In his essay Dr. Bultmann insists that the New Testament provides a world-picture which belongs entirely to Jewish or gnostic mythology and is incredible or even meaningless in a scientific age. In this mythological picture he includes, not only the accounts of Creation and the Fall and the Last Coming, and of a three-storey universe in which the Heaven above the earth and the Hell below it are full of supernatural powers—of angels and demons who intervene constantly in earthly affairs—but also the miracles of Jesus, and even the central doctrines of the Virgin Birth, the Resurrection and Ascension, the Atonement and the Sacraments. He maintains that the myth of a past era is so essential to the whole story that it is no longer possible, as was once thought, to separate the kernel from the husk; and he sets before the theologians the heavy task of 'demythologizing' the Gospel message if it is to be accepted by modern men. This is a problem incomparably more difficult than a commonplace effort to determine ordinary historical facts.

Some may think that the acceptance of such views must mean the end of historical Christianity; but it should be noted that the most radical interpretations of the Gospel story can in fact be held by sincere and devoted Christians. This is already clear from the very names of the authors I have listed; but in order to make it even more clear another quotation may be given—this time from Albert Schweitzer, whose book, *The Quest of the Historical Jesus*, marked a crucial stage in criticism nearly fifty years ago, and whose religion is attested by his life. After saying that the names in which men expressed their recognition of Jesus, such as 'Messiah', 'Son of Man', 'Son of God', have become for us 'historical parables', he goes on:

'He comes to us as One unknown, without a name, as of old, by the lakeside, He came to those men who knew Him not. He speaks to us the same word: "Follow thou me!", and sets us to the tasks which He has to fulfil for our time. He commands. And to those who obey Him, whether they be wise or simple, He will reveal Himself in the toils, the conflicts, the sufferings which they shall pass through in His fellowship, and, as an ineffable mystery, they shall learn in their own experience Who He is'.

§ 4. *The question of value*

If we pass from the question of fact to what I have coldly called the question of evaluation, two different kinds of judgement appear to be necessary. First of all, there are ordinary moral judgements. Although these may be possible only through divine grace, they make no pretence to be other than human; but it is impossible to dispense with them since a history of folly and wickedness cannot be taken as a revelation of God. Secondly, there are what may be called religious judgements or 'immediate utterances of faith'. These, much more than moral or even aesthetic judgements, are strongly emotional; and we have to ask how far men are moved by a religious story to awe and reverence and worship. It is presumably here above all that theologians speak of the inward testimony of the Holy Spirit.

To treat such questions summarily, as is here inevitable, cannot but give an impression of extreme crudity—an appearance of labelling religious stories as a grocer might affix price tickets to sacks of potatoes. What has to be said must be taken only as a series of signposts indicating routes that have been followed; but in these matters every man must find his own way for himself.

In the Old Testament there are many writers of high morality and deep religious insight, but their teaching loses little, if it does not actually gain, by being separated from the history of the Jews. So far as they look forward to the Messiah as an earthly ruler, they throw more light on Jewish nationalism than on religious faith. The historical narrative itself may depict some heroic and religious men, and some of the events may be interpreted as religious parables, but the record is very human and contains a great deal of primitive savagery. The fact that it has been used indiscriminately as a model for human actions has had many unhappy results. There may be traced in it a gradual development of religion, and this may be ascribed to the grace of God; but on the whole its religious influence springs more from its teachings and meditations and prayers than from any historical facts.

It would be even more unseemly to pass a summary judgement on the history of the Christian Church. To some this may be the main ground of their belief, which may even harden into submission to an authority whose utterances have to be accepted as infallible. Yet it has also been said—I think by an Anglican divine—that Church history is the main obstacle to religious faith. This may be contrasted with Boccacio's flippant story of the Jew called Abraham, who was converted after a visit to Rome because he became convinced that so corrupt a Church could have not survived unless it had the Holy Spirit for its foundation and support. There are many conflicting voices, and to some men the record is one of ecclesiastical squabbles and theological intolerance and intellectual obscurantism, of moral obliquity and religious persecution—as if the pride of the Pharisees had all but triumphed over the spirit of Jesus. How many innocent human beings have been slaughtered in the name of the Prince of Peace! It is a terrible thought that men, women, and even children have been bullied and frightened into religion. Nor is it fair to ascribe all European progress to the influence of the Christian Church—a miracle like that of Athens in the fifth century before Christ shows the vast potentialities already present in imperfect human nature. Nevertheless, when all is said, there have been faithful followers of Jesus all down the ages, whose humble service has kept alive the memory and ideals of their Master. Without the influence of the Christian spirit the life of Europe and of the world would have been incomparably poorer than it is. But our judgement of the Church, whatever it may be, must in the long run turn on what is thought of the life of Jesus Himself.

This is the central question, and the only one that matters. There is to-day a new difficulty for human judgement because of the admitted imperfection of our records. Although the moral and religious value of a story may be recognized independently of its historical accuracy, complications arise when we are asked to make up our minds about a life that was actually lived and so extends far beyond the limits of what has been recorded. The question of value cannot be completely separated from the question of fact. The difficulty is not merely that the Evangelists described events with presuppositions—about signs and wonders and angels and demons —which we can no longer share. If the school of Form Criticism is right, it may be hard to determine which of the sayings of Jesus are His own and which of them express rather the thoughts and emotions of His disciples. This difficulty is particularly obvious in St. John's gospel. The reflexions and feelings and message of the early Church stand as a kind of veil between us and the historical reality. Some modern critics even tell us that it was a mistake of the 'liberal' theologians to enquire too closely into what was actually said and done; and from this they take a curious comfort. Yet no one has ever doubted that the early Christians had certain beliefs and feelings about their Master: what men want to know is whether their feelings were justified and their beliefs true. If we think this unnecessary, we might as well accept the story at once as a myth or parable whose foundation in fact we are unable to ascertain.

Although there are difficulties in this historical uncertainty, there can also be some advantage; for we may be able to suppose that some of what may appear to ordinary human judgement as blemishes—such as the praise of eunuchs and the violent denunciations of the Pharisees and the belief in eternal punishment—have been wrongly coloured or imperfectly understood: the narrative itself shows continual misunderstanding on the part of the disciples. Nevertheless, if we speak merely as historians, the imperfections and brevity of our records must render hazardous the claim that we can here have unquestionable empirical knowledge of a completely perfect life. Yet, whatever be the view of scholars, it is hard to believe that a great figure does not shine through all the obscurity. At the very least Jesus was a religious teacher who did not preach either history or theology, but the need for repentance and the coming of the Kingdom of God. He spoke in parables; He was interested in the everyday things of life—the birds, the trees, the flowers, the sower at his sowing, the women at the mill; and He was a friend of publicans and sinners. If we put aside our critical questions and think of Him very simply as He taught the multitudes and healed the sick and blessed the children, as He prayed in Gethsemane and died on the cross, as He talked with Mary in the garden and walked in the evening to Emmaus with His disciples and showed Thomas His hands and His side, we cannot doubt that this is a story which can move men greatly in the way that is characteristic of religion. In view of centuries of religious history it would be foolish to think otherwise. All of this is coloured for us by a long theological and religious tradition, and much will be lost if we have to treat as poetry or parable the attendant wonders—the miraculous birth, the angels, the wise men, and the shepherds, and even the bodily resurrection and ascension—but the moving power of the story is unquestionable; and this moving power has depended to a great extent on the belief that the story is true.

§ 5. *The theological interpretation*

Men are moved by the humanity of Jesus. Yet humanity, although it may be respected and admired and loved and even reverenced, cannot be worshipped or adored. The immediate utterance of faith is said by theologians to go far beyond what we have described. It may be expressed most simply in the words of Simon Peter, 'Thou art the Christ, the Son of the living God'. This is not ordinary human judgement, but religious faith; and it is here that there is a bridge between moral judgement and dogmatic theology—a bridge which is to be crossed only by 'the inward testimony of the Holy Spirit'. Some may think it can be crossed on the sheer authority of the Bible or the Church; but—apart altogether from intellectual objections—this would have no religious value for the individual unless it were accompanied by some direct personal vision; for the religious judgement, like the aesthetic, must be one's own.

On this view dogmatic theology is not itself religious faith: it is an attempt to interpret religious faith and to think out its implications. Divine inspiration is sometimes claimed even for theological thinking; but it would seem more reasonable to hold that it derives what inspiration it may have from the faith it seeks to interpret. The faith itself is not the acceptance of a series of theoretical propositions: it is not so much an interpretation as a direct experience or encounter. Admittedly it may, in its turn, be coloured by its theological inter-pretation; but even so the thinking that is *in* religious experience must be distinguished from the thinking that is only *about* it.

The central doctrine of Christianity is that Jesus of Nazareth is also the Christ, and that Jesus Christ is both Man and God. Traditional theology insists on the full humanity of Jesus; and at the present time even orthodox theologians declare without ambi-guity that not only His knowledge and His healing power, but also His moral and religious life, were as human as our own. Yet at the same time He is said to be 'very God of very God'. Let me quote a passage from Professor Baillie:

'It is impossible to do justice to the truth of the Incarnation without speaking of it as the coming into history of the eternally pre-existent Son of God. This does not mean, it need hardly be said, anything like a conscious continuity of life and memory between Jesus of Nazareth and the pre-existent Son. Nor are we to think of the human personality of Jesus of Nazareth as having had any heavenly and eternal pre-existence. The Church has never taught that the human element in Jesus, His manhood, is consubstantial or co-eternal with God, but that it is consubstantial with ourselves and belongs to the order of created things. But it was the eternal Word, the eternal Son, very God of very God, that was incarnate in Jesus. And the initiative is always with the divine; so that we are bound to say: "God sent forth His Son", and "He came down from heaven and was made flesh and was made man".'

In this way the earthly history of Jesus acquires, as it were, the background of a divine history. The divine history has to be told in what look like temporal terms, but these must be symbolical, and not literal; for otherwise the divine history takes on the character—especially as details are multiplied—of an empirical, but unverifi-able, record of facts. So far as temporal language is used, this record must be described as a myth—a story or parable which expresses a mystery not to be understood in conceptual terms. Yet since men can think only in conceptual terms, the divine history itself has to become more like a philosophy, or metaphysics, which treats of God, not merely as the supreme reality, but as one God who is yet three Persons, the Father, the Son, and the Holy Spirit.

This doctrine had to be expressed in the language of Greek philosophy at a time when there was no other; and it should not be supposed that the word 'Person' has its modern meaning or even that the word 'three' has a literal numerical sense. The mystery of the Incarnation has to be explained in terms of 'Substance'; and bitter controversies raged on the question whether the Son was of the same substance, or only of like substance, with the Father. All the terms employed are of the utmost complexity and subtlety, full of possible ambiguities, and open to different interpretations at different times. Their precise and proper meaning is still subject to dispute among modern theologians, and pitfalls for heresy are open on every side. Yet, although the Church to-day may speak in milder accents, this theological interpretation is traditionally identified with the Faith which, unless one keeps whole and entire, one will without doubt perish everlastingly.

This identification of the Faith with a series of metaphysical propositions may have been forced on religious thinkers by particular controversies in particular historical situations, and perhaps by the practical consequences of certain theological beliefs. Able men have elaborated these doctrines with much searching of heart and honesty of purpose, and have found in them, in spite of all the subtleties, a fresh religious inspiration. Greek philosophy and its developments by such Christian thinkers as Augustine and Aquinas have always to be treated with respect. But the philosophers of Greece made no claim to be divinely inspired; and it would be more in accordance with their spirit, and perhaps more like the practice of the greatest Christian theologians, to think out a new philosophy in the light of modern knowledge and make use of this in theological reflexion rather than to insist on preserving ancient doctrines as far as possible intact.

Something of this more philosophical—and more religious— spirit is already shown in St. Hilary of Poitiers, the great contemporary of Athanasius; although even he does not refrain from applying pejorative terms to those with whom he disagrees. 'The errors of heretics and blasphemers', he writes, 'force us to deal with unlawful matters, to scale perilous heights, to speak unutterable words, to trespass on forbidden ground. Faith ought in silence to fulfil the commandments, worshipping the Father, reverencing with Him the Son, abounding in the Holy Spirit; but we must strain the poor resources of our language to express thoughts too great for words. The error of others compels us to err in daring to embody in human terms truths which ought to be hidden in the silent veneration of the heart'.

The problems of the modern theologian are much more difficult than those which had to be faced by St. Hilary. When the Christian history with all its mythological background was universally accepted as an unquestionable record of fact, a dogmatic theology based on this history might seem to have the solid certainty of a science—of the very queen among the sciences. One of the strangest tendencies of modern times is to reject or belittle the historical facts and yet to construct a dogmatic theology very similar to the old—to gather, as has been said, apologetic figs from sceptical thistles. This too may be an attempt to re-think old thoughts in the light of religious experience; but to plain and simple men theology and history used to give one another mutual support. As each of these is weakened with the increase of knowledge, it tends to produce a corresponding weakness in the other. The currency of theological thinking may have its own inflationary spiral; and it seems as if drastic measures may be necessary if its value is to be restored. Perhaps as theologians reflect afresh on their own experience and the experience of the Church, they may be able to produce a simpler theology which will speak in more gentle tones, will not be afraid to admit uncertainty, and will not make the acceptance of metaphysical propositions the condition of a saving faith. What attracts men to the Christian to-day—and perhaps all down the ages—is not his doctrines or creeds, nor even his rites and sacraments, but the fact that, like the early disciples, he follows a merciful Master, whom he believes to be, although he does not know how, a revelation of the nature and love of God.

The new Biblical learning and the whole scientific outlook has made it necessary for theologians to re-think their theology from its foundations, as some of them are trying to do. Although religion is a life of faith and dedication, it is bound to lose in depth if it does not—so to speak—think seriously about God and the world; and in this task it is not enough to be merely vague and negative—to drop things out and leave men in a kind of golden haze. In the present predicament a new theology may not be enough. If religion is to avoid total eclipse, what the world may require is a religious genius —perhaps one who is also a theologian or a philosopher. But while men can always get on with the humble task of thinking, for the coming of religious genius or religious inspiration they can only wait.

§ 6. *History and faith*

Our enquiry into the relations between history and religion has become a hasty—and some may think an ill-considered—incursion into the realm of dogmatic theology. Is it possible to return from this unlicensed foray with some tentative conclusions, or at least questions, more appropriate to a philosophy of religion?

We may begin with some principles which seem least likely to be a source of controversy.

Belief in historical facts is not to be confused with religious experience or religious faith. In particular it is not to be confused with Christian experience or Christian faith—that is, with a saving faith by which a man feels enabled, through God's grace, to turn from self and the world to the worship and service of God.

It follows that historical belief cannot be a substitute for religious faith or religious experience. The fact of experience must remain central in religion.

If this is true, an appeal to history cannot do away with the need for reflecting about religious experience and trying to interpret it. The whole development of Christian theology is an attempt to meet this need—an attempt which shows that theological reflexion and interpretation must be philosophical. Where this is not so, theology becomes merely legal or historical and in any case superficial.

We may go farther. It seems necessary to conclude that by appealing to history we cannot get rid of philosophical questions about the validity of religious experience itself. If a religious history simply assumes the existence of God, we have still to ask as philosophers how far this assumption is justified and how far it can be supported or refuted by what is known of the universe. If we are told that the assumption is justified by the feelings which the history arouses, we have still to face the difficulty that although feeling can carry conviction, it cannot by itself justify a claim to knowledge.

If it is possible to have historical beliefs without religious faith, is it also possible to have religious faith without historical beliefs? This is a more searching question, and any answer is likely to be controversial.

A religion in which a belief in historical facts is considered essential to faith may be called a historical religion. Christianity has traditionally been preached as a historical religion. It is more doubtful whether this could be said of the teaching of Jesus, which looked more to the future than to the past.

To adherents of a historical religion it must seem that if the history is regarded as non-essential, the whole religion must go, or at the very least must be transformed beyond recognition. Even to more detached observers it will be obvious that to abandon the history, or to regard a great deal of it as myth or parable, must mean the loss of much that has been felt as infinitely precious. Hence it may be in the interests of a religion to preserve a historical belief if this can be done without violence to the truth.

On this view it may be argued that the divine character of a story, or of a person, can be recognized only by religious faith and that the story has been shown in the experience of the believer to be a revelation of God. Since it would already be a miracle if such a story were invented by men, even by men of genius, it is simpler, as well as religiously more satisfying, to believe that the story is true.

Here the argument is from religious faith to historical belief instead of *vice versa*, and it is perhaps the strongest argument that can be found provided that the history can be accepted or rejected as a whole. The strength of the argument is diminished if men think that the different parts must be accepted or rejected separately—if they feel obliged to reject, for example, what has been disproved by historical research or what is incompatible with the fundamental principles of science or what belongs to the mythology of a past age.

Those who hold that historical facts cannot be determined without the elaborate research possible only to scholars must consider it wrong to make belief in historical statements—and belief in a metaphysical theology based on these statements—the necessary condition of a saving faith. They are bound to ask whether a story may not retain its religious value and still be a revelation of God even if it is no longer accepted as an unquestionable statement of fact. The existence of non-historical religions suggests that an affirmative answer is at least not impossible, even if it may be unwelcome both to orthodox believers and to their fiercest critics. And it may be urged that such an answer would at least have the merit of diminishing the exclusiveness and intolerance which are the special bane of religions based on belief in historical facts.

Sincere and able men have interpreted the Christian history as a parable or allegory of timeless religious or moral truths. Others have used it as a guide to a way of religious, and even mystical life, within the Christian community itself. Professor Bultmann, more recently, hopes it may be possible to express the purely religious message (*Kerygma*) of the New Testament in terms of an existentialist philosophy which lays stress on living decisions in the present rather than on traditional beliefs about the past. Those who hold such views seek to find in religious experience, or in some element of religious experience, a faith which may survive the history by which it was originally inspired.

To all this it may be objected that such views either reduce religion to a philosophy or else attempt to retain a faith which will not outlive the historical beliefs it has ceased to regard as essential. More fundamentally, it may be said that all religious faith must depend on a belief that God acts in the world and that such a belief is of necessity historical. A God who does nothing cannot be an object of worship.

Such a contention raises more general problems to which we shall have to return later. Those who maintain that belief in the truth of a past history cannot be made the necessary condition of a saving faith may reply that God does act inasmuch as He enables men to lead a life of dedication and worship which they cannot live in their own strength: to regard belief in historical records as inessential is not to discount that present and living history which is religious experience itself. They may even reply that God must do everything—that the whole universe is a sacramental universe, although some events in it may have more significance to men than others. But these replies are ceasing to regard history as a record of past events, and they formulate afresh the central problems of natural theology as such. They remind us that it is time to get back to our proper business and to leave the warm, personal world of religious history for the colder world of philosophy. And although this discussion has been too brief and too naive, both from the religious and from the philosophical point of view, it will not have failed in its purpose if it has outlined, however crudely, some problems of most pressing concern to religious men in the present age.

Chapter XVI

THE PHILOSOPHERS' WORLD

§ 1. *Science and common sense*

It may seem absurd to talk about the philosophers' world. Why cannot philosophers be like other people and content themselves with the world revealed to science and common sense? There are many reasons other than natural perversity. One reason is that common sense and science so quickly get out of step.

To common sense the world is in the main made up of solid bodies. These bodies are coloured in various ways; they are soft and hard, hot and cold; and they have at any moment a definite size and shape and weight. It is true that both the size and the shape may look different from different distances and different points of view, and even the weight may feel different if we hold the thing weighed in different hands. But we can get over these difficulties by simple processes of measurement. By measuring a body we can find out what we take to be its *real* size and shape and weight; and these we oppose to its *apparent* size and shape and weight. We can even understand by elementary geometry why a penny which is really round must look elliptical when seen from a certain angle and located in a plane other than that in which it is.

The real characteristics determined by measurement may be called *primary* qualities. In the case of colours we cannot make this difference between the real colour and the colour as it appears, nor can we determine what the real colour is by measuring it. Characteristics that cannot be determined by measurement may be called *secondary* qualities; but to common sense they are none the less real qualities of bodies; and here the real quality may be said to coincide with the apparent quality. Grass does not merely look green: it is green. We may even believe that grass not merely looks beautiful but is beautiful. Yet beauty is a different kind of quality from greenness: it seems to depend on a combination of qualities like colour and shape, and it may be called a *tertiary* quality.

Science, unlike common sense, is concerned only with what can be measured: the world of science is a world of primary qualities

239

alone. This at least is—or used to be—the ideal of science and the secret of its success, although the ideal may be fully attained only by the more developed sciences, notably by physics. Hence it is not surprising if scientists, at any rate as they begin to think philosophi- cally, tend to dismiss secondary, and still more tertiary, qualities as unreal. More precisely, greenness is not for them an intrinsic quality of the grass itself: it arises only when certain light waves are focussed on the retina of a normal human eye. These light waves can them- selves be measured, but it would be absurd to say that invisible light waves are green; and the measurement of the waves which cause grass to look green is not a measurement of the green colour itself, even if it may be correlated with differences that can be seen.

Once embarked on this course of measurement science gets more and more out of hand, so far as common sense is concerned. Our comfortable solid bodies are found to be composed mainly of empty space; for they are divided into molecules, and the molecules are divided into atoms, and every atom is a solar system in itself. This has led Eddington into speaking of his two tables—his common- sense table and his scientific table; and it suggests that the world of science is a different world from the world of common sense. Again, even on Newtonian principles, weight is found not to be a property of a body itself: it depends on the relation of the body to other bodies. For Einstein a body does not even have a definite fixed size and shape: what common sense calls its real shape and size differ, and must within certain limits differ, according to the position and velocity of the instrument by which its size and shape are measured— rather like the way in which, on a common-sense level, the seeming size and shape differ, and must differ, according to the position of the observer. The primary qualities of objects have ceased to be absolute and have become relative. All our ordinary concepts of shape, size, motion, energy, and even of space and time, have to be modified or exchanged for others. The talk about atoms as solar systems may itself already be out of date. No wonder we are left breathless: we seem to be plunged headlong into a different world.

But this is not the worst. We ordinarily assume, in spite of diffi- culties, that we are directly and immediately aware of bodies and their qualities. All our knowledge of the external world is built up on this supposition. Even a scientist, we may imagine, regards his measuring instruments more or less in the same way as we regard tables and chairs. All his measurements must in the end be based on what he can see and touch. How could he use a spectroscope unless he were immediately aware of the colours on its surface? Hence his account of what he measures seems to be applied less austerely to his own measuring instruments. But even if this need cause no qualm, a further fact emerges which is truly staggering. As the process of ever exacter measurement goes on, we discover that direct awareness of objects is a myth. When, as we suppose, we see directly the colour and shape of grass, what is really happening is something like this. Certain rays of light are reflected back from a surface to our eye, and this sets up in our nervous system a process which ultimately reaches the brain; and then we see a coloured shape. Seeing, that is to say, is a final effect in a very elaborate chain of causal events. But an effect need not be like its cause, and there seems to be no reason for supposing that the coloured shape we see bears the slightest resemblance to its original cause. We have to abandon our belief in the direct perception of bodies, and we begin to wonder whether we have any contact with reality at all.

It may be replied that the conclusions of science cannot be thus used to discredit the premises from which they are derived. Perhaps not. But we ought at least to note that this is precisely what seems to happen, and the problem cries out for a solution. It should not be solved, as it sometimes is, by a simple appeal to faith in science. We proceed strangely if we first of all reject faith in the name of science and then go on to uphold science in the name of faith.

§ 2. *Materialism*

Philosophers cannot but be dissatisfied when they are left with two separate worlds on their hands—the world of common sense and the world of science. They dislike this bifurcation and the contradictions to which it apparently gives rise—as sober men they have a rooted objection to seeing double. The simplest way of escaping from this is to say that one of the two worlds is illusory or unreal, or at least that it is derivative and subjective. One method of maintaining this is to adopt the philosophy of materialism.

The materialist accepts the world of science—the world of primary qualities—as the real world. Matter is the primary reality. It exists in itself independently of our perceiving and thinking; and it is the source of our sensations, ideas, thoughts, and indeed of mind itself. Mind is thus secondary or derivative or, as is sometimes said, epiphenomenal. In extremer language, the material world is the only reality.

Q

But what then is the material world? For the older materialist the answer was simple. The world was made up of little bodies or particles acting and reacting on one another like billiard balls. It was in short a kind of machine, or mechanism, of which it was possible to construct, or at least to picture, a model in miniature. There was no nonsense or mystery about this straightforward engineer's world, and its laws were completely knowable. Many of its laws were already known, and it only remained to discover more and more of them by the scientific methods which had already justified themselves by success.

This old-fashioned, simple-minded conception of the material world has now gone by the board. The little bodies or particles have been replaced by electrons, which are not particles at all. Causal laws are replaced by statements of statistical averages. All the conceptions which had seemed so fixed and firm, including those of time and space, are transmuted and transmogrified into very different conceptions, for which we can construct no miniature models; and perhaps no one knows how this process is going to end. We cannot be certain that our present scientific conceptions may not in turn be transmuted into something else. Hence we cannot say that we have knowledge of the world as it really is; and some scientific thinkers propound the paradox that although we know our own measurements, we have no idea of what they are supposed to measure.

Those who object to materialism make a great deal of such considerations, but it may not be possible to dispose of this philosophy so easily. The essential character of materialism is not adherence to an exploded scientific theory, but the view that the world revealed to science is the primary, or even the only, reality. This view is still widely held. Admittedly the scientist no longer claims to know the character of the physical world as it really is, and he is prepared for revolutionary changes. He may even wish to abandon words like 'matter' altogether; but such terminological variations are not to be confused with a fundamental change of principle and attitude.

The objections to materialism will have to go deeper than this. On the materialistic view sensation—and also what we call thinking—is said sometimes to be a product, and sometimes to be a reflexion, of what we may still be permitted to call the material world. No doubt a reflexion, though the term seems ambiguous, may also be a product or event caused by the material world; but what we have to explain is how such a caused event can be *knowledge* of the material world. More generally, we have to ask ourselves how the material world, whatever be its character, can be known. If we are told dogmatically that this is just a fact behind which we cannot go, we are left in the presence of an unexplained mystery, a miracle which taxes our powers of credulity to the utmost. Philosophers, as a rule, do not like unexplained mysteries, and it is hard to see why they should accept this one in preference to others; and still harder to see how by so doing they can get rid of mysteries altogether.

But it is not our business here to refute materialism. The one indubitable fact we have to note is this. Materialism is, and is meant to be, and indeed is bound to be, fatal to religion. If the material world is the primary reality, God could at most be a secondary reality; that is to say, He could not be God. Materialism can function as a kind of religion—it can certainly suffer from religious aberrations like fanaticism; but it would be an unnecessary elaboration of the obvious to insist that it is essentially, as well as professedly, atheistic.

§ 3. *Phenomenalism*

If we are dissatisfied with materialism as a philosophy and are still looking for one homogeneous real world unlike the very mixed world of common sense, the obvious alternative is to fall back on what is given directly to sense proper uncontaminated by thought. Let us avoid all unnecessary complications about the causes of our perception and say boldly that the world is what we see and hear and touch and taste and smell. Everything else is derivative or even unreal—the bodies and electrons of the scientist as much as the immortal souls and intelligible universals and unknown substances of traditional philosophy. All of these, if they do not spring from verbal confusion or sheer mystification, are on this view only useful devices which enable us to predict with greater certainty what we are likely to see and hear and touch. We may say that we see tables and hear bells; but we should never lose grip of the fundamental truth that what we see is colours and what we hear is sounds. Only the secondary qualities—if among them we may include also apparent shapes and sizes and so on—can be given immediately to our senses, and we may call them sensa or sense-data, though they are sometimes ambiguously spoken of as sensations.

Those who take the view that the world is composed of sense-data, and that all else is derivative, are known as phenomenalists.

The word 'phenomenon' is simply the Greek for what appears; and on this theory what appears is what appears directly to the senses, namely, sense-data. The classical exponent of phenomenalism is David Hume, although his modern followers are in many ways more sophisticated.

Phenomenalism seems at the moment to be under a cloud, and is sometimes said, even by thorough-going empiricists, to be dead at last. Its funeral oration has been pronounced in *Mind* by Mr. Isaiah Berlin, who has also done something to lay its unquiet ghost. Although its supporters, like most other philosophers, sometimes claim that they are only stating clearly what the ordinary man really believes, the doctrine is manifestly repugnant to common sense. It may seem even more repugnant to science, but this would be a mistake. In point of fact it received a new lease of life when the physicists had to abandon the hope of being able to illustrate their theories by constructing mechanical models.

So much has been written on this topic in recent years, and with such subtle variations, that we must here be satisfied with a bare allusion. Phenomenalism may be taken to deny the existence, not only of the permanent bodies believed in by common sense and of the particles accepted by the old-fashioned materialist, but also of whatever may be said by the modern physicist to fill time and space —if his assertions can be put in these terms. But more recent phenomenalists may reject this language as metaphysical. They prefer to state their position in linguistic terms, which would run something like this.

We employ two languages—a sense-datum language and a material-object language. Everything said in the material-object language can in principle be said in the sense-datum language, just as—to take a rough parallel—everything said about a committee can in principle be translated into statements about members of the committee. Hence a material object need not be regarded as an inferred entity (an entity inferred from sense-data), but as what is called a logical construction.

Whether or not it is possible thus to by-pass metaphysical problems need not here concern us. Phenomenalism, like materialism, is one of the great simplifying philosophies, and as such is worthy of respect. What is important for us is that in the process of simplification mind has to go the same way as matter. Mind, just as much as body, can be taken to be a logical construction (provided we do not ask what does the constructing): anything that can be said of it can in principle be translated into the language of sense-data and images. In the more metaphysical language of Hume a mind can be 'nothing but a bundle or collection of different perceptions, which succeed each other with an inconceivable rapidity, and are in a perpetual flux and movement'.

Some of us may doubt whether these alleged translations from one language into another are possible even in principle—no one pretends that they are possible in practice. We may doubt, not whether we can, perhaps by an effort, see coloured shapes that are only coloured shapes, but whether coloured shapes can be directly given to sense without activity on our part, or can be called sense-data without misleading implications. We may also doubt whether the view that our perceptions are distinct existences can be other than a metaphysical superstition based on faulty analysis and unsupported by empirical evidence. We may even maintain that this philosophy fails to do justice to our knowledge of the world and of ourselves and is unable to explain how it itself could come into existence as a philosophy. But summary criticism and dogmatic rejection are out of place in dealing with any philosophy at which acute thinkers have laboured with the highest degree of subtlety. One thing at least is clear—the only thing that matters for our present purpose. If phenomenalism denies the existence of bodies and minds except as collections of sense-data or bundles of distinct perceptions, it must, to be consistent, deny equally the existence of God. If it reduces bodies and minds to the status of logical constructions, God cannot be more than a logical construction, and perhaps he cannot even be that. Phenomenalism, like materialism, so far as I can see, must be fatal to any kind of theistic religion.

This conclusion, it should be added parenthetically, takes phenomenalism strictly as the doctrine that only what is given to sense can be real. But since the combinations in philosophy are endless, it is possible, whether consistently or not, to be a phenomenalist about the so-called material world and yet to hold that we have a notion of mind—or of minds—which is independent of our senses. Such a view, which finds its most famous advocate in Bishop Berkeley, is manifestly compatible with religion, but it is far from being pure phenomenalism in the sense intended here.

Perhaps phenomenalism and materialism have one thing in common, in spite of their fundamental differences. Both of them take the world to be a mere aggregate—to be, if I may so express myself without disrespect, just one damned thing after another. If we take our world to be an aggregate or sum of parts, and confine our attention to the relations subsisting between one part and another, we may contribute to the philosophy of science, but it is hard to see how we can find any place for religious belief.

§ 4. *Platonism*

It is obvious enough that no philosophically simple world can be satisfactory to the religious consciousness. If we seek to find a world more adaptable to religion, let us try to combine sense-data and material objects within a more Platonic view—how much of it is actually to be found in Plato himself need not here concern us: some of my interpretations would be challenged by many scholars. All I am trying to do is to sketch very roughly the philosophers' world which has in fact been the European background of religion. I will ignore modern developments of mathematics and logic and will use traditional language without criticism, even if it may be sometimes slightly emotive and not always wholly clear.

A material object—let us call it for short 'a body'—always appears to us by means of sensations or sense-data. Sense-data are appearances of a body; a body is the reality which appears. They are apprehended by sense; it is perceived by a combination of sense and thought. They are the sign; it is the thing signified. They are images or reflexions, often distorted, of it; it is their original or model. They cannot be without it; but it can be without them. They are conditioned by it, and it is their condition—the ground of their being and the explanation of their character. It is one; they are many. It is permanent; they are fleeting. It is intelligible; they are sensible. It is real; they are relatively unreal.

On this view sense-data are rather like shadows, or even like the images which appear in dreams.

The passage from the world of sense-data or of changing appearances to the world of real bodies is made, or at least justified, by a process of counting and weighing and measuring, which determines what we now call primary qualities. Although this process is an intellectual one, it must be based on units which are ultimately sensible. As elaborated by modern science, it no longer brings us to knowledge of comfortable solid bodies; but it still brings us to knowledge of what is measurable independently of the observer's personal sensibility. Fresh difficulties do arise, as I have indicated, when we cease to regard sense perception as direct awareness and assert that it is the result of a causal process; but these difficulties must here be ignored.

A more serious objection may be raised from a philosophical point of view. We are distinguishing between appearance and reality and supposing that appearances are unreal, or at any rate less real. We are manifestly preparing the way for a doctrine that there can be degrees of reality, and this—it may be held—is manifestly nonsense. Things cannot be more or less real. They are either real or else they are nothing at all.

This question need not be argued here. It would not be difficult to find support in ordinary language for either usage; but words have always to be understood in their context, and their context here is a whole philosophy. We must simply note that what is opaque to understanding is being treated as less real than what is intelligible—in the sense of being measurable and so describable by mathematics. This seems also to be the view of many scientists and materialistic philosophers, and it involves a distinction between existing and being real: we may say that a thing either exists or does not exist, but if it does exist, it can still be more or less real. We may even have to recognize that the word 'exist' itself may be used in different senses. But with Plato we make the further, and more dubious, assumption that not only the sensible, but the changeable as such, is opaque to the understanding, and that the intelligible must also be the permanent or unchanging.

If we adopt this last assumption, the world of bodies cannot be wholly intelligible or wholly real. Although it is permanent relatively to sense-data, it is for ever changing, or becoming, or being what it is not: 'it tumbles about between being and not-being'—perhaps even more than Plato thought; and our measurements, however mathematical, are still based ultimately on sense. Hence our so-called knowledge of the world of bodies is only fallible opinion. If our craving for knowledge of reality is to be satisfied we must look elsewhere.

Where can we find such knowledge better than in the world of mathematics? Here we can examine by themselves the measurements and numbers and shapes and sizes in virtue of which alone bodies are intelligible. We can count numbers instead of sheep. We can discover the character of triangles and squares and cubes which are really triangles and squares and cubes instead of imperfect approximations to them. We gain genuine knowledge when we pass from the world of the surveyor to the world of the mathematician.

Instead of trying to describe the irregular visible motions of the heavenly bodies, we can think out mathematically the relations of moving bodies to one another. We can deal with shapes and bodies and motions which are unaffected by the changes of their imperfect copies in the material world; which do not come into being or pass out of being; which are, in short, permanent and indeed timeless or eternal. In this way we can attain infallible knowledge of a world which is truly intelligible and truly real. This unchanging world is the condition and explanation of all that is intelligible in the changing world of bodies, just as the world of bodies is the condition and explanation of whatever may be intelligible in the flux of sense-data or sensible images.

But even this world of mathematics fails to satisfy our desire for unity and system and intelligibility. The thinking of the mathematician rests on unproved assumptions, and he is still so much involved with sense that he has to use visible diagrams, although it is not of these that he is thinking. Even his mathematical figures and motions cannot be separated from space and time, which seem to be neither wholly sensible nor wholly intelligible, if indeed they can be said to be at all. Because of this he is still involved in multiplicity: he has to deal with many ones, with many triangles, with many cubes and spheres. If he is to attain complete intelligibility, he must examine his assumptions and definitions and their relations to one another. He must pass to universals, to what Plato called pure Forms or eternal Ideas, to oneness itself, triangularity itself, and so on. Each of these Forms is one and not many: triangularity is the same in all mathematical triangles, in all triangular bodies, and even in all triangular images. The Forms alone are truly intelligible, and are the source of all intelligibility in everything else. According to Plato, they are the ultimate reality and are grasped by pure intelligence without any sensuous aid other than that of words.

Here then beyond the world of images and the world of bodies and the world of mathematical objects we have a fourth world—the real and intelligible world of pure eternal Forms grasped by pure intelligence. Yet though each Form is one, there are many Forms: we have still to understand them as one system and to grasp the principle of their systematic unity. This principle Plato finds in what he calls the Form of the Good, or Goodness itself; and he believes it can be apprehended, or at least approached, through a process of logical thinking which he calls dialectic. In it we find the original or model of all reality, the unconditioned condition, the

ultimate ground and explanation, of the being and nature of everything else.

It will be observed that this whole ascent from sensible images to
the Form of the Good is an intellectual one and in its highest stages
appears almost to be pure logic. When Plato, it is recorded,
gave notice of a public lecture on the Good, the large and fashion-
able audience which came to hear him was disappointed to find
that he talked mostly in mathematical symbols—just like a modern
logician. But there is for him another side to all this. Severe as
is the long intellectual training necessary for philosophy, it must
be accompanied by a practical and moral training no less severe;
and the Form of the Good is a guide to life as well as an explanation
of reality. Furthermore, we are told that the Form of the Good is
beyond knowledge and truth and even beyond being. We are also
told by Plato that he would never commit his deepest thoughts to
writing. For some men perhaps, at the end of the process of dialectic, there blazes out, it may be suddenly, a vision of transcendent
reality, where words are no longer adequate or necessary, and where
verbal description, if employed at all, must take the form of poetry
and myth. There is thus a mystical side to Plato, which was
developed further by some of his successors; but this does not alter
the fact that his philosophy was meant to be accepted or rejected as
a piece of logical thinking.

All this, it may be said, is utterly ingenuous. In a sense it is,
though perhaps it is not more ingenuous than a great deal we have
to listen to to-day. There are still echoes of the doctrine, and more
than echoes, in such modern thinkers as Santayana and Whitehead.
Nevertheless we may agree that Plato was led to claim too much for
the new methods in mathematics and philosophy, perhaps because
of the intense intellectual excitement they aroused. Few of us
realize vividly enough 'the glory that was Greece'—the escape from
the savagery and superstitition of barbarism to the controlled and
reasonable life of free men, the passage from chaos to cosmos (or
order). The escape was not complete—it never is—but no wonder
there was something like a worship of reason and a passionate hope
that by rational methods men could make amazing progress, not
merely in science, but in moral and political life. Perhaps this hope
has never wholly died: it became strong again in Europe in the age
of the Enlightenment after the discoveries of Newton. We may wish
we had more of it to-day. If it led Plato to claim too much for mathematics and philosophy, to plunge beyond the limits of our finite

understanding, to 'hypostatize' an eternal and intelligible world of which the philosopher could have infallible knowledge by means of pure intelligence unmixed with sense, this is no reason why we should belittle it. In spite of weaknesses and obscurities—and what philosophy is free from these?—his attempt to 'carve reality at the joints' still stands out as one of the greatest achievements of the human mind.

§ 5. *Philosophy and religion*

This philosophy is as favourable to religion as phenomenalism and materialism are unfavourable: it is indeed itself almost a religion as well as a philosophy. It formed, at least in its later and more mystical developments, the background of early Christian thinking, very notably in St. Augustine, who did so much to determine the direction of traditional theology. As transmuted by Aristotle and adjusted by Aquinas—in which there was loss as well as gain—it became the official philosophy of the Christian Church. The Reformers were moved by moral rather than theoretical considerations, and they thought, perhaps rightly, that there was a danger of religion being smothered by philosophical subtleties; but almost without question they retained, in the very heart of theological doctrines about the Trinity and the Incarnation, the philosophical concepts of substance and essence which are direct developments of the Platonic Forms. Since then philosophy has gone its own independent way, and in its attempts to keep pace with the advance of science has to its credit achievements based on a far wider knowledge than was possible for Aristotle or for Plato. Theologians have too often either condemned these developments and harked back to Aquinas or else have tried to do without philosophy altogether—or at best have selected out of it whatever seemed to fit their purposes. This may be too harsh a judgement, and there is something to be said for the view that religion should not be committed to any philosophy by which it must stand or fall; but so far as theology is rational, it is in a weak position if it is without any means of philosophical defence. It is in a hopeless position if it attempts to defend itself by philosophical arguments—or still worse by philosophical sophistries—incapable of standing up to any serious rational scrutiny.

From a religious point of view the attraction of the Platonic philosophy is that it claims to give knowledge of an abiding and eternal reality beyond the world of sense and matter and space and time; but it is precisely this claim which modern philosophy has tended more and more to reject. Even Aristotle may be said to have begun this movement when he denied the separate and independent existence of the Forms; but although he was always cavilling at his master Plato, he often finishes up by saying very much the same kind of thing. So long as we hold that there are intelligible universals or Forms or essences or substances which can be grasped by pure intelligence, perhaps it does not greatly matter to religion whether these exist apart from material and sensible objects or only in them. But if we say that all this is only high-falutin' nonsense and that our glorified essences are in fact mere names applied to objects that look alike, then we seem to be confined to a purely sensible or material world of contingent events in space and time; and in such a world there can by definition be no room for God.

In all this nothing has been said of mind or soul, or of the way in which it can know the different grades of reality. Platonism is one form of what is called 'realism'; and, broadly speaking, whatever may have to be done by mind on the way to knowledge, knowledge is supposed to be a direct vision of reality as it is in itself. This is believed possible on the basis of a kinship between mind and its object. So far as the soul is aware of changing sensible objects, it is itself sensuous and changing; so far as it is aware of eternal and intelligible objects, it too is eternal as well as intelligent; and if the eternal is the real, the soul is most real so far as it is directed to eternal objects both in thought and in action. The Form of the Good, the unconditioned reality which is the source of all truth and knowledge and being and yet is somehow beyond all these, may seem to fall short of God in so far as it is nothing more; and the soul of man may seem to cling precariously to the marble façade of a hierarchy of intelligible Forms stretching upwards beyond his vision. But if this supreme Form is not merely supremely real and supremely intelligible in itself, but is also supreme intelligence—as it comes to be in the more mystical developments of the doctrine—then indeed we have a philosophy in which the religious man may find satisfaction, not only for his head, but for his heart.

It is not surprising that in all ages religious thinkers have sought to go back to some kind of Platonism. It is this which in its various modifications is claimed as the perennial philosophy—*philosophia perennis*; and there are some who profess to find it in the East as well as in the West. Yet the predicament of religion to-day lies partly in the fact that most modern philosophy is disposed to question the Platonic claim. Is it really possible for us, with our finite minds and our dependence on sense and matter, to obtain knowledge of the supreme reality? Before we are carried away by the eloquence of the divine Plato, ought we not to turn back and reflect on our own limited capacities and ask ourselves how such knowledge can be possible? The Greeks were less troubled by this question than we are to-day; but, as a matter of historical fact, the Academy which Plato founded, and which lasted for a thousand years until it was closed by an intolerant Church, turned in the end to a doctrine of scepticism. We are still told, though not by many, that it is sheer confusion to ask questions about the possibility of our own knowledge; but perhaps Christian theology, in its concern with the individual human soul and with the need for revelation as opposed to reason, has itself helped to stimulate such questions. The developments of science have made these enquiries inevitable. Even if modern thinking is entirely on the wrong lines—a very difficult assumption—we are compelled to consider, not merely the character of the known world, but also the nature of the mind which knows it.

Perhaps after all it is a mistake to speak of the philosophers' world. There is only one world which we all try to know from our different points of view. Of that world man is only a part, and yet a part which claims to know other parts or even to know the whole. Perhaps the first business of philosophy is to examine this claim and to study the powers and limitations of the fallible creatures who make it.

Chapter XVII

MAN AND HIS EXPERIENCE

§ 1. *The man who knows*

We must now turn our attention from the wheeling galaxies and the whirling electrons, and from the no less dizzying speculations of philosophers, to the strange creature who has propounded these astonishing theories and claims to know this amazing world. Who is it who has set himself to measure alike the immeasurably vast and the immeasurably small? It is a tiny living organism, one of the many animals on the surface of that speck in the universe which we call the earth. No wonder we flatter ourselves that we are rational animals—the paragon of animals, as Shakespeare calls us. And we can echo Hamlet's words—'What a piece of work is man! How noble in reason! How infinite in faculty! In apprehension how like a God!'

Man is a complex being and can be studied from many different points of view. Nearly all the scientists can 'have a go' at him. The molecules and atoms of which his body is composed are subject to the laws of physics and chemistry, and the new science of bio-chemistry may be the great hope of human medicine. Physiology knows more and more about our genes, our glands, and the working of our brain and nervous system. Psychology professes to have plumbed the depths, not only of our individual unconsciousness, but also—if Jung is to be believed—of a collective and hereditary unconsciousness, from which we draw our moods and attitudes and thoughts and symbols. The social sciences attempt to study us in the mass, and hope—according to Karl Mannheim—to develop new techniques which will alter our behaviour, outlook, and feelings by making changes in our environment. Samples of what can be done in the way of transforming men have already been given us by the totalitarian States, and especially by 'the enlightened dictatorship in Russia'.

From all these points of view man is an object to be studied—one object among many others—or even a puppet to be manipulated. We become, as it were, slides under a microscope or vile bodies on an operating table. Yet if this be the whole truth about man, we may be tempted to go back to our Shakespeare again and say to ourselves 'What is this quintessence of dust? man delights not me, no nor woman neither!'

In spite of some frightening possibilities, of which so-called brainwashing is perhaps the worst, it would be absurd not to welcome our increased knowledge of human nature with its high hopes of a more intelligent and healthier life; but we must not let ourselves be so blinded by the blazing light of scientific progress as to forget that in all this something is left out. Who are these divine beings who tell us so confidently what kind of objects we are—or even, with an unconscious arrogance, what kind of objects we must become? Can it be that after all they are not gods, but only men like ourselves? If their statements exhaust the truth about themselves as well as about us, how can they know what they say they know? There must be something more in the world than molecules and atoms and genes and glands and cerebral processes, something more than the unconscious, whether individual or collective, something more than puppets to be manipulated *en masse* by social techniques. There must be thinking, which—however much it may be conditioned or influenced, or in some cases hampered, by the various processes revealed to science—is somehow able to grasp truth and to know reality.

This is not to say that even the least developed of the newer sciences—and it is these that are most ready to tinker with human nature—are without truth. On the contrary, it is because they contain so much truth that they can be a menace in the hands of the irresponsible. Nevertheless, when taken as the whole truth, they suffer from a fatal flaw: they ignore the fact that man is a knowing subject, and not merely a known object. This fact is implied in their every utterance, and our account of man is incomplete unless we recognize that man is a knower and thinker as well as an object known.

It is difficult—some would say impossible—to consider man as a knower, and to ask ourselves how his knowledge is possible. Yet this is precisely what we must try to do. My brief suggestions may be as confused as most of what is said on this topic. If we try to talk about man as a knowing subject, must we not turn him at once into a known object? And how can we examine our powers of knowing except by means of these very same powers?

If we engage in such an enquiry, we may seem to be rather like an absent-minded philosopher hunting for his spectacles and unable to find them because he is wearing them all the time. Even when he discovers they are on his nose, he cannot see them properly unless he takes them off. If we make the impossible assumption that without his spectacles he is totally blind, the spectacles are the one thing he would never be able to see—unless he is fortunate enough to possess a duplicate pair.

Perhaps we should rather compare ourselves to a man trying to see his own eyes. He can find no duplicates for them, but at least he can see them in a mirror, in a reflexion. The late Professor Colling-wood used to speak of the world as the mirror of the mind, and it may be that we can see our mind, as it were, reflected in our world. The question 'How can I know the world?' may not be very different from the question 'How can the world be known?' Whatever the difficulty about knowing ourselves as knowing subjects, we may be able at least to discover some of the conditions under which our knowledge or experience of the world is possible. If to know these conditions is so far to know our powers of knowing by means of our powers of knowing, this is precisely the human situation we have to recognize and to accept.

We must not suppose that our questions could be answered by psychology. So far as psychology describes experience, it is certainly of importance for our enquiry; for we cannot say how experience is possible unless we know what experience is; and if we can know this scientifically, so much the better. But psychology is itself a part of our experience, and when we ask how experience is possible, we also ask how psychology is possible. These are philosophical questions and are not the concern of psychologists as such.

§ 2. *Experience*

The word 'experience' may be used, as I have used it here, for 'empirical knowledge of the world'. But sometimes it is employed, especially by philosophical psychologists like Mr. Farrell, to indicate an element in such knowledge—even a simple element like a sensation, or raw feeling, which cannot be further analysed. There then arises a tendency to say that we ought to 'get rid of experience' in psychology. The business of psychology is to discover the physiological correlates of behaviour, and 'there is nothing else to do'.

This view is reasonable enough if it merely claims the right to develop a psychology which confines itself to a study of human behaviour. But if it denies the possibility of examining experience (in every sense of that word) either psychologically or in any other way, it would be fatal to our enquiry, and we must consider its limitations.

A behaviouristic psychology, whatever its merits, has a special and limited point of view: it treats man, not as a knower, but as an animal organism known. We can use a man as a 'subject' in a laboratory—perhaps it would be better to say as an object. We can show him differently coloured disks and ask him to indicate—either by words or by depressing keys or by opening lids—which colour is red, which is green, and so on. He is then said to 'discriminate' between colours, but this 'discrimination' might be no more than the discrimination manifested by a barometer under different kinds of atmospheric pressure; for we are supposed to know nothing of his 'experience'—of what happens in the gap between the stimulus and the response.

Since this gap is a gap in the experience of the psychologist, not in that of his victim, we might suppose that it could be filled if the psychologist makes himself his own object. For example, he might show himself red and green disks and respond by uttering the appropriate word or depressing the appropriate key. He would then know that the response was preceded by an experience of *seeing* red or green, and would surmise that a similar experience preceded the similar responses of other people. The gap would be filled.

This is surely the plain truth of the matter, but we are sometimes told that the psychologist discovers no more about experience when he experiments with himself than when he experiments with other people. It is impossible here to examine the ingenious arguments for so paradoxical a view: they rest partly on criticism of some absurd ways in which the word 'experience' has been used. Psychologists are sometimes so modest as to forget that they too must be present in the laboratory and that without their own experience of disks and colours and responses there would be no psychology at all.

The element of truth in this attempt to eliminate experience is that we cannot investigate knowings apart from what is known, thinkings apart from what is thought, sensings apart from what is sensed, experiencings apart from what is experienced. This was recognized—perhaps not without some vagueness—by the idealist philosophy which was predominant well into the present century. The opponents of this philosophy protested against what they considered to be a mere confusion, and insisted that we must make a complete separation between the experiencing and the experienced, the sensing and the sensed, or more generally between what has been called the 'ing' and the '-ed'. The result was that all the '-ings'—knowing, thinking, sensing, experiencing—became pure blanks, all exactly alike and indistinguishable apart from their objects. Nothing whatever could be said about them except mythologically. They became an unobservable series of indescribable ghostly events and aroused the ire of some modern philosophers— Professor Ryle is the outstanding example. This is one reason, though it need not be the only one, for rejecting experience—that is, experiencing—altogether.

Nevertheless we cannot as philosophers, though perhaps we may as scientists, be content with a lot of '-eds' existing all by themselves. Even as plain men, nothing could induce us to believe that we do not know and think and question and imagine, or that we do not see, hear, smell, taste, and touch. All these are elements combined in what I call my experience; but my experience is not a series of ghostly events capable of being investigated by themselves: it is experience of the world as it appears to me. In addition to the goings-on in my body which can be studied by the Behaviourist, there is, so to speak, a whole world going on in me or to me or for me—or however you like to put it.

There are here endless complications and difficulties—about feelings and mental images, for example, not to mention actions—but what I am trying to suggest is roughly that my experience in the first instance is my world as seen from a particular point of view or in a particular perspective. It is as if I were a cone of light: whatever falls within its beams is part of my experience, but the light itself is not seen unless indirectly as it illuminates an object. When colours fall within my perspective, I see colours; when bodies fall within my perspective, I see bodies; when arguments fall within my perspective, I see arguments. Here the word 'see' is manifestly being used in different senses; but it goes best with the word 'perspective', which has also to be used in different senses. We may prefer to speak of 'knowing' instead of 'seeing'; but the essential point is that my knowing or seeing is not a seeing double. I may see a succession of colours, but I do not see, as it were, a parallel succession of seeings. In short, my experience—and surely this is only common sense—consists in seeing colours, in seeing bodies, in seeing arguments, and so on. It does not consist in a lot of alleged seeings which can be known apart from what is seen. On the other

R

hand, when I see a colour I know that I see a colour. Experience is not only a conscious, but in some degree a self-conscious, experience. If it were not so, we could not even begin to talk about it.

It is this concrete experience which has to be investigated, but this can be done in different ways. We can approach the experience of an individual from our own point of view as detached observers, supposing we know all about his body and brain and nervous system and about the material world which stimulates his body; and we can try to find out how *his* experience develops in the world as *we* know it. This is the task of philosophical psychology, and its character is admirably indicated by the title of Professor Broad's well-known book '*The Mind and its Place in Nature*'. But there is another, and a logically prior, type of investigation. This would not begin by taking it for granted that a material world exists independently of our knowledge. *A fortiori* it would not begin by supposing that our sensations were effects produced by the action of other bodies on our body and ultimately on our brain. Can we begin instead by asking how our alleged experience of the material world is possible and how it can be justified? Can we ask what our mind must be or do if it is to know the world it seems to know, and indeed what our mind must be or do if it is to know itself? Can we, in short, try to look at the experience of the individual from his own point of view instead of from the point of view of some detached observer who knows a great deal more than he does and tries to put him in his place?

As each of us is an individual who knows and experiences the world from his own point of view, this task, though one of colossal difficulty, should not be wholly beyond our powers.

If we want a name for the kind of philosophy which undertakes this task, we may follow the usage of Immanuel Kant and call it 'Critical' philosophy. But it does not matter whether the doctrines here expounded are to be found in him or not. I am adapting or modifying his views to suit my own purposes.

§ 3. *My point of view*

It is obvious enough that in speaking of my experience and my point of view I am taking for granted a great deal that may be hard to justify and that may not even be consistent with itself. I am proposing to stand away from my experience and try to look at it—in what can only be another experience, and indeed only a part of my experience as a whole. In trying to identify my experience with the world as seen from my point of view, I seem at the same time to be separating myself from my experience. I seem also to be taking for granted that there is a world which exists independently of my experience and my point of view—a world which none the less appears to me, or is experienced by me, from my own point of view. And although I am speaking in the first person—as I must in order to make my meaning clear—I am doing so impersonally: I am expecting that my words may be intelligible, and perhaps even acceptable, to other beings who also make use of the personal pronoun 'I'.

Assumptions of this kind have to be made, so far as I can see, by any one who tries to talk about his experience or about the world as it appears to him. All of these assumptions are in need of clarification, and some of them may become a little clearer as we advance.

What then is my point of view?

At least to begin with, the phrase can be taken literally. My point of view is the point from which I see my world, the point where I am here and now. I look out from here and see perhaps a room full of furniture and people. My own point of view in this literal sense I do not and cannot see—unless I move and see it from a different point of view; but then I have a different vista, a different perspective, a different experience.

My own body is one of the things I can see, though only in part, from my own point of view; and my point of view in space is continually changing as the world on which I stand goes whirling and hurtling through space; but this is a late discovery and for practical purposes can be ignored. Usually I think of my point of view as the same unless I move about—for example, by getting nearer to some object I see. But all movement takes time, and if I am to have a different point of view in space, I can do so only at a later time, and so at a different time.

Space is ordinarily conceived as standing still; and when the uninstructed are told that space is stretching with a speed greater than that of light, they have to think of it as stretching through another space that stands still and does not stretch. But time is thought of as moving inexorably on, so that even if I could keep the same point of view in space, my point of view in time is for ever changing. I always look at my world from the point of time I call 'now'; but the 'now' is always a different 'now', even when the 'here' is supposed to remain the same 'here'.

If this is true, my experience—or the world as experienced by me—is not one momentary perspective: it looks like a whole series, or succession, of perspectives, each of which disappears as the next appears. Yet somehow or other—and this is the great puzzle—the past perspectives must remain with me: they must in some sense be reproduced or remembered; and unless this were so, I could never know that I had a new perspective—still less that I had a new point of view in space and time. When I look out of the window of a moving train, I see a succession of many perspectives, and I could not even know that I was moving unless I were able somehow to hold these perspectives together. Hence, on the one hand, my experience—or my world—seems to be a collection of successive perspectives. On the other hand, this whole collection is still part of one perspective (though not in so literal a sense); for it has still to be viewed by me as a whole here and now: it has still to be reproduced or remembered by me, however imperfectly and however schematically, if I am to be aware of it at all. The railway traveller must be able to say to himself 'I have seen quite a lot of country in the last five minutes'.

Hence, if I am to have the experience I do have, I must continually be holding together, or putting together, different parts of filled time and of filled space. It would be false to suggest that I must remember all the past in detail or reproduce it vividly in my imagination, but I seem always at least to receive my present perspective as part of a whole of past perspectives and, as it were, to attach it to that whole or attach that whole to it. This is true even if I remain at the same point in space and look at objects which do not seem to change; and the process is a kind of treadmill which can never stop while I continue to have experience or while the world continues to appear to me.

This process is sometimes called 'synthesis', which is merely the Greek for 'putting together'. Such language has been criticized on the ground that we do not put things together—we merely know that they are together. But, so far as my experience is concerned, this is not true. My past perspective never was together with my present perspective. The two are together only as I now hold them together or put them together in thought or memory or imagination.

The same principle holds, though less obviously, in regard to parts of space and bodies in space, even when the bodies are supposed to remain in the same place and not to change. Only by putting together and holding together a whole series of different successive perspectives can I know the front, sides, and back of a house: in common-sense language I must walk round the house and remember what I see. When I see the front of a house new to me, I take for granted that it has a back and sides which could be known in the same way. When I look out of my window, I see fields and trees and houses with hills in the distance, all disposed in three-dimensional space. What is going on in my mind it is very hard to say. It is not a simple process of inference, but it is at least an active intellectual process of synthesis which would be impossible without imagination and memory and expectation (or something analogous to these).

The queer thing is that the world as experienced by me seems to stretch out indefinitely in all directions in space and also to stretch indefinitely backwards in time, and perhaps even forwards as well. I perceive only a part, but I am always connecting part with part and pressing on to attain a whole which none the less can never be complete. I take all material objects, even the remotest galaxies, to be ordered in one space continuous with my present space; and I take all events, even the beginning and the end of the solar system, to be ordered in one time continuous with my present time.

Needless to say, this vast universe is not present to me in the same detail as the room in which I stand. At any moment only a very small part of this room—or even of the desk at which I sit—is clearly present to me, but this part is always taken to be only a part, and it shades off into other parts less clearly present. There are parts of the room—for example, the wall behind me—which I do not see at all, but they are taken for granted and may be present to me schematically in imagination. I take it for granted that I am in this room, and this room is in a building, and this building is in a town, and so on indefinitely in one space and time. To experience a world of this kind is manifestly impossible apart from a most elaborate process of synthesis, which yet seems to be guided or directed throughout—consciously or unconsciously—by the principle that my world must be a whole in one space and in one time.

Endless complications are here passed over. There are many, for example, who tell us that there are all sorts of space—visual space, tactual space, psychological space, physical space, and so on. It is hard to see how there can be all these spaces, and how we could ever come to know them and to connect them with one another. But if this view is right, it shows only that the process of synthesis is far more complicated than I have said. Personally I feel more inclined to the view of the Hindu sage who remarked to an impatient European complaining about lack of time 'I suppose you have all the time there is'. I should at least like to think that I have all the space and all the time there is. Then it would be meaningless to say that you had one space (or time) and I had another—although we should be aware of them from different points of view and perhaps measure them by different measures.

§ 4. *Other points of view*

We must now try to envisage the possibility of points of view other than our own—the possibility of other experiences and other minds.

Besides reproducing and remembering and combining past perspectives of my own, I can construct possible new perspectives: when I see the front of a house I can imagine, however vaguely, what the house looks like from the sides or the back, even if I have never seen the house before. In imagination I can, so to speak, place myself in different parts of space and time and construct in fancy the perspectives open from these points of view; and I can sometimes check or verify these products of my fancy, though only by means of another synthesis of the same kind. I am not confined to my own lifetime. I can imagine myself talking to Socrates in the market place at Athens or listening to Cicero in the Senate House at Rome. This power is important when we consider our knowledge of other people—people with perspectives other than our own. A man of genius who grew up alone on a desert island might perhaps be able to imagine a person other than himself—an *alter ego*. In ordinary life I am driven to believe in the existence of other people by knowledge of my own body and of other bodies like it.

The primary qualities of bodies are determined, I suggested earlier, by counting and weighing and measuring. These mathematical processes I can apply to my own body, but in this case I have further sources of information besides my external senses. I have enough in the way of internal sensation to feel that I have an inside as well as an outside, although the feeling is so confused that I could never know my own size and shape apart from external sensations of sight and touch. My body and its feelings are always a very near and intimate part of my total perspective (which is never merely visual); and yet the point of view from which I literally see the world seems to lie in my body. When I close my eyes the visible world is blotted out. Hence it is not difficult to reach the conclusion that I see with my eyes. Similar discoveries are made about hearing, tasting, smelling, and touching.

Among the many material bodies in my world I find some like my own, which behave in much the same sort of way. They open and close their eyes, for example, very much as I do. It is not difficult for me to imagine the perspectives I should see from their point of view. I very naturally suppose they have the same kind of perspectives as I have, and that they put these perspectives together as I do in one time and space. In short I take them to be persons with an experience like my own, and this seems to be confirmed by the possibility of communication. I can say to them 'Look and see'; and they can respond.

This highly intellectual process should not be regarded as the way in which we actually come to know other people. We probably come to know them by cruder processes of fighting and co-operation, of love and hate; and we may have no notion of ourselves till we, as it were, sort ourselves out from others. But at present we are considering in abstraction the cognitive element in our experience. My main point is that even on this cognitive level, although the bodies and experiences of others are in one sense only elements in my complicated system of perspectives, I also think of them as having a complicated system of perspectives like my own. Although I believe that I have privileged access to my point of view as they have to theirs, I can enter into their point of view in imagination— in somewhat the same way as I can construct points of view and perspectives which I might have had if I had lived in some other place at some other time. I can even understand how from their point of view I may be only an element in their system of perspectives and yet may be supposed to have a point of view of my own into which they too can enter in imagination. This means that I can stand to other people in a relation of subject to subject as well as in a relation of subject to object. In Martin Buber's more poetical language—though perhaps he would not agree with this—I can use the primary word '*I-Thou*' as well as the primary word '*I-It*'. And I suppose that other people can do the same. We are in some ways like mirrors reflecting one another *ad infinitum*.

§ 5. *The common world*

It is not very difficult to pass from such considerations to the thought of a comprehensive or ideal experience in which all different systems of actual and possible perspectives could be combined. Such a thought might be regarded as a thought about God, but it would be hard to articulate and would seem to be still necessarily incomplete: it is one of those conceptions almost forced on us by experience and yet seemingly impossible for us to grasp. It is easier for us to think of what is common to all possible and actual human experiences or human perspectives—to think of our common world. We may regard this as primarily a world of material objects determined by scientific measurements in one space and time; but we also know that it must look different from different points of view, and we assume that other people are aware of secondary—and even tertiary—qualities similar in some degree to those we observe ourselves. Hence so far as we can enter in imagination into the point of view of others, our common world is richer and more varied than the world of material objects, although it is only the material objects that can be determined with precision.

On the other hand, my experience—and so presumably that of others—is more than a mirror of the order of physical events. When I watch a moving aeroplane, I see its different positions one after another, and I assume that it passes through these positions one after another; but when I look at a house, although I see its four walls one after another, I assume that they are all there at the same time. The order of my observings is not always the same as the order I attribute to what is observed. In more technical language the subjective order of my perceptions need not be the same as the objective order of what I perceive. Furthermore, when I perceive anything, I may at the same time be conscious of thoughts, images, feelings, and desires, which I do not attribute to the object perceived but to myself.

Into the complications of all this it is impossible to enter here. I measure time—even the time at which I observe objects or entertain thoughts or see images or have feelings or am conscious of desires— by the movement of physical bodies like clocks or stars. Nevertheless, although my experience, whatever else it may be, is always experience of the physical world, the time order of physical events is not the same as the time order at which I come to know these events; it is not the same, that is to say, as the time order of my mental history even if my mental history is reduced to an awareness of physical events. Say if you like—though this is far too simple— that what I call my mental history is only a succession of perspectives of the physical world. These perspectives have nevertheless to be arranged in one time order if they are to constitute my mental history and in a different time order if they are to constitute the world as experienced by me. Here and now I can look back on my own mental history and endeavour to put it in its place in the history of the physical world. I can, for example, remember my first sight of the Roman forum and can ask how many years had then elapsed since the first foundation of Rome.

When I try to do this I am still the centre here and now from which both my mental history and the succession of events in the physical world are viewed. These two series are both of them held together or put together by my act of synthesis here and now. What is more, the two series are not merely parallel—they seem to be inter-connected. The working of my brain I take to be a series of physical events connected causally with other physical events, and yet at the same time I take it to be the cause or condition of my having any mental history at all.

What I believe to be true of my own experience, I believe also to be true of the experience of other people. Hence what I have called the subjective succession of our perceptions—and of our thoughts, feelings, images, and desires—is itself also a part of our common objective world. I cannot know the succession of your perceptions as I know the succession of my own, but I can construct them in imagination in a way that I suppose not to be wholly remote from the reality; and I have some reason to assume that the kind of complications which I find in my own experience will be found equally in yours. Unless I do assume this, I cannot take you to be a person like myself at all, and there would be no possibility of communication between us.

§ 6. *Phenomenalism and materialism*

It may be objected that my perceptions just happen to arrange and co-ordinate themselves into an ordered world: they trip like ballet-dancers into their places in a strange theatre which has no stage and no audience and nothing behind the scenes. Why should we indulge in this elaborate talk about syntheses and imaginative constructions when all that is required is the association of ideas?

It is hard to believe that unordered perceptions and casual associations of ideas could ever constitute knowledge of an ordered world. What is more, this doctrine seems to reduce knowledge to a succession of momentary experiences, each gone before the next appears. It reduces my world to a succession of momentary worlds, each dead before the next is born. But if this were so, how could it ever be *known* that there was a succession of momentary experiences? How could a succession of ideas ever give rise to an idea of succession? And even if I could know the time order of my momentary experiences, how could I pass from this to know the different time order of objects in my world? How could I discover that the walls of a house were not successive but simultaneous?

If answers can be given to these questions, they will be no less elaborate than the doctrine they are intended to replace.

Another possible view is that what I call my experience results from changes in the atoms which happen to have come together in my body and brain in accordance with the laws of physics and of biological evolution.

Such a doctrine assumes that I already know a great deal about my experience and about my body and brain, and it seeks to establish correlations or conjunctions between them. This is a fascinating enquiry, but a quite different one: it does not even begin to ask how the material world of bodies and brains can be known.

If we say that the brain itself does all our thinking and knowing, the word 'does' is used very loosely. What the brain does literally is to manifest electrical activity, sometimes described anthropomorphically as receiving and sending messages. But if we say—as is said by Professor J. Z. Young in his Reith Lectures on *Doubt and Certainty in Science*—that what the brain does is 'to comprehend the pattern of the stars', this is metaphorical or even metaphysical. Comprehending a pattern is a phenomenon unknown to handbooks on electricity and magnetism; and although there may be a pattern of electrical activity in my brain, this is something entirely different from the pattern of the stars which I am supposed to comprehend by means of it.

From the point of view of my experience, the action of my brain is only one of the many things that I can comprehend. I must have experience of the world before I can know anything about my brain or what it does; and such knowledge would be impossible unless my thinking has already principles of its own by which it can distinguish, reflectively or unreflectively, between truth and error, between fact and fancy, between inference and mere association of ideas. From this point of view the causal connexion between my thoughts and the changes in my brain is a connexion between different elements within my total experience.

To all this it may be objected that vague philosophical theories are being pitted against established scientific facts.

Such an objection is due to misunderstanding. A philosopher is not rejecting the facts established by science when he asks how they are to be interpreted and how they can be known. Scientists have no more right than theologians to claim immunity from philosophical questioning. Even if the materialistic view is accepted by simple faith, it remains a miracle that a little eddy in the dust of which this vast universe is composed should be able, because of its changing conformation, to say to itself 'I am only a little eddy of dust, and I know that I am; and indeed I know that in the whole endless universe only a few little eddies like myself have any notion of what is going on'. The knowledge thus claimed is so different from a physical movement that a material world in which it is found is a world in which anything might happen. Perhaps it is a dim feeling of this that makes some scientific thinkers so anxious to get rid of knowledge altogether—to reduce experience and thinking to mere behaviour, or mere talk, considered as a physical movement. A philosopher can speak even of his own talk in this way; but in the long run there must be some one who can *understand* his words and *judge* that they are true or false; and indeed he is presumably able to do so himself. This is a breach in the material order. To a materialistic philosophy it is a perpetual miracle, which must be blindly accepted or blindly denied.

Chapter XVIII

THE LIMITS OF KNOWLEDGE

§ 1. *The given*

Human experience, or human knowledge, has so far been analysed in a rather simple way. More difficult questions have now to be raised, not only about experience itself, but also about the limits of our knowledge and about the status of the world that is known and of the self that knows it. Readers who have found the last chapter difficult enough may be advised to pass straight on to the conclusions outlined in § 8. As human knowledge is still being analysed from the point of view of the knower, the painful practice of speaking in the first person will have to be continued.

If there is any truth in what has been said, my experience (and my world) has to be built up on what is given from moment to moment ; and it is by means of the given that I have what may be called direct contact with reality. But what is it that is so given ?

The word 'given', if it is taken strictly, should be applied only to something of which I am aware without any activity on my part. If sense is supposed to be altogether passive, then the given is what is given to sense alone.

It might be thought easy to describe what is given, yet there are few topics about which philosophers disagree more. The perspectives hitherto taken to be, as it were, the bricks with which I build my experience and my world, cannot possibly be given : like other bricks they have to be made. Many thinkers have held that what is given to sense alone is a 'sense-datum'; and by this they mean, for example, a bulgy red patch or shape or expanse which I see out there now when I am looking at what I believe to be a tomato. For reasons of brevity tactual and auditory sense-data—not to mention others—will have to be ignored.

The sense-datum theory has taken many forms. In spite of opposition, and almost persecution, when it first migrated from Cambridge to Oxford not so many years ago, it rapidly spread, like a prairie fire, over the English-speaking world, but at present it seems almost to have burnt itself out. One of the best accounts of it is to be found in Professor Price's '*Perception*'—a work which retains its value after twenty years ; but he too would probably express his doctrine now in somewhat different language.

When I look at a tomato, I think—though I find it hard to be quite sure—that I can see a definite red bulgy expanse out there now ; and if I were an artist like Professor Price, I could no doubt do this much more easily. As it is, I find it most difficult to see a coloured expanse and not to see a tomato. Difficulties of this kind have given rise to modifications in the doctrine, for which the reader may be referred to Professor Price's recent book called '*Thinking and Experience*'. But if subtleties may be ignored, it is reasonable to hold that while I can be mistaken in believing what I see to be a tomato—it may, for example, be an object made of wax or a mirror image or even a hallucination—I cannot be mistaken in saying that I see a red bulgy expanse out there now. It is also reasonable to hold that I build up my experience of a tomato by means of seen red shapes out there. Only by means of seen and felt shapes can I build up my experience of material objects (although it is true that a blind man can build up his different experience of material objects without the aid of colours).

The fundamental difficulty about all this is already suggested by Professor Northrop's account of Eastern 'nihilism' as outlined in Chapter VI. There is reason to believe that what is given to sense alone is not anything so definite as a seen shape, but is more like an 'undifferentiated continuum'—something vague and obscure and indeterminate, perhaps similar to what I feel within my body when I am hardly conscious that I have a body. According to Professor Northrop, it is possible to apprehend such an undifferentiated continuum by means of sense alone without being aware of any-thing else. Even if few of us are sufficiently practised in ascetic discipline to be capable of such pure apprehension, we may have grounds for accepting his hypothesis about the vagueness of what is given as almost certainly correct.

Many empirical observations might be adduced in support of such a contention. It is borne out, for example, by the experience of blind men who have acquired sight for the first time—they find the utmost difficulty in distinguishing by sight between circles and squares and triangles, although they already know these simple differences by touch. An infant, who lacks this advantage, must find the difficulty still greater. We have to *learn* how to see coloured shapes out there, and still more we have to *learn* how to estimate

their size and distance. The given may be compared to a letter in
invisible ink which can be brought out only by the appropriate
procedure.

If we accept this view and assume at the same time that through
the given we are in direct contact with a reality which is what it is
independently of our experience, it seems impossible to believe that
this reality as it is in itself can be identified either with our sense-
data or with the material objects we know by their help ; for both
of these are not merely given, but are also made what they are by
activity on our part. On the other hand, if we assume that reality is
only what is given, we may be forced to adopt the Eastern doctrine
which has been described as maintaining that what is is what is not.

If we look at things ingenuously, what actually *seems* to be given
is not only more definite and precise than an undifferentiated
continuum, but also more permanent and orderly than a collection
of sense-data. When I look out of my window, what I seem to see
is a steady landscape of fields and trees and houses and hills—part
of my stable, though changing, world, one of the perspectives of
which my experience is made up. But every philosopher would
agree that there must be more to this than mere seeing—more than
can be given to sense : we are not provided, as it were gratuitously,
with slabs of reality which we have only to fit together like a jigsaw
puzzle. Even what seems to be 'given' must somehow be 'taken' as
well. It is possible to look for a pipe on the table and yet fail to see
it, although it is, as it were, staring us straight in the face the whole
time. The word 'given' is highly ambiguous. If anything of which
I am immediately aware can be described as given, no matter what
I may have done to bring it before me, then everything may be
so described—even the present argument.

§ 2. *Space and time*

What I see when I look at a tomato has been described as a
coloured expanse. It might equally well be described as an extended
colour—we cannot see colours that are not extended. We might
also say that it is an enduring colour or—rather more artificially—a
coloured duration. There are no such things as mere colours, for
whatever is a colour must also be spatial and temporal ; and if
colours are given out there now, space and time would seem to be
so far given too. The same statement applies broadly to all sense-
data.

In human experience space and time are all-pervasive. Whatever may be given to me—whether I take this to be an undifferentiated continuum or a red expanse or a tomato or a landscape or even a world—seems to be always a bit of filled time ; and part of what fills time is generally, and perhaps always, a bit of filled space. Every bit of time is for me part of a longer time ; every bit of space is part of a larger space ; and I assume I could go on tacking bit to bit in imagination for ever.

What is given to me can only be given now. But since every 'now' is a different 'now', what is given is not a fixed point on which I can rest a lever that would move the world : it is at best a sliding point—a perpetually vanishing point—and to have anything before me at all I must continually, as it were, attach a past that is no longer to a present that is always ceasing to be. I know my sense-data, as I know my world, only by a synthesis of times and spaces as well as of sense-data—that is, by a kind of double synthesis which itself goes on in time. Without this I could have no experience, nor could I even begin to speak of my point of view. Without this there would be no world for me.

If this is true, the world I know is not merely given : it is also made or constructed—although not created—by me on what seems to be a most precarious foundation, which is entirely concealed by the building that covers it. Nor should it be forgotten that in constructing my world I construct also my own mental history. The world I know seems to be a kind of between-world—the joint product of my activity and an unknown reality. My knowing can never be a mere passive reception of reality as it is in itself. Reality does not migrate into my mind under its own steam : it appears to me under a form imposed by the limitations of my mind.

This contention is independent of philosophical or scientific theories about the nature of space and time—or of space-time, as we are now expected to call it—but it may be strongly reinforced by such theories. On a simple view we can in thought separate space and time from what is in them, and we assume that there can be only one space and one time. These have the curious characteristic of being composed entirely of relations ; and these relations are themselves spaces and times. This does not mean that space and time are things like boxes which can exist apart from what is in them—you cannot make a box out of relations. They are not substances and they are not qualities. They are not even objects, as bodies or minds are objects. They are sometimes spoken of as if they were merely relations between things or even as if they were orders of things ; but they seem to be rather the condition of such relations and orders. Sometimes it is said that the word 'space'— or the word 'time'—stands only for a set of facts, or even a set of propositions, about objects. It is hard to see any difference between 'a fact about' and 'a true proposition about'; and I must confess that this doctrine is to me incomprehensible : to speak ingenuously— how can a body be located in a set of propositions ? But it must at least be recognized that space and time are paradoxical in character —so paradoxical that Kant maintained, and even claimed to demonstrate, that they are contributed by our own minds to the world we know ; that they are, as it were, only the spectacles through which we experience as spatial and temporal a reality that in itself is not in space and time. This is a view which has pressed itself for many reasons on thoughtful men and is not unfamiliar in theology. If it could be upheld, it would establish beyond doubt the contention that we can never know reality as it is in itself.

In any case space and time, beyond the 'here and now' which may be thought to be given with a sense-datum, have to be constructed by an act of synthesis : they cannot possibly be given either as finite or as infinite wholes, although we may think of them as if they were. Even 'here' and 'now' have no meaning apart from 'then' and 'there'.

All of this is complicated by doctrines about what is called the 'specious present'. These attempt to explain the fact that during a relatively short time I may be able to *see* a body moving and not merely to *remember* that it was once in a different place from where it is now. For a brief discussion of this problem I can only refer to my book '*In Defence of Reason*'.

§ 3. *Imagination*

An infant must pass gradually from vague sensation to ordered experience. In spite of having made this journey ourselves we know very little about it, but it should not be confused with what happens in mature experience.

When I see a tomato, it may be said that I must pass from the sign to the thing signified—from the sense-datum to the material object. Yet it would be a mistake to suppose there are two clearly defined stages happening one after another. If this passage occurs, it seems to happen all at once.

But what is it that does happen ? The language employed might suggest that we were making an inference or offering an interpretation, but obviously we are doing nothing so sophisticated. When the validity of mystical experience was discussed in Chapter X, I used words like 'conceiving', 'thinking', 'judging'; but I had to point out that even in describing our experience of finite objects they were not to be taken in the ordinary sense, and that perhaps we had no recognized word for what is meant. Similar difficulties must arise about words for describing the passage, if there is one, from an undifferentiated to a differentiated continuum and from a material object to an ordered world.

It is all too easy to make hay of this over-explicit language, especially if we interpret it as implying some kind of verbal utterance ; but those who concentrate on the inadequacy of the terminology are in danger of missing the problem.

Without entering into these complicated questions, on which Professor Price is probably the best guide, I wish only to call attention to one factor which is too commonly neglected—the factor of imagination.

In our experience we are always doing something more than apprehending what is given here and now ; and it is not nearly enough to say that we supplement this by entertaining, or asserting, a series of theoretical propositions. Such a view is possible only to those who believe that all thinking takes place solely by means of words. Yet nothing can be more certain than that men can think also by means of pictures and images, and by gestures as well. Perhaps there must always be something more than these in our thinking ; but whatever it may be, this 'something more' need not be the utterance, aloud or to ourselves, of verbal propositions.

The very fact that our experience is temporal means that we could have no experience without memory. If we are content to speak in a simple and provisional way, we may say that we must be able to reproduce in imagination what we have sensed and to recognize that the image now produced is like what we sensed before. It should be unnecessary to add that the image need not be visual.

One of the obvious difficulties about this is that such recognition would seem to be impossible unless we *already* remembered what we had sensed. How otherwise could we recognize that our present image is like it ? Some philosophers would be content to say that the image produced feels familiar ; but memory must be more than an inference from a felt familiarity. Yet it is true—to take a rather different case—that when we come into a room we may remember that we have been there before *without* remembering the previous occasion, and presumably without producing any image of what we formerly saw.

In spite of these and other difficulties we may perhaps assume that without images of some kind there could be no memory and no experience. What must be added is that the memory of definite events, which is at least usually accompanied by images, shades off into the other kind of memory which consists in remembering, as we say, *how* to do something—for example, how to ride a bicycle. So too our activity in imagining seems to shade off from the making of images to knowing *how* to make them. Between these extreme limits there may be a whole range of activity, including the making of vague or incomplete or wavering images; and this range, I think, is what Kant had in mind when he maintained that imagination produced 'schemata' for concepts and not merely definite images. It is essential to recognize that our imaginings may be highly schematic and yet that without them our concepts would be meaningless.

If imagination is an ability to have or produce images of what is not immediately present to sense, its function is not confined to memory images. We expect as well as remember. In our experience of material objects we have not only to reproduce in imagination what we formerly sensed: we also have to fill up gaps in experience and to anticipate the future. This too may be done in a highly schematic way.

What I am trying to suggest is this. In the synthesis necessary to any experience which goes on in time the work of imagination is fundamental. It is by means of imagination, however schematic, that we attach the present to the past (or the past to the present) and construct on the basis of immediate sensation an ordered world in one space and time. In so doing we construct also time and space themselves.

This double process of synthesis is most obvious in the counting and measuring by which we determine the relative sizes and shapes and durations of material objects. This cannot be done without concepts and judgements: imagination by itself would at most give us only a picture, not a part of an ordered spatial and temporal world. Such a world could never be given to mere sense or even to sense plus memory of sense-data. So far as we take it to be given, it is given only to beings who imagine and remember and expect and think.

§ 4. *Principles of synthesis*

The synthesis which constructs my experience and my world must take place in accordance with principles. I have to exclude chance associations, casual fancies, dream visions—not to mention illusions and hallucinations. My imagining is not merely wild. It is ordered and controlled and—we might even say—intelligent.

When I recognize that what I am looking at is a house, my imaginative synthesis of the sides and back may be guided in accordance with an empirical concept of 'house' derived from my past experience of houses. But this suggestion merely postpones the real problem ; for I have still to account for the past experience of houses which has enabled me to acquire the empirical concept of 'house' by some process of abstraction. Whatever may be the object recognized—and this is the crucial point—my imaginative synthesis is always controlled in accordance with universal principles which are not derived from experience, but are manifested in experience and are its necessary conditions, although they are at first followed unconsciously and are made clear only by later reflexion.

The most obvious principle manifested in the imaginative synthesis of experience is that I must combine in one time and space whatever it is that may be given—we need not here consider afresh whether what is usually supposed to be given must not also be made. Nothing can be an object of experience, or a part of the world I know, except in so far as it is assigned a position, however vaguely, within the framework of time and also—subject to certain qualifications—within the framework of space.

If this view is correct, it may have far-reaching implications.

Must we not, for example, assume that the parts of space (and of time) are homogeneous, and must we not maintain this homogeneity in our imaginative and conceptual constructions ? It could never be established by any empirical observations. And since we can know time and space only through what is in them, must we not also in our syntheses assume that there is something permanent which fills space and time—something to which what is given successively may be attached as a state or quality ?

This kind of language fits in, not only with ordinary experience, but also with Newtonian physics. We meet with fresh difficulties to-day because modern physics is developing a new language, and it is not clear how far this new language can be used for describing

ordinary experience. But the relation between physics and experience is a problem far beyond our present scope ; and in any case
all physical theories are based on ordinary experience and could not
arise without it. It may be that in the future we shall have to modify
our language, but for most of us at least this time has not yet
arrived.

If in order to be aware of objects in one time and one space we
have to combine the given in accordance with universal principles,
then all objects as known to us must—as a consequence of our
activity—have the characteristic of being so combined. To conceive the principles of our activity is thus to conceive also characteristics which every object *must* have if it is to be an object for us.
That is to say, by making clear to ourselves the principles of the
synthesis necessary for experience we can acquire the concept of
'an object as such'. The concepts of the various characteristics—
such as, for example, causality—which *every* object must have if it
is to be an object are properly known as 'categories', and these
characteristics may be described as 'categorial' characteristics. It
is a great pity that to-day these words are so often used in a much
vaguer and less useful sense.

If this is true, it means that, if we are to have experience of
objects, we must make use of certain *a priori* principles and concepts which are not derived from sense but from our own spontaneous activity.

Such a doctrine, although it is anathema to Logical Positivists,
is not unfamiliar to moderate empiricists such as Professor Price
and Professor Broad, who are prepared to speak of *a priori* concepts
like 'material thinghood' and 'causality'. It is important to trace—
if we can—the origin of such concepts. I have already suggested
that one reason, though not the only reason, why we have to
assume causes and effects in experience is that in our thinking we
must distinguish between grounds and consequents. Similarly it
may be thought that one reason, though not the only reason, why
we assume something permanent underlying the changes in space
and time is that we must in thinking apply predicates to subjects.
Concepts such as 'ground and consequent', or again 'subject and
predicate', can never be derived by abstraction from what is given
to sense : they arise only because they are manifested in thinking
and are subsequently formulated by reflexion—they are not
empirical but *a priori*. The categories, without which we can have
no knowledge of objects, may spring partly from our imaginative

synthesis in one time and space of what is given to sense and partly from the nature of our thinking as such. But these are highly technical questions and must here be left aside.

To some philosophers the language here employed may be unintelligible, and there may be objections to talk about concepts (or principles) 'controlling' or 'guiding' our imaginative synthesis and being 'manifested' or—still worse—'operative' in our thinking. It is therefore with special pleasure that I quote part of a sentence from Professor Price. 'Concepts or abstract ideas may operate *in* our minds (and in our behaviour too) without ever being present *to* our minds'. I should be sorry to ascribe to him my own errors, or even the errors of Immanuel Kant ; but this statement puts in a nutshell an essential part of the doctrine I have been trying to expound.

§ 5. *The phenomenal world*

Whatever be our view of the details, the general doctrine leads to one all-important conclusion.

If the world of objects known to me—and to others—is what it is as the result of a spontaneous synthesis, there can be no reason to believe that this world of ours is the world as it is in itself. We can know the world, not as it is in itself, but only as it must appear to finite minds like our own.

To say this is not to say that we create the world or that it is a product of arbitrary imagination. On the contrary, we are supposing that the synthesis required for experience must conform to principles which are common to all finite human intelligences. Furthermore, we are also supposing that the synthesis is a synthesis of what is given : however indeterminate the given may be, we cannot make it into any sense-data we please, nor can we combine sense-data in a way which ignores their character. And finally we are supposing that what is given is an appearance to us of a reality which is wholly independent of ourselves. This last supposition is admittedly one that can never be demonstrated ; but all three suppositions appear to be necessary if men are to be aware of a common world. If these suppositions are adopted, our common world must be described as a 'phenomenal' world (a world of appearances) or again as an 'in-between' world (one which is the joint product of our minds and an unknown reality). Yet although the world we know is not the world as it is in itself, we must nevertheless take it to be the real world as it must appear to human beings. In spite of the ambiguities of language there are not two worlds, but only one world (1) as it appears to us, and (2) as it is in itself.

To hold this view is not to deny—but, on the contrary, to affirm—that the world as it appears to us is (to speak roughly) a world of bodies occupying a space and time which extend beyond our ken. This is the world explored by science, and we can consistently accept whatever account of it may be given by experts. For purposes of common sense and science we are right to think and act *as if* it were a world of things as they are in themselves. Our doubts about this are metaphysical doubts—the kind we are expected to dismiss when we serve as members of a jury. To those who hold that the beliefs of common sense and science are hard data exempt from philosophical criticism, all such doubts must seem perverse or even woolly. To those who take a different view of philosophy such an attitude appears to be ingenuous—the symptom of a dogmatic slumber that is still unbroken. This is one reason why philosophers of these two schools often seem to be incapable of understanding one another.

Whatever be the difficulties in the doctrine expounded, it is no accident that scientists, and especially biologists, who reflect on their own procedure often come to a similar conclusion. Thus, for example, Professor J. Z. Young in his Reith Lectures can remark : 'At best what we are producing is a system of the universe as conceived by man, the talking animal'. He even goes so far as to use the word 'create' in this connexion, and says his researches can show 'that the brain of each one of us does literally create his or her own world'. If this is so, the world we create cannot be reality as it is in itself—unless we assume that we create all the universe there is.

It will be observed that he prefers to speak of our brains where I speak of our minds. The principles of synthesis about which I talk become for him 'characteristic rules' which each brain 'sets up'; and these are identified with 'patterns of activity' or 'models of action' in the cells of the brain. He combines the language of behaviourism with that of philosophical psychology, though the two go ill together ; and if he really *identifies* electrical activities in the brain with conceiving, it is hard not to think that this is a confusion. Furthermore, we have the very paradoxical result that if the brain creates the world, it must also create itself, for it is only a part, and a very small part, of our world : we have no right, as philosophers, to give it the privileged status of being the sole reality as it is in itself. Professor Young's view, as I see it, does not explain how he can know what he says he knows, and it seems both to recognize and to ignore the limitations of human knowledge in one and the same philosophical theory. What is remarkable is that in spite of using very different languages we seem to arrive at very similar conclusions. At the very least we both agree that 'we are set about with mysteries'; and this is the beginning of philosophy.

§ 6. *Antinomies*

The mysteries of the world we know and of the way we know it and of what may lie beyond our knowledge are endless ; but some thinkers have found especially mysterious the fact that if we try to think about the world as a whole, we seem to fall into contradictions which are known technically as 'antinomies'.

Some indication of this has already been given in our account of the cosmological argument for a first cause or a necessary being. It will be enough here to mention a simpler example from Immanuel Kant. We are tempted to say both that the world must have a beginning in time and equally that it cannot have a beginning in time. Such contradictory theories are commonly opposed as thesis and antithesis, and it seems possible to put up an equally good case for either. Whichever side we adopt, our argument may seem unanswerable so long as we confine ourselves to refuting the other. From this it may be inferred that this world can only be an appearance—an appearance of some reality which presumably could be conceived, at least ideally, without contradictions. This conclusion would be a further confirmation of the doctrine we have expounded.

It is only fair to say that this kind of argument is commonly scouted to-day on the ground that it has been superseded by modern advances in physics, mathematics, and mathematical logic. Mr. Bertrand Russell is the leading exponent of this view, and the simplest statement of it is to be found in his book '*Our Knowledge of the External World*'.

It would be foolish for any one who is not an expert to argue with Mr. Russell on his own ground, and he may be right in saying that this kind of argument should now be abandoned. But he is not infallible as an interpreter of Kant ; and when he imputes to Kant an 'elementary blunder', we may feel inclined to remember that many of the elementary blunders imputed to the sage of Koenigsberg have been blunders on the part of his interpreters.

It is a little surprising—at least at first sight—that Mr. Russell should dispose of the whole argument by refuting the thesis ; for on Kant's view the possibility of refuting the thesis (or the antithesis) is precisely the mark of an antinomy. The refutation consists in rejecting Kant's claim that 'the infinity of a series consists in this —that it can never be completed by a successive synthesis'. Mr. Russell maintains that the notion of infinity is primarily a property of classes and is only derivatively applicable to series. 'Classes which are infinite are *given all at once* by the *defining* property of their members, so that there is no question of "completion" or of "successive synthesis".' The italics are mine.

In reply Kant would, I think, say of Mr. Russell, as he said of Leibniz, that he is lacking in transcendental reflexion ; or—in simpler language—that he fails to ask whether his conceptions are derived from sense or thought. Kant is not talking about mathematical infinity, but about the world in space and time ; and this cannot be *given* by any definition—unless by a strange revival of the ontological argument. On Kant's view—and surely he is right— the world, whether finite or infinite, can be given only by a successive synthesis ; and it is by no means clear that he and Mr. Russell are talking about the same problem.

Curiously enough, Kant's doctrine of the antinomies bears some resemblance to the 'logical paradoxes' which have so exercised modern philosophers, and it might seem to have a similar claim for consideration. But these questions are highly technical, and it must be recognized that mathematics and mathematical logic—to say nothing of physics—have gone far beyond anything known in the eighteenth century. The Kantian doctrine may well require reconsideration and restatement. Nevertheless the plain man may still feel himself faced with a mystery when he asks whether the world has or has not a beginning in time. He may even legitimately wonder whether there may be a reality which is not in time at all.

§ 7. *The self*

If we turn to the self that knows the world, we seem to find further paradoxes, or even contradictions, painfully similar to those already found in Professor Young's account of the brain.

On the view hitherto expounded it is clear enough that not only my body, but also my mental history, can only be part of the phenomenal world I know ; for they too, as we have seen, must be a

product of a spontaneous *a priori* synthesis. So far as I know myself
as an object, I know myself only as I appear to myself under the
limits of finite knowledge. I cannot know what I am in myself any
more than I can know what the world is in itself.

The paradox is this. On the one hand, my mental history, so far
as I am taken to be a knower, is a history of the way in which I
construct my world. On the other hand, my mental history, considered solely as an object known, is only a part of my phenomenal
world ; and—in spite of many puzzles—it appears to be causally
determined by the other parts of my phenomenal world, and in
particular by physical bodies (including my own).

The difficulties become even greater if we ask what is the self
that is supposed to construct its phenomenal world (including its
own mental history) by sensing and imagining and remembering
and thinking.

Some would say that I who think and know must be a permanent
substance ; for only a permanent substance can be aware of a
changing point of view, a changing world, and a changing self. It is
harder to see what this can mean to-day than it was when the word
'substance' had a meaning in physics and could be applied by
analogy to the soul.

Others would say that I who know can be only a structure of
events. But is it possible that a structure of events could know
itself to be such a structure ? The events are continually succeeding
one another and passing away. They can be a structure to a mind
which knows them. It is not so easy to understand how they can
be a structure to themselves.

There appears to be a tendency both to affirm and to deny that I
am something over and above my past thoughts and my present
thinking. If we reject the language of substance, we may be tempted
to say that I who think am, not merely a point of view, but a centre
of activity, or even the unity of an activity. Such statements serve
to call attention to a problem, but it is hard to make them precise.
It looks as if I can know myself only as an object—only as a succession of mental and biological events. Yet what can 'an object' mean
unless it means 'an object to a subject'? And surely I know—if I
know anything—that I am a subject as well as an object, a knower
as well as something known, and am for this reason a person and
not a thing. Although part of the world of nature, I seem to stand
outside of nature and to view it almost as if I were a god. Yet all I
seem able to know of myself as a knower are the principles mani-

fested in my cognitive activity—the principles on which my world
and my own changing history are held together as objects in one
space and time. These principles cannot be causally explained; for
they are the conditions of any attempt at causal explanation. They are
indifferent to time, and they look almost as if they were an intrusion
into our phenomenal world from some other world than this.

All of this is admittedly difficult and obscure. The problem may
have been stated in wrong terms ; but this is better than saying that
there is no problem at all. Part of the difficulty arises from the fact
that even to see the problem requires a revolution in our ordinary
thinking, and especially in our scientific thinking, which is primarily
concerned with known objects and not with our knowing of them.
Thus Professor Young, if I may return to him, wishes to abolish the
word 'consciousness' altogether, because, as he says, if consciousness 'is a thing in the ordinary sense it could be observed directly
like any other object'. Since it cannot be so observed, he concludes
that it must be rejected as an 'occult quality'. But even the simplest
of those who use the word do not mean that consciousness is an
observed object or 'a thing in the ordinary sense'. What they mean
is that there can be no observed objects unless there is observing ;
and they use the word 'consciousness' for the observing, not for
any thing or object observed, and still less for any quality, occult
or otherwise, of an object.

In spite of difficulties there seem to be two points of view—or
two ways of talking—each equally legitimate ; or perhaps we
should say that while the common theory describes the objects
seen from a point of view, the other attempts to consider what is
implied in there being a point of view from which anything can be
seen or described. And if ordinary language is any guide, when
there is thinking there must be an 'I' who think. The assertion that
there must be an 'I'—or even an 'It'—which thinks and knows
presents us at the very least with a question, a puzzle, a problem.
To suppose that it can be solved by any talk about objects and
qualities is to miss the problem altogether.

§ 8. *The limits of knowledge*

This has been a long and troublesome discussion, although it has
touched only on the fringes of the subject. It is to be hoped that the
conclusion will be relatively simple, or at least that it will be easy to
see what is its bearing on religious faith.

An attempt has been made to analyse human experience from its own point of view and to determine the conditions without which it could not be what it is. It looks as if we must be given at every moment something utterly obscure and perpetually changing, and on this precarious basis must construct and hold together our ordered world (including our own mental history) in accordance with spontaneous principles of imagination and thought. This process is dominated throughout by the Idea of a whole—we might almost say by the Idea of *the* whole. Only on the supposition that this idea is operative, whether consciously or unconsciously, in our imagining and thinking can we understand our efforts to construct one world in time and space, and so to construct one time and one space (or one space-time). Such wholes cannot be given, but they seem to be postulated as the necessary conditions of all our experience.

Unless we assume the miracle of a pre-established harmony, a world so constructed cannot be reality as it is in itself, but only reality as it must appear to finite human minds.

This is the main conclusion of our argument. It rests on the prior assumption that there is a world independent of our experience, and that this independent world, as the source or condition of what is given, determines (in conjunction with our own spontaneous activity) the character of the phenomenal world as we know it.

Although this assumption seems natural and almost inevitable, and although without it it is difficult to see how we can know a common world, it may be rejected by philosophers who otherwise attempt to analyse experience in the same sort of way : they may assume instead that there is no reality independent of our experience ; and they will then arrive at a different conclusion.

Some thinkers, for example, may conclude that reality is nothing but a collection of finite experiences. Others—or perhaps we should say simply 'I'—may conclude that reality is nothing but my own finite experience.

Even the first of these views is hard to accept : it seems to run contrary to a natural human instinct, and even the totality of actual finite experiences would appear to be obviously incomplete. The second is wildly paradoxical : it is almost impossible for me to act and think as if I were the sole reality—a single, solitary, imperfect mind. Both views take human knowledge to be absolute and the world to be all of a piece. Here we need only note that neither of them leaves any room for belief in God.

A more complicated view is possible. Even if we hold that there can be no reality beyond experience, we may recognize that our finite experience, and even the experience of the whole human race, is manifestly incomplete. On this basis some thinkers claim to know that finite experiences are parts of one all-embracing experience. They may not treat human knowledge as absolute, but they do treat it at least as if it could approximate to knowledge of absolute reality or to an absolute experience.

This doctrine, which has been developed with the utmost subtlety, is unpopular at the present time : it seems to claim for man a knowledge beyond his finite powers. Like Platonism, it may afford a basis or background for religion—although perhaps for one that must in the long run be replaced by philosophy. But the modern predicament of religion has arisen because the advance of science, which has enabled men to know so much more about the temporal world, has also—whether rightly or wrongly—made them doubt their ability to know a world of eternal reality or an infinite experience other than their own.

The belief that the ordinary world we know by common sense or science is only the appearance to us of an underlying reality which we can never know has been here supported by a variety of arguments which some may think unnecessarily elaborate. It has often been entertained by thoughtful men without a great deal of argument: to some it may seem that there is no initial probability, or even plausibility, in supposing that limited and imperfect minds can grasp reality—or even a bit of reality—as it is in itself. Indeed it is almost a commonplace to-day that all human knowledge is relative ; and it is hard to see what this can mean unless it means that reality as it is in itself can never be known by us. Such a hypothesis is obviously not one that can ever be proved or disproved by science, though it may be suggested by reflexion on scientific procedure ; but at least it is a safeguard against the metaphysical assertion that the bounds of science are the bounds of reality and also against idle speculations to which there can be no end.

It should be noted that the arguments here used are entirely different from the cosmological argument : they make no attempt to pass from knowledge of contingent beings in time and space to knowledge of a necessary being not in time and not in space. Nevertheless if they are accepted, we may find ourselves obliged to use at least the negative concepts of the cosmological argument in order to think about reality in itself as the condition of our experience—if, that is, we allow ourselves to think about it at all. We may even be tempted to conceive it as absolute and unconditioned and self-sufficient, however little meaning we can attach to these phrases, and however impossible it must be to find any confirmation in experience.

From the point of view of religion our doctrine does at least recognize the mysteries by which we are beset. Taken in itself it could only lead to a complete suspension of judgement if man were a purely scientific mind ; but in abandoning a claim to knowledge it may make room for faith. It accords with much that is said by religious men, when they tell us, for example, that the world is not only a manifestation of God's will, but also a veil behind which He is eternally concealed. We might almost say that for all religion the ordinary world as we know it can only be the appearance of a deeper reality which is beyond human comprehension.

Chapter XIX

THE GOOD MAN

§ 1. *Moral scepticism*

In an earlier chapter, when I quoted from Hamlet's eulogy of man, I confined myself to the admiration it expressed for the human intellect. Hamlet himself took a wider view. He describes man also as the beauty of the world, express and admirable alike in form and in motion. This observation, which perhaps is more appropriate to some of us than to others, seems to be concerned with the body, not merely as beautiful to contemplate, but also as adapted to purposes of action. At any rate Shakespeare goes on to couple man the agent with man the thinker—'In action how like an angel ! In apprehension how like a God !' If we consider man only as a being who thinks and knows, we get a distorted picture. We must try to see how he appears to himself from his own point of view as an agent, and particularly as a moral agent.

It is a commonplace of religious thinking that God is revealed both in nature and in the soul of man. In this context the soul of man is sometimes identified with the heart—that is, with religious feeling taken to be an immediate awareness of God ; but it is also, and perhaps more wisely, equated with conscience—with consciousness of our subjection to moral law. To quote Dean Inge, 'The "ought" is the voice of the super-personal spirit within us'. Such an aphorism suggests that there are moral grounds for believing in the existence of God ; and it is with this claim in mind that man as a moral agent has now to be considered.

At this point we are faced with a new difficulty. Although there has been in the world at all times an undercurrent, and perhaps more than an undercurrent, of moral scepticism, we should until recently have been entitled, with general approbation, to take for granted that there is a moral law and that we are acquainted at least with its main provisions. We can no longer, if we make such an assumption, expect to find general agreement either from philosophers or from ordinary men. Agnostics of the nineteenth century did not, as a rule, question the moral code of their time :

they tended rather to make it more exacting. This could not be said to-day ; and apart from criticism of particular moral rules, which is often healthy, there is an inclination to regard all morality as subjective and relative, founded upon emotion or self-interest rather than upon reason.

Moral scepticism has often an intellectual basis. It may rest partly on the findings of particular sciences. Thus psycho-analysis is commonly thought to have shown that reason plays no part in human action, although it should be obvious that by acquiring rational insight into the subconscious man has now greater opportunities for rational self-control than he ever had before. Similarly anthropology is sometimes supposed to establish a complete lack of common moral principles among the different tribes of men. This argument goes back to Herodotus ; but wider knowledge and deeper understanding may deprive it of much of its force. If in reading about primitive societies we make allowance both for their misconceptions of the world and for the inevitable tendency to confine morality within the tribe, we may be surprised to find how rational their moral principles are and indeed how like our own.

These particular problems cannot be examined here, but the reader may be referred to Professor MacBeath's '*Experiments in Living*' if he wishes to find a combination of philosophical insight and common sense in the discussion of primitive morality.

The main intellectual basis of modern scepticism in ethics is perhaps to be found, not so much in particular sciences as in a point of view which assumes, whether as the result of psychological inertia or as the conclusion of philosophical reflexion, that science is the only kind of knowledge there is. If we place ourselves in the position of detached observers and consider man solely as an object of scientific study, his so-called actions, like his so-called knowledge, cannot but be taken as an effect of forces in and outside of his body. We are thus precluded from taking his own point of view as an agent—an agent conscious of a moral law which he ought to obey and may even try to obey. Furthermore, nothing can be more certain than that science tells us only what is : it has no concern with what ought to be. If we confine ourselves to scientific knowledge, all our ethical beliefs must be relegated to some philosophical limbo outside the heaven of knowledge—to the rubbish-heap of emotion or desire, or even, worst fate of all, to the dark domain of metaphysics.

On this view moral judgements, although in fact they always claim to be valid for others as well as for the agent, tend to have their claims dismissed without serious examination. They have to be explained away as the expression of personal emotions or likings, as the product of tradition and religious mystification, as the modern equivalent of taboo, as the effect of social environment, or even as the arrogant manifestation of an irrational super-ego. At best they may be regarded as formulating the rules found practically convenient in a particular social system. The Russians happen to have one code of behaviour and we to have another, and that is all there is to it. It is a mere waste of breath to ask which code is the better or the more right, and we are not entitled to condemn the liquidation of class enemies—if it happens in Russia—as a moral wrong.

Intellectual scepticism about morality may have still deeper foundations in practical scepticism—or at least the two kinds of scepticism may reinforce one another. The plain man is not un-affected by the catchwords of a semi-popular philosophy ; but his ethical doubts may spring more directly from his experience as an agent and so may cut more deeply into his moral life.

§ 2. *The unstable society*

There is a close connexion between moral belief and moral behaviour—a belief on which we never try to act is hardly a belief at all ; and the fact must be faced that moral behaviour, or at least right behaviour, is more common in a stable society. While such a society may tend to complacency or even hypocrisy, it is unfavour-able to the brigand and the man of violence. In this country, in spite of a social revolution, we still have a relatively stable society. Yet nowadays we cannot but be acutely conscious of living also in a world society, and our world society has been in a state of insta-bility for the last forty years.

It is hard to exaggerate the difference in this respect between what may be called the Victorian world—the world before 1914—and the world of to-day. On the 3rd of August in that year, as Sir Edward Grey looked out from a window of the Foreign Office at the gathering dusk, he remarked to those about him 'The lamps are going out all over Europe ; we shall not see them lit again in our life-time'. His prophecy has been amply fulfilled. Let me recall some of the differences in outlook between then and now.

I can remember as a boy hearing some wise old gentlemen—at least they were old to me—talking gravely about the fall of empires.

Former empires, they said, like Babylon, Assyria, and even Rome, had all passed away, and presumably the British Empire would one day pass like the rest, although this was hard to believe when one considered, not merely her power and wealth, but her dispensation of security and justice. In those days the British Empire was regarded, at least in these islands, not as the tyrant and exploiter, but as the bulwark of peace, the destroyer of the slave trade, the bringer of law and freedom to the victims of cruelty, anarchy, and superstition. It was firmly believed, no doubt with too great complacency, that other nations, having once seen these wonderful achievements in practice, would in time come to follow the same ideals. Yet since then not only has our country had to struggle twice for its very existence—and who knows what trials may still lie before us ?—but our very ideals of peace and law and liberty have been spurned and derided over more than half the globe.

In civilized societies, or societies supposed to be civilized, we have seen things happen which to a Victorian were unbelievable. In the First World War the disregard of treaties, the shooting of hostages, and the sinking of passenger ships came as a moral shock which disturbed men's minds more than the far grosser outrages which were still to come. We have seen men, not merely imprisoned without trial, but humiliated and tortured and killed for their opinions. What is even worse, we have seen the same treatment meted out to their wives and children—punishment of relatives is said to be explicitly enjoined in the Russian penal code. One such act is an iniquity ; but the scale on which these enormities have been practised staggers and baffles human imagination. Thousands, and perhaps millions, of innocent men and women have been deported to strange countries and condemned to slavery. Deliberate attempts have been made to kill off the intellectuals in Poland and Abyssinia, not to mention other places, so that whole nations might be reduced to ignorance and servility. The Jewish race in Europe has been almost wiped out. We need not dwell on these horrors, but they have to be looked at with open eyes. The only revival of savagery we have so far been spared is the public burning of heretics ; and we have become almost callous to cruelties which in our innocence we had imagined were embalmed as records in the early books of the Old Testament and the history of oriental tyrannies.

In circumstances like these it is no wonder if private morality declines. Not very long ago an Englishman was sentenced in the Belgian Courts to a long term of imprisonment. The charge against

T

him was that he had informed against Belgian families who had sheltered him as a British soldier during the last war and had helped him to escape. He had been recaptured at the last moment and under threats of torture had betrayed his benefactors to an infamous Nazi revenge. He committed a terrible wrong, to which no punishment could be adequate ; but which of us can be sure that in like circumstances we might not have done the same ?

This is an extreme example, confined, it may be said, to times of war ; but it is difficult to believe that nothing like this happens in what we are pleased nowadays to call peace. Yet even war— whether civil or international, cold or hot—is only the supreme illustration of the way in which social instability tends to weaken morality and, at a less exalted level, to impair manners. Changes, for example, in the value of money tempt some of us to sharp practice, and many of us, if not to jealousy and spite, at least to discontent and grumbling. Incredible as it may seem, there was a time, not so long ago, when it was considered vulgar to talk about one's personal income. To-day the ideal of a gentleman is almost as unfashionable as the ideal of a saint.

The present generation may be no worse than its predecessors : it may only have been exposed to greater temptations. Our own age has not been deficient in military courage, and we are more conscious, sometimes rather smugly, of evils which our fathers took too lightly. But if there is a greater scepticism about moral principles, this should not be too difficult to understand. For most of us what we take to be the good life is a delicate balance between self-interest and duty. In a stable society the way of self-interest may not deviate very far from the path of duty : on the whole it pays to be respectable. When this happy coincidence fails, men tend to lose their bearings, especially as they see advantages gained by others through a lack of scruple. Under the stress of hardship they may speedily abandon, not merely the little airs and graces, but the bigger generosities and even the common decencies of life. If the situation becomes desperate, they may be faced with terrible choices which all but a very few are unprepared to meet.

§ 3. *Total and partial scepticism*

In ethics, as in other subjects, we ought to distinguish between total and partial scepticism. Partial scepticism is healthy as long as it does not lead to paralysis of the will ; but it may be expressed in misleading terms which cause men to imagine that they are totally sceptical when in fact they are nothing of the kind.

Some of those who profess to debunk morality—a fashion perhaps now on the wane—are merely repudiating a Victorian rigorism which they are pleased to associate with the alleged pomposity of our grandfathers—with gold alberts and Dundreary whiskers. A great deal of nonsense is talked under this head, and we ought to be told more precisely what is being repudiated and what is being put in its place. So acute a judge as the late Lord Balfour once remarked in my hearing that while standards of outer decorum varied greatly, the fundamental behaviour of men and women varied little. There was, it is true, in wide circles of Victorian society a prudishness that was really harmful, and Freud has at least helped us to get rid of this. But it is a complete mistake to imagine that all Victorian fathers bullied their wives and terrorized their children—sometimes it was the other way about. It is very hard not to falsify recent history and almost impossible to see it in its true proportions. All of us to-day will seem very funny to the young men of the year two thousand ; but even humour should be kept within bounds.

We ought not to assume that we are all right and our predecessors all wrong. We should rather reflect that if they went wrong, we may do so too ; and such a reminder may be an aid to moral sensitivity. It is not obvious that coarseness is always to be preferred to reticence ; and the modern growth of crime among the young is flattering neither to our family relations nor to our educational practice.

There is plenty of room for differences of opinion, not only about the interpretation of past history and the value of past ideals, but also about quite fundamental topics such as the morality of war, of capital punishment, of euthanasia, of divorce, and of birth control. But even if we admit all this, and even if we condemn as vices what our predecessors may (or may not) have taken to be virtues, it is absurd to suppose that we have thereby freed ourselves from the shackles of morality. We are, on the contrary, whether wisely or foolishly, seeking to replace old moral standards by new ones—perhaps by ones more suited to our new situation. It is a tiresome abuse of language when we describe as moral conduct everything we believe people ought not to do.

It is fair to say that some men profess moral scepticism because of their dislike for harshness and intolerance, which—especially when allied with religion—may be among the aberrations of

morality and may spring from causes too often believed to account
for morality as such. It is sometimes supposed that toleration can
be safeguarded by denying objective moral standards and by making
duty and goodness relative to the wishes of each separate agent.
But if I once free myself from objective standards, there is no
reason why I should not regard it as good to impose my will upon
other people by any means in my power. The only sure safeguard
against intolerance is to recognize the duty of toleration.

In actual practice complete moral scepticism is very rare. There
are plenty of bad men willing to exempt themselves from all moral
obligations, but they are not so willing to extend this exemption to
their neighbours, and then they begin to seem funny as well as
immoral. They can see clearly enough that violence or treachery to
themselves is an intolerable wrong—'you can't do this to me'. Even
Hitler appeared to be morally shocked at any fancied injustice
done to his country. If we could find a genuinely amoral man—
amoral not in some respects but in all—there would be nothing to
do about him. He would just not be human.

As to complete intellectual scepticism about morality, it must be
left to work itself out like any other form of total scepticism. In the
long run it becomes as boring in theory as it is unworkable in
practice. If the sceptic makes any moral admission at all—and he
will find it hard to avoid doing so—it is possible to move on from
this admission. This is why it is so important not to confuse the
repudiation of some moral rules with total scepticism about morality.
We do not say that we have abandoned science when we reject
Newton in favour of Einstein ; and we should not say that we have
abandoned morality if we think that we are putting something
better in its place.

§ 4. *Duty*

Morality was not invented yesterday. Like science itself, it has a
long history behind it. In the face of modern scepticism I propose
to assume that—at least in extreme cases—we are able to distinguish between a good man and a bad, and between right and
wrong actions. Such an assumption is not affected by the fact that
good men are sometimes confused in their moral thinking and may
allow self-interest to mislead them both in their judgements and in
their conduct. This is merely a danger against which we have all to
be on our guard.

On this assumption it is simply untrue to say, whether directly or indirectly, that a good man is one who is good at satisfying his impulses or at furthering his own happiness. Skill in attaining our ends and prudence or enlightened self-love have their own value, and even their own place in a morally good life ; but in themselves they are self-centred and so far are directly opposed to morality. This topic has already been discussed in Chapter VI, especially in §§ 3 and 6, and I will not revert to it.

Similarly it is untrue to say, as religious leaders sometimes do, that a good man is one who is proud and pharisaical. Here again the suggestion is that morality must be self-centred. Distortions of this kind are not likely to further the cause of religion.

To describe morality in terms of self-interest is rather like describing science as if it were mainly the work of medicine-men and witch-doctors. This would no doubt be welcome to the witch-doctors themselves, and we may all have something of the witch-doctor in us when we come to consider the nature of moral goodness. But we try to look at science from the point of view of the scientist ; and similarly we must try to look at morality from the point of view of the moral agent. We do so on the assumption that we already know what a scientist or a good man is.

There is too often a tendency—it is the mark of over-intellectualism—to regard the moral problem mainly as one of criticism, of praising and blaming others, and incidentally of praising and blaming our past selves or our past actions. We forget that there would be no moral problem at all if we did not have to live and act in a society. The primary question of morality for a good man— the one that arises directly in action—is not 'What ought you to do ?' It is not 'What ought you to have done ?' It is not even 'What ought I to have done ?' The primary question is 'What ought I to do now ?' The other questions are derivative ; and it is a mistake to tackle them first and then apply the results to the pressing problem of my own duty here and now. Only such a mistaken method could account for the wide-spread philosophical belief—the remark comes from an acute Australian observer of our country—that moral judgement consists in a lot of individual Englishmen having funny feelings all by themselves.

The question 'What ought I to do ?' may be a question about the best means for securing an already adopted end or for furthering what I take to be my happiness as a whole. If this is all, it has nothing to do with morality. When it is a moral question, it is equivalent to the question 'What is my present duty ?' By asking this a good man already indicates that he is willing to do his duty whatever his duty may be. That is, he is willing to do his duty for the sake of duty as such, and not merely because it chimes with his desires or furthers his ends or promotes his happiness.

Some may think that this makes too much of duty. A saint or a holy man might conceivably be so good as to be immune from temptation and so to rise above duty altogether. But even if this is so, we need not be unduly perturbed. Few of us have any pretensions to be saints, and the problems of saints, if they have any, are not ours.

The path of duty, as Tennyson observes, may be the way to glory—or to wealth or happiness; but if we do our duty solely for the sake of glory or wealth or happiness, we are not good men. We find out our weakness when the two paths diverge and we are faced with the painful choice between duty and self-interest. Duty and self-interest may at such times almost seem like two different persons who press their claims upon us ; and it is then especially that we are tempted to become sophisticated and to pretend that duty is a standard imposed upon us from without, a social device, a traditional taboo, and so on. But our first duty is to be honest with ourselves, and this is a duty which is not imposed on us from without. The claim of this duty, as of duty in general, is absolute and unconditioned—not in any metaphysical sense, but in the very simple sense that it is independent of our likings and dislikings and of what we expect to get out of it. If there is such a thing as duty, it is what I ought to do now, not *if* or *because* I happen to want something else, but no matter what I happen to want. That is what is meant when it is said that the 'ought' of morality is not hypothetical, but categorical : it does not depend on any '*if*'.

The moral judgement 'I ought to do this now' is manifestly not a descriptive judgement : it is quite unlike such judgements as 'I have a red face' or 'I have a wart on my nose'. Even these descriptive judgements, although they are about *me*, are—at least professedly— independent of any whims or fancies of mine. They make a claim to the assent of others. In more technical language they claim to be universally valid or to be objective. The moral judgement 'I ought to do this now' also claims to be objective in this sense, but it claims more. It claims that what I ought to do (and not merely my judgement about it) is independent of my feelings and desires and fancies and of anything peculiar to myself. It claims to state a law binding upon me as a man or as a rational being—a law equally binding upon any other man in my place. That is to say, it claims the agreement of others, not merely to a descriptive statement about myself, but to the statement of a universal law which any rational being would be obliged to follow in the same circumstances. The moral law is impersonal and impartial ; and duty is no respecter of persons. In moral action there can be no special privileges either for me or for you. In asserting that this is what I ought to do, I am asserting that this is what anybody ought to do if he were in my place.

In the modern world it is hard to know whether these statements will be regarded as platitudes or as paradoxes or as sheer illusions. Nevertheless I should be compelled to maintain that if any one denies them, then—although he may be talking most intelligently about some other subject—he has simply no notion of what morality is.

It is too commonly assumed nowadays that if any one claims objectivity for the judgement that a man is good or an action right, he is claiming to possess some mysterious, non-sensuous intuition of an unanalysable and indefinable quality present in men or in actions—or even in things. This interpretation is wholly contrary to the traditional use of the word 'objective': it has arisen solely because of the doctrines of Professor G. E. Moore, which do not have many supporters to-day. It is also wholly contrary to the doctrine expounded here—namely, that an action is morally good only if it is willed in accordance with a principle valid for every reasonable man in the same situation independently of what he happens to like or desire.

This is the doctrine formulated by Kant in what he called 'the categorical imperative'—*Act only on that maxim through which you can at the same time will that it should become a universal law.*

§ 5. *Persons and society*

The principle of moral duty clearly implies that a morally good action, and *a fortiori* a morally good man, is of more value than the particular objects of our desires, the particular products of our actions, and even the attainment of our own happiness. What we have an absolute duty to do or to be must be considered to have an absolute value, with which no other value can be compared. Yet to describe moral action in the abstract as obedience to universal law may seem arid and unconvincing to those more concerned with action than with thinking. Hence it may be well to add that men who seek to follow a universal law, or even are capable of following it, are worthy of respect and indeed of reverence, and so are never to be used merely as a means to the satisfaction of our desires. In more technical language it is our duty to treat them as persons or as ends in themselves, and never merely as a means. If we use the language of religion, we may say that every human soul is of infinite or supreme value, and that this should never be forgotten in dealing with others or even with ourselves.

In moral action the relation of person to person is of fundamental importance—it is here above all that we have to use the language of *I-Thou*, and each person has to be treated as his own individual self. But we are also related to persons as members of a society ; and so it is the duty of a good man to aim at establishing a society where all men, in seeking to realize in their actions the same universal law, will respect each other and respect themselves. This ideal society has been described in technical terms as a kingdom of ends in themselves. It is what is known to the religious man as the kingdom of God ; and so far as it is realized in earth or heaven, it is the communion of saints.

If this principle is applied to the mundane field of politics, it enjoins also that so far as men constitute a political society, they ought to aim at establishing as much external freedom under law as is compatible with the like freedom for others ; for this is the condition of the fullest realization of the moral society itself.

When the moral principle of obeying a universal law for its own sake, and not for the sake of any gain to ourselves or others, is interpreted in terms of respect for human personality and the realization of a society of persons as ends in themselves, it becomes warmer and more vivid to our imagination, and—although it still remains highly abstract—it may seem to express better the motives on which good men act. Men find their place in a well ordered society, or perhaps we should say in a society of societies, and in this way they know, even at the most primitive level, what their duty is. They do not ordinarily attempt to disentangle the motives or justifications for their moral actions, and they may seem to be moved only by loyalty to persons and to the particular society of which they form a part. If they can find no place or function in their society, the result is likely to be maladjustment and frustration and deep unhappiness, such as we see too often in the vast and machine-like States of to-day; and it is very easy to assume that what men seek is their own happiness, as indeed they very often do—their motives are generally mixed. Certainly they do not start from scratch in morals any more than they do in science: they have to accept the social structure as given and endeavour to fit in with it, and perhaps to improve it—the scientist does something very like this with his science. But if there is to be any criticism or reform of an existing society, or even of an individual way of life, it is necessary to get back to first principles; and here above all the principle that a moral law is universal becomes of supreme importance—it must hold for *all* men in like circumstances and cannot be confined within the limits of one privileged society, still less within the relation between one individual and another.

§ 6. *Moral principles*

Into the intricacies and implications of this doctrine it is impossible to enter here. The man who adopts these moral principles as his *supreme* rule of life is no longer an average sensual man whose highest rule is at the best the principle of self-interest: he has undergone a spiritual conversion, a kind of new birth; and if he is possessed of common sense and sound judgement, he will be able in many, or even in most, ordinary situations to recognize without much difficulty where his duty lies.

We must indeed distinguish between such ultimate principles and particular moral laws or moral rules. Since moral laws (such as 'Thou shalt not lie') and moral rules (such as 'A soldier may have a duty to kill') are confined in a lesser or greater degree to particular situations, the question may have to be considered whether a given situation properly falls under some accepted law or rule. A moral *principle* is absolute—that is, it holds in all situations. A moral *law*, and still more a moral *rule*, is only one application of a moral principle and must also be relative to a special kind of situation. Thus even a law or rule may be called absolute in the sense of not being dependent on the likings or dislikings of the agent and of holding for all men in a like situation; but it is not absolute in the sense of holding for all situations whatsoever.

Only by making a distinction of this kind can we avoid an absurd rigidity which leads men—often through misunderstanding—to reject out of hand the doctrine that moral principles are absolute and universal. Such a distinction also compels a good man—and this too is wholesome—to recognize that his judgements about his duty in a particular situation are not infallible although he has to act as if they were. All he can claim is that they may be right or wrong, true or false (unless we confine truth and falsity to scientific statements). How such a claim can be tested is too large a question to examine here ; but in doubtful cases we have to start from common beliefs and practices and criticize these in the light of our ultimate principles. In the end there may come a time for decision or experiment. It would be absurd to deny that even moral principles can have their full meaning only in relation to a whole system of rights and duties. In this sense they may be enriched, expanded, and illuminated with a wider experience and with that deeper moral insight which can be attained only in action. We must always assume that we have made some way already ; and each moral discovery may become, as it were, the instrument of further advance.

Belief in the absolute claims of duty does not prevent us from being tolerant or from recognizing both that our judgement is fallible and that the principles of morality have to be applied differently in different circumstances. But it does assume that there are ultimate moral principles by which a good man must judge and on which he is obliged to act. These principles may be difficult to formulate, difficult to apply, and still more difficult to justify ; but they must nevertheless be presupposed in our moral judgements and moral actions, and without them there is no morality at all.

Moral principles bear a certain resemblance to the theoretical principles of synthesis discussed in Chapter XVIII § 4, or again—if something more familiar is wanted—to the principles of induction, without which there could be no science. All such principles (including the so-called Principle of Verification) have to be distinguished from generalizations about the way men in fact think and behave—most men think incompetently and behave badly. On the other hand, men may think and act on principles which they cannot clearly formulate ; and it is only by principles, however vaguely grasped, that they distinguish sound scientific thinking or good moral action from their opposites. Is it not partly an unreasoned intellectualistic prejudice that makes so many thinkers to-day boggle at moral principles even when they are prepared to swallow theoretical principles without a qualm ? It is hard to see why moral principles should be regarded as less intelligible or less rational than are, for example, Mr. Russell's five postulates of scientific inference on his book on *Human Knowledge*.

In spite of their resemblance we should not forget the difference between moral and scientific principles ; for moral principles are principles of acting and not merely of thinking. This is the reason why moral judgements arouse stronger feelings—so much so that they are often thought to be founded on emotion. Moral judgement makes a claim, not merely for theoretical assent, but for practical co-operation as well ; and the refusal of practical co-operation, still more an attempt at practical opposition, will arouse more passion than is found in our not always unemotional theoretical disputes. This is true even when practical co-operation is required below the level of morality. When rowing men are bent on winning a boatrace, they will not love the oarsman who prefers his own style or who deliberately rocks the boat. It is easy for one powerful man—or one powerful nation—to rock the ship of State ; and those who care passionately for law and order will have no tepid emotions about a disturber of the peace. They may even be tempted to harshness and cruelty ; for badness—like goodness—may be highly infectious. If they succumb to the temptation, they depart from their own principles ; but perhaps at a time when so much sympathy is lavished on the criminal rather than on his victim, we may be able to spare some sympathy even for the criminally good.

§ 7. *Material principles*

Ultimate moral principles must be highly abstract and formal. If you expect the wrong things from them—such as detailed instructions or emotional uplift—you are doomed to disappointment. They can no more provide a mechanical solution for moral problems than the principles of induction can for scientific problems. But it may be maintained that as they have been formulated here, they are too thin and empty to receive the assent or allegiance of men. Moral principles, we are told, should not be formal, but material—that is, they should put before us some specific, concrete end.

No sensible person would deny that moral principles have to be embodied in specific laws and rules—and, I would add, in actual concrete living—if they are to win the full allegiance of men. But the question here is whether it is possible to adopt some material principle as the sole and sufficient standard of morality. I think not.

The oldest and best of these material principles (though it has had refinements in recent years) is that a good man is one who aims at the happiness of mankind.

This doctrine has at least the merit of formulating one of the main obligations of good men—the duty of benevolence or kindness. It may even afford a rough criterion for the progress of morality, for there is probably something morally wrong with a society in which there is widespread unhappiness. But is it plausible to maintain that the only moral relation between man and man is that of benefactor and beneficiary ? Can this principle give an adequate account of virtues like gratitude, good faith, justice, perseverance, courage ? These virtues, and indeed virtue as such, seem to have a value incomparably greater than any happiness they may bestow. To regard happiness as the end, and virtue only as the means to it, is not to give a convincing account of moral goodness. And however amiable be such a doctrine, it is too soft for the rigours of actual life. Unless men value freedom and virtue and duty above happiness—and even above such great goods as personal affection or aesthetic enjoyment—they will not have enough virtue in them to defend the goods they cherish.

Some of those who uphold material principles do so because they admire the power and energy exhibited by enthusiasts who make some cause, such as communism or fascism, their sole end and the criterion by which all actions are to be judged. We no longer hear this claim on behalf of fascism ; but there are still some who would maintain that communism, with all its cruelties and treacheries, is a higher morality than ours or is at least as high. Yet although admittedly men may be attracted to a popular movement by some moral element within it, they are never more in need of the restraints of morality than when they espouse a cause.

The greatest stains in our human history have been inflicted by those who have given themselves totally to some respectable cause—be it race or class or country or Church—and have subordinated everything to that one end. Totalitarianism, under whatever guise we find it, is not an alternative system of morality : it is a repudiation of morality, and we should not be afraid to say so. Or perhaps we should say that it is the setting up of a false morality and so corresponds to that worship of false gods which is known in religion as idolatry.

§ 8. *Practical reason*

If we hold that moral principles are universal in the sense that they are binding upon all men as men—and without this there may be *mores*, but not morality—we are not talking of man as 'a forked radish with a head fantastically carved upon it': we are talking of him as a rational or reasonable being. There must be something common to men in virtue of which they can be moral agents and can be treated as such. This cannot be merely their common desires, for these, the more they are alike, may the more easily lead to antagonism and conflict. It is best described as reason, and when it is concerned with action, as practical reason.

There are many to-day who dislike such language, partly because they mistranslate it into a statement about some occult faculty. Practical reason is in no way occult, nor does it differ except in its application from the reason displayed in human thinking. We think and act well only in accordance with principles which claim to be valid for all rational agents ; and to do this is to be reasonable alike in thought and in action. If we are inclined to seek support for philosophical doctrines in ordinary language, we should not ignore the fact that we speak of reasonable and unreasonable actions at least as much as we speak of reasonable and unreasonable thoughts. And it is no paradox to say that a morally good man is essentially a reasonable one. Unless this is so, there can be no objective and binding moral standards.

It is impossible to discuss here either this doctrine itself or the objections to which it lays itself open ; but I am compelled to add that the function of reason in morality is closely connected with what I described in Chapter XIII as the drive in our thinking towards wholeness or completeness. In our thoughts this drive leads us, as we saw, to the conception of a first cause and an unconditioned reality with all its paradoxes and even contradictions. In our actions it leads us to the conception of an unconditioned good and an absolute obligation—we cannot be content to pursue one thing for the sake of another and so on indefinitely. But there is a difference between the two cases. For the theoretical notion of an unconditioned reality, even if we can conceive it consistently, we can find no corresponding object in experience ; but in action we can provide, however imperfectly, an object corresponding to the notions of unconditioned good and absolute obligation so far as we succeed in doing our duty for its own sake.

It is perhaps because this is dimly grasped that men attach a supreme and over-riding value to moral goodness and blame their moral failures as they do not blame their intellectual errors and aesthetic defects. In moral action above all they seem able to attain freedom from determination by external causes and so to rise to the full dignity of man. Failure to fulfil so absolute an obligation and to realize so supreme an ideal must bring with it a conviction of unworthiness.

To those committed exclusively to a scientific point of view all this must appear as emotive utterance and metaphysical nonsense. Even men who adopt the moral standpoint may be content to think that they do so by a personal decision or commitment—'Here I stand, I cannot do otherwise'. For purposes of action this is enough. But whatever be our intellectual attitude to these matters, one claim may perhaps be generally admitted—that an ethics of the type so summarily expounded here is at least as likely as any other to afford a basis for theological argument.

Chapter XX

SCIENCE AND ETHICS

§ 1. *'Is' and 'ought'*

According to some modern thinkers it is the business of science to supply us with moral guidance.

This view is directly opposed to my contention that if man is regarded merely as one of many objects for scientific study, it will be impossible to understand him either as a moral agent or even as a person who knows his world and knows himself. So direct a challenge can hardly be ignored, especially as some among those who make it are apt to speak as if professional philosophers who disagree with them can be dismissed as incompetent at their own job. Any discussion here must be elementary and over-simple; but after the heavy going of the last chapters we are perhaps entitled to a little light relief.

A scientific judgement is always about what is, was, will be, or would be. A moral judgement is about what I *ought* to be—or, perhaps better, about what I ought to do. To identify scientific and moral judgements is sheer confusion, and to infer the second from the first is a patent fallacy. If we admit—and who can deny it?—that men often do what they ought not to do, we cannot infer from what they do to what they ought to do.

If this be granted, then *a fortiori* we cannot infer what men ought to do from what animals do or what stars do or what atoms do. In short, we cannot infer what men ought to do from what nature does. Hence however much science tells us about what nature does, or even about what men do, by itself this teaches us nothing about what we ought to do. If we are determined to confine ourselves to scientific thinking, then the only logical course is to say, with the Logical Positivists, that when we make moral judgements so-called, we are not thinking. We are certainly not thinking scientifically.

Popular morality—or perhaps we should say nursery morality—does not always adhere to this wise restraint: it sometimes professes to find in nature the models or norms for human conduct. Are we not urged to emulate the busy bee, the industrious ant? And does not even an unconventional thinker like Mr. Gerald Heard maintain that we may have to revise our attitude to landed property because of recent discoveries about the territorial claims of robins? I was once informed by a clerical friend that a moral lesson was to be drawn from sea-gulls: just as they always face the wind and rain, so we ought always to face our difficulties. One objection to this is that gulls have other habits less worthy of moral imitation; and what are we to make of cattle who—if I may so express myself—always face the wind and rain with their rumps?

Is it not obvious that in such exhortations we already know, or think we know, what we ought to do, and then proceed to pick and choose in nature what seem to be illustrations of our moral principles? There is no harm in this if we are merely trying to make moral ideas vivid to youthful imaginations; but if we are seeking moral guidance from nature, no procedure could be less scientific. Yet it is by no means certain that some of our eminent scientific thinkers, when they turn their attention to morality and advise us to be guided by the process of evolution, do not fall into a very similar trap.

If we take a teleological view and attribute purposes to nature, the fallacy is at least not so obvious. Indeed if God has made every thing for a purpose, then it may be good for each thing to fulfil that purpose. Even so, it will be good for man to fulfil the purpose for which he himself was created, if we can discover what that purpose is. We are not entitled to assume we can discover the purpose of man by the study of ants, bees, and sea-gulls, which were presumably created for a different purpose. This is familiar to a teleologist like Dr. Watts, who can use an animal, not merely as a model of morality, but as an awful warning. Thus he can say

'Let dogs delight to bark and bite,
For God hath made them so;
Let bears and lions growl and fight
For 'tis their nature too!'

But he can also add, quite consistently,

'Your little hands were never made
To tear each other's eyes.'

Doctrines of this teleological kind have been expounded with a high degree of intelligence by thinkers like St. Thomas Aquinas, and they are found in a less theological form in Plato and Aristotle. But the modern scientist, I am assuming, excludes teleology from nature, and he should be on his guard against re-introducing it surreptitiously when he reflects about morality.

For the sake of clarity this should be added. If you have already chosen, or even envisaged, an end, science may be able to tell you the most efficient means to that end. In this sense science will tell you what you ought to do. But the 'ought' here is technical, and the reason *why* you ought is merely because you want the end. Indeed even when you know the means to your end, you have still to decide whether you want the end together with this means or not—you might dislike the means more than you wanted the end. All this is below the level of moral judgement. Granted that you want to do the action which consists in using the best known means to a particular desired end or even to a moral end, you have still to ask the question whether such an action would be right. Similarly an artist, however much he may learn from science about technique, has always to decide for himself what will be a good picture. On this problem science can give him no aesthetic guidance whatever. The distinction between means and ends, between the technical on the one hand and the moral or aesthetic on the other, requires more examination, but I believe that this would confirm rather than weaken my main contention.

§ 2. *The super-ego*

The question before us is whether we can get moral guidance from the study of nature—that is, of nature, not in any metaphysical sense, but as it is known by modern science. Can we substitute a scientific moral philosophy for the dim gropings and emotive utterances and metaphysical speculations of the past? Some distinguished scientific thinkers tell us that we can do this by studying the direction of the evolutionary process; and the prestige of modern science is so great that we are bound to listen to them. So far as I know, the doctrine has never been worked out systematically in this country since the time of Herbert Spencer—a philosopher no longer in high repute; but it has been expounded briefly by Dr. Julian Huxley in a rather sophisticated and eclectic way and by Professor Waddington much more bluntly. Both these thinkers believe that their doctrines are confirmed, if not established, by a study of psycho-analysis; and although I am at a loss to understand why they should think this, we must at least pause to note that psycho-analysis is supposed by some to be one of the pillars of the new scientific moral philosophy.

It is perhaps doubtful whether Freud himself would support such

U

a claim: his philosophical interests seem limited mainly to a rather amateurish concern with his own presuppositions. The theories of the ego, the super-ego, and the id are based on a vast clinical experience which the layman cannot have, and it is hard to say whether they offer us more than a useful mythology. But even if they give us a correct account of infantile conflicts and of a proto-ethical mechanism which results from them, this establishes nothing about the nature and validity of our moral judgements. We might indeed argue that if moral judgements arise from this mechanism, they cannot have any validity whatsoever—this, as I have maintained throughout, is always a possible result of treating man merely as one object among others; but at present we are supposing on the contrary—in deference to certain scientific thinkers—that we *can* get correct moral guidance from our scientific studies. Freud regards morality as the control and restriction of instinct; and he tells us that from the point of view of morality 'it may be said of the id that it is totally non-moral, of the ego that it strives to be moral, and of the super-ego that it can be hyper-moral and then becomes as ruthless as only the id can be'. From this it appears that Freud himself has a point of view—the point of view of morality—from which he is able to pass moral judgements on the ego, the super-ego, and the id, as these are portrayed by his science. If this is so, there is no reason why we should not be able to do the same.

One thing is abundantly clear—we can get no assurance that our moral judgements will be sound if we take them over from the super-ego, who appears to be a thoroughly unpleasant and unreasonable sort of person. Nor is there any evidence—if I may revert to our main line of enquiry—that the super-ego bases his judgements on the general direction of the evolutionary process, which is what we are being recommended to do. He is himself no doubt one of the infinitely varied outcomes of the evolutionary process, but this does not guarantee that he knows anything about it; nor does it afford any ground for listening to his moral exhortations. So far as I can see, he could be properly used only to discredit moral judgements—he is sometimes used to discredit the categorical imperative by people who have not even begun to grasp what the categorical imperative is. If the super-ego, with all his savagery and cruelty, is part of the psychological mechanism which is supposed to be produced by evolution, then the sooner we get him under rational control the better. Freud may give us valuable information about what we have to control and the kinds of treatment likely to be effective; but this is something wholly different from determining the principles and purpose of rational control itself.

§ 3.   *The ethics of evolution*

We must now turn back to consider, without the aid of psycho-analysis, the naked contention that good moral action consists in following the general direction of the evolutionary process. This raises two questions: (1) What is the direction of the evolutionary process? And (2) Why ought we to follow it?

On the first point it is already possible to be entirely sceptical. I quote Professor A. D. Ritchie, who can speak as a scientist, and not merely as a philosopher. 'The direction of the evolutionary process', he says, 'may have been revealed to Spencer or Dr. Waddington, but not by science'. On this point I think he is right, but it is hard to discuss it without passing on to our second question.

All arguments of the type we are considering are trying to argue from what is to what ought to be. I have suggested on an elementary level that those who imagine themselves to be doing this are really picking out from nature certain phenomena which seem to them to illustrate moral principles already accepted on quite different grounds. With the utmost respect for our distinguished scientists, they appear to be doing very much the same thing on a more magnificent scale.

If we are going to argue from what is to what ought to be, we ought to argue from all that is, without any arbitrary picking and choosing. That is to say, we ought to argue from the evolutionary direction of the whole cosmos, not of any particular part. But what can we say of this alleged direction if we extend our vision beyond the spectacle of life on our own particular earth? Sometimes it is suggested that the evolutionary process of the cosmos is from the more simple to the more complex. At other times it is suggested that the universe began with an explosion and is gradually running down. But even if we suppose one or other of these views to be established, what moral guidance could they give us? To speak very crudely—there seems to be no more reason for concluding that we ought to prefer the complex to the simple, than for concluding that we ought first to explode and then let ourselves gradually run down. And if there were any reason, it would certainly not be a scientific one.

But let us suppose, though it is hard to see why we should, that a good man ought to follow the evolutionary trend only of life on this planet. The difficulty then arises that there is no one trend—there are hundreds of trends—so once more we have to pick and choose.

Many species have become extinct, and that is one trend of evolution. Why should we not follow their example and aim at our own extinction? We might even secure psycho-analytic support for doing so: there appears to be some evidence for a 'death-instinct'. It might, however, be argued that as extinct species can no longer be evolving, we should not be following the present trend of evolution if we modelled ourselves on them. This would look very like sophistry, and the conclusion seems to rest on the non-scientific and purely ethical assumption that continuing to evolve is a good thing; but as these lost species are no longer here to plead their own cause, we may let their case go by default.

Other species, like insects, have been so successful in their evolution that they have come to a dead-end. They were here long before man arrived, and they will be here long after he is gone. Why should we not imitate them? When we are told that we ought not to do this because they have stopped evolving, it becomes as clear as day that those who argue thus are not supplying the required inference from what is to what ought to be. They have, on the contrary, some principle of preference, rational or irrational, but certainly one which has nothing to do with science. Unlike Plato they prefer to be dynamic rather than static; they prefer the changing to the stationary; and so they look round the world, they pick out the things which accord with their preferences, and they tell us that from these things alone we shall be able to get real moral guidance at last. They imagine they are distilling moral principles out of evolution, when all they are doing is to inject, or project, moral principles into evolution. No procedure could be less scientific, or less philosophic. We are back again in the nursery.

I have stated this fallacy crudely—perhaps too crudely—because I believe it to be an elementary fallacy concealed under scientific statements and moral judgements which are logically unconnected although they may have their own independent validity. When Dr. Huxley says that what we may legitimately call progress 'consists in the capacity to attain a higher degree of organization, but without closing the door to a further advance', he is not making a scientific, but an ethical judgement, as we can see from his use of words like 'higher' and 'advance'. Only because he has done so is there any plausibility in the inference that 'it is right to realize ever new possibilities in evolution, notably those which are valued for their own sake'. The discovery that possibilities may be 'valued for their own sake' is an independent ethical judgement which cannot be inferred from any scientific facts. Dr. Huxley propounds some admirable moral principles because he is a civilized man able to think and act morally; but he makes a profound mistake in supposing, as he does, that 'the ultimate guarantees for the correctness of our labels of rightness and wrongness are to be sought for among the facts of evolutionary direction'. It cannot be too strongly insisted that science as such is absolutely neutral as between good and evil. Even if evolution had a direction, the policy of climbing on to the band wagon would have nothing to do with morality, though it might be recommended by self-interest. We cannot make our morality depend on the way the cat is going to jump.

§ 4. *The ethics of communism*

There is a far more formidable and more philosophic school of thought which attempts to derive morality from the scientific study of nature. The dialectical materialism of Karl Marx proposes in the name of science to root out our bourgeois morality as well as our bourgeois religion; and we cannot afford to ignore its challenge. From the Marxist point of view the liberal doctrines of Dr. Huxley are merely idealistic philosophies invented by the lackeys of capitalism in order to exploit the working proletariat. It is interesting to observe how opposing systems of ethics may be professedly derived from a study of the same scientific facts; and this by itself suggests that the whole method is grounded on an illusion.

According to the communists, traditional morality is deduced from the alleged commandments of God in order to protect the interests of the bourgeoisie as exploiters. Idealistic philosophy is merely a more sophisticated attempt to do precisely the same thing. In modern society, we are told, a professor of philosophy is, in most cases, nothing but 'the diploma-ed lackey of clericalism'. The communist on the other hand—I take this from Lenin himself—deduces morality 'from the facts and needs of the class struggle of the proletariat'. For him 'morality is subordinated to the interests of the proletarian class struggle'. A statement of this kind implies that man's only duty is to adopt the most efficient means to success in the class struggle. It is easy to see what dreadful results, from a bourgeois point of view, are likely to follow from the contention that this end justifies the means; but here we are concerned with communism as a philosophy, not as a political movement. It will be noted that bourgeois morality is condemned precisely because it is alleged to recommend the means to the success of the bourgeoisie in the class struggle. Hence there is in communism a prior assumption, namely, that the success of the bourgeoisie in the class struggle is a bad thing, while the success of the proletariat is a good one. How is this assumption to be justified by science?

We may suspect that the choice of proletarian success as an overriding end springs from a passion for justice which is present in men as men and is independent of the interests of persons or classes. In his choice of end the communist, like the idealists he despises, is appealing to an absolute or objective standard, though we may think that his revolutionary ardour leads him to adopt an end that is unduly narrow. This is borne out by the authors of '*The God that Failed*', all of whom seem to have been attracted to communism by a passion for justice together with the ingenuous belief that a scientific method of securing justice by means of violence had at last been discovered. They were soon disillusioned.

The official doctrine of communism cannot admit the idealistic view that men *as men* may be able to seek justice for its own sake independently of their class. Hence they have to put forward an elaborate philosophy which attempts to derive moral standards from the study of nature. It is this philosophy, the philosophy of dialectical materialism, that we have now briefly to consider.

§ 5. *Dialectical materialism*

Dialectical materialism sets up to be scientific. As a typical product of the nineteenth century it takes a materialistic view of nature, but it professes to study nature by a dialectical method derived originally from Hegel.

It is impossible to describe the dialectical method of Hegel in a few words. Speaking very roughly, we may say that on the Hegelian view the advance of thought consists in overcoming contradictory or opposing theories. This is done by discovering a wider point of view, a more comprehensive theory, in which they can be reconciled. This wider theory is called a higher synthesis, in which the previous contradictions find their proper place and so cease to be contradictions. This can be done most effectively, not by blurring the contradictions, but by making them as extreme as possible. Indeed Hegel holds that if you think out one of your apparently contradictory theories to its logical conclusion it will pass over into its opposite, and so prepare the way for a higher synthesis. This process he finds actually working out in the history of thought and of civilization. It is confirmed by the popular belief that extremes meet. Perhaps we may find something like it in politics in what is called the swing of the pendulum.

There is in all this at least a germ of truth, though most people hold to-day that Hegel made far too much of it. What is much more dubious is the extension of these ideas to nature, where—again speaking roughly—the opposition of forces takes the place of logical contradiction.

Dialectical materialism takes over a good deal of its method from Hegel, but its special task is to apply the doctrine to nature. For it the oppositions or contradictions in material nature are fundamental, and it is they which give rise to oppositions and contradictions in human thought and behaviour. This materialistic contention is directly opposed to the idealism of Hegel. It turns Hegel upside down and is thus itself an illustration of the Hegelian doctrine that philosophical theories tend to pass over into their precise opposite. But there is no suggestion of any higher synthesis.

The principal question before us is this. Does Marxist dialectic give a scientific account of nature and subsequently extract from this its moral and political ideals; or does it, on the contrary, pick and choose in nature precisely those phenomena which look as if they provide support for moral and political ideals independently formed? Wherever we find in a professedly scientific account the use of words like 'important', 'higher', 'onward' and 'upward', we may be sure that the author is not being scientific, but is on the contrary injecting his own moral ideals into his science. It is interesting to apply this clue to the official account of dialectical materialism as expounded by Stalin himself. It will be sufficient if we print in italics the words that give the show away.

According to the official doctrine, nature is an integral and developing whole in which every part is conditioned by every other part and in which some things are always coming to be and others are ceasing to be. The things which are coming to be are of primary *importance* for the dialectical method, even when they are not yet fully established. The process of development in nature is one in which a series of *insignificant* quantitative changes lead to rapid and abrupt qualitative changes; for example, imperceptible changes of temperature result suddenly in water changing into ice or steam.

Therefore this development is an '*onward and upward movement*' from the simple to the complex, from the *lower* to the *higher*. What a jump!

At this point we are introduced to the internal contradictions in nature—the essential mark of dialectic. All phenomena have their positive and negative sides. They are positive so far as they are coming into being, and negative so far as they are going out of being. Hence we conclude that development consists in a *struggle* between these opposites, between the old and the new. Development from the *lower* to the *higher* is in short not a harmonious process: it is rather 'a *struggle* of opposite tendencies' based on the contradictions inherent in phenomena.

The conclusion may appear to be a trifle hurried, but it is not difficult to see where we are going.

§ 6. *Historical materialism*

According to the official theory, it is easy to apply these methods to the history of society and so to turn history, and even socialism itself, into a science. Indeed if social life is determined by matter, we know beforehand that we shall find in society the same principles of development already found in the material world.

If everything is conditioned by everything else, if all phenomena are interdependent, we have to *evaluate* systems of society, not by reference to eternal justice, but by reference to the conditions which give rise to each system. Thus under certain conditions slavery may be an *advance* on a primitive communal system, feudalism may be an advance on slavery, capitalism an advance on feudalism, and socialism an advance on capitalism. In determining what is an advance we base our orientation, not on the social classes which are disintegrating, but on those which are developing—in other words, at present on the proletariat. Here we have a very clear statement of the morality of the band wagon, or the jumping cat, based on a scientific knowledge of the direction of evolution. 'In order not to err in policy, one must look forward, not backward'.

The remaining principles are, from a bourgeois point of view, more sinister, but they are interesting as specimens of Marxist inference.

If it is a law of development in nature that slow quantitative changes pass into rapid and abrupt qualitative changes, 'then it is clear that revolutions made by oppressed classes are a quite natural and inevitable phenomenon'. Hence the liberation of the working class from the yoke of capitalism cannot be effected by slow changes, that is, by reforms, but only by a qualitative change of the capitalist system, by revolution. Similarly, if development in nature is a struggle between opposites, the class struggle of the proletariat is a quite natural and inevitable phenomenon. Hence we must not try to check the class struggle but rather carry it to its conclusion. We must pursue an uncompromising proletarian class policy. We must always be revolutionaries and not reformers.

There is much more both of logical and political interest in the development of this philosophy, which is too little studied to-day. In particular, it should be noted that although social ideas are the *product* of the material conditions of life, they can nevertheless, once they are formed, *react* upon the material conditions of life. This doctrine distinguishes dialectical materialism from vulgar material- ism. In the words of Marx himself 'Theory becomes a material force as soon as it has gripped the masses'. Such a doctrine must inevi- tably be held by revolutionaries whose business is to spread theories and translate them into action.

In spite of the interesting features and occasional truths of the Marxist philosophy, and in spite of the hushed awe and bated breath with which it is often mentioned by modern intellectuals, it is surely obvious that while this doctrine may be a potent instru- ment of revolution among the uneducated, it is in its central core nothing but a nest of fallacies. These revolutionary ideals are no more derived from the scientific study of nature than are the liberal and humanitarian ideals of Dr. Huxley: they are, on the contrary, read into nature by people who have arrived at them on quite other grounds. The whole method of equating logical contradictions with opposing forces in nature, and with the passage from the old to the new, is a piece of mythology designed to support a political theory. Furthermore, it would be possible to reverse the argument. If small quantitative changes gradually produce abrupt qualitative ones, why should we not argue that by making small and gradual quantitative changes—for example, in income tax—we shall be able to produce quite suddenly a new heaven and a new earth and that this is the method of nature we ought to follow? Such might be the reformer's argument, and it would be no less valid, and no more valid, than the revolutionary's. Neither argument has any validity at all—they are both totally irrevelant to any political decision.

The plain fact is that you cannot make any inference whatever from what nature is or does to what man ought to be or ought to do. Until this is realized, ethical discussion will be bedevilled by intellectual confusions. There is and can be no way of arriving at moral principles except by analysing the implications of moral judgements and moral actions. This passion for basing morality on some kind of external authority seems to be one of the deep-rooted mental diseases of the human race. Those who cannot base their morality on divine revelation seek to base it instead on scientific revelation. There is no scientific revelation; but if we had to choose, it is obviously more rational to believe in divine revelation. God is at least supposed to be good and intelligent, while nature—considered as the object of science and not as the creation of God—is not supposed to have any goodness or intelligence at all.

The belief that morality rests only on a divine revelation which is beyond ethical criticism has done great moral harm: in our own country we have only to think of the injunction 'Thou shalt not suffer a witch to live'. But although the scientific revelation of dialectical materialism has had a shorter run, in the production of iniquities it seems to be rapidly overtaking, if it has not already outstripped, its predecessor.

§ 7. *Science and morality*

I can see no direct way of controverting the very simple considerations I have put forward, but it may be thought that there are indirect ways. Those who seek moral guidance from science tend to assume that the only alternative to their view is an obscurantist ethics which supposes that a good man, alike in his moral judgements and his moral actions, need take no account of science whatsoever. Such a contention is one more example of the same confusion of thought.

All action, including moral action, takes place in the world, must be adjusted to the world, and must vary as the world varies: no sane man wears a heavy over-coat in the height of summer. This means for intelligent agents that their practical and moral judgements must be made in the light of their knowledge of the world, and can be made best when they have the fullest and most scientific knowledge. It is even in a sense true that the world in which we act varies as our knowledge varies; for each man has to decide on his actions in the world as he knows it, not as it might be known by somebody else. Science gives us knowledge of the world, of how it is, was, and will be, of its actual and possible variations, of the causes of effects and the means to possible ends. Thus—quite apart from the physical changes effected by applied science and the vastly different situations to which these changes give rise—the mere theoretical knowledge of science may be said to give us a new world in which to act; for the world as known to modern man is utterly different from the world as known to our primitive ancestors. All this is equally true of our own nature considered as part of the world. Inadequate knowledge of our selves and of our world may lead to the misdirection of our energies and the complete frustration of our efforts. For purposes of action we cannot have too much scientific knowledge, and nothing that I have said has been opposed to this even in the slightest degree.

What I am maintaining is that when you have acquired all the knowledge (including scientific knowledge) possible for you in any given situation, you have still to make up your mind how you ought to act. This is an entirely different process: the moral judgement involved in it is different in kind from a purely theoretical or scientific judgement. You may say, if you like, that scientific know-ledge gives you guidance; but the guidance it gives you is guidance as to facts—guidance as to the situation in which you are, the passions and potentialities of yourself and others, the possible alternative courses open to you and their probable results, the best means to your desired ends (including your moral ends), and so on. Such guidance is of the utmost importance to action, and to suppose we can neglect it is the extreme of folly; but to call it moral guidance is utterly misleading; for moral guidance is concerned, not with the situation which you have to meet, but with the ideal which in that situation you ought to pursue. The two kinds of guidance are funda-mentally different, and there is no simple passage by way of infer-ence from one to the other.

To accept these elementary truths does not commit you to an obscurantist ethics. It does not commit you, as Dr. Huxley appears to think, to standards 'grounded in Authority, Absolute, or Revela-tion' (all with capital letters). It does not commit you, as Professor Waddington appears to think, to the intuitions of priests, poets, and prophets. It does not even commit you, as Lenin appears to think, to the superhuman and non-class conceptions which are a swindle, a deception, a befogging of the minds of the workers and peasants in the interests of landlords and capitalists. In fact it does not commit you to any particular system of ethics at all. It merely states that there is a moral problem, and that this is quite distinct from a scientific problem. You may think that the problem admits of no rational solution and that for the purposes of action men must fall back upon arbitrary choices or emotional attitudes or self-interest, or upon the external authority of prophets and priests, of a Holy Book or an Infallible Church. You may think, as I do, that the problem is not one of theoretical insight or logical deduction, but of rational action and its implications. All these and perhaps many other views remain open. What does not remain open is the possibility that knowledge of what I do or you do, of what bees, ants, or robins do, of what water, ice, and steam do, or even of what nature does in the general direction of evolution, can be, or be a substitute for, any kind of moral judgement.

I hope I have not spoken too strongly, but this seems to me to be one of the few questions on which all philosophers ought to agree. Science is ethically neutral. It enlarges, beyond the wildest dreams of our ancestors, the scope and possibility of human action, both moral and immoral; but—except in technical questions, where the end is already given—it can never by itself tell us what we ought to do.

Chapter XXI

MORALITY AND RELIGION

§ 1. *Moral goodness*

As men become less hopeful of proving the existence of God by metaphysical arguments, they are almost bound to base their theology on moral conviction rather than on theoretical knowledge. In so doing they come closer to religious experience; and it is commonly held that God reveals Himself in the heart and conscience of the believer. This is the contention that has now to be examined.

Such a doctrine must seem unconvincing if we take moral action to have little or no value in itself—if we regard it at the best as only a necessary means to the furtherance of art or science or social intercourse, which do have value in themselves. The argument from morality to religion, if it is an argument, must proceed on assumptions similar to those that have already been expounded in summary form. A good man, on this view, is one who follows for their own sake universal moral principles no less rational or reasonable than the principles of scientific thinking; who treats all men with respect as persons or ends in themselves; and who seeks to establish and promote a society whose members in following such principles will respect themselves and respect one another. Moral goodness is for him of supreme value, and all other goods have to be subordinated to it in action.

To live in this way is not to deny the value of art or science or personal affection: it is not to reject, but to accept, the vigour and spontaneity and creativeness of life. All these things are parts of the good life and elements in the ideal society. It is our duty to further and foster them so far as we may. But even the skill of the scientist and the genius of the artist and the devotion of person to person may be hateful, when they are directed, as they can be, to evil and cruel ends. And, as we know only too well, it may sometimes be the overriding duty of a good man to set aside even these most precious possessions for some painful task such as fighting in defence of liberty.

It is from this point of view—the point of view of a moral agent, not of a detached observer—that we must try to consider the bearing of morality on religious faith.

§ 2. *Freedom*

To adopt a point of view is to make certain assumptions, which may or may not be clear to ourselves. One of the main tasks of philosophy is to bring out the character of such assumptions. Here we are concerned with the assumptions of the moral agent or the good man, and the first thing he seems to assume is that he is free. Unless we are free to act on moral principles and so to realize a supreme good, it is absurd to speak of duty or moral obligation or moral responsibility. We can have no duty to do what we are not free to do. 'I ought' implies 'I can'.

This is not commonly denied, but one modern theologian has maintained that 'I ought' always implies 'I can't'. This paradox, whatever be the theological motive behind it, has no plausibility unless we hold that it is always our duty to be perfect. If we are not prepared to lose all contact with common sense, we must insist that a duty to be perfect must be understood as a duty to aim at, and if possible to progress towards, perfection. If even this duty is known to be beyond our powers, it is not properly described as a duty at all.

The man who assumes himself free to act in accordance with moral principles assumes also that his action is not determined (even although it may be influenced) by natural causes, such as impulses and desires. Freedom has both a positive and a negative side: to be free *for* something is also to be free *from* something else. A moral agent seems to take it for granted that he can stand above nature and be in certain respects exempt from its endless chain of causes and effects.

This assumption of freedom is not confined to man as a moral agent: in a lesser degree it is present wherever men act on rational principles—for example, on principles of skill or self-love. Here too they recognize an 'ought'. They think that they ought to use the best means to their adopted ends and ought to combine their ends in such a way that these do not clash. Such an 'I ought' has by itself nothing to do with morality; but it too implies 'I can' and so assumes at least some degree of freedom—even if we believe that human ends are imposed from without.

Although men may, and often do, fail to follow their principles of skill and self-love—not to mention those of morality—there is a sense in which they always act on principles: that is, they are aware of the *kind* of action they are doing, and they *will* it as an action of a certain kind. There are thus, so to speak, concepts operative— generally without words—in human conduct as well as in human thought; and it is this conceptual factor that makes all human actions so far rational and distinguishes them from mere animal behaviour. Because of this we can say that human actions have a reason and not merely a cause; and we seem thereby to assume at least the beginnings of freedom.

The word 'principle' is here being applied loosely. If we wish to use it, as we should, only for a first or supreme principle, we may say that men always act on general 'maxims', of which they are at least potentially aware: they do not merely conform, like animals, to laws of which only other people can be aware. If this is ignored or denied, it will be impossible to admit freedom or to distinguish human conduct from animal behaviour.

So far as men act on principles, they are aiming, however imperfectly, at some sort of coherent teleological whole (which is analogous to the coherent logical whole aimed at by theoretical reason). This is obvious in the principles of skill, and still more in those of self-love, but most of all in the principles of morality since these are concerned with the whole of human society. Here too we may find different degrees of rationality and may assume different degrees of freedom.

The drug addict, for example, may be most rational, and so far presumably free, in providing means to satisfy his needs; and yet he may feel himself enslaved by some over-mastering passion. He is, so to speak, free only in a cage. The man who refuses to wreck his happiness in order to satisfy a sudden impulse or a persistent craving, and who seeks to fulfil his various needs in an organized life, assumes himself to be more rational and more free. The morally good man seems, at least ideally, able to rise above his own needs and passions altogether. His aim is to obey a law which any reasonable man would be obliged to follow in the same circumstances. So far as he can attain to this ideal, he assumes himself to be most rational and most free.

The assumption of freedom serves at least to bring out the negative side of rational action—its freedom from determination by purely external causes. On the positive side it is hard to be sure whether the thought of freedom adds anything to the thought of rational action.

§ 3. *Saints and sinners*

If we assume as moral agents that we are free to act rationally, there arises a further question. Is it really in our power to decide how rationally, or how freely, we can act? Or is the extent of our rationality, and so of our freedom, determined for us by something else?

According to some theological doctrines freedom is granted to the saint—and denied to the sinner—solely by the grace of God. Even apart from theology it might be considered theoretically possible for a man to become so good that he could not but act on moral principles—it would be impossible for him to sin. A holy and perfect will, such as is reserved by theologians for the saints in Heaven and is also attributed by analogy to God, might be described as free to act on moral principles, and yet it might not be free to do otherwise.

This problem is of no practical concern to us as sinful men; but it might be held that for unholy wills like our own the partial freedom of skill and self-love is illusory, and that a man is not free except in so far as he does act on moral principles. This question does concern us very closely. It is not unplausible to say that in immoral action—perhaps even in non-moral action—man's reason is merely a slave to his impulses and desires, which are themselves only events caused by external objects. If this were true, the defaulter could always claim that it was impossible for him not to sin. As a sinner he would not be a person at all, but merely a thing: all his movements would be determined in accordance with causal law.

This view has at least the merit of drawing attention to the limits of human freedom. Apart from the obvious fact that our bodily actions must conform to physical laws, we feel ourselves, as it were, pushed and pulled by impulses and desires, and even by circumstances; and at times these forces seem to get beyond our control. By yielding to some forms of temptation a moral agent may reduce himself almost to the state of a beast or even of a thing. Some men are mentally deficient and so can hardly be called human at all: they may have no power to rise above the level of the brutes. In this matter too there are all sorts of degrees, and the sharp antithesis which we make between the *causes* of our behaviour and the *reasons* for our conduct seems at times to be blurred.

Such considerations may serve to remind us that a man's degree of freedom may be reduced to zero by foolish actions or congenital defects or even by physical accidents; but they do not affect the supposition that distinctively human action has always some degree of rationality and is so far free. What is more, we must still hold that if any one is rational enough to recognize his duty and yet fails to do it, this is not to be attributed to external causes, but to his own free choice. Otherwise we make nonsense of duty and responsibility. If a man is in no way responsible for his bad actions, it is impossible to see how he could be responsible for his good ones. Our ordinary moral judgements can have meaning only on the supposition that so long as we are in possession of our faculties, we are responsible in some degree for all our actions, good and bad alike.

Hence it looks as if freedom to act well carries with it also—at least under human conditions—a freedom to act badly. Freedom to act badly may be a lower or lesser freedom; but even if it consists only (though this is far too simple) in an ability to let ourselves be dominated by passion or self-interest, it cannot be eliminated from the assumptions we make as moral agents.

We thus appear to be faced with the need to assume a double freedom. On the one hand, we take ourselves to be free so far as we act morally—this view we cannot abandon. On the other hand, we seem to assume also that the extent of this freedom (or the lack of it) must be determined by ourselves, not by anything outside ourselves. This means that we must regard ourselves as free (in a new sense) to choose between acting well and acting badly.

These two freedoms have at least something negative in common: by taking them for granted we assume that our actions are *not* determined by anything outside ourselves. But whereas the old freedom depended on the extent to which we acted reasonably, the new freedom to choose between acting reasonably and acting un-reasonably (or—perhaps better—between acting more reasonably and acting less reasonably) looks like an ability to act for no reason, but from mere caprice. So far at least as we choose to act unreason-ably (or less reasonably), we seem to be acting capriciously for no reason at all. Even if we still claim that our actions are not deter-mined by any outside cause, we appear to be at the mercy of chance; and it is not easy to discover any sense in which an action done for no reason can be regarded as positively free.

It is only fair that the difficulties of these conceptions should at least be indicated. Nevertheless for our present purposes we must hold to the view that a moral agent must assume himself to be free so far as he recognizes a duty to act on moral principles; and he must, it would seem, adhere to this assumption, whether in fact he acts well or ill. Hence he must assume that he is not merely one object among other objects—that he is a subject who can somehow rise above the causal events of nature and mould them, if only within narrow limits, to his own rational will.

§ 4. *Freedom and nature*

If we abandon the agent's point of view for that of the detached observer, human behaviour must appear to be only a part of nature and so to be determined by causal law. In the world as known to science there can be no place for freedom.

This is sometimes questioned on various grounds. We are told, for example, that the principle of uncertainty is now admitted in microphysics and that old-fashioned materialism, with its particles pushing and pulling one another, has long been superseded. We are also told—with more relevance—that 'cause' is no longer a scientific concept, or at least that a cause is not to be regarded as the ground of its effect, and so any talk about determinism must be out of date. We should say only that the succession of events is regular and so can in principle be predicted. Nothing is made, or compelled, to be what it is.

It is impossible to examine these contentions here or their bearing upon human action—we should have to ask how far they are scientific and how far they rest on metaphysical assumptions which may or may not be justified. But it should be noted that they are not always confirmed by the language of practising psychologists. The rank and file of psychiatrists, for example, have been said by one of themselves to believe in absolute determinism; and when they tell us that all crime is a symptom of mental disease, they appear to hold that free will is an illusion and that no one can ever help doing what he does. Even our most rational judgements are believed by some, however inconsistently, to be nothing but the tools of the unconscious—nothing but the inevitable effect of causes which lie buried in the unconscious levels of the individual psyche. I take these illustrations from an article by Professor A. G. N. Flew.

The case for determinism—or fatalism—is stronger than it is made to appear in some modern accounts. Those thinkers, for example, who imagine they can dispose of it by saying that I could —or would—have acted otherwise *if I had chosen to do so* are evading the difficulties. The question about freedom is whether I can choose between different ways of acting here and now.

Even if we deny that human actions are determined, but maintain that they are in principle predictable, we do not escape from troubles about freedom. We are in the same position as those theologians who rejected divine predestination, but accepted divine foreknowledge. Was Adam free not to fall, even although God knew from all eternity the precise place and moment of his disobedience? Can complete foreknowledge, whether human or divine, be compatible with freedom?

A rough kind of prediction is manifestly compatible with our ordinary assumptions of freedom. We can say beforehand that a good chess player will play in accordance with the rules of the game —provided he is not inventing a new one—and he will not imagine that his freedom is threatened by such a prediction. But if we handed him a sealed envelope to be opened only after the game was over, and if he discovered that his every move had been written down before he started, he would begin to doubt his freedom and even his sanity. Anyone can predict that Beethoven will write good music, but what scientific genius will predict the Ninth Symphony? And who will foretell that St. Francis will kiss the sores of the leper?

The fact that a prediction is said to be only 'in principle' makes no difference to the problem: it would be foolish to comfort ourselves with the thought that it cannot in fact be made because no one has enough knowledge to do so. The important question is whether the prediction claimed—either in principle or in fact—is vague or precise. No sensible person would deny that a good man is unlikely to steal money from a child; for we know that this is incompatible with the very principles on which his life is built.

There is no problem at all unless it is claimed that at least all large-scale movements can be predicted—in principle—with absolute precision. This claim has in fact been made, and perhaps it must be made. It is still not uncommonly held that the only explanations worthy of the name must be scientific; that all events can be scientifically explained; and that to explain scientifically is to be able to predict precisely what will happen and to do so solely on the basis of observed regularities.

If we interpret this as meaning that the word 'explanation' is to be used in an arbitrarily restricted way, the contention becomes trivial. If it is not trivial, it appears to exclude the view that human actions can be understood as the expression of rational principles and so as free.

On the other hand, if we are allowed to treat the adoption of principles, and even human character, as if they were observed events, the claim to exact prediction begins to seem at once more plausible and less menacing, although perhaps also less scientific; and Kant, who did take such considerations into account, was prepared to believe that if we knew enough, we could predict all human action as surely as an eclipse. He also held, for reasons into which we cannot enter here, that this was compatible with human freedom; but it is not easy to believe that he was right.

The assumption of freedom has been discussed here, not so much for its own sake, but in order to prepare us for the religious assumptions said to be bound up with the moral point of view. With this in mind it may be enough to put the case hypothetically. If, as seems probable, the scientific point of view is incompatible with freedom —or even if, as is certain, it has no more use for the concept of freedom than for the concept of God—then as moral agents we have to maintain that the scientific point of view is not enough. There are two points of view—the moral and the scientific—and while each may be valid within its own sphere, it is from the moral point of view that we get the fullest insight into human action.

This is a large claim, but it is not without parallel. Only the artist can be in a position to understand artistic creation. What is more, only the scientist can understand scientific thinking; and even if, for purposes of his science, he is content to regard all men (including himself) as objects and so as causally determined, he may be forced, if he becomes a philosopher, to reflect on the fact that besides being a known object, he is also a knowing subject. As a knowing subject he, and every other thinker, must assume himself to be free—free to *think* in accordance with rational principles. Hence it is neither an outrage nor a paradox if a moral agent, as a moral agent, also assumes himself to be free—free to *act* in accordance with moral principles no less rational than those of science.

A good man may be unable to find a philosophy that will justify his assumptions, but—like the artist and the scientist himself—he has to act on the assumption of freedom. This assumption becomes easier to accept if we believe that the world of nature, which seems to exclude freedom, is itself, as known to us, in part a product of our own spontaneous thinking in accordance with rational principles. As such a product it cannot properly be used to disprove the very assumption of freedom without which it could not exist for us at all.

If there is any truth in these contentions, a finite subject may, and indeed must, regard himself as more than a part of nature and as able to rise, as it were, above nature. This implies that he cannot take the world of nature to be all the reality there is. Such a view is manifestly unlike any scientific theory of natural objects: it bears more resemblance to a religious faith.

§ 5. *The existence of God*

In acting morally a rational agent does not assume the existence of God in the same direct way as he assumes his own freedom; but it has been thought that the two assumptions are sufficiently akin for one of them to throw light on the other.

The so-called moral argument for the existence of God is sometimes put crudely as if God's existence were necessary in order that the appropriate amount of happiness might be granted to each individual as a reward for virtue—a curiously humble office to assign to the Almighty. It is put less crudely when it is said that unless the universe is divinely governed, the justice which it is our duty to pursue can never be realized. Perhaps it is best put by saying something like this—that it is our duty to seek the highest good, namely, the realization of an ideal society in which the good will of its citizens may be fully effective; that it is impossible to attain this end unless the universe is divinely governed; and that since a good man must suppose duty to be capable of fulfilment, he must thereby postulate the existence, not only of an all-powerful God, but of a God who is wholly wise, benevolent, and just—the existence in short of a holy God, who alone can be an object of worship.

It is possible to argue thus without abandoning the view that a good will is of supreme value in itself altogether apart from the results it may produce. If a man strives to do his duty, he is good even although his efforts have little or no effect. But this does not mean that he is striving only to strive. On the contrary, he is endeavouring to produce results and attain ends—in particular he is struggling to establish and maintain and serve an ideal community; and this end, which it is his duty to seek, cannot be realized without the co-operation of other men and ultimately of nature itself. If we are to conceive it as capable of realization—and how otherwise can we regard it as an end which it is our duty to seek?— we can do so only on the assumption that the world is created and governed by God.

There remains indeed the obvious difficulty that the ideal community can, at the best, be realized only imperfectly in this world, which seems indifferent to moral considerations and will in any case be at some time wholly destroyed. This is one reason why it has been maintained that a moral agent must postulate the immortality of the soul as well as the existence of God; but this claim must be considered later.

These moral arguments for the existence of God may seem no more convincing than the metaphysical arguments already examined—they may seem less convincing, for they do not even pretend to be scientific. The phenomenal world, it may be said, cannot provide complete satisfaction for our intellectual aspirations any more than for our moral ones. As we have seen, men may find the infinite series of temporal causes and effects unintelligible and may tend to postulate as its unconditioned condition a non-temporal reality which may be intelligible in itself. If the validity of this procedure was questioned, are we not obliged to treat the moral arguments with equal caution?

Those who uphold the moral argument in spite of distrusting metaphysics would reply in some such way as this.

To seek the realization of an ideal community is to do more than aim at satisfying moral aspirations—it is to perform an absolute and unconditioned duty laid on us as rational agents. Our intellectual aspirations do not impose on us a similar duty to find a world that is completely intelligible, which is indeed impossible. Furthermore, the metaphysical arguments are arguments from object to object, but they fail to satisfy the conditions without which there can be no human knowledge. The moral argument is not an argument from object to object, and it does not pretend to give us knowledge: it is concerned only with what a moral agent may reasonably hope or believe—perhaps with what he cannot but hope or believe as subject to the absolute claims of duty.

If we regard moral judgements and moral actions merely as phenomena to be explained by psychology—and from the narrowly scientific point of view this is all they can be—then manifestly any alleged religious assumptions bound up with morality are mere moonshine, or at least are only further phenomena in need of psychological investigation. So too if we base morality on casual likings and dislikings, or again on self-interest, the so-called moral argument for the existence of God may reasonably be dismissed as nonsense. Even if we hold an objective view, like that of Professor G. E. Moore, which takes the greatest goods to be personal affections and aesthetic enjoyments, we can attach no weight to theological thinking of this kind. Its cogency, if it has any, must depend on the view that the claims of duty are absolute and that moral goodness is of supreme value.

Even on this view we are still not free from difficulties. It might be said—I take this from a critical friend—that it is quite possible, and nowadays fairly common, to believe that it is one's duty to make the best of a fundamentally bad job, an enterprise in which nothing and nobody is going to co-operate except a few other men and women of good will. It might be said also that even if the religious assumption were forced on the man who seeks to do his duty, it would still be an illusion, although perhaps a comforting and helpful one. We should be like children who invent for themselves an imaginary friend, but have to abandon this fiction as they grow up.

Such a criticism is bound to be felt forcibly by those who are occupied with science and are oppressed—as most of us are—by human insignificance in a vast and apparently purposeless world. Perhaps they are letting the moral point of view be dimmed by the scientific one, but it would certainly be false to say that there can be no moral action without explicitly religious assumptions. There is no direct and valid inference from belief in morality and freedom to belief in the existence of God. Even if there is a natural tendency to pass from one to the other, and even if religious belief is interpreted as an assumption—or a hope—on which good men act, we have to regard it, not as a logical inference, but as a leap of faith. Whether this leap is to be considered reasonable or unreasonable must depend, not only on moral convictions, but also on our view of human reason and of the world as a whole.

§ 6. *Immortality*

Similar arguments—if this misleading word may still be used— are sometimes put forward in order to justify or defend a belief in personal immortality.

Since modern science has abandoned the category of substance, the old metaphysical demonstration that the soul is a substance, and therefore must be immortal, has lost what plausibility it may have had in a less sophisticated world. There remains the appeal to moral conviction, and this may take different forms. It is sometimes said, for example, that there can be no justice in the world unless there is another life in which the wrongs of our present state may be redressed. A perhaps more plausible form of the argument may be put as follows. We have an absolute duty to strive towards a perfection which can never be attained in this life, and therefore in seeking to do our duty we must assume that our life here on earth is only a preparation for another life in which such perfection may be attained.

Contentions of this kind manifestly depend on a prior belief in the existence and goodness of God. Yet they rest also on a specifically moral assumption. We do not normally argue for immortality on the ground that in this world we are unable to attain the highest possible development of our capacities for art or science: we rather accept it as one of the limitations of our human state that we can realize only some few of the amazing potentialities we have when we are young. Here too the argument must rest on the supposition that moral goodness is of supreme value, and that our duty to attain it ultimately is absolute.

Considered strictly as an argument, this train of thought looks like an inference from what ought to be to what is; and this is as invalid as the counter argument from what is to what ought to be. From a scientific point of view nothing could be more naive. If we look on man as one object among others, his life is inseparable from his body, and considerations of duty and perfection, justice and injustice, do not arise. The question of survival after death is at the most a problem for psychical research.

On the other hand, we go too far if we say that survival can be disproved by science. Curiously enough, from the subject's point of view immortality (or at least survival) is something that might be empirically verified, but can never be empirically disproved. If we survive death, we shall presumably know that we have survived; but if we do not survive death, we shall not be in a position to know that we have not survived.

It is sometimes maintained that belief in immortality must be rejected on *a priori* grounds. No doubt if we define thinking and acting as functions of the body, we preclude ourselves from saying that we might be able to think and act after the body has perished. But unless we claim insight into a necessary connexion between nerve changes and mental activity—an insight which would seem to be miraculous—we are attempting to settle problems of fact by arbitrary definitions. To say that a man might survive death is not meaningless. From the point of view of man as a thinker and agent his body is only one object among many; and to survive would presumably be to continue thinking and acting with reference to a world of which his body is no longer a part. We have no empirical grounds for believing this to be possible, and if we consider man solely as an object, we are entitled to say that such a belief cannot be verified; but if this is all that is intended when we say that it is meaningless, our language is likely to mislead others if it does not mislead ourselves.

What has to be admitted is that we cannot have more than the vaguest conception of what it would be like to survive death. This must remain a mystery, and it becomes still more of a mystery if it is thought that life after death is not in time but in eternity.

If we talk this language, it may not be illegitimate to say that a good man may realize eternal values in the world of time and space —this is only another way of saying that moral values are unconditioned and so far are independent of time. We may be tempted to go on from this and declare that a good man ought to live *as if* he were immortal and that so to live must be to cherish the hope of immortality. This may be psychologically true, but it can hardly pass muster as a logical inference. As Aristotle sagely remarked, a thing is not any whiter if it is white for a long time, and the same principle seems to apply to goodness. Yet it is a deep human desire that the most precious things in life should be lasting; and it is at least natural, if not necessary, for a good man to hope that those in whom supreme value is, or may be, manifested will not be utterly blotted out. But this hope—even if science cannot prove it to be in vain—must at best be dim except to those who believe in the existence and goodness of God.

From a religious point of view some may think that men should be ready to accept either life or death in accordance with a divine will which they believe to be wholly good.

This may be an appropriate attitude for a religious man to take towards himself: he may recognize his own unworthiness, and he may be selfless enough to contribute what he can to the world, and so to a divine enterprise, without asking that either he or his work should survive. But even the most selfless of men must think also of other people; and there is a risk of a too smug complacency if those who have warmed both hands before the fire of life commend to their less fortunate brethren a willingness to depart without the hope of anything beyond. When we think of spastic and crippled children, of those to whom the enjoyment of life is denied, and of those who have suffered grievous wrongs, it may seem a mockery of divine justice and a frustration of moral endeavour that there should be no other life than this. Belief in personal immortality, though often held for self-centred reasons and less essential to religion than the belief in God, may yet have its own moral and religious grounds; and—unless in face of conclusive evidence against it—a good man who believes in divine justice may reasonably seek to live *as if* he were immortal, and in so doing may cherish a not unworthy hope.

It can hardly be denied that this hope or belief has become less widely held during the present century—perhaps sometimes in reaction against its cruder forms. Apart from the doubtful aid of psychical research there is no scientific evidence for human survival, and from the scientific point of view the only reasonable attitude is a suspension of judgement. I have suggested that we may be entitled to take into account other points of view as well—especially the point of view of moral agents. The present decay of the belief in immortality may spring partly from the weakness of our moral convictions, and this in turn may have its roots in a widespread feeling of exhaustion and in the heavy pressure of the times. But it is the business of philosophers to rise, if they can, above the passing moods of individuals and the fashions of a particular age. Our beliefs on this subject must ultimately depend on our attitude to religion as a whole. Men are not morally good if they do their duty only for the sake of future reward; but it is hard to see why they should abandon the hope of immortality if their assumption of human freedom has led them to a belief in the goodness of God.

§ 7. *Religion and philosophy*

From what has been said it should be already clear that the question to be discussed is not whether it is possible to infer from the existence of moral agents to the reality of freedom, the existence of God, and the immortality of the soul. Such inferences, if they profess to give us knowledge of empirical facts, must seem childish to any one impressed by the methods of modern science. The question before us is whether in adopting the moral standpoint we can reasonably act in accordance with the assumptions, or even hopes, which appear to be bound up with moral action.

The assumption of freedom is not specifically religious: some theologians have come very near to denying it altogether. But at least it suggests, if we accept it, that the world as known to science is not all the world there is, and that there may be other assumptions, perhaps not so intimately connected with moral action, which are not to be rejected on grounds equally fatal to freedom. The assumption of immortality is, as we have seen, subsidiary. The prior and central question of religion is concerned with the existence and nature of God.

All these questions are questions for philosophy, not for science, although they cannot be answered by ignoring scientific knowledge.

If we hold that the world of observed objects and events in time and space is the sole reality, religious belief seems to become impossible. Those who look at things only from the scientific point of view will see no freedom, no immortality, and no God; but then— if they are sufficiently consistent—they will see no goodness, no justice, no beauty, and perhaps no truth either; for these things have to be understood, not in relation to observed objects, but in relation to subjects who think and act and feel.

I have argued that when we reflect on our own experience, it may become impossible to believe that the world of science and common sense is all the world there is—the world as it is in itself. We are faced with the thought that the world of objects, as we know it, may be only a kind of between-world—a world lying, so to speak, between finite centres of intelligence and an unknown reality. Without some assumption of this kind it is hard to see any room for belief in the existence of God.

Such a thought is admittedly obscure and dangerous: it may provide scope for those who like religion to be quaint and so discredit it by peopling the unknown reality with the strange monsters of their own imagination. Yet in recognizing the limits of human knowledge and the mystery of the world as it is known to us, a doctrine of this kind can at least supply a defence against dogmatic attempts to rule out religious belief altogether on the ground that it can never be established by science. It may also find an echo in religious experience itself.

In spite of all this those who worship a merely unknown reality lay themselves open to Bradley's gibe at Herbert Spencer's attitude towards his Unknowable—that 'it seems a proposal to take something for God simply and solely because we do not know what the devil it can be'. Men must have some concepts by which they try to think about what they cannot know, and some grounds for supposing so great a leap to be at least not unreasonable.

Some may believe that the leap can be made on the ground of

moral conviction alone, but its justification will be stronger if it can have some support from a view of the world as a whole and so from metaphysics. We must venture for a moment on these slippery paths.

It is here that the cosmological proof—and perhaps even the ontological proof—may begin to appear in a new light. If our argument has been sound, it is clear that the unknown reality cannot be thought of by the categories we apply to—and impose on—objects of experience. We may think of it as the condition—though not the cause—of our phenomenal world, but we cannot take it to be itself temporal or caused or conditioned. It is indeed difficult to see how we can pass from this to the positive assertion that it is eternal and self-caused and unconditioned; for apart from the impossibility of finding in experience any objects for such concepts, we may suspect that the concepts themselves have no intelligible meaning. On the other hand, it may seem that they are the product of a demand of reason for completeness—a demand which is the basis of all our thinking. They also appear to be themselves a source of religious or numinous emotion.

If we venture further on the paths of speculation, it may seem to some that only a mind can be intelligibly conceived as self-sufficient and unconditioned—a mind which is creative and does not, like ours, have to construct its world, in imagination and thought, on the basis of what is obscurely given to sense and is for ever being replaced by something equally obscure. But perhaps it is from our moral judgements that these metaphysical concepts appear most likely to acquire a meaning, if only by analogy. So far as we act in accordance with the moral law, we can perform actions which, however inadequately, do fall under our conceptions of an unconditioned obligation which has no further ground and an absolute goodness which is not good merely as a means to something else. In this way we can give some sort of meaning, even in the world of time, to our vague notions of the absolute and unconditioned; and we may pass from this to the thought that only a holy God can be conceived as an absolute and unconditioned reality. All these concepts spring from the drive of reason towards wholeness or completeness in thought and action. As good men strive in action for wholeness or completeness in the practical end which it is their duty to seek, they entertain the notion of an ideal society under a divine head.

From the point of view of science all such speculations must be regarded as unverifiable assumption and wishful thinking. Even from a philosophic point of view it has to be recognized that they are not valid logical inferences from one finite reality to another. They are not even thoughts which can be made lucid and precise and consistent in themselves, and they cannot pretend to give us knowledge. Yet in a way they carry on the work of reason and offer a basis or a background, or at least a possible defence, for faith.

Theoretical speculation leads at most only to *deism*—to belief in a supreme and self-sufficient reality which is the ground of all appearances. This has to be supplemented by moral conviction and by reflexion on the nature of subjects (not merely of objects) if it is to lead to *theism*—to belief that the supreme reality has to be conceived, on the analogy of a free human agent, as a wise and beneficent creator. The first view may find its embodiment in Buddhism and other religions of the East; the second in the religions of the West and above all in Christianity, where the perfect man is taken to be also the Son of God.

From a Western point of view we may put the position in this way. A critical philosophy can only leave beyond experience a blank in which by metaphysical thinking we can obscurely *conceive* the existence of the unconditioned. On the basis of moral conviction we may *believe* that this blank may be filled by the existence of a holy God.

If men were purely intellectual beings, any such belief would be a matter only of idle speculation. But they are not purely intellectual beings—they have to lead their lives on certain assumptions. If they take this world to be all the world there is, they may allow themselves to float with the stream. They may make self-interest their guide or give themselves whole-heartedly to some personal ambition or public cause. More philosophically, they may decide in a harsh world to be cheerful Stoics or melancholy Epicureans. If, on the other hand, they have grounds—as I have maintained they do—for thinking this world to be only the appearance to finite men of some deeper reality and for holding the claims of duty to be absolute, they are at least no less reasonable when they take instead a decision to make the venture of belief in God and to live their lives in such a faith. Yet from a religious point of view this decision is not just one decision like the others. It is rather a self-surrender which is the beginning of a new life.

§ 8. *Religion and morality*

It may seem to the plain man, even to the plain religious man, that all these moral considerations are as remote and empty as the theoretical arguments of the scholastics. But he too must remember that he is not being offered theoretical proof to buttress his religious beliefs. As far as he is concerned, the doctrine may run rather like this. If a man believes that the supreme value in life, the one which claims priority above all others, is to do his duty; if he believes also that it is his supreme duty to live, so far as he may, as a free citizen of an ideal community and to seek its realization; if, further, he not only believes this, but strives to act on his belief; then he will find that he is not merely accepting the world as the environment in which he must act, but is obeying moral laws *as if* they were the principles on which the universe is governed—*as if* they were the expression, not merely of his own will, but of the will of a divine creator and governor. These assumptions—like the scientist's assumption of universal law in nature—are not the result of inference; but they may become convictions which are confirmed, and even made necessary—they may almost seem to be forced upon him —by the course of action in which he is engaged. They will give rise to new emotional experiences and will open up new theoretical possibilities. He may feel himself to be sustained by a divine grace, to be acting in a strength not his own, to be possessed, at least sometimes, of a peace which seems not of this world, to be moved by the beauty of nature as a revelation of the divine, even to be intoxicated like Spinoza with the mere thought of God. He may seem to himself to have a new and deeper vision of the world, of himself, and of his fellow men. Such experiences may strengthen and confirm his convictions till he passes beyond conviction altogether and feels himself—in the supreme case—to be overwhelmed by God's love for him, and his love for God, in a consciousness of union which seems more like knowledge than like faith.

There may be few who go more than a short distance along this path, but many go far enough to have some inkling of what is reported by those who have gone farther—and even to gain from these reports a better understanding of what they have found in their own lives. In this case too the dusty and abstract arguments of philosophers may reflect a more concrete and intimate process within religious experience itself. There is no need to suppose that morality is the only way to religion. Nevertheless moral action is an essential strand in the religious life; and in days when emotion is distrusted and metaphysics despised and religious histories subjected to question, this may prove to be the strongest strand of all.

All of this, as I have said, offers no proof of the existence and goodness of God. Most men hanker for knowledge in these matters, but if they grasp the problem aright, they will understand that such knowledge must be impossible for finite minds. They have to live by faith, and to be content if this faith can be shown not to be unreasonable, but rather to accord with the demands of reason for wholeness and completeness alike in action and in thought.

§ 9. *Some objections*

From the religious point of view some may think that too much is made of morality when it is treated as if it were independent of religion: they may hold that without religion there can be no morality at all. It is perhaps true that without religion a moral life may tend, through human weakness, to become a thankless and joyless struggle in the face of overwhelming odds. Nevertheless to deny the independence, or at least the interdependence, of morality and religion is to discredit both and to deprive each of the other's support.

What this denial amounts to in its naked horror is this. Unless men were instructed by some authority claiming a divine revelation, they would be totally unable to distinguish between right and wrong; and even after the instruction had been imparted, they could never be induced to do the right except by promises of future rewards and threats of eternal punishment.

History lends little support to so cynical a contention. There have been many good men who have had no use for religious dogmatism. In the ages of faith, when the authority of the Church was unquestioned, human beings seem to have behaved, if anything, with even more brutality than they do now—witness the hideous legal punishment of hanging, drawing, and quartering. But, in any case, to obey the law from hopes of bliss and fears of torment has nothing to do with morality or with religion either. And if any one says that unless he had a special communication from God on the subject, he would never have dreamt there could be anything wrong in savaging an old woman because he disliked her husband's opinions, he is either a monster or a lunatic or a liar—or at best a philosopher. But even the most sceptical of philosophers will perhaps agree that slavish obedience to the arbitrary decrees of an irrational but all-powerful God has no claim to be described as either moral or religious—unless these words are to be employed as terms of abuse.

Nor need we be moved by those who would tell us that religion comes rather to the sinner than to the righteous. They are presumably thinking of the experience known as conversion, when a man is first seized by a sense of guilt and by despair. This belongs to the psychology of religion; but a feeling of guilt and despair, if it is not merely a dread of punishment, may, as we now know too well, be pathological. So far as it is healthy, it means that a sinner has seen his own unworthiness in comparison with a binding moral law or with the majesty of God's holiness. It would be strange to regard such an experience as independent of morality.

As for the countless objections to our brief attempt at a philosophical defence of religious faith, only one can here be mentioned. Religious men who cling to the older metaphysics, and even to a rather crude materialism, are sometimes inclined to say that if the world of time and space is only a between-world—only the world as it must appear to finite human minds—then all our moral struggles and endeavours are illusory, and this whole argument must defeat itself.

It is hard to see why this should be so. On the traditional view itself the world of time and space has been created, but will one day cease to be, and time will be merged in eternity, which is the ultimate reality. Those who feel entitled to speculate on the methods of creation should refrain from laying down rules for the guidance of the Almighty. If God should choose to create the world in time and space partly through the activity of finite minds, who is to show that this economy is inconsistent with the divine wisdom? And why should we proclaim that moral action in a world so created must be an illusion? Is not this like saying that the masterpieces of a painter must be illusory because colours exist only in the mind of the beholder?

The difficulties are indeed insurmountable if we fail to distinguish between appearance and hallucination, and if we try to construct a pseudo-scientific theory of two independent worlds. The duty of a good man is to act in this world of time and space in accordance with moral principles; but if he is entitled to assume that in so doing he is a free agent and not merely a part of nature, he may reasonably entertain the hope or the belief that these principles may be also the principles on which the universe is governed. To believe this is to believe, however vaguely, in the existence and goodness of God.

Chapter XXII

GRACE

§ 1. *The meaning of 'grace'*

If a morally good man acts on religious or semi-religious assumptions, and if morality leads—or tends to lead—to religion, we have to ask in what way religious life differs from moral life. Perhaps the simplest answer is that the religious life is distinguished by grace.

The concept of grace has played a great part in Christian theology, which differentiates, for example, between prevenient grace, sufficient grace, and efficacious grace. We must try to consider the subject in a more general way.

The word 'grace'—like the Greek χάρις and the Latin *gratia*—is rich in meaning and in subtle gradations both of emotion and of thought. The historical development of its various senses must here be ignored, but we may take the primary meaning to be 'beauty': grace is, in the first place, a beauty of proportion, movement, and expression which attracts and charms.

Grace in this sense seems to be a gift. Those who possess beauty do not work for it or deserve it: it comes without effort and without thought. To those also who are attracted and charmed by it, it comes as a boon to which they have no right. Beauty, like kisses, goes by favour, not by merit; and a grace is a favour given and received. Hence the second meaning of the word is 'favour': he who shows grace or favour is not obliged to do so, and he who receives it receives something on which he has no claim.

On the side of the giver grace or favour is a free gift—it is given gratuitously or *gratis*, if we may go back to our Latin. On the side of the receiver it has to be received with gratitude and thanks. This third meaning of 'grace' as 'gratitude' or even 'gratification', so prominent in Latin, has almost disappeared from English except in the one phrase 'to say grace'—that is, to return thanks.

It may be said then that the three main senses of 'grace' are first 'beauty', secondly 'favour', and thirdly 'gratitude'. But these are not equivalents: the word 'grace' combines these meanings in itself, and it has an aura that is all its own.

337

338 THE MODERN PREDICAMENT [XXII § 2

In considering grace as the special mark of religion, we shall have to take religion at its best and ignore the manifold aberrations which are opposed to grace and may be called disgraceful.

§ 2. *The grace of beauty*

One English writer who takes a special interest in grace, though in an anti-theological way, is Samuel Butler. He laid stress on the unconscious before Freud, and in spite of his anti-intellectualistic exaggerations he brings out well the unconscious element in grace: we do not acquire grace by taking thought. 'Dog-fanciers', he says, 'tell us that performing dogs never carry their tails; such dogs have eaten of the tree of knowledge, and are convinced of sin accordingly —they know that they know things, in respect of which, therefore, they are no longer under grace, but under the law, and they have yet so much grace left as to be ashamed. So with the human clever dog; he may speak with the tongues of men and angels, but so long as he knows that he knows, his tail will droop'.

Whatever may be thought of this in other spheres, it is true that grace in religion does not come by cleverness, but is rather opposed to it. In pleas for religion there is no room for the clever dogs—not even if they wear dog collars. Nothing could be more out of place than the condescending assumption that if only we will attend to some obvious considerations, if only we will rid ourselves of a few elementary misunderstandings, all the difficulties about religion will disappear. The mark of religion is not sophistication or intellectual superiority, but a kind of unconscious simplicity such as is found also in the poet and in the man of genius. Such simplicity is not shallow: it may be the outcome, as well as the condition, of a rich experience, and it would ill become me to suggest that in this experience thinking can play no part. Yet there is no room for self-consciousness in the bad sense or for self-complacency. The religious man is humble; and what we value in him is a kind of unconscious grace.

For Butler himself grace is essentially Pagan, as will be seen from one passage of his magnificent English.

'And grace is best, for where grace is, love is not distant. Grace! the old Pagan ideal whose charm even unlovely Paul could not withstand, but, as the legend tells us, his soul fainted within him, his heart misgave him, and, standing alone on the sea-shore at dusk, he "troubled deaf heaven with his bootless cries", his thin voice pleading for grace after the flesh.'

'The waves came in one after another, the sea-gulls cried together after their kind, the wind rustled among the dried canes
upon the sandbanks, and there came a voice from heaven saying
"Let My grace be sufficient for thee". Whereon, failing of the
thing itself, he stole the word and strove to crush its meaning to
the measure of his own limitations. But the true grace, with her
groves and high places, and troups of young men and maidens
crowned with flowers, and singing of love and youth and wine—
the true grace he drove out into the wilderness—high up, it may
be, into Piora, and into such-like places. Happy they who har-
boured her in her ill-report.'

From a religious point of view this may be regarded as deplorable
—as glorifying 'the lust of the flesh, the lust of the eyes, and the
pride of life'. But we must remember that Paganism also is a
religion, and that, at least in Greece, it was under the discipline of
beauty. We may even think that Pagan grace was too readily extru-
ded from the Christian religion—that the snares of loveliness loomed
too large in the minds of celibate priests. Yet by itself the religion of
Paganism is too narrow: it is a religion only for the young and
beautiful, not for the sick and the sorry. And, in spite of Butler, the
grace which is beauty is present in all religion worthy of the name—
a beauty even more precious than the beauty of the body. Beauty, as
I suggested earlier, is to be found in the ritual and myth and
language by which a religion is expressed. It is to be found in the
art which religion has inspired. But it is surely to be found above all
in the simple religious life itself, a life of unself-conscious service and
kindness which seems to be encompassed by a kind of holy peace.

Virtue also has its own beauty. Even Aristotle could say of justice
that neither the evening nor the morning star is so wonderful; and
the Stoics could claim that the sage, the ideally good man, has
complete peace in the midst of misfortune. But the beauty of moral
excellence may seem to be won and maintained by human effort.
Are we going beyond the empirical evidence if we say that what
distinguishes the beauty of the saint is that it seems to be given and
received rather than fought for and won?

This brings us to our second sense of the word 'grace'—the sense
of a free gift that comes by favour and not by effort or by merit.

§ 3. *Divine grace*

When we speak of the beauty of the saintly life, we do not use the language of the saint himself. He is too humble to claim merit for his actions, and they would be less beautiful if he did. For him all beauty is in God or comes from God. He regards himself as a sinner and feels himself sustained by an invisible power. Every virtue, every victory, 'every thought of holiness'—to quote the well-known hymn—seems to belong to God alone and to come to man only by divine grace.

Such an attitude has a special religious value. Morality is an appeal for effort, an appeal to be strong; but religion can appeal also to those who feel that they have no strength in themselves, that they are incapable of effort and in need of help. The drawing power of religion, and perhaps also its healing power, depends on its ability to make this appeal.

Yet we must not look at religion through rose-coloured spectacles. The struggle in morality seems at times to be intensified in religion —perhaps because the religious man is more vividly aware of the ideal and is less content to approximate to it by degrees. The peace he enjoys may still be only a peace in the midst of strife, and—as becomes clear from study of the mystics—even that peace seems to be only intermittent. The beauty of the religious life—if I may go back to the first sense of 'grace'—is not a superficial beauty: it contains within it elements of pain, and so is more akin to tragedy. This does not mean that the religious life, or even the way to it, should be represented as a kind of hysteria, as in some modern versions. A religious man, like his less favoured brethren, has to be steady in affliction; but if he is not always sustained by conscious-ness of divine help, perhaps he is always assured of final victory.

The doctrine of grace has its own theoretical difficulties and practical dangers. Some have found it hard to reconcile divine grace with human freedom—although we need not suppose the omnipo-tence of God to be so straitened that He cannot give to men the grace of being free. More serious is the objection that if grace is given and received apart from merit, then the will of God must be arbitrary and unjust. It may even be supposed that in religion we can avoid the effort necessary for virtue—or abandon virtue alto-gether—by adopting some creed, or experiencing some emotional change, or submitting ourselves to some mystical or ritual cleansing. Into these darker errors it is impossible to enter here. A religion becomes self-frustrating if it denies human freedom in order to magnify the grace of God. It becomes idolatry and superstition if it throws virtue overboard as unnecessary lumber. It becomes devilish if it makes God as arbitrary as He is powerful. The word 'favour' may suggest favouritism, but a God who has favourites could not be a God of grace. Divine grace must be open to all who are willing to accept it with gratitude.

§ 4. *Acceptance*

Whatever special graces may be given to the religious man, he accepts them gratefully and gladly. In his attitude there is no place for vanity. When we find this unaffected humility and self-forget-fulness in any one, we all value it, even the most sceptical. If we found it more often, religion would incur less odium than it does.

So much is obvious, but it is to be remembered that from the religious point of view divine grace is not confined to the help or comfort or peace by which a man may be favoured—it is manifested in every happening in life and indeed throughout the universe. Here too the attitude of the religious man is one of willing and, if possible, grateful acceptance—not mere acquiescence in the inevitable.

It was once reported to Carlyle that Margaret Fuller had expressed her attitude to life by saying 'I accept the universe'. He replied, 'Gad, she'd better!' This may have been a just protest against pretentiousness, but the problem is not so simple.

Even on the level of self-interest—not to speak of morality—there are countless men and women who get into all sorts of trouble because they refuse to accept the universe. They will not take the limitations of human life, and the special limitations of their own life, as a basis for action, but are always envying other people and yearning for opportunities they suppose themselves to have missed. It would be wrong to speak unsympathetically, since there are many who, through no fault of their own, but through the pressure of life, perhaps even in early childhood, have to suffer painful experiences for which modern psychology may be able to find a diagnosis and in some cases a cure. Yet the popularization of psycho-analysis may foster a tendency to evade present responsibilities on the ground of real or imaginary infantile conflicts. It is hard not to be impatient when we find people, especially young people, graced apparently with every gift of nature and of fortune, healthy, intelligent, and well-educated, complaining bitterly that they have never had a chance. The amateurs of psycho-analysis have much to answer for —including a lack of humour and of common sense. In the presence of futility and flabbiness we have to remember that there is such a virtue as courage. If I may say so without undue sententiousness, life is rather like swimming: you must be brave enough to give yourself to the water and learn that it will bear you up.

It is here that the religious man receives a very special grace. He is able to accept his circumstances, and even his limitations, as a manifestation of the divine will. This acceptance is not primarily a theory—he does not pretend to understand the divine will or to know why things are as they are: it is rather a way of taking the world gratefully as a basis for his action. To take things thus is to transform them: circumstances, however painful or even degraded, may then become the setting of a holy life, and willing acceptance of them may be a source of strength. This can be best expressed in the language of poetry, which is also the language of religion—in such an affirmation as 'If thou wilt carry thy cross, thy cross will carry thee'.

In these matters it is easy to indulge in false emotion; but it is perhaps in some such way as this—especially if the cross is taken as a symbol of suffering also for others—that the healing power of religion is to be conceived. In some respects we have to-day a clearer understanding of the spiritual conflict, the sense of sin and guilt and despair, the anguish or the *Angst*, from which religion may set men free. To glorify these trials—still more to seek them—is wrong, and seems sometimes to spring from morbidity or vanity; but they have to be looked at dispassionately and accepted willingly, if a cure is to be found. In a desperate situation men must use whatever remedies may be provided by science or religion; nor need they think it unscientific to consult the recorded experiences of the saints.

§ 5. *Service*

Gratitude as an emotion is not enough: it has to be displayed in action if it is not to turn sour. The gratitude of the religious man is manifested in service to his fellows, which for him is also service to God. It is in this way that his moral life takes on, as it were, a third dimension so that he may be tempted to decry a morality that is without religion and to speak of it contemptuously as what is sometimes called 'works' as opposed to 'faith'.

In the religious life 'good works' may no doubt become too absorbing: if they are not tempered by prayer and meditation and even humour, they may stifle the spirit of religion. A life of service is not one of grim efficiency or bustling officiousness, nor even one of bubbling spirits and overflowing amiability—still less is it a life of self-complacency and pride. All this is a religious aberration, but it is also a moral aberration. Moral goodness too depends upon the spirit that is manifested in action. If it is taken up into religion, it becomes something like saintliness or even holiness, and it is then a form of worship—some may find it the most selfless form of worship.

There is another way in which morality may be enriched by religion. As we have seen, in practice moral action is more than obedience to an abstract universal principle: it is also a fitting in with a pattern— a moving or changing pattern, for which we seem to have no special name—and it merges into loyalty to comrades, perhaps especially to a captain or leader, and also to society. The religious man's pattern is consciously wider than his society or even than the visible Church—it becomes for him the pattern of the universe, and the captain of his faith is God. Obedience and loyalty seem to be merged into awe and love.

A more technical point may be added. Because of the imperfection of earthly persons and earthly societies—and indeed of a visible Church—moral loyalty has always to be checked and corrected by an appeal to universal principles. There is no such separation for those who love God, since He is conceived as both universal and individual—as we saw, it has been thought better to say of Him that He is goodness rather than that He is good. It is curious how in this respect metaphysical speculation seems to find an echo in moral and religious conviction. This is shown also by the way in which moral conviction, like theoretical speculation, seems to strive towards a whole which is complete and perfect and unconditioned—a whole accepted by religious faith, in spite of paradoxes and even contradictions, as actual and not merely ideal.

It is in this way that faith becomes more than the adoption of a moral attitude—it seems to become a complete self-surrender, a waiting upon God. It is described as like the opening of a door that He may enter. This waiting is easier for the Christian since he thinks of God, at least in part, under the figure of a man in whom self-surrender was complete—a man who loves him and seeks him and demands his love and service. Other Western religions seem to share at least something of this view of God and this emotional experience. In Buddhism, if not in the other religions of the East, the theoretical interpretation is different; but there too the moral life, although apparently more self-sufficient, is a way to absorption in the ultimate reality and is accompanied by something like the same emotional experience of self-surrender. It is perhaps this that constitutes the distinctively religious attitude, so that ways of life may be classed together as religious in spite of opposing doctrines. Perhaps there is no religion which does not believe in the Real Presence, however differently this may be interpreted and however varied may be the speculations about the way in which it is felt or known.

Some may think that this account is too rational and too moralistic, that it neglects the numinous, that it fails to allow sufficiently for awe and dread, and says nothing of the wrath of God. For the last omission I make no apology, for I think that much of what is said on this subject is diseased. Otherwise there is no necessary conflict with Otto's analysis of the *mysterium tremendum* and of its rational schemata, as he unhappily calls them, although there may be a difference of emphasis; but while awe may be felt in the presence of the overpowering and the incomprehensible, it is most fully religious—at least from a Western point of view—when it is felt in the presence of absolute holiness.

It may be true that in the Western world even religious men tend to make too much of action and too little of contemplation and adoration. But adoration is to be distinguished from adulation; and it may be found most fully in a life of humble devotion and service—not in the repetition of fulsome praises in which (to judge by human analogies) the Almighty is not likely to find satisfaction. Nor should it be forgotten that for the religious man virtues and victories as well as thoughts of holiness come only by divine grace.

§ 6. *Religious assumptions*

So far an attempt has been made to describe grace from the point of view of the religious man himself. He is not interested in philosophical difficulties; and if he becomes too curiously concerned with questions of ways and means—if he enquires, in Martin Buber's language, not about man's way to God, but about God's way to man—he seems to move into new territory and enter on the doubtful paths of speculation.

It may seem ungracious here not to follow his wise restraint, but one thing must be said from a more philosophical point of view.

There can be no doubt about the nature and reality of religious experience—the experience of grace. But it is always possible, and indeed inevitable, for a scientist to maintain that consciousness of divine help, or even consciousness of the divine presence, is the result of preceding actions and states of mind or of the hidden workings of the unconscious. He may take in a special sense the saying of Jesus, 'Thy faith hath made thee whole', and argue that belief in God gives rise to the experience so that the experience cannot be used to justify the belief. Those who feel free to indulge in psychological surmises may even hold that the religious man draws upon a collective unconsciousness which seems to be a great deal cruder than his own conscious life. It is not easy to see why this should be thought a more acceptable theory than the view that the religious man draws, as it were, on a divine consciousness which is as much above his own as the collective unconsciousness of Jung is below it. Neither view, so far as I can see, can be regarded as a scientific theory to be verified by empirical evidence; but it is a pity that those who explore the unconscious restrict themselves so much to abnormal experiences. Their explanations can discover little but the irrational or even the monstrous, although it seems obvious enough that unless there were more rationality in the unconscious than is usually admitted, we could not think the thoughts, or enjoy the experiences, which are common in the normal man.

There can be no hope of defending religion by means of pseudo-scientific theories, which in any case would be opposed to religion in so far as they must treat God as if He were only one object among others. The religious man has to live his life on principles which cannot be turned into scientific hypotheses: it has to be enough for him that his assumption of divine grace is necessary to a way of life which has its own achievements, its own consistency, its own system, and its own satisfaction. Can we say much more about the assumptions of the scientist himself?

§ 7. *The factor of emotion*

If religious experience is taken to be an experience of grace, it must contain emotion as well as thought and action; and it may be advisable to return briefly to this topic, now that we perhaps have a clearer view of the intellectual and moral factors in religion. This is a more hopeful task than an attempt to speculate about the ways in which God may act upon man; but we must not forget that any account that is given must be inadequate from a religious point of view.

All human activity has what may be called a feeling-tone. Pleasures, so far as we can speak of them by themselves, take their character and, as it were, their colour from the activity they accompany, whether this be regarded as belonging to the body or the mind. Broadly speaking, if our bodies are functioning well, we have a sense of well-being. If our minds are functioning well, we have a sense of ease and satisfaction. Feelings of pleasure or pain, satisfaction or dissatisfaction, may be a kind of reflexion, however blurred, of success or failure in our activities. They may thus form a kind of clue or guide to our success or failure: an uneasy feeling, for example, may suggest to us that something has gone wrong with our thinking.

This connexion between feeling and activity extends beyond feelings of pleasure or pain in any narrow sense. In athletic exercise, for example, if our bodies are balanced, we feel balanced; and this may suggest that a harmony of feeling—or a feeling of harmony—may reflect, or even further, a harmony in our actions. To suppose this is to follow, or perhaps to go beyond, Aristotle's well-known doctrine of the mean. Thus in the face of danger a brave man acts in a way adjusted to the circumstances: he strikes a sort of mean between reckless and cowardly behaviour. This is what we may call an outer mean or harmony. But according to Aristotle—and his analysis was confirmed by the late Professor J. L. Stocks as a result of battle experience—there is also an inner mean, a mean or harmony or equilibrium of feeling: the feelings of a brave man may be a compound of confidence and fear in due proportion. This suggests that a harmony of emotion, a harmony which may be felt, is the condition of harmony in action. The conception is admittedly vague and in need of further analysis, but it corresponds to something in our ordinary experience.

A similar view may be taken of aesthetic enjoyment. The aim of the music lover is to hear a complex succession of sounds as an aesthetic whole, one in which—if vague words may again be pardoned—there is a balance or mean or proportion. This proportion must be in the sounds themselves; but the ultimate criterion of the success or failure of the music lies, not in any theory or measurement, but in the satisfaction or feeling of the hearer. The music may arouse emotions of joy or sorrow, cheerfulness or gloom, but these are not the criterion of musical excellence—to use them as such is the main source of bad taste. What makes these emotions aesthetic seems to be a feeling of harmony in our activity of listening. Kant thought this might be the feeling of a harmony between our power of conceiving and the imaginative activity of combining successively given sensations into a whole. This combining is what we do when we make our most prosaic judgements of perception; but there we are concerned with bringing objects under concepts, whereas in listening to music we are hardly concerned with concepts at all. Whatever be the correct theory of these difficult matters, there does seem to be in aesthetic experience an outer and inner harmony (which may contain elements of disharmony and be all the richer for them). You cannot separate the harmony of feeling from the heard harmony of the sounds, but without the feeling there would be no aesthetic enjoyment or aesthetic judgement at all.

Many philosophers to-day jib—and even gibe—at the suggestion that there might be a specifically aesthetic feeling. No doubt they are right if this is regarded as simply one among many other feelings; but however many emotions may be present—perhaps emotions recollected in tranquillity—it seems pretty obvious that unless we can distinguish the feeling-tone of aesthetic appreciation from sheer raw emotion as such, we are not likely to be good judges of art.

The details of all this may be highly questionable, but one point I take to be sure. Feeling is an essential basis for aesthetic judgements, and yet—if modern scepticism may be discounted—these judgements claim to be valid for others as well as for ourselves. If we adopt a wide, rather than a narrow, conception of truth, feeling is an essential basis for some judgements that claim to be true.

Less need be said of love, for love is notoriously blind. In its possibilities of frenzy and despair it resembles religious aberrations, and religious emotion is itself sometimes considered to be sexual in character. This may be used against the present line of argument. Yet even the tense emotions of love may help to give a vision of the world, of the value of personality, and of the possible union of two minds, which brings us nearer to reality than the detached observations and abstract generalizations of the scientist. If we are seeking for truth in a wide sense, and not merely in a scientific one, emotion, although it must be subject to criticism and control, is not to be rejected or disregarded.

In moral judgements also there is an element of feeling—so much so that some philosophers have thought they must be based on feeling and so must be akin to aesthetic judgements or even to judgements of personal likings and dislikings. All this I believe to be a profound mistake, but it arises because in moral judgements there really is—along with more fundamental factors of thought and volition—a moral feeling which is, not only a spur to action, but also perhaps a rough criterion or guide. And moral achievement may also bring with it its own satisfaction—a quiet contentment and peace of mind which is not to be mistaken for complacency and may at least be suggestive of rightness in our actions and in the judgements which preceded action.

It is in view of such considerations that we have to ask ourselves what is to be said for those who tell us that the heart has its reasons which the head can never know. How far can we accept the claims of those who seek to base religion on feeling, and perhaps on numinous feeling ?

If these claims are intended to exclude all rational thinking and moral judgements, they must be repudiated. We are not obliged to succumb to advocates of religion who occasionally hint that their obscure reflexions must be profound because their emotions keep on interfering with their thoughts; and there is Biblical as well as psycho-analytical warrant for saying that out of the heart proceed evil thoughts and other horrors which need not be further particularized. Nevertheless, if we take feeling as one element in a wider experience which is also intellectual and moral, we may be able to accord to claims made on its behalf at least some measure of justification.

Religious feeling, as we have seen, may run through the whole gamut from despair to ecstasy. Like art, religion may give rise to all sorts of emotion, and some of these may be deplorable, especially if they are used as a criterion of religious insight. There may be no specifically religious feeling if this is taken to be one feeling among many others; but it may still be possible, as it is in aesthetic appreciation, to distinguish the feeling-tone of religious experience, no matter what further emotions may also be present. It can hardly be doubted that religious men sometimes feel themselves to be in the presence of God—the saints may feel this more continuously, although the feeling of God's presence may be withdrawn even from them, and they have to fall back on mere belief or will. It is this feeling that theologians explain to themselves by a special sense, a power of intuition, a faculty of divination. No immediate feeling, however intense, can by itself give us any kind of knowledge—let alone knowledge of God. But if we suppose the goal of religion to be a harmony of the whole man—of mind and will, and even of mind and body—in harmony with the ultimate whole, may not even an imperfect attainment of this ideal be reflected in feeling, perhaps in a feeling closely akin to the feeling of beauty which at times comes so near to a feeling of divine grace?

A suggestion so vague, so summary, so open to objections is not to be compared with a scientific theory—or perhaps even with a philosophic one; but it would be strange if the religious man did not take a felt emotion which he alone has experienced to be a confirmation of his faith or even a revelation imparted to him by the grace of God.

Chapter XXIII

THE WORLD AND GOD

§ 1. *Grace in the world*

From a religious point of view it is not too difficult to find God in the heart of man—in the experience of what seems to be divine grace. Even if the picture painted may be thought too rosy, and even if it is susceptible of very different interpretations, there is here at least a solid foundation of fact. It is far more difficult to find God in the world—to believe that His grace is present in every detail of the physical universe and of human society. There are many who would say that such a belief has no foundation whatever or even that it is opposed to the clear deliverances of science. Although it may be true that religious men accept the world as a manifestation of the divine will and build their lives on such acceptance, this does not mean that they can justify their attitude by any appeal to scientific knowledge.

It may seem a tiresome habit of philosophers to be always inventing fresh difficulties, always giving something with one hand and then taking it away with the other. Nevertheless there is here a problem—some may think a dreary problem—that cannot be passed over in silence.

Thoughtful men have not always found it easy to regard either the world or human society as a manifestation of divine justice and divine love, but the difficulties are greatly increased with the spread of scientific knowledge. Theology, so far as it was independent of revelation, used to rest on three main supports—it was rather like a tripod. The first leg was metaphysical speculation about ultimate reality; the second was moral conviction; and the third was the belief that purpose can be discovered by science in the physical world. Nowadays the first leg is considered rickety; even the second one is thought to show signs of weakness; but the third seems to have collapsed altogether. How then can the tripod expect to stand?

As we saw in examining the argument from design, modern biologists reject the concept of purpose or purposiveness, although they continue to talk about organisms as self-regulating systems. However we are to interpret this, they are no longer tempted to extend such conceptions to the world as a whole, and so to facilitate, if not to prove, the assumptions of theology. Hence the age-long background of teleological science—or scientific teleology—which was taken over from the Greeks by Christian theologians has now disappeared, and the religious man has to face a new situation.

In examining this situation we are no longer attempting to argue from the design in nature to the existence and attributes of God: we are looking at theology, so to speak, from the other end. If a man already has faith in the goodness of God, he has still to ask what—in view of all that is known about the world—he can reasonably believe and hope. It is his duty not to talk nonsense and not to make assumptions which are untenable in the light of scientific knowledge—otherwise he will bring discredit upon his religion as well as upon himself.

Thus, even if we are still trying to look at the world from a religious point of view, it is necessary to take into account the intellectual impediments to faith. We have to consider, however briefly, what can be believed about God as He is thought to manifest Himself in the world. It should be unnecessary to add that a belief about God is something very different from a belief in God.

§ 2. *Religious assumptions*

In a scientific age it is natural to suppose that when we ask what can reasonably be believed about God's presence in the world, we are asking what hypotheses can be verified—or even what hypotheses can be established by means of experiment. This supposition is not confined to a scientific age: it is characteristic of primitive religion itself—as when Elijah sought to prove that Jehovah was superior to Baal because He alone was able to set a sacrifice on fire. One of the modern impediments to faith is that primitive religions—and even religions by no means primitive—were bound up with beliefs which have now to be abandoned.

Although the grounds for faith are no longer sought in scientific experiments, it may still seem a proper question if we ask what evidence would count either for or against a religious belief; but even in this there is a risk of confusion. The propositions in which theology seems to formulate religious beliefs are more akin to what I have called 'principles' than to the propositions of empirical science or to those of logic and mathematics. This means that the evidence for them—if 'evidence' is a suitable word—cannot be dependent on simple methods of verification.

Consider, for example, such a principle as the scientific assumption that there is universal law in nature. If we ask what evidence is to count for or against such an assumption, the answer may be that there is none. We may say that our principle is confirmed by every scientific success, but we do not say that it is overthrown by any scientific failure. If we are unable to bring any phenomena under law, we merely suppose that we do not know enough about them. To abandon our principle would be to abandon science—and perhaps even to make all experience impossible.

The same considerations obviously apply to theological propositions so far as these rest on the cosmological argument. If this argument is taken to be valid—if it is supposed to prove that a necessary being exists or even that the notion of a necessary being is not inconceivable—then no observed changes in the world could possibly count either for or against it. The only conceivable change that could count against it, would be the disappearance of all finite or imperfect or contingent beings; and this would be the end of all experience and all argument.

The man whose religion can be formulated in such theological terms is wholly unaffected by any facts or laws that science may discover. Nor should it be thought that this is true only because he is concerned with a reality supposed to lie beyond the observable world. On the contrary, he not only lives differently in the world because of his religion, but he sees all things differently. He may also indulge in quasi-empirical beliefs—for example, he may assume the transmigration of souls—but these, besides being unaffected by scientific discoveries, seem to belong to the periphery of his vision, perhaps even to be only the myth in which the vision is expressed. If a man is enough of a thinker, he may be able, like Spinoza, to do without mythology altogether.

The problem becomes more difficult when God is conceived, not merely as a necessary being, but also as a creator who is all-wise and all-holy. On this view the world has to be accepted as the working out of a divine plan; but—in spite of traditional beliefs to the contrary—it seems that such an assumption can neither be supported nor overthrown by scientific evidence. This admission may not be alien to the spirit of religion. The believer may be convinced that not a sparrow falls to the ground without his Father; but he holds to this conviction in spite of the fact (and not because of it) that sparrows do fall to the ground.

Religious principles can be confirmed only in the life of religion, just as scientific principles can be confirmed only by a successful pursuit of science. Indeed the nature of science is such that it cannot conceivably provide support for religion. Although a scientist may be a saint, or a saint a scientist, this is no reason why we should muddle up two different kinds of outlook or expect them both to have the same kind of confirmation; nor should it be forgotten that even the principles of science are not to be confirmed in the same way as the empirical generalizations of natural history.

These distinctions have to be clearly grasped if theology is to maintain itself in the modern world; but it has also to be admitted that they will give rise to difficulties, not only for theologians, but for religious men themselves. These difficulties will have to be considered here only from the Western point of view. For most Eastern religions they either would not arise or would arise in a different form.

§ 3. *Providence*

As I have said, it should not be thought that a belief in God offers only a basis for action: it also affords a new vision of the world. This vision may be regarded as a dream and may be opposed to the reality of common sense and science, but from the religious point of view it is the other way round. Such a reversal has been well expressed— in spite of occasional queernesses—by Simone Weil in her *Attente de Dieu*, especially in what she calls the Forms of the Implicit Love of God. Here is her final summing up. 'Our neighbours, our friends, religious rites, the beauty of the world—these do not sink to the level of unreal things after direct contact between the soul and God. On the contrary, it is only then that these things become real. Before that there was no reality.'

For the religious man all the different facets of the world—even its sadness and its tragedy—seem to fall into place and to shine with a new light as a result of his experience, or rather in his experience itself. This is something quite unlike a scientific theory: it is far more concrete and direct, like being in love. But if he is also a thinker, he appears to require a theology more than the good man or the good citizen requires a moral or political philosophy. This is presumably because the scope of religion is so much wider. At times the theology is pursued in horrifying detail and hardens into something like an empirical science, when its shallowness and superficiality may do great disservice to religion.

x

It cannot be denied that scientific absurdities penetrate into theology and so—what is much worse—into religion itself. This is particularly obvious in the statements sometimes made about divine Providence.

For misplaced condescension and sheer nonsense it would be hard to beat the preacher who assured his congregation that if only they would think more, they would find many hitherto unnoticed manifestations of the divine benevolence—for example, that God had been considerate enough to fix the day of rest at the end of the week when we are tired, and not in the middle of the week when we are less in need of repose. Against such individual puerilities there can be no safeguard: they serve only to illustrate the folly of which the unintelligent are capable when they try to think about matters too high for them. What is really disturbing is the blandly optimistic tone of much devotional writing. In a popular hymn a man so intelligent and so religious as William Cowper can give utterance to the following sentiment:

'Beneath the spreading heavens,
No creature but is fed;
And He who feeds the ravens
Will give His children bread.'

And the Psalmist too can tell us that although he has been young and now is old, he has never seen the righteous forsaken nor his seed begging bread. We who have seen so much cannot but think he was very lucky or very blind.

All such survivals of primitive religion are bound to come up against the hard facts of science. The facile optimists—though Cowper was far from that—who assert that all creatures are fed, are able to do so only because the creatures that were unfed are no longer beneath the spreading heavens. Religion must be purified of absurdities if it is not to be regarded in the modern world as a fool's paradise.

There are some who claim to recognize the divine plan, to trace the divine pattern, if not in the events of the physical universe, at least in the working of human society.

We need not be facile optimists to believe that man has made some progress since the days of primitive savagery, certainly in knowledge, but also in morals, in art, and in political life. There is indeed no such inevitable progress as the Victorians sometimes fondly imagined, and the history of the human race may be regarded pessimistically as a series of catastrophes with brief periods of civilization in between. But apart from conscious human purpose it is possible to understand how violence and treachery and injustice tend in the long run to defeat themselves; how conflict can be a spur to ingenuity and so to mechanical improvements; and how, as a result of conflict, men may sometimes shake down into an uneasy equilibrium which might have been attained almost without effort by the exercise of justice, or even of common sense. In such happenings philosophers like Kant and Hegel have thought to see evidence of a divine plan or a divine cunning which uses men for ends other and better than their own.

All of this may give some ground for hope in progress and may at least seem compatible with a divine plan: it does not baffle our minds or shock our aspirations, as do the apparently wasteful processes of the physical universe and of animal life, when we attempt to judge them by the standards of human action. But even on such a supposition, which may appeal more to philosophers than to historians, divine Providence would work through natural laws, not through direct interventions; and the mills of God grind far too slowly for us to see that they grind exceeding small. In this world happiness is not always adjusted to virtue, nor unhappiness to vice; and the issues of justice and injustice seem to lie in human hands. How little justice there is in the world has been brought painfully home to us in recent years.

The religious man has to act on the assumption that the divine will is manifested in every happening throughout the universe; and he has to accept it all as given by God's grace. But it is an impertinence to claim that he understands the divine will; and it is childish, if not dishonest, to support his claim by singling out some events and ignoring others.

§ 4. *Special providences*

The divine plan for all creation is of more concern to the theologian than to the saint, but it used to be the fashion to speak, not only of Providence, but of special providences. This belief has been a comfort to many simple souls and has entered deeply into religious life itself. It might seem a pity to disturb it, were it not for the fact that it is already disturbed.

If we think dispassionately, it is hard to see what the doctrine of special providences can mean. A man who does not believe in general providence will be unlikely to believe in special ones; but if

he has faith that God's will is manifest in all creation, what can he
mean by saying that there is a special providence in any particular
case?

Is it too harsh to suggest that the term is often used merely of
happenings which we regard as advantageous to ourselves? We need
not count blatant examples like the story of the ship-wrecked sailor
who was clinging, along with another, to a floating log too small to
support them both. 'Providentially', he reported later, 'I managed
to get hold of a piece of wood and knock the other man into the
water'. But many of us would consider we had had a providential
escape if some miscalculation or mishap prevented us from catching
an aeroplane which subsequently crashed with all on board. We
should perhaps feel this more strongly about a child—for example,
if he happened to leave a room just before the roof fell in. These are
natural human feelings, and in such circumstances a religious man
will feel special thankfulness; but he has to recognize that Providence was equally at work in the case of the passengers who did *not*
miss the aeroplane, and in the case of the child who walked *into* the
room instead of out of it. To think otherwise is not religion but
superstition—it is rather like a belief in one's star. Admittedly a
religious man would not be human if he felt the same gratitude for
bad fortune as for good; but he must at least try to believe that even
the worst of ill fortune is in accordance with the same divine and
beneficent will.

We have here a clear illustration of the difficulty which arises for
religious men themselves when their picture of a world full of supernatural powers intervening constantly in human affairs becomes
incredible or meaningless in a scientific age. Whatever may have
been thought in the past, no one, however saintly, has any reason to
assume that God will save him from the typhoid bacillus if men have
neglected sanitary precautions, or from the concentration camp if
they have allowed wickedness to triumph. To abandon a false, but
comforting, sense of security may be the hardest lesson of all for
modern men to learn, but may it not also mark a spiritual, as well as
a scientific, advance? A genuinely religious faith is not a belief in
exemption from personal misfortunes: it carries with it only the
assurance—however difficult to retain—that even in suffering it may
still be possible to serve God and so to realize an absolute good.

There is a similar difficulty with regard to prayer, if we consider
this, not as worship and dedication, but as a plea for special favours
and special interventions. It would be inhuman to forbid a mother

to pray for her sick child, or even to forbid men to pray for themselves or others in time of danger. Yet must not such prayers be regarded as the satisfaction of a human need rather than as a means to instruct or influence the divine will?

§ 5. *The problem of evil*

The questions raised about divine Providence come, as it were, into focus in what is traditionally known as the problem of evil—that is, the problem of reconciling the existence of evil with the goodness of God.

From the religious point of view this problem is very primitive and very old. There is an African belief that the Supreme Spirit is wholly kind, but He has an idiot brother who follows Him about and spoils much of what He has done. These obstacles to faith have been familiar at least since the time of Job, and probably far earlier in the first dim gropings of the human race towards what was later to emerge as philosophy. Yet with the advance of knowledge they seem to become, not more easy, but more difficult. Those who slur them over in the supposed interests of religion help to spread the opinion that theology is too superficial to be taken seriously by intelligent men.

This is not the kind of problem that can be 'solved'—like a problem in chess or mathematics. Yet if we are to have a picture of religion, it cannot be ignored. It has manifestly two aspects—the problem of pain and the problem of moral evil.

Of the two the problem of pain seems, at least at first sight, the more difficult. Pain appears to be so wanton and so unnecessary, and those who make light of it give the impression that they have never suffered or observed it themselves. Up to a point, no doubt, pain may serve a useful function as a warning of danger; but in the evolutionary process it appears to have gone far beyond this point and to perform at times no useful function whatever. If we are to judge by human standards, it would seem so easy to set a limit to the amount of pain that can be felt, or to lower the level at which it passes over into death. It is incomprehensible that a beneficient creator should allow so many of His creatures, both animal and human, to die in agony: human beings are not often so cruel, though they sometimes show more consideration for animals than for men. It sounds a mere evasion to insist that pain may always be an occasion for the exercise of human virtue. This does not apply at all to animals, and some pain is so great that the victim may cease to be human. Nor can we ignore the utter waste of life, the deformed and idiot children, those who go through their whole existence maimed and crippled through no fault of their own. If we look for justice or benevolence in these things, we shall not find it. A religious man may be enabled to accept his own pain, and perhaps the pain of the world, as the cross he has to carry; he may believe that all of this could be seen as the product of wisdom and goodness if only he knew the whole; but he deceives himself and others with a superficial piety if he pretends to see this now.

The problem of moral evil may seem less incomprehensible; for if men are to be good men, they must be free; and if they are free, they must be free to do wrong; and it is impossible to separate wrong-doing from wrong-suffering.

It is not obviously incompatible with a benevolent will that human beings should be left to establish justice by themselves without continual divine intervention. They may have to do this at a frightful cost; but at least they are engaged in a serious enterprise that is worthy of free men. In the process the innocent may suffer, but suffering is inevitable where we all stand together to win or lose; and a good man may be willing to suffer if the success of the enterprise may thereby be attained. This is the characteristic virtue of the soldier as well as of the saint. Although such sentiments may be uttered too complacently by the prosperous, there can at least be no right to complain against omnipotence that justice has to be won by human efforts. We cannot demand a world in which wrong-doing would be miraculously prevented from affecting other people.

The deeper trouble is the fact of wrong-doing—not its effects. It is hard to see why a divine plan should have given us so many proclivities to evil—why we should be the product of animal evolution and so have to control inherited instincts akin to those of the ape and the tiger. Why could not creation have been confined to animals innocent of sin and rational beings either without passions or with adequate means of control?

A kind of answer might be given if it could be maintained both that goodness is the most precious of all things and that it can be manifested only in a struggle, only in the overcoming of strong temptation. But while to human eyes goodness may become more conspicuous in the face of difficulties, we cannot reasonably say that the degrees of goodness vary with the intensity of the struggle. If we did say so, we should have to regard goodness as self-frustrating

—the man who had won full control would be a less good man. We should also have to reject any analogy between human and divine goodness. Hence there seems to be no satisfactory answer to our question. We are not in a position to know that this is the best of all possible worlds, nor can we understand why God made the world as He did.

Questions of this kind are alien to the spirit of philosophy in a scientific age, but are they not also in some ways a departure from the spirit of religion? The religious man has to accept the world as it is given to him and to live in it a life of dedication. It is not his business to yearn for imaginary worlds or to mitigate the harsh features of the existing one. If he has some vision of God in contemplating the beauty of nature or even the universe as a whole, he may be devoutly thankful; but his vision must be touched with tragedy and his faith with doubt. He may speculate—for some it may be a duty to do so—in the hope of making his assumptions consistent with themselves and with the rest of his beliefs; but he cannot expect to explain God's ways to man or to transform religious faith into scientific knowledge. For his finite mind the pattern of the world must be obscure and incomplete, and while he may vaguely conceive the whole, he cannot know it. It must be sufficient for him if he can understand and complete his own little bit of the pattern, and believe that this may be his contribution to the whole. If he can gather anything of the divine purpose from his study of nature and society, it would seem to be that man is intended to use his own brains and his own will in order to master his own problems. And if in this endeavour he is able to meet with some success, this too he will put down to the grace of God.

§ 6. *The charge of vagueness*

To religious and scientific minds alike all this may seem to result in hopeless vagueness. In trying to free religion from crudities there may be a risk of making it empty.

This process may be illustrated by the primitive belief that men who are religious will be rewarded in this life with earthly goods— with flocks and herds and sons and daughters. When this is not borne out by experience, the reward is postponed to a later time— to the last times, which are supposed to be at hand. When the expected millennium fails to arrive, the reward is postponed still farther—to a life after death. Finally, the life after death ceases to be conceived crudely as a continuation of life on earth: time is replaced by eternity, and mere survival becomes an eternal life of which we can have no picture. We can no longer say what empirical observations of this world would give support to our belief.

There is a similar purification of the religious attitude itself. It may be too harsh to speak of primitive religion as if its motive were mere self-interest—as if it were a kind of bargain with the gods like the vow of Jacob at Bethel; for it may, like the desire for revenge, contain within it a demand for justice. This demand for justice gradually becomes less crude: it extends beyond the interest of the individual and his tribe to all mankind. Justice itself may no longer be conceived as a distribution of appropriate pleasures and pains, but as affording opportunity for further worship and service. All this is a spiritual advance; but it means also a loss of the definite—and erroneous—beliefs which characterize primitive religion and still attract the simple minded who want their theology to have all the precision of an empirical science.

Religion cannot give men factual knowledge about events in space and time—this is the function of science. What is more, it cannot give them factual knowledge of a world outside space and time: it cannot set itself up to be the empirical science of another world than this. To religious men the world as revealed to science is a mystery—the appearance of a deeper reality—but it is in this world that they have to live. They may live as if the laws of duty were the commands of God and leave all else to Him—some thinkers have believed that this is enough. But they may also have a vision, not of new facts, but of new values, in the world. All the world's beauty, all the excellence of man, will seem to them more precious. They will find a new wholeness in themselves, and will believe that this comes from God—they know not how. All these things they will experience as a revelation of God, and it is by this experience alone that their faith is confirmed. To most, if not to all, the experience will be intermittent and imperfect, subject to lapses and to doubts; but such as it is, they will cherish the hope that it is only the prelude to a fuller experience and a fuller life.

The charge of vagueness, and even of incomprehensibility, must in a sense be admitted. To finite minds it might be more satisfying if God could be known as another finite being whose actions might be observed and tested like those of any mortal man. Then they would obtain all the definiteness for which they hanker, but it would be definiteness in error. If men think about God at all, they have to strain their human concepts to the bursting point; but if they are philosophically wise, they will understand that these can be applied to Him only by analogy so that all pretence of empirical demonstrations must be abandoned. A demand for scientific precision and scientific verification can never be satisfied even if it is made by religious men. This becomes clear enough to those who have gone far in religion itself, as can be observed in the passage already quoted from St. John of the Cross. 'One of the greatest favours bestowed on the soul transiently in this life is to enable it to see so distinctly and to feel so profoundly that it cannot comprehend God at all'.

It may seem high-handed, if not disingenuous, to dismiss serious problems by an appeal to divine incomprehensibility. Yet surely those who ask these questions are expecting too much. If we do not understand the relation between our own mind and body, how can we understand the relation between God and the physical universe? We may entertain the notion that if we could grasp the nature of the whole world in its real setting, we might be able to see every event in it as a manifestation of divine goodness—as something analogous to an action by a good man. The notion is obscure in itself, as are all human analogies extended to the world as a whole; for a good man has to act on given material and adjust himself to a given situation outside himself—that is, he acts subject to conditions which cannot conceivably apply to God. Nevertheless, obscure as it is, this notion might seem in a way to be confirmed—it could never be proved—if science proceeded on the assumption that events were to be explained, not only as happening in accordance with law, but as happening in the best possible way. When this teleological principle is abandoned, theology has lost what appeared to be its only possible scientific support. This can never be replaced by any casual pseudo-scientific observations.

Religious men may indeed fall back on the assumption that the world is always intelligible, the knowledge that it is sometimes beautiful, the suspicion that mechanical explanations of animal life are inadequate, the assurance that minds are not merely the result of a chance collocation of atoms. These are at least not incompatible with belief in a divine creator and governor. But the belief itself must rest on religious experience—it cannot become a scientific hypothesis. Some may think that if it is not a scientific hypothesis capable of verification, it is empty; but there remains at least the conviction that in this world it is possible by divine grace to serve God, and the hope that this service will not be in vain.

Chapter XXIV

MAN AND GOD

§ 1. *Humanism*

Throughout the whole of this enquiry the fundamental questions of religion have been approached, as was proposed at the outset, 'from the side of man, with his obscure experience, his confused conceptions, his imperfect ideals'. Even with this modest approach it has been possible to touch only on the fringes of the subject: little has been said, for example, of its social implications—partly because there is a danger that we may seem to degrade religion if we emphasize its importance as a kind of cement for holding society together. The aesthetic factor is also in need of a much fuller examination. But—apart from the inadequacies of my attempt to say something on this basis 'about the nature and principles of religion, its present predicament, its grounds in experience, and its philosophical defence'—it may be thought that the whole discussion suffers from a fundamental defect. The very character of the approach, it may be said, must lead to a kind of humanism concerned with man's needs and aspirations and hopes rather than with the nature and activity of God.

If this means that religion has been examined from a human point of view, the charge has to be admitted. Natural theology must not attempt with the aid of a special revelation to see God and the world and man as God Himself sees them; and if there are any able to do this by sheer metaphysical insight, I cannot profess to be among them. But while modesty demands that philosophers should not pretend to escape from human limitations, they are not thereby restricted from the beginning to a brand of humanism which rejects God and makes for man the preposterous claim to be master of the universe. The study of religious experience is already a study of possible views about the divine nature; for every human attitude involves an assumption about the character of the object to which it is directed.

Human attitudes and emotions do not indeed guarantee the existence of their professed object: belief in the existence of God, so far as it is rational, must have a wider basis. Attitudes and emotions are no sure guide even to the character of their object: their deliverances must be subject to criticism even when the existence of their object is admitted. It is here that theologians are in need of the most scrupulous intellectual honesty in what may be an ungrateful task. Those who have been brought up in a particular religious tradition and have absorbed its influence may at times be moved, perhaps even greatly moved, by hearing familiar words or tunes which they may yet recognize to be emotionally false or false in other ways. Apart from the extremer cases of spurious sentiment—and in this there are all sorts of gradations—it is possible that an attitude felt to be emotionally right may yet carry with it theological implications which are indefensible. There can be few more moving prayers than that in the burial service of the Church of England: 'Suffer us not at our last hour for any pains of death to fall from Thee'. Yet the thought—if this thought be present—that God would turn away from a dying creature because of anything said or done in his final agony is theologically intolerable, no matter what may be its basis in religious tradition.

Criticism of traditional beliefs and attitudes is always necessary if religion is to be kept pure—and if theology is to be kept in touch with religious experience. So far as such criticism is an enquiry into the principles of religion, it is not merely a study of human nature, but an attempt, however imperfect, to examine what can be reasonably believed about the nature of God and His relation to man.

§ 2. *Divine action*

To all this it may be replied that the real point is still being missed. We are talking only about what man may believe, and about the implications of his thoughts and actions and emotions; but the real business of theology is to talk about what God does.

This type of complaint comes mainly from Karl Barth and his followers. He has levelled a similar charge against even the most orthodox 'Anglo-Saxon' theology, which he accuses of being two-dimensional and concerned only with principles. Theology, on his view, ought to be three-dimensional: it ought to deal with events that happen once and for all—with the unique, concrete acts of the living God.

This contention has already been examined, and it is a sufficient reply to say here that, as Barth himself insists, it means the end of natural theology—the end of all philosophical reflexion about religion and about God. But perhaps the criticism can be considered more generally. So far as it asks whether God can be said to do anything, it is putting a fair question which any philosophy of religion must attempt to answer.

An answer, for what it is worth, has already been given, but it may be useful to pull the loose ends together.

If God is conceived only as a necessary being, it would be misleading to say that He acts. This is why Buddhism seems to be so consistent.

If God is also conceived, on the basis of moral conviction, under the analogy of a perfect man—and this is the view of all Western religion—the relation between God and man must be regarded as analogous to the relation between person and person. This means that God must be conceived as acting, although it must be added that His 'acts' can only be analogous to our own: we cannot pretend to know His acts as they are in themselves.

If we try to be more specific about these acts in their relation to men, we seem almost to be abandoning the religious point of view for one of speculation. Nevertheless the religious man may be said to accept God's acts both in his experience of grace and in his attitude to the world as a manifestation of divine wisdom. It is for theology to formulate the assumptions made by such acceptance and so to construct a theory which will certainly be inadequate and may easily be absurd.

On this basis what God does—if traditional language may be used—is to reveal Himself to man and in so doing to heal and save. He alone can make man whole—at one with God and so at one with himself.

If we are rash enough to speculate about the way in which God acts upon men—to imagine that we can see, as it were, God's action from His own point of view—we fall into palpable absurdities both religious and scientific. All that theory can do is to indicate the occasions on which God manifests His grace, to consider man's way to God and not God's way to man, to describe religious experience and try to understand why it is taken to be God's revelation of Himself.

This is the task that has been attempted here with the aid of evidence from many sources. If we are to use the language of divine action rather than of human experience, we must assert that God reveals Himself in many ways. He may come to some men in an

emptying of sense and emotion and thought and will; to others in a
humble endeavour to lead a good life, in an intense vision of natural
beauty, in studying a sacred book, in contemplating the history of a
perfect man, or even in the course of philosophical speculation. He
may make His presence known in the luxuriance of an Indian forest
or in the blankness of an Arabian desert. To some He may show
Himself in the beauty of a cathedral and in elaborate religious rites;
but He may also come in the bareness and simplicity of a Quaker
meeting or a Highland kirk. He may reveal Himself to some in
prayer and meditation; but He may also give Himself unasked and
unexpected in the ordinary course of life. Some men, it would
appear, may be seized or grasped by a power that there is no with-
standing; but these experiences are granted to very few and have
too many spurious imitations.

We do not know how far all these ways are genuine, and there
may be a mixture of religious experience with much that is irrelevant. But it befits religious men to be charitable to one another.

In whatever way God comes, He reveals Himself always to the
whole man—not to mere thinking or mere willing or mere feeling
by itself. Because man *feels* himself to be made whole by being at
one with God, it can be said with truth that God reveals Himself
only to the heart. Yet the union itself is better described—with St.
Teresa and St. John of the Cross—as a union of wills, or as a
surrender of man's will to God's, if indeed it can be described at all.

This is true also of a religious acceptance which takes the world
to be given by divine wisdom as an occasion for service to God.
Here too there would seem to be a union of wills which is also a
revelation to the whole man and so to the heart. But when an
attempt is made to turn this into theory, the simple language of
religion has to be mixed up with that of philosophy and even science.
This is why there is a greater danger of falling into absurdity.

§ 3. *Divine action in the world*

Some religious thinkers may wish to insist that God must reveal
Himself in the world as well as in the heart of man. But here the
word 'reveal' seems to be used in two different senses. Without its
appeal to the heart a revelation becomes more like a theory, or even
a set of facts alleged to support a theory. Facts are the concern of
science; and if the theory contains anything like a moral judgement
on the facts, it seems wholly out of place as a theory about nature.

The world of nature can indeed arouse many emotions and give rise to judgements about its overwhelming vastness and energy, about the all-pervasiveness of law, about its amazing beauty, and so on. So far as these experiences contain numinous emotion or a sense of oneness with God, they may be regarded as a revelation, but once again as a revelation to the heart. The scientists, as we have seen, now forbid us to make judgements of purposiveness in general; but even without this our own good sense tells us that nothing could be more inappropriate than to judge nature by moral standards. We do not expect nature, or any part of nature, to do its duty: this is a privilege reserved for man. A moral theory about the physical world as it is known to science or even to ordinary experience is manifest nonsense.

In a sense this ground has been already traversed, and it would be superfluous to discuss again the difficulty of arguing from design in the world to a beneficent creator, and even of reconciling the goodness of the Creator with the character of His creation. But some fresh points must be added.

If it is possible to accept the world as the working of divine grace, it may be supposed that we can know God's acts as they are manifested in space and time. Yet it is here that the analogy with human persons breaks down. The difficulty is not that the acts of God considered as events in the temporal world can be only finite objects of science and can be understood only in accordance with the laws of nature. A similar difficulty arises even in regard to human thought and action, and it can be surmounted if we consider that from the agent's point of view the scientific treatment of these subjects is by its very nature too abstract and incomplete to take any account of human freedom or of moral excellence. But God does not reveal Himself in the world as human beings reveal themselves by their bodily actions. We can distinguish between what a man does and what merely happens to him, and human activity is only a tiny fraction of the events in the world of nature. God, if He does anything, must do everything—possibly with some exceptions made for human freedom; and it may seem—from a human point of view —as if doing everything is equivalent to doing nothing. No man can hope to understand divine action from God's own point of view— if such absurdly misleading words can be used for God's knowledge of Himself.

At Geneva in 1935 the late Archbishop Temple is alleged to have shocked the Barthians by saying—I have seen only a German translation—that 'unless all existence is a medium of revelation, no special revelation is possible . . . only if nothing is profane can anything be sacred.' If this is accepted, it is still hard to see what can be meant by a special revelation. All of God's acts—if we allow ourselves to indulge in speculation—would presumably be revelations of His nature, although they might not appear so to a finite mind. There can here be no comparison with the way in which a man may reveal himself more in an act of kindness than in a routine operation like brushing his hair. For God there can presumably be no routine operations.

It is easier to understand how a revelation is special, if this means that it is special relatively to us. God may reveal Himself to us in a good man more than in the explosion of a supernova; for moral action, however imperfectly, is part of our own life. The special revelations are to be found, not in the world, but in the experience of what is taken to be divine grace, no matter what be the occasion of such experience. And if men have found a special revelation in the life and death of one good man, is not this because the grace of God present in him can find an echo even in sinful hearts?

§ 4. *Contradictions*

If God is to be conceived under the analogy of a perfect man, it is inevitable that He should be regarded as just and merciful and loving in all His actions, whether in the giving—and withdrawing—of divine grace or in the creation and government of the world. This judgement can be supported only by religious experience itself and not by any scientific study of natural events. But words like 'love' and 'mercy' are applied to God only by analogy: if they are used literally, they will give rise to paradoxes and contradictions with which the religious man as such need not be troubled.

Human analogies and finite concepts have to be used in order to bring the infinite within the range of finite minds and make it vivid to pictorial imaginations; but, since these analogies and concepts are bound to be inadequate, all theological statements about God cannot but contain an element of contradiction. If we think of God as one object among others, or even as a subject who can be regarded as also one object among others, we are treating Him as a finite being—that is, as what He is not. Yet how can we avoid doing so if we think of Him at all?

At the very beginning of our enquiry we saw that God was con-

ceived as the Whole and yet also as the Other. This is only one
sample of the contradictions which arise in speculative theology—
they might be multiplied indefinitely. Even in speaking of God as a
Person, it is necessary to add that He cannot be subject to the
limitations of finite personality, which alone we are able to understand.

There is a short way of dealing with all this. We can say that all
theology is nonsense—not merely in the trivial sense that its assertions are not factual statements about finite events in space and
time, but in the more serious sense that it cannot say anything at all
without falling into self-contradiction.

This contention even in its more serious aspect seems to spring
partly from a determination to confine all thinking to the methods
of common sense: it appears to assume that theological contradictions are on the same footing as those in history or science. But
may not this be compared—I am not enough of a mathematician to
know—with a determination so to restrict the methods of arithmetic
that it becomes impossible to deal with transfinite numbers? The
methods of thinking have to be adjusted to what we are trying to
think about; and we have to distinguish between arbitrary and
necessary contradictions. It is not too difficult to understand how in
trying to think about God we have to apply finite concepts to the
infinite, and so to fall into contradictions which do not arise if we
confine our thought within a narrower range. It is the great merit
of Kant to have made this clear.

If this is sound, it means that religious faith can never be knowledge. Such a view is familiar to religious faith itself, which may
seem partly to live in straining towards a knowledge that can never
be attained. If some men are thereby encouraged to indulge in wild
imaginings and fanciful speculations and genuine nonsense, this is
a pity; but they can still be asked to state the grounds for their
oracular utterances and to show that their contradictions are not
arbitrary but necessary.

There are some who maintain that these problems can be solved
by a kind of dialectic which enables us to say both 'Yes' and 'No',
and to reconcile these in a higher synthesis. The dialectic of Hegel
is certainly to be treated by those who are not its votaries with a
respect not wholly void of suspicion. But there is a danger that
lesser men may use these devices mechanically as a kind of gadget
to make the commonplace appear profound and the ridiculous intelligible. The danger is increased when the system of the master is

twisted or corrected into something quite different, as it is by later
thinkers who reject the thought but cling to the terminology. When
followers of Kierkegaard and Marx are seen sobbing on each others'
shoulders at the wonders of dialectic, it is difficult to avoid a feeling
of acute discomfort. Whatever benefits dialectical thinking may have
contributed to theology, it remains desirable to keep an open mind
and a modest remembrance of our limitations, even if this confronts
us with puzzles that we are admittedly unable to solve.

§ 5. *Intuitive understanding*

It may be said that the analogies under which men try to think of
God are meaningless if they have to be immediately cancelled. What
is the use of saying 'God acts', and then adding at once 'but not as
we act'? Should there not be an attempt to indicate what is conceived to be the difference between His activity and ours?

This seems a reasonable demand, and within limits it can perhaps
be met. If an analogy is seen to be inadequate, it should be possible
to say something of the contrast that is assumed as well as the likeness, although this may be hard to do without getting lost in the
vast ocean of speculative theology. Here it is possible only to offer
a hurried and dogmatic sample of the kind of answer that may
be given.

Our dim and even contradictory thoughts of God could never
arise unless we were conscious of our own limitations. All human
thought is limited since in order to know our world we must have
something given to our senses, however obscurely, in each successive
moment of time; and this obscure material we have to work up by
imaginative construction and conceptual thinking into an ordered
world which for us can never be complete. The ultimate principles
by which we do this cannot themselves be derived from what is
given; and the world we build up can only be a between-world—
only reality as we assume it must appear to finite minds like our own.

To recognize these limitations is to entertain, however vaguely, a
concept of reality as it is in itself—a reality which is not merely
relative to us; and there may be grounds for conceiving this as absolute and unconditioned. But it is also to entertain the concept of a
mind not subject to finite limitations, nor even restricted to an ideal
experience in which all possible and actual human experiences would
be combined—a mind which knows reality as it is in itself and is
indeed the unconditioned reality it knows.

Y

Such thoughts may still be negative: we may understand only what they deny, and we cannot claim that we know any corresponding object to exist. Nevertheless, if we are not afraid to speculate, it may be possible to interpret them in a more positive way.

An infinite mind would not, like ours, have to wait for something to be given, out of which it could construct a universe; and its universe would not be an indefinite extension in space and time of a momentarily present here and now. It would not be partly passive and receptive, but wholly active and creative. The distinctions in our finite thinking between active thought and passive sense, and again between abstract concepts and concrete individual objects, would disappear. Its abstract thinking—in the self-contradictory language that must be used—would be at the same time a direct intuiting of individual reality; and the individual reality it intuited it would also understand. Even the distinction between subject and object would be overcome if the object were not an object given to be thought about, but present, and indeed created, in the very act of thinking itself. Such a mind would not have *both* a power of understanding *and* a power of intuiting, as we have: it would be itself an intuitive understanding; its intuitions would be not sensuous but intellectual; and what we call its thinking would not be a discursive process in time. Perhaps such a mind alone can be conceived as a self-sufficient reality, and the reality it would know would be itself.

From so summary a statement we can see at the most that the concept of an intuitive understanding need not be purely negative. On the other hand, as we do not possess an intuitive understanding —although some philosophers have claimed to do so—we cannot make the concept clear to ourselves or supply it with an object in our own thinking. If we could do so, we should ourselves be God.

Another antithesis bound to disappear would be our distinction between thinking and acting, or thinking and doing. Thinking would itself be a creative act, a creation out of nothing: considered as action it would not require a given matter to mould or alter, any more than it would require a given matter about which to think. Action also—if we continue to think of it as analogous to human action—would not admit our distinction between abstract principles and concrete doing, and would not be exposed to a conflict between inclination and duty. An intuitive understanding has to be conceived as also a holy will.

The divine activity which would be both thinking and acting

might also be compared with the creative activity of a human artist; but here too our ordinary distinctions would have to be abandoned.

If we care to pursue such abstract speculations, we may even be tempted to ask whether God can be conceived as having feelings in any way analogous to ours.

The pantheist may be inclined to say that God feels in all the joys and sufferings of His creatures; but we are at present presuming to think our finite thoughts only about God as He is in Himself, and all we can say is that in Him feeling is not to be distinguished from what must be at once both thought and action. If feeling is taken to be passive suffering, it is impossible to think of this in what is envisaged as pure activity or to understand how the self-sufficient could be in need of others or in need of love. But so far as we consider human feeling to be something immediate in which distinctions have not yet arisen, we may take this as analogous to a divine immediacy in which all our finite distinctions are overcome. This analogy has been used by some thinkers in their metaphysics, but it bears no relation to religious views of God as a Father who loves His children. Such views spring entirely from the moral approach to the conception of God and not at all from metaphysical thinking.

Speculations of this kind become more and more difficult if we attempt to conceive with their aid the relation which we suppose to exist between God and His creation as this is known to us in our temporal experience; for then they are applied to what looks like a relation between part and part and so begin to resemble scientific hypotheses.

The whole creation would have to be the thought or action of God, but we ourselves should know it only as it appeared to finite and temporal minds, only as something different from what it is in itself. God's thinking cannot, like ours, be a process in time carried on from a particular point in space. Yet we ourselves should somehow have to be God's thoughts, or rather God's thinkings, although we should be unable to know even ourselves as we really are. A view of this kind has been attractive to many religious men, but it is only another attempt to conceive the inconceivable by means of analogies drawn from human experience of the relation between person and person. We must suppose that human minds have some degree of independence both in thought and in action. It would be foolish to say that the creation of such independent beings is beyond the power of an intuitive understanding; but it would be equally foolish to say that it was intelligible to ourselves.

This discussion may throw new light on the ontological argument for the existence of God. I have urged against it that no concept of perfection (or of anything else) can guarantee the existence of its object. It is possible to go farther and to take this as a disproof of God's existence; for it may be maintained that God can be conceived only as a being whose concept (or essence) is the ground of His existence, and that if this is impossible, God's existence must be impossible. Such a contention seems to spring from misunderstanding. The objections to the ontological argument are concerned with human concepts which can be applied to objects only if these objects are independently given. For an intuitive understanding there could be no such distinction: what we describe as its concepts would necessarily guarantee the existence of their object—the very concept would be also an intuition, and even a creation, of the object conceived. The same principle would necessarily hold for the concept of divine perfection. If we presume to speak about God's intuitive understanding of Himself, the objections raised against an argument falsely supposed to be valid for finite thinking cease at once to have any force.

§ 6. *Speculative theology*

In response to charges of meaningless talk I have permitted myself to deviate into a speculative theology which attempts to envisage God's actions as they are in themselves. This is far more temerarious —some may think even more meaningless—than an effort to examine the religious experience of grace and to ask whether such experience may be accepted as the way in which God reveals Himself. Yet it would not be unreasonable to claim that the more modest enquiry needs to be completed by a bolder flight of thought; and a purely speculative theology, so long as it does not profess to be a science, may have more importance from a religious point of view that I was inclined to allow when I started out on this enquiry. It certainly has a kind of grammar of its own, and the relation of this grammar to the grammar of scientific thinking might deserve some attention from linguistic philosophers.

On the other hand, a theology which abandons all contact with experience and refuses to acknowledge its own limitations may go completely wild. It may lead to a degradation of philosophy and so to a corruption of religion itself. Although we suppose that to God His own nature and that of the created universe must be supremely intelligible, we must also recognize that the divine nature, not only is, but must be, beyond our understanding. For the practical purposes of religion, at least as it has developed in the West, God has to be conceived under the analogy or image of a perfectly good man, utterly inadequate as this must be. In that sense Western religion is anthropomorphic; and one main use of speculative theology is to rob this anthropomorphism of its crudity and to make men conscious that their analogies are only analogies and can be nothing more.

Chapter XXV

THE MODERN PREDICAMENT

§ 1. *The modern predicament*

The modern predicament, if I may try to sum up this long discussion, is that man seems to be faced with an unbridgeable gulf between science and religion or—it might be better to say—between knowledge and faith. This is a permanent human predicament as well as a modern one, but at the present time it is particularly cruel. Religion was born and bred in a world different from ours—a tiny, comfortable world, full of signs and wonders and divine interventions, where it was easy for man to consider himself the end for which all things were made. That ancient world has been nibbled away by science, and the question arises whether against a new and scientific background religion in any form will find it possible to survive.

The present situation is not to be taken too crudely. Scientific discoveries cannot be said to contradict the doctrines of theology except when theologians are rash enough to make pseudo-scientific assertions about events in the world of nature. Within science itself the problems of religion—like those of morality and art—simply do not arise: they are merely irrelevant. The conflict, so far as there is one, is not between abstractions like science and theology nor even between two different sets of men. It is a conflict of different attitudes in the soul of each individual man. This struggle is not to be easily described, yet it is very real and very obvious to many at the present time. Catherine Carswell, for example, the Scottish writer, speaks of herself as 'religious of heart, but profoundly sceptical in mind.' A divorce between mind and heart is bound to be unhealthy.

For those who are wholly satisfied with the findings of science there is no theoretical predicament; and if they are practising scientists, their minds may be more than fully occupied at their own job. But is there perhaps a practical predicament? If we suppose that moral judgements, because they are not scientific, must be based on sheer emotion, it may be hard to keep our faith in goodness and in the duty of respecting other men even to our own loss. If, on

374

the other hand, like the Marxists, we are confused enough to extract
moral judgements from supposedly scientific ones, we may find a
faith for which we are willing to live and die, but one which makes
us indifferent to justice and mercy and even to truth—a process in
which science suffers as well as religion. From this last desperate
error the English are usually saved by their distrust of philosophy
and their love of fair play—perhaps even by a sense of humour. But
there are among intellectuals many who speak of our sick society,
and who feel themselves lost as individuals because they are without
faith in the value of human living.

The divorce between mind and heart is far more dangerous to
religion than to science; for it is directly opposed to that very wholeness at which religion aims. The religious man cannot afford to
sweep aside science as the scientist can sweep aside religion.
Whether he likes it or not, scientific knowledge must now provide
the bony structure of the world in which he has to live and act; and
it is foolish of him to shudder as if science were the skeleton at the
feast of life. At every feast we are all skeletons underneath; but
without our bony structure we should be too flabby to be interesting.
Although we may prefer to look at the human body as artists rather
than as anatomists, we shall do this all the better if we are anatomists
as well.

§ 2. *Points of view*

The relation between art and anatomy already shows that it may
be legitimate to look at the same thing from different points of view.
Is it possible that this may afford a clue to the more complicated
relations between science and religion? The question has forced
itself upon us during the whole course of our enquiry, and perhaps
we should try to bring together in short compass some of the
answers that have suggested themselves. Readers who dislike jejune
repetitions may go straight on to § 6.

There are different points of view even within science itself. The
physicist, the chemist, the biologist, and the psychologist—each has
his own special point of view, his particular assumptions, his appropriate methods; and consequently he finds different things, or at
least different laws, in the world he studies. But each, as a scientist,
assumes that these different laws are compatible with one another
and can be combined in one whole. This assumption is not itself a
scientific discovery but a kind of faith; and if we ask how the

combination can be effected, we are already asking a philosophical question. If we are empirical philosophers, we should not assume *a priori* that all scientific laws can be reduced to the laws of physics.

If there is uncertainty about the way in which the points of view appropriate to different sciences can be combined in one whole, there is greater uncertainty about the way in which the scientific point of view is to be combined with points of view appropriate to the artist, the good man, and the saint. The danger is that each type of man, when he tries to consider this problem philosophically, will assume that his own point of view is the only possible one. This is legitimate and necessary as long as he is conducting his own business. When carried into philosophy it substitutes inertia for insight.

Philosophy too, as it actually exists, has always its own point of view, and every philosopher suffers from a kind of narrowness more obvious to other people than to himself—perhaps even painfully obvious. Yet it is the aim of philosophy, or at least of one powerful tradition in philosophy, to enter into different points of view, to formulate their assumptions, to examine the world as seen from each of them, and to fit the different vistas as far as possible into one coherent whole. This is why the problems we have been considering are philosophical problems—not scientific ones. It is also why the task of philosophy is almost beyond human strength.

The prestige of science is now so great that some philosophers are tempted to concern themselves exclusively with the scientific point of view and even to adopt it as their own. In so doing they have contributed much to the study of scientific method and scientific language—including the method and language of mathematics and mathematical logic—and also to the theory of knowledge. But there has been a danger of neglecting other problems or treating them superficially or even distorting them by the application of inappropriate standards borrowed from elsewhere. A narrowness not unnatural in the excitement of new discoveries may also react unfavourably on theories about science itself. There are signs that this narrowness is gradually being overcome.

All this is a matter of controversy, but one thing is beyond dispute. A philosophy that restricts itself to a scientific point of view can have no use for religion.

§ 3. *The scientific point of view*

Within its own limits science is, and must be, supreme: it can be contradicted only by better science; and there is no observable part of reality or of human life that can claim immunity from its investigations. Nevertheless the scientific point of view is, like others, still partial and limited.

First of all, science is concerned only with certain aspects of reality, however hard they may be to describe. Fifty years ago we might have said that it was concerned only with quantity and measurement, but to-day we are sometimes told that it is turning instead to concepts of shape and structure and is becoming more geometrical, like the early science of the Greeks. What remains clear is that it has, and can have, no concern with judgements of value or with judgements of what ought to be: it can treat these only as emotive utterances or psychological events.

In the second place, it is occupied only with the relation of part to part within the whole of reality: it does not pretend to make judgements about reality as a whole. Scientists may assume for their own purposes that reality as a whole consists only of more and more of the sort of thing that they investigate; but if they assert this explicitly, they are making, not a scientific, but a metaphysical statement, and one open to question, as all metaphysical statements are.

It is often held that the scientist makes assumptions only about his own methods and not about the reality he proposes to investigate. This is one reason why we have to say that explicit assumptions about reality are metaphysical, not scientific; and it is right to insist that if the scientist makes any such assumptions, they are only provisional. Nevertheless it seems clear that any suppositions about a method of investigation must take for granted certain characteristics in the objects to be investigated—for example, that they conform to law.

What is not so commonly recognized is that to adopt a method of investigation is also to make assumptions about the character of the investigator. These assumptions are so different from suppositions about the character of the objects investigated that they may never come officially within the purview of the investigator himself. Science seeks to be objective—to concern itself solely with objects and to eliminate all merely personal points of view. Yet to adopt such an aim is itself to take up a point of view—a point of view from which things can be seen objectively and impersonally. However much we may attribute this to the method rather than to the individual, it raises questions about how such an objective point of view is possible for imperfect human beings. This is a question for philosophy, not for science, but it is one we cannot afford to neglect.

Similarly, a scientist may take it for granted that his objects are in some sense determined, and of this assumption he may be fully aware. But he also takes it for granted that he himself is free—free to think in accordance with rational principles and so to distinguish between truth and error. Of this assumption he need hardly be aware at all—it is certainly no object of his science—but it should not be ignored by philosophers. Hence it is philosophically false—though it may be scientifically true—to say that there is no freedom in his world. And although truth is not one of the objects he investigates, it is always truth that he is seeking. Hence it is philosophically false—though it may be scientifically true—to say that there is no truth in his world. The contradiction arises only because the word 'world' is being used in two senses; but the point is that the world of science is one from which something is being systematically left out.

§ 4. *A critical philosophy*

A critical philosophy cannot afford to leave out what is properly ignored by science: it must take into account, not only the world as known to the scientist, but also the scientist as claiming to know the world. Nor is there any reason why it should confine itself to scientists and neglect all other forms of human experience. It has to recognize that human activity is not confined to science and that all men in all their activities are subjects as well as objects.

Unless we screw ourselves religiously to the scientific point of view and regard all deviations as temptations of the devil, we may reasonably ask ourselves what kind of world we should know if our scientific investigations were as successful as possible. Although this is rank heresy to-day, I have maintained that even then our world of objects would be incomplete: it would leave out too much. If we take the relativity of science seriously, we have to say that we can have knowledge only of reality as it must appear to finite minds like our own, and not of reality as it is in itself. We should still be haunted with the thought of something beyond, possibly of something not contingent, but unconditioned and absolute—not intelligible merely in relation to something else, but intelligible in itself. Such a thought is admittedly obscure and may even contain contradictions. Whether rightly or wrongly, I have insisted that it can give us no knowledge of ultimate reality: it can certainly never be confirmed by any conceivable development of scientific observations. Nevertheless we are at least entitled to regard our between-world, as I have called it, as leaving a blank—perhaps even a God-shaped blank—beyond itself.

This view I take to be more than confirmed if we consider human knowledge, not as a series of subsistent propositions nor as a succession of events looked at from outside, but as it can be analysed from within. It is not enough to say, as some do, that the world we know must be relative to our sense-organs and to a brain which does not merely receive impressions but is always itself continually active. This is indeed a puzzle, but it appears to assume that the brain itself is a kind of absolute, whereas it can on this hypothesis only be part of the relative world we know. The real crux is that we seem to start from given impressions which, apart from our own activity, are indeterminate and constantly changing (so far as the indeterminate can change); and on this precarious basis we have to construct, in accordance with spontaneous principles of thought and imagination, an ordered world which is always a perspective viewed from a particular, and changing, point in time and space. To suppose that this world of ours is reality as it is in itself, or is all the world there is, may appear on reflexion to be useful and necessary for practical purposes and yet to be theoretically indefensible.

Farther than this it seems impossible to go in a philosophical theory based only on the character of our knowledge; but on such suppositions we can at least admit that points of view other than the scientific may be possible and legitimate. Of these the moral point of view is the most fundamental for our purposes so far as it recognizes the possibility of obeying an absolute moral law and fulfilling an unconditioned duty; for moral action so understood seems to give a concrete meaning to terms which might otherwise be supposed to be unintelligible. In spite of admitted difficulties I have maintained that the moral point of view is as rational and as legitimate as that of science itself. Its assumption of freedom and value is closely akin to a very similar assumption made by the scientific thinker (and perhaps also in some ways by the artist). In all such assumptions man is committed to the view that the world of objects known to science is not all the world there is.

We trespass upon more difficult ground if we seek to pass from this to theological beliefs. The passage is certainly a natural one, and it has been held to be logically necessary; but perhaps it requires what may be called a rational leap of faith more like our assurance that physical objects and other minds exist than like any scientific theory or logical proof, and yet different from all of these. I must here describe it without qualifications.

A good man—if this term may be applied to a man who is trying to do his duty—must assume that his duty can be done; and, at least if he has a religious bent, he will find himself acting as if the laws of duty were the commands of God—as if God existed and man were immortal. He will find himself thinking of God, not merely as unconditioned and self-sufficient, but as all-wise and all-holy. To think thus is to conceive God under the analogy of a perfect human being, and not merely as the supreme reality. By the aid of such concepts man is able, however confusedly, to think about God, and to act as if the God-shaped blank in reality as he knows it (and perhaps also in his own life) were filled by God himself. Such a practical belief can never become knowledge, and if he fails to recognize this, he will have to meet overwhelming theoretical difficulties; but considered as a living faith it will be confirmed, or perhaps we should rather say aroused and strengthened, by his experience of what he takes to be divine grace.

Such processes of thought, here summarily outlined, may reflect on an abstract level some deeper and more obscure religious experience. They will not prove either God's existence or His goodness; but they may provide some assurance that religious belief is not unreasonable and is not to be disproved by any extension of scientific knowledge.

To the saint and the sceptic alike this may seem a lame conclusion to draw from a halting argument; but both may be asked to remember that theology is not a substitute for religion. Religion is simple, while theology is complicated; religion is a rich experience, and theology—especially natural theology—only abstract thinking. It is not the business of a natural theologian to persuade the sceptic or to edify the saint. What should be clear to them both is that in the modern world religion is desperately in need of some philosophic defence if it is to survive without taking refuge in absurdity; and if the saints are dissatisfied with the line of defence suggested here, it is high time they should find a better.

As for those who hold that the world as revealed to science is all the world there is and that anything else is frills and furbelows, they are unanswerable—like Karl Barth—so long as they stick to their own point of view. But the question is whether we should stick to one point of view.

§ 5. *Psychology*

There are many who suppose that we must look to psychology for the explanation of religious experience—and even of such philosophical considerations as I have put forward on its behalf. One word must be added about this if we are to avoid the charge of ignoring the obvious answer to all our questions.

It is certainly right and proper that psychology should concern itself with the whole of human experience, and it would be absurd to claim any exemption for religion. As a science psychology indeed is only in its infancy; it has as yet not attained to one consistent point of view; it suffers too often from a jargon which is lacking in precision; and it appears to hesitate between admitting and excluding judgements of value. Broadly speaking, it has had greater success in dealing with the more elementary mental activities than with the more developed, and with the abnormal rather than with the normal. A behaviouristic approach to religion must be superficial; and although some thinkers not unsympathetic to religion are inclined to look to psycho-analysis for help, this type of enquiry is more likely to illuminate religious aberrations than religious sanity, or even to treat all religion as an aberration. However it may explain, or explain away, his experience, the religious man will still insist that the same experience may be understood differently from different points of view, and even that psychology can touch only on its accidental concomitants and outer fringes—not on its inner core of rationality.

The plain fact is that an appeal to psychology is merely another example of the assumption that the scientific point of view is completely adequate by itself and that all other points of view can be ignored. This is the assumption that is being questioned.

On this topic it is desirable to avoid dogmatism, for as psychology develops, it may have to adopt a point of view and a method peculiar to itself—all I say must be taken as provisional. But—subject to this qualification—it would seem that so far as psychology is a science, it must take the view of a detached spectator; it must regard mental events as a causal succession; it must refrain from all judgements of value and ignore the function of rational principles; it must look on the individual as one object among others, and consider his experience, not as it appears to the individual himself, but as it appears to the psychologist, who sees it from outside and seeks to determine its place in nature.

The legitimacy and value of all this is not to be questioned; but it leaves too much out, and it can be no substitute for an attempt, however imperfect, to analyse experience from the subject's own point of view. Such an analysis is not an attempt to trace causal connexions between successive mental events or even to follow the growth of a mind from infancy to maturity. It is rather an endeavour to formulate the principles without which there could be no rational experience at all—no science, no psychology, and, if we suppose religion to be rational, no religion.

Analysis of this kind is not easy. It means that we have to abandon our ordinary habit of looking at objects without reflecting on their relation to subjects. If the effort is made, all our thinking will undergo a complete revolution, and we shall see everything (including religion) in a different light.

§ 6. *The scientific attitude to life*

Perhaps in conclusion we may be allowed to leave these dusty regions and survey again the human situation with its practical difficulties and varying responses. What is to be said about the scientific and religious attitudes to life?

The scientific attitude, while wholly beneficent in its own realm, must here be taken as one which looks to science for all practical guidance and refuses to have any truck with religion or metaphysics. This is perhaps the dominant mood of the present age.

If man were a purely intellectual being, there would be much to recommend this view. Those who adopt it have ample warrant for preferring the solid certainty of science to the misty speculation of theology, especially where these seem to conflict; and they may be well advised to devote themselves to urgent scientific work instead of wasting their time on insoluble problems. Even as regards the practical business of life, they are seeking to act in the world with the most accurate knowledge that is available to man. If the world as known to science is a less agreeable world than we might wish, this— they may hold—is no reason for indulging in vague yearnings and rosy dreams. If men want poetry, let them take it as poetry, and not as philosophy or science. It is more manly to face the world in all its harshness and not delude ourselves and others with false hopes. We must free ourselves from the foolish superstitions by which religion has been riddled and progress impeded. An honest man should live in the open-air world of science with all its chill, and not in the

opium den of religious hallucinations. Even in the hour of danger
or death he should fall back on natural human courage; for he
certainly has nothing more.

This view—although, like any other, it may be held in a superficial way—is at least a manly and honest one: intellectual honesty,
as well as moral toleration, has been greatly fostered by the development of scientific method. On the intellectual side the most it can
be charged with is a lack of philosophical curiosity—an unwillingness to explore first principles and to look beyond the solution of
particular problems; but, so far as theory is concerned, there may be
more important things to do, and the unwillingness may rest on the
considered conviction that there are no first principles to explore.

The fundamental difficulty here is that although we are provided
with much, we do not seem to be offered any philosophy of life.

This contention should not be exaggerated. Every way of life has
in it a kind of unreflective philosophy; and although, as I have
insisted, we cannot extract principles of action (other than technical
ones) from what scientists discover, perhaps we can from what
they do.

The detachment and impersonality of science—the willingness to
consider evidence from every source and to set aside all prejudice
and self-interest—is closely akin to the detachment and impersonality necessary to moral judgement: this is one ground for the claim
that it is legitimate to speak of practical, as well as of theoretical,
reason. To see our situation and ourselves objectively is the first
condition of spiritual health and good action: even without judgements of value it may offer a substitute for that self-examination
which, although practised at times in an unbalanced way, is necessary to a religious life. And since scientists are also men, they do in
fact make judgements of value about their own activity: they recognize their duty as scientists, and devotion to truth is sometimes
taken as an absolute duty and even as a kind of religion.

Attitudes and judgements of this kind are not objects or discoveries of science, and they are as much in need of philosophical
criticism as any other moral attitudes and moral judgements. Some
scientists, for example, being rightly exercised at their part in the
creation of the hydrogen bomb, insist that they have an absolute
duty to publish the truth, since they alone know it. If they mean
that they should make the public aware of its devastating effects,
this can probably be better done by trained journalists. If they mean
that the physical theory behind its construction should be made

more widely known, this task, although laudable enough, can affect only the few who have the necessary training and intelligence to understand them. If they mean that they should impart technical secrets to an unscrupulous enemy of their country and of human freedom, they are merely showing that a scientific education does not always equip men for making political and moral judgements.

Whatever the scientific attitude may take for granted without reflexion, it can, by its very nature, give no account of any objective standards by which we may guide our lives. The artist need not be greatly perturbed if he is told in consequence that one man's taste is as good as another's: in practice he knows very well that this is nonsense, that aesthetic judgements are not dependent on scientific measurements, and that a good scientist may be an arrant philistine. In any case the artist can live happily with his dreams. The man of action is not in the same comfortable position: it is a serious matter, both for the individual and for society, if men are to be told that there can be no objective moral principles because these are not the same as scientific generalizations. Science provides man with a most potent instrument, but it can provide no directions for its use. This is like putting a hydrogen bomb in the hands of a child.

So far as this is true, the scientific attitude, in the sense here employed, leaves men in a practical predicament, if not in a theoretical one; for vast ranges of human life are abandoned to mere impulse or emotion, and we are left to struggle blindly for we know not what. It is not surprising if this should produce our modern discontent and even despair.

Within its own sphere science is the most astounding achievement of modern man. Any philosopher who seeks to condemn it, or even to correct it, merely makes himself a laughing-stock. Yet science by itself cannot satisfy the whole of man's needs: for purposes of action he requires at least a system of moral beliefs. In an age of criticism such a system is unable to stand unless it is supported by a rational ethics, which cannot conceivably be merely an inductive science. Whether wisely or unwisely, I have maintained that moral action and ethical beliefs bring men at least to the threshold of religion, and that rational ethics has to face the problems of theology. If we act consistently on the assumption that science is to be a substitute for all our other ways of thinking, there is a danger of falling, not merely into philosophical error, but into practical disaster. Such consistency is not likely to be found in human action; but if it were, man would tend to become an ill-balanced, divided, dissatisfied, and possibly heartless creature, incapable of spiritual wholeness and spiritual health. He might even end in self-destruction.

§ 7. *The religious attitude to life*

The religious attitude leads to a different predicament—to one which in its origin is mainly theoretical.

The climate of the modern world is unfavourable to religion, partly because the habits and attitudes of scientific investigation are different from the habits and attitudes of religious life, but mainly because so many of us assume, consciously or unconsciously, that science is the only source of knowledge and rational belief. This assumption, in spite of its psychological influence, is, I have maintained, a philosophical error and not a scientific truth. Nevertheless it has to be admitted that religious faith cannot pretend to be knowledge, and that theology does not provide us either with scientific knowledge or with a super-scientific knowledge such as has been ascribed in the past to metaphysics. The utmost we can claim is that our moral judgements may reasonably be regarded as providing knowledge and rational beliefs of a non-scientific kind; and that moral and speculative philosophy together may be able to supply a defence of religious faith and a protection against religious aberrations. Yet even if this be granted—and many philosophers would reject it—there remains a wide-spread impression that religion, as we know it, is opposed, not only to a scientific attitude which claims too much, but to science itself. If this belief is to be dispelled, it can only be by a supreme effort of religious thinking; for the belief has its roots in a theological obscurantism which has ignored or controverted or even persecuted scientific discovery. This may be the main source, although not the only one, of modern indifference.

Religious leaders are already conscious of living in what they call a pagan world: they regard themselves as missionaries to the heathen and are seeking to recover territory which they once held, even if with light forces, and have now lost. For this purpose they have their own well-tried methods of prayer and meditation and religious rites, as well as of preaching and teaching; and the best of them know that success will come, if it comes at all, only from a whole-hearted devotion—from scrupulous toleration and kindness, from a continual battle for justice, from genuine love of others and complete forgetfulness of self. Some of them may believe that man cannot seek for God, or that seeking he will not find, but can only

z

await the divine condescension. Yet even this waiting is a kind of
seeking—a turning away from too much absorption in the goods of
this world, a retiral into the self and a readiness to receive what may
be given. In these matters it is to be presumed that religious men
know their own business: they are in no need of advice or criticism,
but only of God's grace.

When all this is said, it may still be true that in its present predicament religion is in dire need of an intellectual reformation. The
great teachers of religion have always had to get rid of the useless
lumber which accumulates in its progress—the rigid dogmatism,
the narrow legalism, the mechanical rites, the silly superstitions
which may become a substitute for religious life. But in our times
there is a special need for intellectual honesty, or intellectual scrupu-
lousness. These words have to be used in no crude sense: they must
not be taken to suggest that religious men, or religious leaders, are
guilty of rank dishonesty or wilful unscrupulousness—that in short
they are conscious hypocrites. This would be far from the truth and
would merely be insulting. Yet the fact remains that many men
to-day are encouraged to regard religion as a cheat because they
suspect their preceptors of failing to face the results of scientific
discovery and Biblical criticism, of imposing moral rules based on
chance texts accepted blindly without regard to their setting, and
even of not telling the whole truth as they see it. Religious teachers
must be humble enough to face intellectual difficulties and to admit
how little they can know; and in their arguments they must not give
the impression that they accept the conclusions first and select or
twist the premises to fit them. The tasks that lie before theology are
not for every one—there are many who, however transparently
sincere, are lacking in the necessary intellectual equipment. These
tasks are being tackled by the courageous few against inertia and
opposition within the Church itself; but the world is not convinced
of their success.

The work of intellectual reformation is bound to be a thankless
one. It may have to lay its hands on the dearest idols of the past—
to break with much that is embedded, not only in the language of
theology, but in the traditional language of religion itself. Criticism
is not a religious exercise, even though it may be carried on in a
religious spirit; and it may seem to empty religion and so to weaken
its appeal. Yet religion, which has always to struggle against spurious sentiment and twisted morality, must to-day free itself also from
the primitive science and false history it has taken over from an

earlier age. In the ancient and mediaeval worlds, where there was no vast gulf between the religious and the secular views, it was easier to adjust them to one another than it is under present conditions. Good men who reject theological dogmatism may still attach themselves to religious institutions in which they find the elements of grace; but until theology can be adapted to its modern scientific background and so can recover its ancient integrity, not only will the indifferent masses remain indifferent, but many men and women who either are, or long to be, religious in heart will continue to live their lives outside the Churches, especially if these treat honest attempts at criticism—not to mention one another—with hostility or intolerance. Simone Weil, for example, who combined a deeply religious spirit with a passion for intellectual integrity, found herself in many ways—in spite of her wider sympathies and her queer ideas of history—astonishingly close to the doctrines and rites of the Roman Catholic Church; and yet felt herself obliged to remain outside—perhaps most of all because of the two little words 'anathema sit'.

A revival of religion will never come by mere thinking, not even by religious thinking; but without a supreme effort of thought which will satisfy the mind as well as the heart, religion will not easily recover its former influence or restore to men the spiritual wholeness which many of them prize but seek in vain.

§ 8. *Faith and knowledge*

What I have said is unlikely to please either the sceptics or the orthodox, especially if they expect more from natural theology than it can give. Both may regard the whole discussion as an attempt to defend the pale relics of an earlier and more full-blooded doctrine, which to the first is sheer superstitition and to the second is true religion. If a complaint about lack of intellectual honesty is to be bandied about, they may perhaps even unite to bring this charge against a plea for seeking to combine the religious and scientific points of view.

Such a plea, it may be said, is only an effort to revive a double standard of truth or—in the blunter language of to-day—to defend the dishonest practice of double-talk or double-thinking. I have suggested that a binocular rather than a monocular vision may give us the most satisfactory view of reality—perhaps a stereoscopic view. When one eye becomes much weaker than the other, there is a tendency for the weaker eye not to be used at all; and something like this seems to be happening to modern man. His scientific eye is, so to speak, ousting his religious eye, while in the old days it was the other way about. If it is retorted that such contentions can lead only to a spiritual intoxication in which men are reduced to seeing double, I must reply that they are seeing double now and are in need of an operation to adjust the focus of their eyes to one another.

These metaphors take us nowhere. Whatever my errors in detail, the theoretical question is this: If, as I think, it is the business of philosophy to look at the world from different points of view and try to see how far these views can be consistently combined, can this be done in the case of religion and science? An honest attempt at an answer, however imperfect, may at least help others to see what the problem is. But the question of religion, like that of morality, is not one of theory: it is a question of the life a man is going to lead. This is a matter for personal decision and personal commitment in a world of which we can know only the surface appearance, although there is no need to surround this with an atmosphere of portentousness and despair. For the religious man the decision may come only by the grace of God, but even so it should not be taken blindly in the dark. The leap of faith—or the leap of doubt—should be made in the light of all that each man can know, not merely of science, but of action and of art and of religion itself.

The predicament caused by the gulf between faith and knowledge is acute in the modern world, but it is also very old. Perhaps I cannot do better than conclude with some words which in the *Phaedo* Plato puts into the mouth of Simmias:

'I think, Socrates, as perhaps you do yourself, that about such matters it is either impossible or supremely difficult to acquire clear knowledge in our present life. Yet it is cowardly not to test in every way what we are told about them, or to give up before we are worn out with studying them from every point of view. For we ought to do one of the following things: either we should learn the truth about them from others; or we should find it out for ourselves; or, if this is impossible, we should take what is at least the best human account of them, the one hardest to disprove, and sailing on it, as on a raft, we should voyage through life in the face of risks—unless one might be able on some stouter vessel, some divine account, to make the journey with more assurance and with fewer perils'.

INDEX

Mr. George Unwin is responsible for the index

GEORGE ALLEN & UNWIN LTD
London: 40 Museum Street, W.C.1

Auckland: Haddon Hall, City Road
Sydney, N.S.W.: Bradbury House, 55 York Street
Cape Town: 58–60 Long Street
Bombay: 15 Graham Road, Ballard Estate, Bombay 1
Calcutta: 17 Chittaranjan Avenue, Calcutta 13
New Delhi: 13–14 Ajmere Gate Extension, New Delhi 1
Karachi: Haroon Chambers, South Napier Road, Karachi 2
Toronto: 91 Wellington Street West
Sao Paulo: Avenida 9 de Julho 11388–Ap. 51

MORAL JUDGEMENT

By D. DAICHES RAPHAEL

This book deals with most of the problems of Moral Philosophy by concentrating on two of them : the criterion of right action and the nature of moral judgement. Rejecting Utilitarianism, it shows how principles of moral obligation may be unified under Kant's formula of treating persons as ends-in-themselves. But this formula is interpreted in terms of a new, naturalistic theory of moral obligation, which occupies the central chapter of the book ; the concept of moral obligation is held to arise from the sympathetic imagination of the interests of other persons. Throughout the book the social reference of ethics is stressed. Moral obligation is discussed in relation to rights, justice, liberty, and equality ; and different social ideologies are compared to alternative logical systems resting on different postulates. As regards logical and epistemological issues, the author follows for the most part a broadly Empiricist approach, taking account of recent developments in logic. He argues that Ethical Rationalists have been justified in drawing an analogy between moral principles and mathematical propositions, but that this need not imply the Rationalist theory of knowledge. He concludes, however, that the ultimate metaphysical issue between Rationalists and Empiricists in ethics is still unresolved.

Demy 8vo. *about 15s. net.*

THE CONTEMPLATIVE ACTIVITY

By DR. P. HAEZRAHI

Dr. Haezrahi analyses our present knowledge of aesthetic experience, consisting of a particular mode of perception plus a particular attitude adopted towards the object. The senses and the mind co-operate in this experience, which is completely non-emotional ; the person who undergoes this experience retains the role of a contemplative spectator to the last. But in his pure contemplation he is deeply indebted to all subsidiary disciplines, which are therefore—as well as methods of objective evaluation of the aesthetic experience—carefully examined.

Demy 8vo. *12s. 6d. net.*

SPINOZA

By LEON ROTH

A cheap re-issue of a well-known book, long out of print, on one of the great classical philosophers.

Demy 8vo. *10s. 6d. net.*

CHRISTIANITY AND THE NEW SITUATION

By E. G. LEE

"All who would be inclined to bear the yoke of Christian witness will be conscious that in these pages a mind attuned alike the glory of the past and the demands of the present has but to tread that path which may lead on to the recovery of faith to a closing of the gap between the Christian and non-Christian societies."—*Hibbert Journal*

"If there is a quarrel between Christianity and Humanism, what is it really about? . . . We have here a sensitive appreciation of the issues at stake and a courageous attempt to find a way of reconciliation."—*Manchester Guardian.*

Demy 8vo.   *12s. 6d. net.*

PAIN AND OTHER PROBLEMS

By J. C. WORDSWORTH

"This is a book which the scientifically of philosophically-minded layman should read and enjoy ; and it would be well for every young science student to read this book and find it is just as difficult to find certainty in science when we come to the problems of life as it is to find it in orthodox beliefs."—*British Weekly.*

Demy 8vo.   *12s. 6d. net.*

FAITH AND CULTURE

By BERNARD MELAND

'Faith and Culture' is a valuable contribution to contemporary thought about the nature of faith, man, the church and about the relation between religion and culture.

Lg. Cr. 8vo.   *about 12s. 6d. net.*

LONDON: GEORGE ALLEN & UNWIN LTD